Praise for *Lead With We*

"*Lead With We* is what business desperately needs today to rise to the moment. It does not dwell on the WHY (those who still need a business case 'are not paying attention'), and while it brings the WHAT to life with hundreds of well-researched examples, what is unique about Mainwaring's book is the HOW blueprint it offers, with practical frameworks and potent questions that will inspire and enable all of us, and especially business leaders, to co-create an inclusive and regenerative future."

—Virginie Helias, Chief Sustainability Officer, Procter & Gamble

"Companies cannot survive in societies that fail. We need a new narrative for business—and for our lives. In this passionate and powerful book, Simon Mainwaring draws from years of experience working with leading-edge companies to show us what this looks like in practice— demonstrating how aligning our interests with those of the entire society can catalyze growth, build powerful brands, and ultimately create a private sector whose central goal is the good of the whole. The result is a roadmap for change that is both eminently actionable and deeply inspiring."

—Rebecca Henderson, professor, Harvard Business School & author, *Reimagining Capitalism in a World on Fire*

"The challenges facing humankind today are too big and too complex for government or philanthropy to meet alone. Business must step up. *Lead With We* is both a rally cry and a roadmap for collaborative leadership and how to harness that power in business to transform our lives and future."

—Deval Patrick, former Governor of Massachusetts & Founder, Bain Capital Double Impact

"COVID-19—like the climate crisis, inequality, and so many of the world's challenges—has proved that we must work together for the future of our planet. With a vacuum of coherent political leadership, who can step in to provide the narratives and actions that will bind us together? In this deeply insightful book, Simon Mainwaring argues that every one of us can lead with 'we,' breaking down false barriers and working toward a common goal. With clear guidelines and specific steps, this is not only an inspiring call to action, but a practical blueprint for a better future—and the role we can all play in getting there."

—Philip Thomas, Chairman, Cannes Lions International Festival of Creativity

"*Lead With We* gets it right. We need a new narrative of what it means to lead: who leads, how, and to what end. It all begins [with] a shared collective purpose to create shared well-being on a healthy planet. Society needs—and the market is demanding—leaders who design for inter-dependence, invest for justice, and account for all stakeholders."

—Jay Coen Gilbert, CEO, Imperative 21 and Cofounder, B Lab & the B Corp movement

"There's never been a better opportunity, and more dire need, to rewire capitalism. In *Lead With We*, Simon Mainwaring shows how we can engage all stakeholders in transformative change and embrace purpose as a competitive edge. The pandemic helped illustrate how every-one has a role to play in healing our economic system and our ecosystem—this is the playbook."

—Seth Goldman, Cofounder, Honest Tea, Eat the Change & PLNT Burger & Chair, Beyond Meat

"If you are a business leader or entrepreneur that's passionate about solving today's social and environmental challenges, grab *Lead With We*. It reveals a radical new vision for the role of business and how it works, and provides us the confidence and guidance to make it happen. Visionary, inspirational, actionable; it's what business and our world needs now."

—Amy Smith, Chief Strategy & Impact Officer, TOMS Shoes

"Three assumptions. The crises (from inequality to climate) are now. Politicians can't take them on alone. The business community must and will step up. To lead with transparency and collaboratively in the interests of the planet. And then Mainwaring offers much practical wisdom: Business needs to support science and deny cynicism. Corporations don't need to look to their better angels. If there are no people, there'll be no commerce. Mainwaring lays it out, as he must, from data. But it's a compelling read as a prayer book as much as a playbook. I hope his readers take heed."

—Sherry Turkle, professor, MIT & author of *Alone Together*, *Reclaiming Conversation* & most recently, *The Empathy Diaries*

"The global pandemic and recent cultural crises have shined a brighter, more deliberate light on the need for businesses to lead with their purpose rather than what drives the bottom line. Simon has long been a leading voice signaling that, without brand purpose, businesses will be left behind. In many of my conversations with Simon, we've discussed at length that brands can no longer sit safely on the sidelines of important cultural and societal issues, but must instead become beacons for positive change by leveraging their platforms, resources, and initiatives to take a stand. To do this is not only the right thing to do as human beings but has now become an expectation of today's consumer, as more are choosing to align with brands that share personal beliefs. While the decision to commit to action on societal issues may result in some consumers choosing to no longer support your business, you must have the intestinal fortitude to be OK with that. As we all continue to navigate the intersection of consumer expectations and the role of brands in leading with purpose, Simon's book—*Lead With We*—is a must-have resource for any business leader or decision maker to have on hand."

—Doug Palladini, Global Brand President, Vans

"The relationship between society and business is fundamentally changing. *Lead With We* not only explains why this is happening, it provides a clear blueprint for how leadership can shape this process today and into the future. The central message—that business and leadership can and must be part of the solution to society's greatest challenges—has never been more important."

—Martin Whitaker, CEO, Just Capital

"In the wake of the devastation caused by COVID-19, we all have an unparalleled opportunity to enable a deep transformation of our society, our economy, and our lives once and for all. Now is the time to face the challenges that were there pre-COVID, from the climate emergency to deep, structural racism and inequality, but in a COVID world have come into sharp relief, with the seemingly futile past attempts to solve for these challenges laid bare. We now understand planetary health equals human health and it just isn't possible to have a healthy economy without healthy people and a healthy planet. But how exactly do we seize this moment of profound and unsettling change and create the future we all want to see? This book goes a long way to spell out that blueprint. It provides practical guidance that could enable us to rewire the world around us to create the conditions in which all people flourish, and our fragile planet flourishes too. From shifting mindsets and narratives to shifting the very purpose of business and brands, Simon Mainwaring shows us the way. And the most important takeaway from this book? We all have a role to play. Every single one of us has agency. It's time to unlock our passion, our desire for something better, now. And create the future we want."

—Dr. Sally Uren, OBE, Chief Executive, Forum for the Future

"*Lead With We* is a roll up your sleeves, let's get to work, real results guide to leveraging business's ingenuity, influence, and power to transform our society. The visionary ideas are grounded in research, case studies, and practical recommendations so that businesses of any size can start their journey. With this book, everyone can be part of the solution and improve our communities and environment in ways that also build their business."

—Letitia Webster, Managing Director, Chief Sustainability Officer, Goldman Sachs Asset Management

"*Lead With We* challenges leaders to take the concepts of stakeholder capitalism and collective action to a higher standard. To a level that hearts and minds must reach to meet the challenges of addressing the planetary and social challenges we face today. This book can help inspire and instruct everyone in the business sector to be an agent of change."

—Ilze Melngailis, Senior Director, Business Council for the UN & Private Sector Engagement

"In 2011, Simon's first book, *We First*, made my short list of the best business books of the year. In it, he elegantly made the case for the need—and opportunity—to evolve capitalism into a force for good in the world. In his new book, *Lead With We*, Simon provides an elegant roadmap for brand leaders who are compelled to take action against this vision. Why is this book a must-read now? Because as Simon says, 'companies cannot survive in societies that fail,' and sadly, the environmental and social ecosystems we depend on are now being stretched to the breaking point. Furthermore, as more of us realize this, the expectation for brands to help drive change is escalating. In fact, the competitive landscape for marketers is now changing so swiftly that brands that do not equip themselves to meet rapidly shifting stakeholder expectations are not likely to survive in the years ahead. If you're looking to equip yourself for thriving in today's challenging context, do yourself a favor and buy this book today."

—KoAnn Vikoren Skrzyniarz, Founder/CEO, Sustainable Life Media/Sustainable Brands Worldwide

"From pandemics to climate change, the crises of our time won't be met by any one person, community, company, or country—they require collective action and for each of us to play a role. Simon Mainwaring's *Lead With We* is at once a stirring call to arms, a handbook for action, and an expert tour through a new Good Economy being born before our very eyes."

—Andrei Cherny, CEO & Cofounder, Aspiration & author of *The Next Deal* and *The Candy Bombers*

"Today's social and environmental challenges represent an enormous opportunity for business leaders who can seize this moment to lead collaboratively. Mainwaring emphasizes the importance of collective impact and helps us reimagine business and work together, in ways that serve everyone. This is the great imperative of our times and *Lead With We* shows us how we can get there."

—Sophie Bambuck, Chief Marketing Officer, Everlane

"As moral and market forces align for the betterment of humanity and restoration of the planet, businesses of every size have a historic opportunity to bring human and living systems into harmony. *Lead With We* is an indispensable guide for business leaders seeking to thrive while serving humanity and our planet."

—Lynne Twist, Cofounder, Pachamama Alliance and President & Founder, Soul of Money Institute

"We face some critical and daunting challenges, sadly compounded by the COVID-19 crisis. To create a positive future for our children, a stable climate, a fair and equal economy, and thriving communities, we need to act now and collaborate at an unprecedented scale and speed. Businesses, policymakers, NGOs, communities, innovators, and all parts of society need to come together with a shared vision and purpose to scale solutions together—no one can solve these challenges alone. Yet many have been saying this for decades. The difference with Simon Mainwaring's book *Lead With We* is that he offers a tangible and compelling roadmap for how we can design this radical collaboration process that inspires hope, optimism, and urgency."

—Simon Henzell-Thomas, Director of Public Affairs & Advocacy,
Ingka Group (IKEA)

LEAD WITH WE

Also by Simon Mainwaring

*We First: How Brands and Consumers
Use Social Media to Build a Better World* (coming in 2022 in a
substantially revised new edition)

LEAD WITH WE

THE BUSINESS REVOLUTION THAT WILL SAVE OUR FUTURE

SIMON MAINWARING

Matt Holt Books
An Imprint of BenBella Books, Inc.
Dallas, TX

Matt Holt Books is an imprint of BenBella Books, Inc.
10440 N. Central Expressway, Suite 800
Dallas, TX 75231
benbellabooks.com
Send feedback to feedback@benbellabooks.com

BenBella is a federally registered trademark. MATT HOLT and logo are trademarks of BenBella Books.

Printed in the United States of America
10 9 8 7 6 5 4 3 2 1

Library of Congress Control Number: 2021026228
ISBN 9781953295699 (trade cloth)
ISBN 9781637740033 (ebook)

Editing by Ian Blake Newhem and Camille Cline
Copyediting by James Fraleigh
Proofreading by Marissa Uhrina and Cape Cod Compositors, Inc.
Indexing by WordCo Indexing Services, Inc.
Text design and composition by PerfecType, Nashville, TN
Spiral illustration by Curio Co., LLC
Cover design by Teresa Muniz
Printed by Lake Book Manufacturing

To loved ones lost around the world during the pandemic
To my loved ones: Monna, Aisha, and Talia
To future loved ones for whom we LEAD WITH WE

Contents

Notes on Case Studies, Language & Resources

We're going to explore case studies of many companies through multiple lenses at each stage of the *Lead With We* process. These companies, big and small, from all over the world, have become vanguards in this revolution.

One legacy of the antiquated mindset we're about to explore is in long-accepted vocabulary. Regarding gender and sexism (pronouns, titles, terminology), I've endeavored to be inclusive, but have kept the original language wherever it might appear in quotes. When it comes to the unhelpful and inaccurate term "consumer," I offer this proviso: The word implies either a certain passivity or lack of judgment—someone simply being fed as though buying against their own will—or more actively devouring, monopolizing, and squandering limited resources. Either way, the term is an artifact of the Old World economy, and doesn't describe today's highly aware, hyper-connected, and increasingly conscious shopper.[1] Nevertheless, for simplicity's sake, I'm going to use "consumer" herein to refer to people using the products and services of business.

Visit *LeadWithWe.com* for access to a suite of enhanced resources, including a self-assessment tool, brand case studies, key performance indicators, leadership interviews and insights, and other resources useful for your own business evolution. You can also find downloadable assets used by the world's top brands to guide you through the process as you commit to *Lead With We*.

Additional Resources

Visit *LeadWithWe.com* for access to a suite of enhanced resources, including a self-assessment tool, brand case studies, key performance indicators, leadership interviews and insights, and other resources useful for your own business evolution. You can also find a host of downloadable assets used by the world's best brands to guide you through the process now that you've committed to *LEAD WITH WE*.

Also go to *WeFirstBranding.com* for guidance on how we can help your brand put purpose, people, and planet—the Higher We—First.

Introduction

*We First—Serving Our Collective
Best Interests*

An ambition as lofty as reengineering capitalism provokes questions. How do we repurpose market forces to drive positive change? How does our company not only survive, but *grow* while we act as a responsible steward of our part of the world and the rest of it? How do we attract savvy talent in a competitive marketplace, among new generations mostly guided by purpose and values? How do we market our company's conscience along with its services or wares without sounding pandering or self-congratulatory? How do we maintain our fiduciary responsibility to our shareholders while living up to our moral responsibility as human beings on a planet in dire straits?

Most urgent of all, how do we make money *and* make the world a better place? Specifically, how can our business ensure the betterment and perpetuation of just and fair political systems, and help transmute and promote human health and happiness? The answer to all these questions is to tell a new story called *Lead With We*.

In my last book, *We First*, I declared, "The future of profit is purpose," as enabled by the wide adoption of digital technologies and social media. That future is now, but two major shifts have occurred since then. The first is the bad news: The challenges we were solving for have only gotten worse in the past decade—to the degree that we now find ourselves at a tipping point. Thrive in business, survive as a species—or don't. Our choices are glaring: The climate emergency is upon us. Biodiversity is dramatically depleting. The oceans are suffocating. The escalating

1

well-being of a few comes at the unconscionable cost of far too many, including the natural world. Humanity must either steel itself to endure a growing number of social, environmental, and natural disasters—or, instead, *LEAD*.

The choice to *LEAD* is the second major shift, and it's the good news: Businesses across the planet are confronting the constellation of crises the world faces with proactive, collaborative, and innovative solutions. All signs so far point to significant potential headway in resolving our most pressing challenges. But we must understand both *why* and *how* these businesses succeed, then multiply their efforts to *LEAD WITH WE*.

To start, we don't just kick the idea of "responsible," "conscious," or "sustainable" capitalism slightly farther down the road. *LEAD WITH WE* offers a total reset—a provocative paradigm for how we live and do business that is at once urgent, regenerative, and all-encompassing, because anything less is simply unrealistic.

It's increasingly necessary to expand all our ideas about business's role in making a better world. After recent shocks and disorientation across the global economic landscape, a sudden and profound reckoning is now underway, one that can no longer be written off. Yes, a revolution is occurring among companies of all sizes, as they transform their core businesses and weave social and environmental responsibility deep into the fabric of their organizations. Brands like IBM, Starbucks, Procter & Gamble, and Nike are commingling profit and purpose—and reaping rewards by elevating their brands far above competitors' in the eyes of employees, customers, consumers, investors, the media, and Wall Street. Such firms are thinking longer term, acting more responsibly, becoming transparent and accountable, and collaborating in partnerships with other companies—even competitors—to foster a new, more creative mindset focused on addressing the social and environmental challenges we face, not as an afterthought of doing business, but as the very reason for it.

From all regions around the globe, these revolutionary companies are acting with new conviction, new drive. *LEAD WITH WE* offers effective instructions to all leaders, wherever they sit, and all businesses, whatever their size, to thrive as those companies thrive, and propel this movement with greater velocity. It offers a different decision-making filter and engine to anticipate and pilot the change our world desperately needs today—a *universal, collectivized purpose* for business and all its stakeholders. It's a three-part method for codifying, integrating, and acting on purpose and impact.

LEAD WITH WE is a rallying cry. A call to action reminding us that we're all in this together. Even before the COVID-19 pandemic ravaged the world, we were in profound trouble. Even as economies worldwide contracted or collapsed—and, before the first vaccines arrived, two million people died—all was not well. The coronavirus disaster only hastened a process already far along: widespread economic, environmental, cultural, and infrastructural calamities caused by a toxic combination of irresponsibility, inattention, and outright avarice—not to mention gross economic inequalities. In fact, the virus drew an indelible line connecting purpose and profit, economy and ecology, people and the planet. "The number of people affected by humanitarian crises has more than doubled over the past decade," the *Guardian* reported in 2016, and the scale, intensity, and frequency of these global crises will only continue to explode.[1] Although individuals' attitudes and behaviors have surely contributed to these interrelated crises, we can lay much of the responsibility for our multifaceted disaster—and therefore the opportunity to solve it—at the foot of businesses, large and small.

The virus reminded us unambiguously—with boarded-up businesses, bread lines, and body bags—what happens to the global economy when many crises collide. By April 2020, nationwide lockdowns had cost the US economy 20.5 million jobs, the steepest and deepest decline since employment-data tracking began in 1939.[2]

Inequities in access to good and affordable healthcare, brought into stark reality by news coverage of COVID-19—and paired with uneven public health responses—proved we were not prepared to combat any kind of global health emergency. Employment, housing, immigration status, political exclusion, access to healthcare, comorbidities, disability, religious affiliations, and sexual and gender identities have played a major part in COVID-19 outcomes—and are all strongly influenced by class.[3] In short, according to economics writer Mike Davis, "the coronavirus crisis is a monster fueled by capitalism."[4] One monster of many.

In the US, the pandemic recession also revealed that the Black–White economic gap in 2020 is still as wide as it was in 1968.[5] We witnessed race-based police brutality and experienced increased awareness of systemic racism inherent in the criminal justice system. This reality ignited a surge of civil rights protests that culminated in massive nationwide demonstrations led primarily by the Black Lives Matter movement—perhaps "the largest movement in US history."[6] In June 2020, beginning the same week many merchants were just reopening after the devastating, initial months-long lockdowns, they suddenly found themselves shut-tering again, hastily nailing plywood over their doors and windows to avoid the extensive fires, vandalism, and looting that swept the US and beyond, perpetrated by a small minority of the otherwise peaceful demonstrators. Some business own-ers dodged direct damage from the civil unrest. Some did not. And all of us got a long overdue wakeup call. The Insurance Information Institute designated the riots the first "multi-state catastrophe event" in US history.[7] But we didn't need insurance analytics to know that. We all felt it. We still feel it.

The good news is many business leaders finally realized it was time to take action. We must end the duplicity and ineffectiveness of current business and eco-nomic strategies. Our "Me First" approach no longer works. In short, it's now or never. After this recent worldwide health and economic disaster—not to mention the preexisting environmental, political, and cultural cataclysms—we're primed for the most expansive and substantive global change we've seen since the Indus-trial Revolution. And who shall *Lead* us?

WE Are the Answer We've Been Looking For

From the COVID-19 catastrophe to the Australian bush fires that consumed large swaths of my home country in 2019, we have all experienced how little "We the People" can rely on government in a crisis of expansive proportions. In my adopted home, the US, we couldn't even agree on the basic facts of "the most secure elec-tion in American history."[8] On the other hand, we sometimes see relatively swift action on items such as healthcare and the environment, as we did beginning with a new US administration in 2021. But we cannot rely on the vagaries of flip-flopping party politics, can we?

Why can't our politically privileged lead this movement toward a self-sustaining, even regenerative economy and environment, so we can get on with what we do best—running our businesses? Recent state-centered geopolitical trends—consolidation and ever-increasing national control—have eroded collaborative global efforts to overcome our shared challenges. Governments around the world are now riddled with corruption, bias, and rising nationalism, rather than embracing our shared mandate to address issues such as the climate emergency.[9] Yet a recent survey shows that half the business community still thinks government should address the 2015 "Sustainable Development Goals"[10] (SDGs), the United Nations' (UN's) seventeen-point blueprint to achieve a better and more sustainable future for all. The other half already understands that we can no longer wait for others to secure our future, that we need to move with more urgency, and that the business world can and should do more on its own and in partnership with other entities.

Why not government? The public sector will not—cannot—take on these challenges on its own. Politics in general has been hampered by, well, politicking, along with unshakable vested interests that have frustrated efforts to address the climate crisis, global health concerns, economic disparities, and many other key issues. In the US and other Western nations, the electoral process is compromised by misinformation, gerrymandering, lobbying, gridlock, overt corruption, and, as the 2020 US presidential election proved, "fake news." Political beliefs aside, the net result is that government, the traditional custodian of social change in service of its constituents, has proven unwilling or unable to respond rapidly enough to stall the mounting crises.

So how about nonprofit foundations (NPFs) and nongovernmental organizations (NGOs), born out of the mission to fill critical gaps for unwary civil authorities? We've learned how resource strapped and stretched most NGOs find themselves; hard working and deeply invested, yes, but insufficient on their own in the face of sprawling calamities. Citing internal challenges, lack of funding, partnering problems, and the absence of adequate willpower, most of the CEOs in charge of more than two hundred of the US's largest foundations don't believe their industry is making a significant difference in the world, a recent report revealed.[11] Alone, they possess neither the resources nor the infrastructure to supply global solutions at scale, and historically have been limited by inefficiencies, lack of collaboration, even misappropriation of funds. For all their efforts and trillions in spending, the combined impact of these NPFs has barely scratched the surface, especially in the developing world.

In light of the failure of states and foundations to combat existential threats, WE together now need to take responsibility for our own healing, restoration, and regeneration. Reengineering from the ground up. A whole new operating system. These problems we face—social, economic, ecological—are not discrete. They require a more holistic approach that includes all stakeholders in our society; a cooperative, global effort undertaken by organizations in the trenches that will reshape our daily lives.

Why do I say "holistic"? Because each distinct issue is intimately connected to all others. An example: The journal *Environmental Research* estimates fossil fuel pollution is the cause of nearly one out of every five deaths, killing 8.7 million people a year.[12] A new global study has also linked depression and suicide to air pollution; reducing toxic air could prevent millions of depression cases, the research suggests.[13] During the COVID-19 crisis, we saw indisputable proof of the interconnectedness of all things—a fact environmentalists had been yelling from the rooftops for fifty years as temperatures and waters rose, skies darkened, and our collective lungs drowned in industrial pollution.

Weeks into 2020 and through 2021, we all understood, practically and viscerally, how our physical health drives our economic health—and vice versa. We also now know for certain that all but the wealthiest of our global citizens are but a small step away from a shock that knocks them into sheer survival mode. Even the heartiest multinational companies—not to mention the millions of mom-and-pop shops—are vulnerable to sudden, devastating shifts in the marketplace or a complete economic shutdown. Big and small firms alike must adapt to sudden, costly new rules for doing business.

Yet the pandemic also reminded us of the best of us. We've seen large-scale solutions to combat a global threat enacted with alacrity and intensity. As in the past, humans tend to respond together in the face of imminent catastrophe. For instance, on May 8, 1980, the thirty-third World Health Assembly (WHA) officially declared the planet liberated of smallpox—maybe the greatest international public health achievement in history.[14] This landmark stood until the advent of the Pfizer/BioNTech, Moderna, AstraZeneca, and Johnson & Johnson (J&J) COVID-19 vaccines at the end of 2020, after less than a year of development. The lesson is so simple that it's deceptively obvious: When we work together, when the stakes are high, when we change the narrative of our lives to *Lead With We*, there are few limits to what we can achieve. Even rivals J&J and Merck began working together around the clock in 2021 to produce vaccines on an unprecedented scale.[15]

Since the start of the pandemic, we've witnessed unparalleled cooperation in response to the novel coronavirus. We've observed dramatic successes not only in public–private partnerships, but also in business alone leading the way in solving crises, even when that required 180-degree pivots. We've seen business rising to the challenge innovatively and in real time, fast-tracking personal protective equipment (PPE), ventilators, and supplies for the medical front line. Why? Because industry, companies, brands—*business leaders*—are best positioned to facilitate meaningful change for the good of all. Business possesses the infrastructure, relationships, and logistics, as well as the talent, expertise, and pressure to innovate. In contrast to the NPF or public sectors, the private sector can leverage its extensive resources, reach, and global footprint to mobilize employees, innovation, supply chains—as well as consumers—around the world to rapidly provide solutions at scale.

Business manages products throughout their entire life cycle, and so is therefore best positioned to do less harm and more good at every stage of the process. Business is also both more formidable and more durable than government, which is subject to political and electoral swings, not to mention partisan-only support. Business enjoys real-time feedback from the citizenry—enhanced by its direct access to increasingly precise consumer psychographic data—and can nimbly adjust to marketplace imperatives more effectively than governments and NGOs working independently. Its brands have earned the hard-won position of being the most knowledgeable and influential responders to and framers of consumer priorities: what they buy and, therefore, how they live. Last, only business faces relentless competitive forces, as well as stakeholder expectations, to satisfy public demands and do it more effectively, accountably, and transparently over time. Examples and case studies abound in this book and, in almost every case, these businesses outperform competitors and the market, to boot—even as they protect our collective future.

Take a lesson from Yvon Chouinard, founder of outdoor clothing and gear giant Patagonia, who told the crowd at Expo West in 2019 that "if your business is not helping to regenerate the Earth, start a new business." The company even changed its mission statement to reflect this dedication to social and environmental responsibility and long-term sustainability: "[Patagonia is] in business to save our home planet."[16] How can we all do the same?

We Need Business at the Vanguard, Solving Crises at Scale

As we find ourselves transitioning toward new kinds of leaders with new ways of thinking, we might ask, "Why now?"—and in some cases, "Why me?" Is it fair that we have to worry about the *WE* when so few others did before us? Why can't we just coast and let a select few big dogs take responsibility? What about the developing world and their outsized ambitions to enjoy the same spoils? What if our competitors take advantage of us in the meantime? What's wrong with the status quo if it's working, pretty much, for *us*?

These vectors and voices of resistance fall into three main categories. The first is that a small percentage of the "1 percent" benefits most from holding back transformative efforts. The fifty richest people in the world—the billionaires, investment bankers, and captains of the financial sector—own more wealth than more than half of all other humans. That's fifty individuals versus 3.8 billion people,[17] half of whom live on less than $5.50 a day. Second, the rising middle classes around the world in countries like China, India, and Brazil want their shot at upward mobility and affluence. And third, we must account for those who are barely surviving from paycheck to paycheck, or who are government dependent and outright impoverished, for whom changing the world seems so far outside their scope of influence and ability to even consider.

In fact, the three wealthiest people in the world as of this writing are now substantively committed to saving the planet: Bill Gates through his longstanding foundation with Melinda Gates, Elon Musk through his myriad companies, and Jeff Bezos via his funding efforts. Consider also that 220 other billionaires have signed on to give away half of their immense fortunes to social causes as part of the Giving Pledge launched by the Gateses and Warren Buffett in 2010.[18] Now WE must *all* act within our ranges of impact—and work to expand them—before it's too late. The great news is it can be a mammoth opportunity to redefine growth so that it encompasses profit, purpose, *and* the overall well-being of the Earth and all its inhabitants.

Collectively, we have to get to work—or else we business leaders, along with the rest of the world, will find ourselves still "sleepwalking into a crisis."[19] It is *because* we've been telling ourselves that these problems have nothing to do with us, that they're too big, or that someone else will swoop in, that we've accelerated the negative forces of change, disruption, and destruction. It's time we adjust our goggles and work toward greater returns both on our company balance sheets and within the communities we serve.

Why? And why should the business world care? Not to put too fine a point on it, but we learned during the pandemic that we're all connected. Sick and dying customers buy fewer apps, cans of soda, sneakers, and cars. Even citizens who are merely *afraid* of each other or stepping outside are not good consumers. Certainly, a few well-positioned and lucky companies such as Amazon manage to grow during a pandemic. Notwithstanding criticism and multinational investigations about its possible anti-competitive practices, Amazon's first quarter 2021 revenue leapt 44 percent year over year to a whopping $108 billion. The company's profits tripled in that same period to $8.1 billion—even after it hired about 400,000 new workers and invested heavily.[20] Most companies, of course, do not fare so well in times of health, social, and economic crises. Risks and trends in the business world are all interconnected, such as PPE and vaccine supply-chain issues relating to regional, national, and global well-being. Community health is coupled with clean water and sustainable agriculture. Sales routes depend on robust and resilient infrastructure. Rising sea levels will affect the bakery business just as surely as it will distress the tech sector. Businesses large and small cannot run without the physical and financial survival of often-overlooked "essential" workers that make all busy supply chains and stocked store shelves possible. The point is that the hip bone's connected to the backbone.

Business executives worldwide woke up to this reality in 2020, and began to enhance their roles to encompass more ethical decision making in solving the world's problems. In 2021, the UN undertook the world's most extensive survey of public opinion on the climate emergency, which revealed that 59 percent of respondents from fifty countries believe urgent and wide-ranging action is necessary.[21] We can learn from these leaders, and expand overall efforts within our own company, industry, or sector, especially by collaborating.

And companies have been succeeding at such collaboration. How a brand shows up during a crisis like COVID-19 is key to its own survival and the long-term viability of the communities and society it serves. For instance, early on, Ford and Dyson began to retool their production facilities to make virus test kits, hand sanitizer, and PPE. Thousands of other firms also began responding willingly, on their own, and jumped en masse at the chance to serve. After having to shutter all its brick-and-mortar locations, huge Swedish multinational retailer H&M quickly pivoted not only with massive in-kind donations of bedding and clothes to local organizations hard hit by the shutdown, but also by adapting its supply chain to produce PPE for hospitals and healthcare workers. H&M allowed global aid organizations to piggyback on its considerable social media network and expanded its foundation arm.[22] The brand also managed to stay relevant and in front of the masses, and kept its employees productive and its resources and reach leveraged, even though its stores were shut. H&M did the right thing *and* maintained revenue streams.

We Must Take Care of Our Home Planet

Corporate contingency planning for Earth's survival must start now. Yesterday. We must learn to treat our businesses as "first responders"; more on that in chapter two, "Urgency." Advocating for her generation, in September 2019 teenage climate-emergency activist Greta Thunberg goaded the UN, "People are suffering, people are dying, entire ecosystems are collapsing. We are in the beginning of a mass extinction and all you can talk about is money and fairytales of eternal economic growth."[23]

The world population hit one billion in 1804, and took 126 years to double, then only fifty to double again. Our population has doubled a third time since 1970, just in my lifetime.[24] It's estimated to reach eleven billion by 2100. It's not a question of land alone—we're utilizing only about half of the usable part of it—but terminable *resources*, given the exponential rate at which we devour them. The "number of consumers and the scale and nature of their consumption,"[25] according to population expert David Satterthwaite of the International Institute for Environment and Development, makes overpopulation and human–environmental interactions not just a bothersome reality we have to live with while continuing on our merry way to the bank—but an existential threat.[26]

And it's not just us humans we have to worry about. Our influence on other species and our shared home is unprecedented in scope, speed, and growth. For instance, humanity is causing mass marine extinction that will take millions of years to ameliorate.[27] In fact, on land, in the sea, and in the air, we're in the midst of what some experts have called "the Earth's sixth mass extinction crisis."[28]

We can't pass the buck. "The next few years are probably the most important in our history," says a leader of the UN's assessment of human impact on the natural environment.[29]

The massive, three-year, UN-backed landmark study by the Intergovernmental Science-Policy Platform on Biodiversity and Ecosystem Services, assembled by 150 experts in fifty countries, concluded that governments *and* the business community will have to respond post haste—or join the list of endangered entities.[30] Now that human-caused mass extinction has taken hold, the UN warns us that we have a mere decade to save the Earth's biodiversity.[31] Ten years.

But, you might be saying, I'm out there manufacturing bowling balls. I provide temp services to accounting firms. I'm the president of a university system. What does any of this have to do with me?

Everything.

A 2020 World Wildlife Fund (WWF) report projects a $10 trillion hit to the global economy by 2050 if we continue down this road. Sustainable Brands (SB), a global community of brand innovators who are shaping the future of commerce worldwide, did an analysis:

> The Global Futures report—a partnership between WWF, the Global Trade Analysis Project at Purdue University, and the University of Minnesota's Natural Capital Project—includes first-of-its-kind analysis that calculated the economic cost of nature's decline across 140 countries. The findings show that if the world carries on with "business as usual," the US would see the largest losses of annual GDP in absolute terms, with $83 billion wiped off its economy each year by 2050—an amount equivalent to the entire annual GDP of Guatemala.[32]

And here's an entrée into the great opportunity in our hands: We can start by helping all kinds of consumers to keep altering our old, unproductive, hyper-consumerist behaviors. But let's not put all the responsibility on consumers. Business producers and providers must do their part to heal an unhealthy system for which they're largely responsible. Consider that 165 million tons of plastic now swamp the world's oceans, and that by 2050, the amount of plastic will outweigh the volume of sea life.[33] Every single minute, the equivalent of a truckload of plastic enters the ocean.[34] Beyond the well-documented damage to marine wildlife,[35] tests show billions of people globally are drinking water contaminated by plastic particles, with 83 percent of samples thus polluted.[36] Surely we can discover ways— ideally in collaboration with all our stakeholders—that our businesses and every link in our supply chains can halt the harm in these and adjacent arenas.

We also need to continue this healing by slowing the rate of woodland destruction required to build the vast plantations and ranches that feed our insatiable demand. Clearcutting for farming, livestock grazing, mining, or lumber are key factors in the degradation of our environment, and a major culprit in intermediate and long-term human suffering—including the spread of viruses from animals to people. In the last five years, humans have cut down an average of twenty-eight million hectares of forest every year—that's "one football field of forest lost *every single second around the clock*"; In just forty years, a forest area the size of Europe has been destroyed.[37] Cutting trees in particular both adds carbon dioxide to an air supply already choked with the gas and removes the Earth's ability to absorb existing CO_2. If the territory subject to tropical deforestation were a country, according to the World Resources Institute, it would rank third in carbon dioxide–equivalent emissions, behind only China and the US.[38]

Now, let's think about industrial animal ("factory") farming. "Stressed animals, immunologically compromised and crowded together in unhygienic conditions, create ideal conditions for the propagation of disease."[39] On top of that, the widespread and mostly unregulated prophylactic use of antibiotics to tamp down disease outbreaks among animals jammed together ultimately causes downline antibiotic-resistant superbugs in humans. Diseases that were once under control will suddenly start killing again.[40] Large-scale livestock operations and farms even cause significant ocean "dead zones" off US shores and other coastlines from manure and fertilizer runoff. Taking on this public health issue is well within the mandate of the World Health Organization, but it will require business and consumers to change their behaviors. Addressing the WHA a few years ago, Margaret Chan, the organization's outgoing director general, referred to antibiotic-resistant microbes, chronic diseases, and the climate emergency as "three slow-motion disasters" shaping the global health landscape. Factory farming connects the dots among them.[41]

We Need to Redefine the Purpose of Business

COVID-19 and increased consciousness about the associated climate emergency recently catalyzed our great, preexisting sense of urgency, but focused on a repurposing of business. This movement is driven by a coalition of employees, consumers, customers, investors, and the media, all scrutinizing every move business makes. When urgency met higher expectations, the ongoing change accelerated. So, the present and intermediate future requires more "proof of purpose" (POP)— the actions our company takes, our products or services as the embodiment of our values, and our ability to effectively communicate our impact. Because we truly intend to build lasting trust, establish integrity, and become part of the solution to our grave collection of coming disasters,[42] we should focus on bolstering our POP.

Yet today, though many companies are providing valuable LEAD WITH WE models, we still suffer from a POP famine. "While many big businesses communicate a clear purpose, only a quarter link this purpose to sustainable development. And of those that do, fewer still appear to truly live that purpose," according to the important *2030 Purpose* study undertaken by Deloitte.[43] Perhaps this is owing to the political warzone our world's become, with real and imagined mines under leaders' feet at every turn. But these conditions remain our reality on the ground. Employees, consumers, and investors have connected with the dramatic response by business of all sizes to COVID-19, which raised the bar of expectation for every company—and business at large—as we grapple with a challenging (to say the least) future.

For instance, like Ford and Dyson, apparel company SanMar pivoted its manufacturing—in this case from mass-producing T-shirts to making masks— not only to survive, but to help others survive, too. "I wasn't sure we could do it," CEO Jeremy Lott told me. "Our largest yarn vendor said, 'We're putting together a coalition of American textile companies to make protective masks. We want you to be part of it.' I was all in."[44] SanMar's story mimics thousands of other corporate journeys.

When PPE was running out, these companies stepped between us and harm. They saved themselves, too, rendering themselves more resistant to negative market forces. They worked to save us all. This was true of countless small businesses, including fashion stores that sewed masks, local restaurants that fed medical practitioners, and solopreneurs struggling to survive simply sending messages of gratitude and support to those taking care of the infected.

In recent years, we've seen a ramp-up to corporate accountability regarding environmental sustainability, too, a cornerstone of the SDG list, with large European companies in the vanguard. For example, Swedish global furniture giant IKEA powers most of its stores with solar energy, aiming not only to become electricity neutral, but actually to build a surplus of juice to share with local communities.[45] We also see this commitment in IKEA's supply chain, where almost half its wood comes from sustainable foresters, and all its cotton from farms that meet the Better Cotton standards.[46] Those are just a few of the many regenerative acts IKEA enacted by following a simple set of efficient, resourceful instructions: "People and Planet Positive."[47]

All that we achieved in 2020 in response to an "invisible enemy" is emblematic of what we *can* do, a test run for solving our other challenges. Every system has a breaking point, and ours has reached it. Let's not lose our momentum, our willingness to push ourselves, to come together and get creative, to take the kind of risks that personify most successful entrepreneurs, businesses, and industries. The good news is the COVID-19 pandemic has mandated a moonshot to redefine the conversation around humanity, business, and the planet. The crisis enabled unprecedented agility in terms of the business response. Many businesses placed primary importance on protecting the health and safety of their employees (which means they can do the same for the communities they serve, all of humanity, and the planet). Starbucks offered employees "catastrophe pay" for working during the lockdowns.[48] Dollar General became, in January 2021, the first major retailer to incentivize inoculations through bonus pay.[49] (Contrast this with retailers like Primark, Zara, and H&M, which faced employee and media backlash over garment worker layoffs and union busting during the crisis.[50]) Moving forward, capitalism and the other bastions of our way of life can be redefined around LEAD WITH WE thinking: cooperation, collaboration, and partnership in service of a business *repurposed*. It focuses on what it means to LEAD. (Much more on this in chapter four, "Purpose.")

We Must Share a Story We Can All Believe In

Purpose is at the core of our human story. It's the *meaning* of our lives. And what's the plot of this story? Of all our stories? We exist to look out for each other. In fact, our very survival depends on it.[51] And here's the thing: We don't write our stories on stone anymore. They can change, intentionally, whether they're the ones we're telling ourselves or hearing from others. So, it's time to change the story. We're starting with business, because business is at the nucleus of the ballooning challenges we all face, and as we've seen, it's best positioned to defuse those problems at scale.

Think this can't be done? Consider how the Rev. Dr. Martin Luther King Jr. fundamentally changed the narrative around economic justice and the African American experience with his "I Have a Dream" speech and other teachings. The power of his language—his "profound advocacy of the social gospel"[52]—unlocked hearts and minds, and fundamentally shifted the course of history. Or how John F. Kennedy changed the story of the space race and Cold War with his stirring "Ask not what your country can do for you" and his "We chose to go to the moon in this decade" speeches. They rallied large blocks of society around singular foci, motivated them to make sacrifices and take unaccustomed actions to achieve extraordinary deeds. Examples are legion: Mother Teresa's story of universal love. Rosa Parks's story of justifiable civil disobedience in the name of what was right and true. We can do this.

Business leaders, from founders and solopreneurs to CEOs and CMOs (chief marketing officers) of global corporations, hold in their hands the power to frame a new, more productive narrative, and to institutionalize it through internal and external storytelling in all its forms, redirecting and rewarding new behaviors that will improve our lives and our future. We must reimagine, craft, and share revised stories to co-create an abundant future of humankind. By doing so, we also make such a future more possible for ourselves. The act of telling a story affects not only the listener; it also strengthens the resolve of, and otherwise transforms, the teller.[53]

We need to forge a new narrative originating in meaningful and measurable positive impact supported by transparency and accountability. *WE* are *respons-ible*. *WE* can and must respond to the forces around us. *WE* need to *LEAD*. And only *WE*, collectively, collaboratively, creatively, can solve the immense real-world problems we've occasioned by our prior misguided narratives. Language is a virus.[54] We've variously infected the world with our injudicious attitudes. But we're also the only potential cure.

This movement is a *fait accompli*. We're seeing massive and simultaneous shifts within all key business constituencies, from investors to employees to consumers, finally enabling a new system, an alternative to the prevailing narrative and practices. Together, we're telling that new story, rooted in all-new, *LEAD WITH WE* language. The requisite coalitions required to affect real change are aligning. Only all of us, together, with everyone doing their part, can get us out of the mess we've collectively created.

WE Must Now *LEAD*

To reengineer capitalism for the benefit of all, this is what business must do, starting today. It's simple. And hard. We must:

LEAD.
WITH.
WE.

What does that mean?

⟶   *LEAD*: To go before or with, to show the way, to conduct, escort, or guide. To progress. To act, and to act proactively, with forward thinking; to take responsibility and shoulder burdens. To envision and realize a regenerative future. To extend scope of impact.

⟶   *WITH*: To consider all stakeholders, to assemble and associate, to collaborate unreservedly, to conjoin and partner, to bring along, to correspond.

To lead consistently with ethical, moral, and natural laws that involve elements within, beside, or beyond ourselves. To exponentially expand our relationships, reach, and results.

➡   *WE*: To aim in every decision toward serving the entire collective. To share responsibility, burden, and benefits. To remember the whole is greater than the sum of its parts. To transcend the typical ranges of impact and transform the future for the betterment of all. *WE* is an initial assumption, a process, and the ultimate aim for our leadership expansion. It should be paramount in all decision making, all policy, and all communication, internal and out.

Consider these prophetic words by Salesforce's CEO Marc Benioff:

This idea that somebody put into our heads—that companies are somehow these kind of individuated units that are separate from society and don't have to be paying attention to the communities they're in—that is incorrect . . . Are we not all connected? Are we not all one? Isn't that the point?[55]

We Can Envision What It Means to *Lead With We*

Here we find a graphic representation of the essence of the *Lead With We* methodology, its principles and practice. This graph, called "Collectivized Purpose in Action" or "the Spiral," is a simple, consistent, but powerful schema with huge dimensions to it, encompassing us as individual leaders, our companies, communities, society, and the planet. My intention is that this model should travel well across all stakeholders and cultures, regardless of nationality, industry, economic theory, or one's particular position in the business hierarchy.

Think of the Spiral as a complete matrix of mutualized business responsibilities and rewards, with three basic but profound reminders built in, to *Lead. With. We.* This "Virtuous Spiral" model and its taxonomy loosely derive from the natural world. In each successive chapter, we'll dissect different, ever-widening levels of the Spiral and see what's inside. But, by activating our unique version of the collectivized purpose—serving the *We*, *With*, and for all stakeholders involved in as many of our decisions and actions as possible—we essentially ascend the Spiral from "Me to *We*," collecting more collaborators and expanding our compass of

VIRTUOUS SPIRAL

COLLECTIVIZED PURPOSE IN ACTION

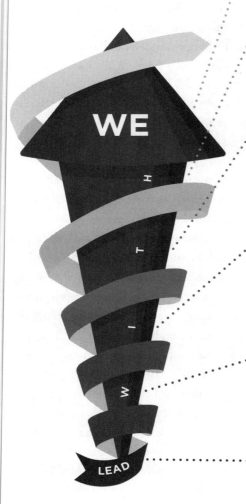

TRANSCENDENCE
FOSTER REGENERATIVE & ABUNDANT FUTURE
Evolve principles & practices to scale human & planetary health
Humanity & Planet

SOCIETY
COLLABORATE CROSS-SECTOR & SHAPE CULTURE
Drive cultural conversations & coalitions that improve society
Citizens, Collaborators & Sectors

COMMUNITY
MOBILIZE BRAND COMMUNITIES & BUILD MOVEMENTS
Engage external stakeholders around purpose-led movements
Customers, Consumers & Partners

COMPANY
ACTIVATE PURPOSE & ALIGN INTERNAL STAKEHOLDERS
Integrate & apply purpose throughout company
Execs, Employees & Supply Chain

LEADERS
DEFINE COMPANY PURPOSE & GOALS
Conduct honest audit & determine reason for being
Corporations, Businesses & Startups

ME
ADOPT *LEAD WITH WE* MINDSET & BEHAVIOR
Recognize new reality, grasp urgency & shift thinking
Every Individual

impact. Our lives and our businesses will change forever, for the better. Let's dive in for more details.

The *LEAD WITH WE* paradigm model is a three-dimensional Spiral. The shape contains three basic elements: (1) a bottom center point—the "hub"; (2) a curving ribbon deriving from the hub and rising; and (3) space(s) between the line(s) of the ribbon—the various levels.

1. ***LEAD* new thinking and action.** At the hub of the Spiral, we find ourselves: a stakeholder ready to interact optimally for or on behalf of a business. We gain the right mindset, understand and embody the urgency, and become willing to tell a new story, to shift any remnants of legacy thinking (e.g., "Greed is good"). We're ready to *LEAD*, to work in collaboration *WITH* others, to serve the collective *WE*. Note that it's critical that wherever we sit—even if we're not working within a business at all—we can and must *LEAD*. This is not on others—it's on all of us (This means you!).

2. ***WITH* internal stakeholders.** Under proactive leadership, we and all the other business stakeholders cooperate and work together to form a cohesive business unit built around a clear and meaningful *purpose* related to facts. We work *WITH* each other (C-suite with staff, customer service with sales, etc.), beginning with the vital premise that it's not about "Me"—it starts and ends with *WE*. Likely this means our business as well as its suppliers, distributors, and strategic partners are all collaborating effectively. We're taking our first steps up the Spiral, creating a corporate *culture* that reflects our collective core values, our shared business purpose. Our leadership and middle managers, for instance, are working in tandem with our frontline; our PR department is aligned with our customers' cares and concerns; our stockholders are getting behind our new programs. *WE* comprises all the stakeholders, human and natural, that make up our business. The more and better we consider and collaborate *WITH* all the other stakeholders inside our business, the more we expand upward and outward on the Spiral beyond ostensible limitations. As "Me" becomes *WE*—as the arrow widens outward with our increased collaboration—we exponentially expand our influence and our impact. This starts coming to fruition when each member of our internal crew becomes a local emissary of our brand's purpose.

3. **WITH external communities.** Next, we start working with others outside our business offices/website. People within our business entity work *WITH* its customers/consumers/clients. So, we're taking that well-integrated business purpose—to *LEAD WITH WE*—and we're aiming together, first, to build community beyond our business. We're building a brand movement, but we're not running the show on our own. Our business responds to the needs and cares of citizens, celebrates its consumers, and collaborates with them as brand ambassadors who co-own the purpose, co-create content, and collaborate on its execution.

4. **WITH society.** At this level, we're working in partnership *WITH* others to lead cultural conversations among consumers and citizens beyond. In turn, this shapes the culture at large and exercises a measurable, positive impact on society. Here we work *WITH*—not against—positive trends and pressing needs in that wider culture—political, environmental, social, and economic. We seek to drive—not just react to—that conversation, and the shifts in thinking and behavior it inspires. And we work *WITH* partners. Multiple businesses further interact with each other, forming interconnected coalitions—wider *WEs*—thereby broadening our combined reach and scope of impact. Within our industry and then, of course, cross-sector. These clusters of cooperation in the business world are the next significant *WITH*, especially effective if and when our business works *WITH* appropriate partners, with government agencies, with competitors, with NPFs and/or NGOs.

5. **WE.** Now, when *WE* are all optimally engaged in this process, we can surpass the usual boundaries of possibility, ultimately entering together a transcendent realm of *WE*, The Higher *WE*, where there's zero limit to what we can accomplish, and no problems we cannot, together, solve.

In this new conception of what it means to *LEAD*, we follow the broadening Virtuous Spiral, expanding the "Breadth of Our *WITH*," and encompassing a wider and wider *WE*. We always continue to move upward and outward, progressing further, always enlarging our compass of influence—because it's not a self-limited sphere; it's an infinitely expandable Spiral—while ensuring our decisions and actions accord *WITH* natural laws, *WITH* justice, *WITH* the best interests of the collective. In so doing, we always exert a net positive effect on the local and global environments—on the whole world. On The Higher *WE*.

Ultimately, when we continue to *Lead* in this manner, our behavior transcends the present challenges, opening up limitless potential impact. All driven by business.

The logarithmic pattern of our Spiral, mimicking nature, serves to illustrate the idea that we and our business (large or small) are but a small component of a much larger ecosystem, a larger whole: a *We* that necessitates maximal interaction *With* all other stakeholders with the collective to function optimally. This is business reengineered. When we choose to *Lead*, our business—what we make or do—becomes a launching pad for major change affecting domains and provinces far beyond the limited scope of our work walls, home offices, or IP address. This is how your home landscaping business in Sydney or your bookbinding business in Boise can ultimately influence the overall environment, the economy, or politics at large—all of us.

Now, it's worth noting the current practice of Me First business sees this same Spiral working in reverse, with individuals or organizations thinking only of themselves, depleting the abundance of nature and others, further compromising the whole. With a "We First" movement, on the other hand, the ribbon twines upward and outward from the hub at the bottom. As we lead and grow by accumulating more elements of *With*, each level gets more significant, into the infinite possibilities of a much-improved future with business leadership at the helm. The survival of the stakeholder units that make up our businesses depends upon other businesses in our and related industries, as well as the fitness of the overall environment, just as much as its own intramural health, in the same way that if bees went on strike, penguins would ultimately die. All species and organisms depend on each other and the health of the whole.

In an analogous manner, our leadership moves along the ribbon, expanding outward from our springboard of *With We*. The increasing space between the lines represents broadening levels into and through which our business and every other business can and should grow with We First leadership. We measure success here by the Breadth of Our *With* and the "Width of Our *We*": its dimension and expansiveness, how much of the collective we have incorporated into our business activities.

Remember, our business progresses forward—grows—along the line of the Spiral, expanding into newer, wider levels, *only* when we accept and practice working *With* all constituents in the center (all interested parties), then expands into as many levels of the Spiral as we can practicably reach. This second step is where *Lead With We* differs from most of the purpose paradigms available: It means we need to rethink the traditional idea of "stakeholder." Maybe we should even reconsider what "shareholder" means: all parties with a share in the future, which includes, well, everyone. Yes, everyone, from our investors to our line workers and everyone in between, still counts. But so does our local community. So do the citizens who are not yet our customers and might not ever be. So do other species. So does the planet itself. All of these entities deserve a share of the abundant benefits. But remember, all stakeholders share accountability and the responsibility with us. In every decision, strategy, and practice, we ask, "Is this WITH?" or better yet, "Who is this WITH?" The more constituents *and* levels our business can reach, the better. Are we working WITH our consumers? WITH competitors? WITH environmental goals? WITH cultural trends and needs? WITH positive political influencers? The span of our WITH, or the extent of our collaboration, is determined by how far along the Spiral levels our decisions and actions exert appreciable impact.

No one's expecting that your small shoe store can literally transform the world at the outermost edges of the Spiral. But if we all continually question the Breadth of Our WITH, and the Width of Our WE, and if we strive to adapt and do more still, we'll win at this new game of growth because everyone wins.

Note also that although I'm breaking the Spiral down for the sake of clarity, we can and will, and must, sometimes "skip" steps. At any point we find ourselves on the ribbon, we can use the center ascending arrow to go anywhere. In other words, we mustn't worry if we haven't quite gotten all our suppliers on board; that doesn't mean we can't start caring about, and acting in accordance with, say, responsible environmental practices. This is important, so worth stressing: *We may start with the whole rather than build up from the parts.* This is a new point of departure from all the other purpose prescriptions. Think of the center ascending arrow, a constant access to the abundant Higher WE, like a turbolift accessed from any level—the Higher *We* has on-ramps at any point.

And keep in mind that the LEAD line of the Spiral moves in both directions, too. Our LEAD WITH WE actions move our business growth outward, but in so doing, the Spiral moves inward, too, meaning we gain greater rewards the farther out we reach. When our business enlarges and enriches our community, for example, our community can serve our business in turn with higher profits. When our actions and messaging truly serve society, stakeholders critical to our business open their wallets with loyalty, goodwill, and a willingness to spread our brand's message and impact. When we improve our brand's influence over culture, the culture amplifies our messaging, and we sell more of our beneficial stuff. When we nurture rather than deplete nature, the natural world repays us with abundance: a salubrious environment, vigorous economy, healthy workers, vibrant and plentiful resources. *Growth* goes both ways. So does contribution.

The *LEAD WITH WE* movement *collectivizes purpose*. The *process becomes the purpose*. It's important to clarify that I'm not advocating communism or even socialism here, just a far better form of capitalism, and a more just and fair democracy. Some of the impact work that's been celebrated in the "purpose" space is nevertheless limited in scope. Recycle your coffee cups. Be kind to suppliers. Hire diverse staff. These efforts got a lot of well-deserved traction over the years, paving the way for the modern, global, purpose-driven business movement. We've also seen many fine books about finding purpose, as well as countless great programs and paradigms for adopting a more purpose-based business model, from Harvard's Michael Porter to Simon Sinek's *Start With Why*. We've even seen a growing body of evidence about shared purpose, too, such as in General Stanley McChrystal's *Team of Teams*.

But what I propose the world needs more than anything right now goes beyond a shared purpose. It needs to be a *collective purpose*, a single rocket ship we can all fuel, board, and navigate together. Unless *WE*—together—embrace the critical prioritization of the whole, our most well-intended efforts will continue to be undone by others choosing not to play along. And we certainly won't meet the contracting timelines drawn by the crises we face. *LEAD WITH WE* builds on previous notions of purpose-based capitalism, then thrusts it light-years forward, because this prescription calls for all of us to act on a single purpose. I know that might at first sound unrealistic or naïve. But hear me out. The purpose *is* the process, not the destination. And that's right—I'm saying *everyone's purpose is the same*: It's *WE*. To put We First and then to *LEAD WITH WE*. That's our only hope for continued business relevance. For our very survival. That's the collective business purpose fueling this ongoing revolution.

The process of building a collective purpose gets sparked by the formation, execution, and maintenance of *your* core business purpose, around which all the stakeholders of *your* business circulate, while *all* business—everyone—contributes in this way to the common purpose. We're defining here the overarching or foundational purpose of business itself—to *LEAD WITH WE*, after which each company has the opportunity to define, integrate, and execute its own unique expression of it. So that a just, equitable, and prosperous future in which human and natural systems symbiotically regenerate and flourish becomes not only possible but sustainable.

It's why companies across all sectors, from Honda to Land O'Lakes, from Hilton to Disney—with Musk's Tesla in the pole position—have committed to decreasing their carbon footprints and modeling for their competitors how to turn major profits while innovating solutions and setting aggressive operational standards.[56] They make money and change the world—for the better.

In *We First*, I outlined the concept of a Global Brand Initiative (GBI), through which companies leveraged social media and combined their efforts to collaboratively address pressing and interrelated issues. *LEAD WITH WE* goes much further, because we know those crises have worsened and we need a wholesale repurposing of business. Whereas GBI posited a collaborative mindset and practice of business with a singular impact focus, *LEAD WITH WE* prescribes a collectivized purpose for business itself—to serve the *WE*.

Remember, for this revolution to continue to work, we must all *LEAD* (proactively decide to do something meaningful, to affect change) *WITH* (accumulate like-minded collaborators along the way) *WE* (aim toward a collective, positive future, encompassing all). All grounded in a quest for trustworthiness, both in terms of the integrity of our intent and the soundness of the system our combined efforts build. The needs are self-evident. Expectations continue to rise. And a leadership opportunity awaits for companies that seize this moment most fully, and execute accordingly. Let's explore how to get there, starting with how to *LEAD* in this new paradigm.

PART
ONE

LEAD

We now see why leadership has never been more important, nor in greater need of redefinition. A combination of ongoing global crises today requires that we expand the term as it's traditionally applied, especially with respect to all aspects of business. New imperatives occasioned by our world in turmoil mean we must now magnify the definition of leadership to become *Lead With We*. Without a radical reimagining of the philosophy, form, and function of business, its leaders of today will become its coffin bearers of tomorrow.

This book's three parts will elucidate a mindset and methodology based on the three-word prescription, *Lead With We*, and will consider each word in the phrase individually, starting with *Lead*. Think of *Lead* as the ribbon on which we as individuals move (through our attitudes, decisions, and actions), wider and wider—meaning more collaboratively—up the Virtuous Spiral, motivated by a service-oriented purpose. The following bullets can help frame your thinking about what it means to *Lead* in this new world:

➠ ***First***, we *must Lead*. All of us. We don't have a choice anymore. We can't sit by as enormous changes in culture, climate, politics, and economics happen to us. We can't hope someone else will fix the problems for us. We must act and act now, before it's too late for us and everyone else.

➠ **Second**, the business world—including consumers—is the ideal sphere to manage this major revolution in leadership. Business can best handle it. The reach and power of its experience, infrastructure, and resources, combined with social and exponential technologies, mean that we in the business world have never been better equipped to find, enable, and execute world-changing solutions.

➠ **Third**, future-facing leadership necessitates a radically new kind of thinking about the roles and potentials of leaders. We're no longer just trying to keep our companies together and the books in the black. Instead, we're all on the hook now for (literally) saving each other, the planet, and our future. We have to LEAD . . . "WITH WE" by taking into account all stakeholders in as many of our decisions as practicable. The initial assumption, WITH WE, thus becomes a springboard, a continuous action, and an aspirational end state throughout all our leadership.

➠ **Fourth**, leadership in this redefinition means piloting people and processes toward the exercise of a net-beneficial (not just "less bad" but "more good") influence over local and global phenomena—presupposing the existence of a transcendent, Higher WE. We must continually endeavor to extend and expand our compasses of impact, most often through effectual and broad collaboration, both inside and beyond our businesses. We must LEAD WITH WE.

➠ **Fifth**, we don't need to be in the C-suite to LEAD. We can—and should—lead from wherever we sit. As suppliers, employees, and consumers, we must all lead through our decisions and actions. No less than the future of humanity and the planet we share depends on our ability to work together to solve our communal problems at scale. We're all part of the WE, WITH which we must all LEAD.

➠ **Sixth**—and we've likely all encountered this idea already—leadership and management are two entirely different processes. Management is when we handle responsibilities; people might "work for" us in this capacity in service of systems that defend the status quo. But people "follow" those who LEAD—they come along WITH leaders who guide people and organizations toward a shared vision, based on an articulated purpose and vision.

➡ **Seventh**, wise and effectual leadership cannot be disentangled from moral and ethical obligations—principles of health, prosperity, and equity—for all, not just our businesses' returns and personal ledgers. To LEAD means to take responsibility for all stakeholders, meaning any entity that shares a stake in our collective future: the WE.

➡ **Eighth, and finally,** the most productive leadership is neither unilateral nor strictly hierarchical, but a holistic, synergistic, and multidimensional practice undertaken collaboratively by all stakeholders.

In this first part, we'll begin by shifting our posture, our mentality, and our behavior around what it means to LEAD in this new landscape. Ready? Let's go.

MY PERSPECTIVE

WE

LEAD

WITH WE

TRANSCENDENCE
FOSTER REGENERATIVE
& ABUNDANT FUTURE
Evolve principles & practices to
scale human & planetary health
Humanity & Planet

SOCIETY
COLLABORATE CROSS-
SECTOR & SHAPE CULTURE
Drive cultural conversations &
coalitions that improve society
Citizens, Collaborators & Sectors

COMMUNITY
MOBILIZE BRAND
COMMUNITIES &
BUILD MOVEMENTS
Engage external stakeholders
around purpose-led movements
Customers, Consumers & Partners

COMPANY
ACTIVATE PURPOSE
& ALIGN INTERNAL
STAKEHOLDERS
Integrate & apply purpose
throughout company
Execs, Employees & Supply Chain

LEADERS
DEFINE COMPANY
PURPOSE & GOALS
Conduct honest audit &
determine reason for being
Corporations, Businesses & Startups

ME
ADOPT *LEAD WITH WE*
MINDSET & BEHAVIOR
Recognize new reality, grasp
urgency & shift thinking

1

The Rise of
We First Capitalism

We Begin Our *LEAD WITH WE* Ascendance

Here at the hub of the Virtuous Spiral, we find ourselves changing our mind and reassessing the scope of our considerable agency, reframing how we see the world and the role of business and ourselves within it. Of course, we all wish to climb—to "succeed" in our business, and for the world to work. But what does that mean?

People around us still measure our relative success by the rising stock market, which is in no way an accurate measure of the health of an economy, despite persistent political assertions.[1] The GDP, a particular bugbear of Nobel-winning economist Joseph Stiglitz,[2] similarly falls wide of the mark. Both these measures overlook the considerable effects on economic "value" caused by environmental degradation, resource exhaustion, inequality, middle-class misery, lower standards of living, rioting cities, hungry masses, and the panoply of other real-world problems real people regularly face in countries with healthy GDPs and stock markets.[3] It's created a bizarre disconnect between rosy financial reporting and the bleaker experiences of real people. Abundance for a few comes at the cost of scarcity for the many, and the engine will soon seize.

By contrast, a new breed of capitalism—We First Capitalism—presumes the well-being of the entire environmental and economic ecosystem should be primary, rather than focusing on the attainment of monetary wealth for a few elites. We're suddenly seeing billionaires such as Warren Buffett, Bill and Melinda Gates, and MacKenzie Scott (the ex-wife of Jeff Bezos), along with 220 signatories to the Giving Pledge, plan to donate the bulk of their wealth to solving significant challenges, including global health emergencies. We've seen whole countries such as Iceland[4] and New Zealand[5] reexamining quality of life—happiness and health—as more essential than GDP. This makes sense, given the so-called leading nations did not rate as the happiest on the World Happiness Report 2020.[6] Businesses, along with billionaires and nations, have begun to ask the question, "What do we want—wealth or well-being?

We Don't Need to Abandon Capitalism—Quite the Opposite

I agree with Ben & Jerry's co-founder, Ben Cohen, that "the end result of capitalism is not unlike a Monopoly game. One guy gets all the bucks, and everybody else loses."[7] But, again, this is not some socialist manifesto. What I'm proposing is that we must reevaluate and reframe capitalism in light of some cavernous gaps intrinsic to its current practice. Note that over the years and across the miles, multiple expressions of capitalism have existed, each allowing for varying gradations of free markets, public ownership, obstacles to open competition, state-sanctioned social policies, and intervention. And the 2010s spawned several new frameworks explored in many excellent books by economists and academics.

As we'll see (and as business authors assert, such as John Elkington, a thought leader in the environmentalist-business space, in his excellent 2020 book, *Green Swans*), capitalism, along with "democracy" and "sustainability," represent fiercely contested territories. The average climate activist, for example, will decry an "evil" economic system that has nearly wrecked the natural environment. At the same time, many citizens of the Western world will not brook any denunciation of "their" system—even those most neglected or exploited by their respective countries' form of capitalism, and even when it demonstrably "does them and others little discernible good."[8] Large cohorts of US citizens, for example, have literally voted against their own economic interests over the years, for paramount motives rooted in a proud (if outdated, illogical, or nationalist) sense of ownership over the essence of "American" values—capitalism.

Let me be clear: I am not proposing a new economic theory. My argument is simpler: Companies cannot survive in societies that fail. Brands cannot boom without a vigorous middle class. There's no place in a healthy economy for masses of people to suffer lack of access, resources, and agency. Yes, capitalism's development has evolved from shareholder primacy, through to a recognition of value in others, such as customers and employees, toward a broader *stakeholder* model. But, in practical terms, we're still essentially where we started. Perhaps the worst consequence of conventional capitalism is the kind of gross economic inequality, in which "'the 1%' [make] out like bandits at the expense of 'the 99%,'"[9] owning nearly half the entire world's wealth[10]—and rising. In 2017, 82 percent of the world's wealth went to that "lucky" super-minority.[11] And before the first year of the pandemic was over, the coffers of the US's 659 billionaires increased by $1 trillion, which means their wealth is now about double that of the entire bottom half of their less elite compatriots, even as four hundred thousand small businesses shut their doors forever and millions of workers lost their jobs.

Just as this is a shared human crisis, the reengineering of capitalism to better serve all stakeholders requires a collective solution. And business leaders are ideally positioned to effect real, positive change on behalf of the world's constituents, even as they develop innovative new ways to simultaneously grow their companies, industries, and the economy as a whole. Our entire way of life—including democracy itself—is at stake if we continue with a persistent Me First mindset. Global surveys show younger people losing faith at a rapid clip.[13] "Economies are not delivering for most citizens because of weak competition, feeble productivity growth and tax loopholes," and this radically threatens liberal democracy, writes Martin Wolf, chief economics commentator at the *Financial Times*.[14]

So, we needn't abandon capitalism, but we absolutely need a repurposed capitalism to protect our cherished democracy—an imperfect experiment, yes, but a worthwhile one. Let's rethink the word "experiment" as not only a static noun, but an active verb. Let's get it working again for the betterment of all. We should start with the fundamentals by at least recognizing the damage we're doing before we acquire ways to stop and change direction. Even if capitalism, or "business as usual," has so far bettered our own bank account, our *collective* remains at an impasse, where we must all reconsider all the ways our individual actions affect the whole. At best, the popular idea of capitalism is a mirage. Regulations, monopolies, lack of real competition, and the like are the reality, and "free markets" aren't free.

A We First framework will preserve a more equitable capitalism. Any more radical, unscripted shift in response to our obvious economic and social challenges could, in fact, lead to an entirely different economic model, such as regressive communism. The LEAD WITH WE evolution therefore mends and protects capitalistic society for the next generations, the doubters, and the disenfranchised. Let's also remember that opposite the downside of the worst excesses of capitalism, there's a huge, missed opportunity in the upside of optimizing capitalism to better serve more people and the planet we all depend on.

This shift is not a stretch. It's begun in earnest. Scores of millionaires and billionaires alike are volunteering to pay more in taxes: "The COVID-19 crisis has revealed the fragility of our system and shown that no one—rich or poor—is better off in a society with massive inequality and a failing social safety net," declares Morris Pearl, investor and chairperson of the Patriotic Millionaires collective. "We must reset our tax structure to one that values the contribution of labor as much as the contribution of capital."[15] Economists like Milton Friedman; former US presidential candidates such as Andrew Yang; current and former heads of state and government officials such as Spain's minister for economic affairs, Nadia Calviño; former US president Barack Obama; Bill Clinton's former secretary of labor, Robert Reich; tech giants such as Facebook founder and CEO, Mark Zuckerberg; and Tesla's Elon Musk—even Pope Francis—join a litany of other giants all calling for universal basic income (UBI), which raises the floor for everyone by providing a small, guaranteed income. Studies, such as one done in Finland, suggest a UBI helps people financially, psychologically, and even cognitively.[16] Direct payments and other government subsidies and stimuli related to COVID-19 in the US, UK, Denmark, and Austria, among other places, have begun to offer a "level unifier"[17] en route to a UBI. The *New Yorker*, the *Atlantic*, and the *Washington Examiner* all recently reported on a new US experiment with a federal UBI, through a provision in the March 2021 rescue package that extended the child tax credit, sending monthly payments directly to families, regardless of their employment status. California, reports the *Los Angeles Times*, has even more radical pilot programs, with local governments providing randomly selected low-income families $500 a month, "no strings attached." In one carefully studied Stockton, California, program, full-time work rates rose substantially among recipients, who also reported feeling "healthier, happier, and less anxious."[18]

We Must Expand on "Stakeholder Capitalism"

The economically disadvantaged are a great place to begin this revolution, but we also need to put the environment up front in our thinking. To *LEAD*, to move up the Spiral, we must change our minds and actions about who and what we include as shareholders in our collective future, as well as what motivates us in the first place. Marc Benioff of Salesforce declared at Davos 2020 that "capitalism as we have known it is dead. This obsession that we have with maximizing profits for shareholders alone has led to incredible inequality and a planetary emergency."[19]

Benioff, worth $7.7 billion that year according to *Forbes*,[20] no doubt can afford to ignore such concerns. Yet he's chosen to *LEAD WITH WE*. "My goals for the company are to do well and do good," he told *Fast Company*. "The most important thing to me is that we bring along all our stakeholders with us."[21] "And yes," Benioff reminded us at Davos, "the planet is a key stakeholder."[22] Among his many initiatives (including solving homelessness and maximizing opportunities for his employees), Benioff has joined more than three hundred companies to work with BirdLife International, the Wildlife Conservation Society, and the World Wildlife Fund (WWF) to plant one trillion trees by the end of the decade.[23] The Trillion Trees mission is founded on a vision of the world where tree cover is expanding—not shrinking. And because it's a global vision, it "requires commitment and action from governments, businesses, non-government organizations, communities, and individuals all across the world . . . a collective effort . . . to drive real change on the ground, by demonstrating approaches that others can replicate, and by inspiring sectoral change."[24] It's a great example of what it means to *LEAD* (proactively decide to do something meaningful, to effect change) *WITH* (accumulate like-minded collaborators along the way) *WE* (aim toward a collective, positive future, encompassing all). We'll discuss such top levels of cross-sector collaboration more in chapter seven, "Society."

The planet itself as a key stakeholder might seem the jurisdiction of progressive "green" companies alone. Does Salesforce fit the bill? Isn't it a tech company? Sort of. But its customer relationship management software platform makes it a company built on understanding and enhancing *relationships*. And Benioff also understands that leadership, especially in a polarized world, demands new approaches, a reimagining. "Business is the greatest platform for change, and CEOs have an obligation to use their leadership to create that change of the world," Benioff told the *Harvard Business Review* (*HBR*). "It could be around LGBTQ [equity], it could be about schools, it could be about the environment. These are things where CEOs can take simple and concrete actions, and I'm encouraging them to do that."[25]

Stakeholder capitalism "gives life to how to measure [a] company['s] progress towards serving all stakeholders, doing a great job for its customers, clients, team-mates, and shareholders, and doing a great job for society—and it's that 'and' that is critical," Bank of America CEO Brian Moynihan told us at Davos in 2020.[26] According to Klaus Schwab, founder and executive chairperson of the World Economic Forum (WEF), stakeholder capitalism is the best hope of reviving "the crumbling legitimacy of business and political institutions" because "people are revolting against the economic 'elites' they believed have betrayed them."[27] Companies should aim to create long-term value rather than short-term profits, Schwab argues; governments should collaborate to create "the greatest possible prosperity for their people, and civil society and international organizations complete the stakeholder dialogue, helping balance the interests of people and the planet."[28] Without a swift and well-attended shift from Benioff's, Moynihan's, and Schwab's ways of transforming a business into its next natural iteration—without everyone willing to *LEAD WITH WE*—we'll still face a crisis of leadership. All the sustainability and circular economy efforts to date have taken us from "do no harm" at first, to a net-neutral impact at best. But we must now progress from our remedial mentality to a proactive stance, where we prevent problems before they occur. Major institutions such as the WEF are calling for an urgent reengineering, a "Great Reset"[29] of capitalism. Again, Benioff at Davos 2021:

> CEOs around the world need to realize they must mandate for all stake-holders, not just shareholders. And there has been a mantra for too long that the business of business is business, but today the business about business is improving the state of the world.[30]

More and more businesses have started to stress "the need for a triple or even quadruple bottom line, creating value for customers, employees, and society in addition to shareholders . . . Society is demanding that companies, both public and private, serve a social purpose," Larry Fink, CEO of BlackRock—the world's largest asset manager, overseeing almost $9 billion in assets—wrote in a 2018 open letter to corporate CEOs. "To prosper over time, every company must not only deliver financial performance, but also show how it makes a positive contribution to society. Companies must benefit all of their stakeholders, including shareholders, employees, customers, and the communities in which they operate."[31] In 2021, Fink told a virtual crowd at Davos:

> The transition that we are . . . undergoing . . . is a huge economic opportunity. We're going to be creating new technologies, new industries, as other industries are going to become less important.[32]

That's better capitalism, which will make the world a better place. And the more companies that sign on, the more competitive it will get for other companies to do the same—so it will become a self-fulfilling prophecy, the new twenty-first-century standard.[33]

I'm calling for a major distinction here, a significant build on stakeholder capitalism: We First Capitalism. It's not just that all stakeholders must be considered in the tally of beneficiaries—but that *all stakeholders share equally the responsibilities and benefits.* That all decisions derive from mutual self-interest, from the good of the collective. And efforts by one leader, one company, one industry, won't be enough. Unless *WE* all work *WITH* each other in mutual trust, this won't work.

We Must Reanimate Trust to Truly *LEAD*

Naturally, a huge obstacle to the widespread adoption of *LEAD WITH WE* at any level is lack of trust all around. In 2020, none of the four societal institutions that the Edelman Trust Barometer (ETB) study measures annually—government, business, nongovernmental organizations (NGOs), and media—was trusted (*seen as both ethical and competent*) by the public.[34] But by 2021, in response to COVID-19, the public's trust in business changed, and it became the *most* trusted of all the institutions. Business still has some distance to travel, though. Maybe it only *seems* true that business doesn't suffer as much from a diminishment of trust, owing to the kind of disinformation people perceive coming from the media, private sector, and government. The obvious fracturing and polarization of the information ecosystem evident in recent US political campaigns already extends into business communications and relationships. And I'd argue the upcoming exponential advancement of supercompetitive AI is going to only deepen a disinformation ocean that's already swamping the average consumer's consciousness, mostly through social media. See the 2020 docudrama *The Social Dilemma* for shockers in that department.

Tristan Harris, former product ethicist at Google and co-founder of the Center for Humane Technology, steered the film's narrative. He argues that social media and the misinformation it propagates have warped our understanding (and even our experience) of "reality," thereby stymieing our ability to solve common global challenges. If we can't even agree on the world we live in, how can we possibly fix it?[35] This necessitates, perhaps, what Adam Grant, author of *Think Again: The Power of Knowing What You Don't Know* and an organizational psychologist at The Wharton School, calls "complexifying" this binary distortion of reality, especially after a year of widespread reflection inspired the global pandemic.[36] The handwriting (and code) are on the wall: Disinformation, deliberate or unintended, has become and will continue to be a huge obstacle to all authentic connections. And this will inevitably continue to erode trust in companies reliant on authentic communication.

When we look further into the last six years' worth of ETB reports,[37] we see that erosion of trust in all institutions, including business, followed by a loss of trust specifically in CEOs and other business leaders (with people trusting only other employees and peers). Given the life-or-death upheavals and polarization of 2020–21, people don't even trust each other anymore.[38] But the 2021 study revealed a rise in *expectations* on the part of consumers toward the business world. Consumers across all demographics understand just how determinative business can be as a force to make their lives and the greater world far better—or worse.

Seventy percent of all 2020 ETB respondents said that trusting a brand is more important today than in the past. And even more—74 percent—said a brand's impact on society is a reason why brand trust has become more important to them. Finally, "81 percent say personal vulnerability (around health, financial stability, and privacy) is a reason why brand trust has become more important."[39] Business leaders cannot disentangle their "Me" interests with the interests of the *We*.

And here, the annual Edelman's No Brand's Land Report is especially instructive. It reveals three key data points that drive home the *Lead With We* mentality as it concerns consumers:

- ⮕ 64 percent of belief-driven buyers would buy *or* boycott a brand based on its position on a social or political issue;
- ⮕ 65 percent of belief-driven buyers would *not* buy a brand that stayed silent on an issue they felt it was obliged to address; and
- ⮕ 67 percent of consumers bought a brand for the first time *because* of its position on a controversial issue.[40]

That last statistic is remarkable. Such data on the corrosion of trust provides a blow-by-blow account of exactly why we need more LEAD WITH WE processes and collaborations in place—and why they will, on the whole, work wonders. Capitalism as traditionally practiced in the West has increasingly failed to meet the expectations, hopes, and needs of all stakeholders—of the common WE. We need a new narrative that can inspire and equip the problem solvers: Us.

A few months into the pandemic, a special appendix to Edelman's twentieth annual survey uncovered that a mere 38 percent of people believe business was doing well or very well at putting people before profits.[41] That's unacceptable. We must take responsibility for this perception, and the actions we leaders are taking to contribute to it. Lack of trust in business hinges heavily on a legacy of generalized skepticism of monolithic and powerful institutions, as well as a multitude of tangible, traceable causes.[42] The survey also revealed that well more than half of people globally think capitalism does more harm than good, with only 20 percent believing the system is actually benefiting them.[43]

What's trust based on? These five LEAD WITH WE maxims:

1. **Non-presupposition.** Bottom line, we can't presume trust—we have to deserve it, earn it, through consistent ethical actions. So, we infuse trust metrics and trust messaging in all our storytelling. We build, as the saying goes, a reputation that withstands scrutiny when we're not in the room.

2. **Truth & transparency.** We do our best not to lie. Of course, "the truth" in business is often mutable. When our business makes a major mistake or suffers a manageable or "uncontrollable organizational failure,"[44] we tell the truth, and prove to the public they can trust that we've learned a significant lesson and are better now for it. The cynics among us might still characterize such a premium on truth as unsophisticated, unrealistic, or even foolish. But consider the cost of exposure in terms of employee trust, brand reputation, investor confidence, consumer goodwill, and more. Legacies of trust, coupled with transparent and meaningful apologies, are how the likes of VW, Uber, and Wells Fargo survive scandals—and WorldCom does not.

3. **Mutuality & mutual respect.** Trust is rooted in shared values. All the parties act in service of each other at least, and ideally, the whole. So we ask, "Who's this WITH?" And we work WITH and for the WE.

4. ***Fair & equitable power dynamics.*** One side isn't substantially disadvantaged economically, legally, or in terms of level of influence. Others don't have to lose so that you can win.

5. ***Guardrails against violations.*** Just because there's no law per se that says we can't slowly kill a consumer with boatloads of sugar, fat, nicotine, and bullets doesn't mean we *should*. Regulations, policies, codes of ethics, and purpose or mission statements provide the structure we need to operate.

The US Business Roundtable (BRT) is an organization of CEOs of large US companies deeply aligned with LEAD WITH WE values. Along with the Arthur W. Page Society, an organization for senior public relations executives, it undertook a task force in 2009 to explore the erosion of the public trust in business, and opportunities to improve it. "The general distrust of business hurts all companies, and, indeed, all participants in the global economy," their report concludes. "Both trust and mistrust in firms can be irrationally contagious."[45] The solution?

> Leaders need to become as expert in the trust environment as they are in the technological, economic, political, and competitive environments. Just as it is difficult for an individual firm to succeed if the whole economy is in trouble, so it is difficult for an individual firm to be trusted if all of business is mistrusted.[46]

Keeping always in mind that age and gender play a role in stakeholder trust, they continue, "Business leaders should be cognizant of these differences when assessing the status of their relationships with various stakeholders."[47] For example, research shows men and younger people are much more likely to trust business than their older, female compatriots.[48] So let's adapt our storytelling accordingly for all our authentic actions.

If we're either a consumer or a business leader looking for models to increase trust, many lists and awards have emerged since I wrote *We First*. In 2021, the for-profit Ethisphere Institute of Scottsdale, Arizona, recognized 135 companies for "setting the global standards of business integrity and corporate citizenship," and the list included Japan's cosmetics and personal care giant, Kao; Greece's telecom company, OTE; Poland's Orlen, in the gas, oil, and renewables business; Baptist Health of South Florida; France's consulting group, Capgemini; Paraguay's construction company, Cementos Progreso; and Thailand's food and beverage leader, CP Group.[49] Let's get our businesses on such a list—in our industry, region, or associated with some relevant ethos—by demonstrating a proven track record of good governance and leadership; a culture of ethics; and positive societal and environmental impact. Better yet, we can join a coalition or subscribe to the tenets of an organization that measures LEAD WITH WE efforts. We don't have to reinvent the wheel.

We Should Think of Ourselves as Corporate Ecologists

Yes, the system has to change. But here's some good news. The complexity that makes the natural world so astonishing turns on the interdependence and mutual benefits of its myriad parts. The same can be said for the capitalist ecosystem. When functioning well, its complexity benefits all constituents, as Alex Edmans, professor of finance at the London Business School, shows us in his 2020 book, *Grow the Pie*. It's not a dichotomous choice of either profit *or* serve; rather, companies can make money *and* provide social value.[50] In fact, the most successful companies don't target profit directly, but are driven by meaningful, LEAD WITH WE purpose that resonates with society and ultimately benefits them financially.

We could even gamify this process along the way. Let's open-source our solutions to the world, as the revolutionary "comprehensive anticipatory design scientist" Buckminster Fuller did in his ongoing "World Game" experiment, begun in the 1960s, where the instructions are to "make the world work, for 100% of humanity, in the shortest possible time, through spontaneous cooperation, without ecological offense or the disadvantage of anyone."[51] Compounding results demonstrate time and time again Fuller's vision of a world that can supply everything we require. We need a reset that builds on this revelation.

To reach this ultimate aim of serving The Higher WE—not some unachievable utopia, but a real potential future—and to rewrite our business story in line with "Bucky's" several blueprints for the survival of humanity, we must begin by retelling the story of business so that it encompasses this central theme. Humanity and nature are intimately connected, but only one depends on the other's thriving. According to Fuller, our actions much be "salutogenic, contributing to both human and the planetary health . . . synergistically linked into cooperative networks . . . across every scale; and . . . follow nature's design principles."[52] This is how we must build an ecological economy at the heart of capitalism—an idea later promulgated in 1993 by business strategist James F. Moore, in a seminal *HBR* article.[53] Nothing could be more important or urgent.

To understand this form of corporate ecology, We First Capitalism, we must fundamentally rethink the way we run our companies on the basis of all our separate fears of scarcity, rather than the pursuit of collective sufficiency. We must grow out of that notion. One of Fuller's mantras was *Not you OR me—You AND me*.[54] We're oriented toward individualism, but we must grow into mutuality. I wear *my* mask to protect *you*—and you do the same. We need to evolve beyond the restraints of the assumption of competition, into a field of cooperation. Grow from greed to generosity. From accumulation to allocation, from exploitation to service.[55] In this way, our businesses and our lives will become less fragile and more resilient.

We should think of ourselves more as servant members of a large and interdependent ecosystem, a collective in which all members can lead, thrive, and benefit. "One thing I know," wrote physician and humanitarian, Albert Schweitzer: "The only ones among you who will be really happy are those who will have sought and found how to serve."[56] Note that to "serve" and to *LEAD* are one and the same in this new paradigm. As business leaders, we need to think of ourselves as organisms belonging to a species interacting with others in our species, those outside it, and our shared environment. We measure success here by the *scope of our service* to the collective—by the Breadth of Our *WITH* and the Width of Our *WE*. This doesn't mean every CEO, contractor, middle manager, and consumer has to shape themselves after patron saints. Service and self-abnegation are not the same thing. In fact, our interests are interdependent.

More and more, we're seeing investors, consumers, citizens, and leaders of all stripes, all wanting the same changes, willing and able to *LEAD WITH WE*, for the betterment of the collective. Our individual actions, some of which might seem unfair or inconvenient now, will signal others to join the effort. We should allow others to encourage us in the same way. This will ultimately influence market forces—and that's how the world changes. "Apocalypse got you down?" asks *New York Times* (*NYT*) reporter Cara Buckley. "Live like the crisis is urgent. Embrace the pain, but don't stop there. Seek out a spiritual path to forge gratitude, compassion and acceptance, because operating out of denial, anger or fear only hurts us in the end."[57] Proactivity tamps down pessimism. Action cures fear.[58] There's so much hope.

We should be excited, not despondent. There is a tremendous cause for optimism, particularly in the context of the reach and resources of today's global marketplace. Since the first Earth Day half a century ago, much has changed for the better. In April 2020, CEOs and other leaders convened virtually for the Yale Business Sustainability Summit. Leaders from Walmart, Trane Technologies, Unilever, and the WWF, among others, recounted that business is now an advocate rather than an antagonist toward sustainability aims. A new generation of leaders and consumers is demanding further action, they noted, spurred of late by the COVID-19 pandemic, with many companies "doubling down on their commitments or even shifting their strategies to better address systemic risks."[59] Unprecedented collaboration is a major key to solving these problems at scale, Walmart's Jane Ewing said at the conference, echoing others: "Collaboration is everything. We can't achieve true systems change without collaboration across sectors, across NGOs, and even with our competitors."[60]

WE Must Act Accordingly, Collectively

Notice how this process of reframing begins with the conscious use of communal language.[61] This is no longer an "us" versus "them" business landscape. It's all about the *collective* us—WE—together, effecting major change. The twin emergencies of the climate crisis and a deadly virus pose a real-time and real-world "acid test"[62] for this reengineering of capitalism, according to the *Financial Times*. It's increasingly clear that the various ways that business leadership responds to this and other crises "will have a lasting impact on their reputation among both employees and external stakeholders for years to come," according to Dallas Mavericks owner Mark Cuban[63] and other business experts, including *Fast Company*.[64] This new path for humanity is a return to our natural state in terms of our neurologically hardwired connection to each other and the planet. It's also a moral imperative, as the logical conclusion of the current path is our own self-destruction or extinction owing to the "natural" forces we have unleashed against ourselves.

We must start with WE. Begin with the collective, following the ways of nature that we'll get into further in chapter two, "Urgency." Not only by putting all stakeholders on equal footing, but also by considering them as *one*, as WE. Each part survives owing to the success of the sum, as in a natural ecosystem in which the sum cannot survive with only a few of the parts intact. This We First mentality and practice subsume the individual stakeholders' needs in favor of the ecosystem. Integrity of the whole comes first.

We need to see how much leadership can accomplish when it works together, what competitors can do together, what partners can do together, what employees can do together, what brands and consumers can do, *together*. In short, what we *can* do when we LEAD WITH WE, and how we *must* if we are to survive.

The future of profit is peoples' purpose aligned.

But LEAD WITH WE takes leadership that quantum step further, to a mandate that today sits at the heart of all thriving business: to unlock the radically scalable and collaboratively effective Virtuous Spiral of not only "doing well by doing good," but of doing so at an expanding scale, through which we drive business growth *by* solving the world's most pressing challenges. To make decisions that take into account the whole web of entities that make up the collective *WE*. To practice We First Capitalism, and serve the interests of all stakeholders, from investors and employees to consumers, local communities, and the planet itself.

This has been the focus of the BRT over the past few years. In August 2019, half a year before the pandemic hit us, the BRT announced (in grand fashion, in a full-page *NYT* ad) that "the purpose of business is no longer to uphold shareholder primacy, as its mission statement has declared for decades, and is instead to prioritize and care for all stakeholders."[65] The COVID-19 pandemic really put the BRT principles to the test. Were companies moving fast enough, doing enough? What more can we all, collectively, be doing?

We are also seeing legions of new entrepreneurs, startups, and small businesses launching ventures whose sole directive is to address social pain points. Companies like New York City's Solgaard, which has so far upcycled more than 75,000 pounds of ocean-bound plastic into solar-powered luggage, bike locks, and other gear, recycling about five pounds of sea plastic for every product it sells. The company aims to halve the volume of plastic in the ocean by 2025.[66] Solgaard isn't alone. Unburdened by the complexity of retrofitting purpose to profit, and inspired by the willingness of millennials and Generation Z customers to reward them for it, these new ventures are launching products, services, and industries whose whole *raison d'être* is to exert a positive impact on lives and our planet.

In short, leading companies large and small have recognized that the business and social responsibility cases are increasingly one and the same given the context of a planet challenged by social inequity and finite resources. They've seen how consumer activism through digital and social media can harm or destroy their credibility, and yes, even their bottom-line revenue. Consider H&M, Nike, and other retailers that in 2021 faced the dilemma of choosing between sourcing cotton from the controversial Xinjiang region of China—and weathering attacks in the West over forced labor and racist politics—or refusing it and fighting a boycott by consumers in the world's second-largest market, causing share prices to plummet. Experts predicted potential 4.4 percent drops in Stockholm and 5.4 percent in New York,[67] all of that action taking place in the venue of our pocket-based electronic court.

Even social media companies themselves aren't immune, especially when consumer activism is inflamed by celebrities who represent significant global brands in their own right. Take the 2018 case of Snapchat, which suffered backlash for an offensive and insensitive ad for its mobile game called "Would You Rather?" (i.e., rather slap Rihanna or punch Chris Brown). The former, and legions of her fans, called the company out for its ignorant and callous depiction of domestic abuse. The company lost $1 billion in market value within days.[68] And this came just one month after Kylie Jenner joined Snapchat users in criticizing its new interface, which had wiped an additional $1.3 billion in value.[69] LEAD WITH WE companies are constantly redefining and reengineering how business builds purposeful companies, effective cultures, and loyal communities that all deliver responsible growth and impact.

The best news is that not only do conscious business leaders not lose profits for the effort, but their companies grow much faster than their competitors by expanding their overall markets and even stealing market share from their more self-serving competition.[70] Mindful companies not only do good things for the world, they reward their stakeholders with extraordinary returns—more from nine[71] to fourteen times higher than the S&P 500.[72]

We Must Rewrite Capitalism from a *WE FIRST* Mindset

Remember, to *LEAD* up the Spiral, we must redefine the story of business from the default of "So it has been, and so it shall ever be." If some of us are still skeptical about our collective ability to reframe entrenched narratives, let me remind you that we've already, together, radically evolved certain germane narratives. Cultural narratives tend to be fluid, evolving over time, typically in line with the beliefs of the power brokers of the day. Consider the quaintness of geocentrism, the belief that the Earth is fixed at the center of the universe. Global narratives have frequently been driven by power, control, and money, rather than "truth." Today is no different, as evidenced by current terms now evolving before our eyes:

Sustainability

Across industries, sectors, and platforms, this concept morphed from the juris-diction of a few "green" companies to de rigueur for everyone. But what does "sustainability" really mean? Maybe more than any other concept related to the intersection of business, technology, and the environment, sustainability has evolved its meaning several times in the past quarter century alone.[73] From its origins in early 1700s Germany (*Nachhaltigkeit*—"sustained yields" that foresters should aim for by cutting enough trees to meet demand, while not outpacing growth[74]) to the North American forestry industry a hundred years later, the idea expanded from forests to plants, fish, animals, deserts, and so on. Later examples include the *Ecologist*'s 1972 "Blueprint for Survival," offering radical suggestions for sustainable practices encompassing a complete economic and environmental overhaul,[75] and the United Nations' (UN's) 1987 Brundtland Commission's hon-ing the definition of sustainability to encompass practices that "meet the needs of the present [generation] without compromising the ability of future generations to meet their own needs."[76] In 2005, the World Summit on Social Development changed the meaning of sustainability once again, incorporating profits, people, and the planet. Then, in a major milestone, the UN's Guiding Principles on Busi-ness and Human Rights established in 2011 a global standard for preventing and addressing the risk of human rights abuse linked to business activity:[77] Sustain-ability should focus on sustaining human life, health, and dignity.

We seem to be progressing now out of traditional sustainability into the idea of "full-spectrum flourishing,"[78] a "bright green restorative economy" wherein we "re-[design] the entire material basis of our civilization—successfully."[79] Or, at the least, we are embracing author and environmentalist John Ehrenfeld's daring redefinition of sustainability as "the possibility that humans and other life will flourish on Earth forever."[80] Buckminster Fuller would approve.

It's clear that sustainability as we currently understand it goes nowhere near far enough. In chapter seven, "Society," we'll discuss sustainability's evolution into restorative, *regenerative* practices at *LEAD WITH WE* businesses. For now, know that nature isn't naturally "sustainable," per se. Rather, it's *regenerative*, and that's the model we should follow, as Californian environmental activist and entrepreneur Paul Hawken reminds us: "When you stop scraping, poisoning, burning, logging, clearcutting—*harming* nature—the default mode of nature is to regenerate."[81]

Corporate Social Responsibility (CSR)

Along those same lines, it's instructive to consider a timeline from CSR, through sustainability, to purpose, toward where we need to head now—regeneration and collective flourishing. Over the past decades, there's been a slow but steady rise in awareness and engagement around "responsible" business. But as we've seen, there's been a much more accelerated rise in urgency of late around the problems that we need to solve. We saw business leaders start to talk about "purpose" in earnest around 2008, as a means by which progressive companies defined *why they exist* and, by extension, their roles in the world of business and beyond.[82] It was a clear delineation, a shift from businesses not just doing what they've always done (but with less negative impact) to doing what they've always done (but with more purpose).

Clearly the right direction. But still not far enough. In most cases that process translated to merely mitigating business risk, then alleviating reputational risk and building company culture—with profits always a primary goal—coupled with halfhearted attempts to serve the environment or social justice. The new movement we're talking about here—to LEAD WITH WE—takes a giant leap. It's about building condominiums that clean the air, for example. It's about energy-positive firms that repurpose waste as a valuable and beneficial resource. Companies like Cleancult, based in Puerto Rico, delivering nontoxic, plant-based, and eco-friendly cleaning products in zero-waste refillable packaging. Or CleanWell in Denver, a small business winning market share by selling plant-based, regenerative cleaning and personal "products from the Earth" that tackle everything from floor cleaning to killing COVID-19 on surfaces. Says CEO Stew Lawrence, "We have focused on the *regenerative* nature of our supply chain. We use products from the Earth. When we use them, we're putting those products back into the ground."[83] For these LEAD WITH WE companies, purpose is no longer an inconvenient, even if necessary, cost—it's a solid and reliable profit center.

Global Warming/Climate Change–Or Climate Emergency?

What was at one time referred to as "inadvertent climate modification"[84] became, in the 1970s, "climate change," caused, for the most part, by "global warming." But as *Quartz* editor Elijah Wolfson said in the 2019 article "'Global Warming' and 'Climate Change' Are Disasters at Conveying Our Environmental Predicament":

that term, "global warming," is too easily misconstrued, too easily manip-
ulated by bad-faith actors who point to cold weather events or rainstorms
and say, "how could Earth be turning hot and dry when it's colder and
raining more than ever?" These science deniers are disingenuous, of
course; just take a peek underneath the hood of any politician spouting
climate-change denials and you'll find vainglorious party operatives and
avaricious industry influencers lodged in the machinery.[85]

The strongest predictor of climate denial, Wolfson explains, is a free-market ideology. He goes on to argue that "global warming" was never an appropriate term to
convey "the catastrophe that's in our foyer and about to sweep through the house."

The replacement term, "climate change," in wide use for the past decade, is
subject to the same underestimations and outright dismissal. In another *Quartz*
article, Michael Coren details how deep-red mayors in the crimson Mississippi
River Valley of the US, confronted with hundreds of billions in climate-related
damages over the past ten years, have recently parted with their Republican colleagues in Washington, DC, insisting on "climate-change adaptation policies."
The good news is they've succeeded somewhat. But only by eschewing the term
"climate change." The terms they use now? "Disaster resistance" and "disaster preparedness."[86] That's more on the money, isn't it?

Politico reported on the 2019 meeting of the American Meteorological Society, which focused on how much language matters in communicating the message
to a small but influential minority refusing to respond to record rainfall, drought,
temperature, and other weather pattern shifts that threaten humankind. The scientists concluded that the term "climate change" could no longer be extricated from
partisan politics.[87] I have long agreed that the term fails to generate sufficient and
sustained emotional resonance in the average person. Psychologist and economist
Per Espen Stoknes gave a notable TED talk in 2017, in which he implored us all
to "step away from the doomsday narratives and learn how to make caring for the
Earth feel personable, do-able and empowering."[88] Indeed, many environmental
leaders are now promoting the new strategy in their messaging, highlighting the
novelty and *conflict* of the problem, the *impact* on *people*, both to their health and
finances—and its *proximity* to our back door—all elements of newsworthiness.

For example, when it comes to responding to the climate emergency, a thera-
peutic social worker and executive committee member with the Climate Psychology Alliance, proposes in *Fast Company*, "if we block out our emotions, then we

are unable to connect with the urgency of the crisis." In this way, as Hickman titled her piece, "our environmental problem is also a *mental* problem."[89] Timothy Morton, controversial philosopher and ecological theorist, explains the uniqueness of the challenge by asserting that global warming represents a "hyperobject," meaning a phenomenon that exists on too vast a scale for human comprehension.[90] If we want to transform business to change the world for the better, writes Joel Makower in *Green Biz,* we need to change from the inside out the story we tell—and that will alter the behavior that it's meant to elicit:

> For decades, the main argument against climate action has been economic: Even if the climate is changing, the argument went, addressing it at the scale needed would force companies, cities and institutions into bankruptcy. In short, it would tank the economy.[91]

Makower's review of "capitalism's change of climate" goes on to show how that standard of care has damaged both the environment and the bottom line of business. Now, in just a few years, the story is entirely different: "Today, the fear is that corporate and institutional *inaction* [my italics] on climate could lead to a global recession, or worse."[92]

"The need for a new language that bridges sustainability and finance is now," writes Mark R. Kramer, senior lecturer at Harvard Business School.[93] "The new language taking root is meant to instill this sense of urgency about what is happening in ways to which everyday citizens can relate."[94] The new story is positive, not negative. Emotional, not neutral. Relevant, not vague. So, the story is jobs. The story is housing. The story is farming. The story is funds. The story is our children. The story is the collective "Us" and how *WE* better clean up our act.

Thus, a team of global corporate and scientific "namers" got together in 2019 to propose more meaningful and motivating monikers for our climate crisis. "The new name needs to speak to a global threat affecting 7.5 billion humans," they said. The group devised three options that speak of the reality: Global Meltdown/Global Melting; Climate Collapse/Climate Chaos; and Boiling Point/Melting Point.[95] Beginning in 2020, the *Guardian, Scientific American, Oxford Dictionaries*, and other respected publications followed more than 13,000 scientists,[96] and recommended using the term "climate emergency." "We want to ensure that we are being scientifically precise," said the *Guardian*'s editor-in-chief, Katharine Viner, because "what scientists are talking about is a catastrophe for humanity."[97]

Circularity

As it's traditionally understood, circularity refers to a rising commitment in key sustainability efforts throughout all aspects of a business, from design to disposal. These efforts help companies ameliorate the climate crisis by, for example, reducing waste and pollution while better conserving valuable natural resources. LEAD WITH WE circularity expands this practice by enlisting not just the company's suppliers, employees, and consumers, but also maintaining cross-sector collaboration between all stakeholders in our collective future, by sharing mutual and codependent responsibilities and rewards. This means adopting mindsets and practices that prioritize restoration, renewal, recommerce, preserving and bolstering the integrity of living systems, and not always assuming we constantly need *new* everything. Circularity goes beyond monitoring products and waste to encompass regenerative mindsets and processes affecting all aspects of society and culture.

Capitalism

This whole book is a treatise on our collective ability to rewrite the future story of capitalism using a LEAD WITH WE model. But major changes have already occurred. The US economy and our national cultural identity both derive from the depths of the capitalist creed: *All boats rise. Pull yourself up by your bootstraps.* For two hundred–plus years, every schoolchild has been inculcated with the idea that if only they work hard, there's no goal out of their reach. The very recent upsurge in this thing called "prosperity" differentiates the last fifteen or so generations from all those preceding. The average of all countries' GDPs per capita now is more than ten times its historical average.[98] For millions of migrants, the gravitational pull of the Western capitalist system is so powerful that despite its obvious shortcomings, they have risked it all to float over on makeshift rafts, traverse deserts waterless, navigate bureaucratic minefields, leave family behind, and face open xenophobia and hostility, "coming to America" (or Europe) to achieve financial triumphs inconceivable in their homelands. They know there are no guarantees, but they assume that, at least, the market is "free," and so will they be.

But we're hardly free. Capitalism has masqueraded as democratic, egalitarian, fair, and just. Yet there's a dark side of capitalism, especially as it concerns the death of competition at the hands of digital and other monopolies, as documented by business insiders and economists, and outlined in several recent books, including *The Myth of Capitalism* by Jonathan Tapper with Denise Hearn.[99] The thinking and execution behind Adam Smith's *The Wealth of Nations* necessitates class antagonism (read: conflict). Capitalism inevitably leads to objectification. It's inherently absent of any but its own internal "morality." And it's prone to crises, including those born from supply–demand dysfunction, such as the mask and ventilator shortages in early 2020.

"Markets require adult supervision," as Harvard business professor Rebecca Henderson wrote in *Reimagining Capitalism in a World on Fire*. "In the last seventy years, the world has changed almost beyond recognition," she argues. Free markets are not free when inequality of opportunity reigns supreme, when genuine competition does not exist, and when we still cling tenaciously to the Reagan-era, Milton Friedman–esque injunction that it's all about maximizing profits for shareholders—at any cost.[100]

Let's take this unprecedented opportunity occasioned by the recent pandemic and impending environmental collapse to reevaluate and ultimately reengineer our prevailing economic paradigm. To edit, rewrite, and revise this story. Who should take the vanguard as author? Business leaders, from companies of all sizes and in collaboration with all of their stakeholders, are uniquely positioned to effect real progress on behalf of the world's constituents, even as they uncover or develop innovative new ways to simultaneously grow their companies, industries, and the economy as a whole. The time for building on the past is over. We must now revise our economic and environmental destiny. The best way to future-proof our business is to future-proof the future—the people and the planet.

Technology will be critical to rapidly scaling and deploying the solutions that enable reengineered thinking and behaviors. That said, a question remains as to whether such technology and the companies that create them will finally embrace this ethical use of its assets. They certainly haven't yet, at least not full bore. We have seen powerhouses such as Google and Facebook mine data and violate privacy in order to accelerate exponential profits. At the same time, social media has compounded divisions between us, and created self-serving echo chambers that have compromised elections around the world—and our faith in the political process. The choice for business and its bewildering array of technology is whether it will authentically embrace the needs of others and support the flourishing of the planet.

The alternative direction—the prospect of a few elites cloistered in ever taller ivory towers—is not only amoral, it's unsustainable. If history is any guide, as Peter

Diamandis explores in his book *Abundance*, we have never been better equipped to provide effective solutions at scale than through the power of emerging technologies.[101] We just can't forget that technology's ideal purpose is *to serve humanity*— not the other way around. "How can enterprises redefine the capitalism vision and unleash their potential in the meeting of social needs? . . . The solution, as espoused by Michael Porter," Bishop William Lawrence University Professor at Harvard Business School, and head of the Institute for Strategy and Competitiveness,[102] centers not only on making money, but also on what Porter (and Mark Kramer in their 2011 *HBR* article of the same name) call *creating shared value*[103] for the collective, global *WE*. As we climb up the Virtuous Spiral, "economic value could expand while simultaneously solving societal challenges and needs," in line with Porter and Kramer's teachings.[104] *LEAD WITH WE* goes even further, mobilizing the collective to solve shared challenges based on our shared responsibility.

The co-founders of the B Lab–certified B Corp movement—in which businesses meet strict standards to balance profit and purpose—elucidated in *Fast Company* the collective approach I'm calling *LEAD WITH WE*: "It's a significant sign of our shifting culture that the country's largest corporations and the organization representing their interests are revising their definition of the purpose of the corporation from profit maximization to leading their companies 'for the benefit of all stakeholders—customers, employees, suppliers, communities and shareholders.'"[105]

Writing in *HBR* in the early days of the pandemic, Hubert Joly, executive chairperson and former CEO of Best Buy (whose successor signed the BRT pledge), wrote that there's never been a better time to lead with humanity, empathy, and purpose.[106] Again, if COVID-19 taught us anything, it is the fundamental and fragile codependence of people and planet, of ecology and economy—*as well as the indivisible marriage of purpose and profit*. Our maniacal fixation on short-term gains (profit) has utterly failed to create a fair, just, and prosperous society (purpose).

It's especially failed those masses at the bottom. As Dr. King famously argued, "it's a cruel jest to say to a bootless man that he ought to lift himself up by his bootstraps."[107] Where we once considered the natural environment limitless and robust, we know now that it's always been fragile and limited. Even our most prized Western possession—our freedom—has suffered under burdensome taxes on the least wealthy citizens, mass incarceration, gross racial inequities, and extreme political polarization. And, in times of crisis, like the pandemic, those who benefit least from the current practice of capitalism struggled without safety nets, while the wealthiest profited.

To recast the narrative of capitalism, we must preserve financial rigor while solving for systemic crises. It's not like growth drivers are any less important. The profit purpose must sustain the business and drive growth to then scale impact. We have to demonstrate defensible financial growth before our leadership team, shareholders, or even the marketplace will support the financial and other resource investments we make in service of purpose. Becoming purposeful doesn't at all let us off the hook in terms of financial attention, but rather it demands that we be more accountable for it.

Let's examine one of the fastest-growing and most purposeful tea companies in the US, the brand that pioneered the category of wellness tea in North America—Traditional Medicinals (TM) of Sebastopol, California. Since 1974, its passion has been to connect people with the power of plants, building a thriving business around an ecologically responsible product and a promise to keep consumer prices stable for ten years between 2007 and 2017. The company leverages its business to catalyze authentic social and environmental impact. TM's journey is thus a prime example of how to intertwine social impact with consistent financial growth. It supplies the continent with sustainably grown, non-GMO, plant-based herbs and teas. It uses 100 percent renewable electricity in its manufacturing facilities. The business also bolsters underprivileged indigenous communities in India and elsewhere, supporting education, healthcare, economic development, eco-friendly transportation, and more. The company's specific mission is *to inspire active connection to plant wisdom in service of people and planet*. Simple. Clear. Purposeful.

Now—how do you monetize that purpose? Because at TM, CEO Blair Kellison tells me, "We're not making tea. We are deeply dedicated to changing lives." An ethos that supports human health and source-community growth. TM has expanded that purpose-based core across its supply chains, corporate culture, and communications. Not that it's been easy, says Kellison: "After 10 years, in 2017, we took a 3% price increase and during that time we quadrupled the size of the company, and we moved profits 500% all from internal capital. We are an efficiently run company today, but it was really hard."[108]

Every business leader must stare clear-eyed at the fault lines of capitalism, business, and their brand—at wealth inequality, racial injustice, and the climate emergency, to begin with—and commit to a course of action that will rewrite the future. This new "monomyth" will constitute a hero's odyssey with business and all its stakeholders as collective leaders. Our storytelling, like all our actions from now on, must be a collaborative effort, a *We* effort. When companies act and speak together, people listen twice as hard. But the key is, we must act.

We Must Acknowledge Neutrality Is Complicity

Still think a business can best weather these storms by staying out of the rain? The time for business to play Switzerland is long over. The climate emergency is demolishing corporate supply chains. Generations are born with anxiety, depression, and hopelessness about the fate of their future. Why can't business remain impartial, unaligned, objective on political and cultural issues? Because neutrality now makes us complicit. Denial is indefensible. Consumers nowadays mostly expect companies to take a stand, even if the issue is highly politicized. But not with empty platitudes. We communicate our business purpose through our public actions. For instance, "take a page from Timberland's book. The outdoor lifestyle brand launched its largest-ever global campaign, 'Nature Needs Heroes,' which aims to plant 50 million trees around the world by 2025."[109]

Sure, but who'd object to tree planting? What about real hot-button issues? We don't want the public to perceive we're on the wrong side of history by overtly supporting candidates, sitting politicians, or other lightning rods. Just ask Under Armour's founder and former CEO, Kevin Plank, who, in February 2017, drew instant wrath from critics for calling former president Donald Trump an "asset to the country" owing to his ostensible pro-business posture, even joining Trump's since-disbanded manufacturing council.[110] Billionaire philanthropist Plank and the sports apparel company he founded faced massive online opposition to the political stance, dropped endorsements, effective boycotts, and bad press. He left the president's advisory board and was forced to retire,[111] and three years later, the company still struggles to emerge from its association with a polarizing figure like Trump. Likewise, MyPillow founder and CEO Mike Lindell received serious blowback for his avid support of Trump. His product was taken off major retail shelves, and he was banned from Twitter for falsely alleging fraud in the 2020 election. These and other companies, such as Goya, take their stands at a cost.

Yet a stand you must take. After blood was shed when White supremacists attacked and killed[112] regular citizens at the "Unite the Right" rally in Charlottesville, Virginia, in 2017, Trump told the nation there were "very fine people on both sides."[113] In response, a flood of chief executives, from Walmart CEO Doug McMillon to JPMorgan head Jamie Dimon, publicly excoriated hate groups and called for tolerance and inclusion. The flood became a torrent that washed away two key White House business advisory groups.[114] Other respected business leaders took an even harder line. PayPal proclaimed that it would thwart alt-right hate groups such as those who participated in Charlottesville from transferring funds via its platform. Inge Thulin of 3M quit Trump's business council, and Airbnb kicked hateful extremists out of their accommodations.[115] Similarly, before President-elect Joe Biden's inauguration, a reformed Airbnb, having recovered and learned from the Unite the Right violence, canceled all its Washington, DC–area reservations. It didn't want to contribute in any way to ensuing violence encouraged by certain government officials, and marked the beginning of a significant cultural/political shift. The pendulum swung toward business, which started to take from government the reins of *moral* leadership. Attempting neutrality is at best a miscalculation, and at worst, a death sentence.

The opposite of neutrality is aiming for purposeful, collaborative impact on important problems. Are we willing to take certain hits in service of our stated purpose? What higher cost, short and long term, could we face if we don't? When we make promises to our communities, for how long must we commit ourselves to the response or achievement? We can't maintain a long-term movement if we're planning a finite campaign tied to a marketing calendar. That's why, according to Jay Curley at Unilever's semi-autonomous Ben & Jerry's brand, the company chooses to align with existing movements and bring stakeholders and resources to the table to ensure their efforts long outlast any timely media buy or single marketing campaign.[116]

As a small start, the manufacturing sector could simply produce a net-positive product. How about floor tiles that pull excess carbon from the air? Interface, a global manufacturer of commercial flooring, and the world's largest manufacturer of carpet tile, launched such a carbon-negative flooring product in 2020.[117] The company has been purpose driven for more than a quarter century, starting with the "Mission Zero" plan its founder, Ray C. Anderson, instituted in 1994, after reading ecologist and entrepreneur Paul Hawken's *The Ecology of Commerce*—what Anderson described as a "spear in the chest moment" for him and his company. Interface set aggressive zero targets in many areas: zero waste to landfill, zero fossil-fuel energy use, zero process water use, and zero greenhouse gas emissions. By 2018, Interface reported it had greatly reduced its footprint in these and related areas.[118] "I was kind of looking for a pat on the back" for continuing the company's commitments, Jay Gould, president and CEO, says of his decision to come onboard Interface in 2014. "Instead, I got a stern lecture from . . . Hawken. He said, 'Interface is the kind of company that takes on the world's greatest challenges. I'm happy that you're going to deliver on Mission Zero . . . But doing no harm is simply not enough. We have to move to positive action.'" In response, Gould asked Hawken, "What do you expect us to do? We're a small company." And Hawken said, "Reverse global warming."[119]

So, Interface realigned its intention with the ethos of We First Capitalism. It wouldn't be complicit anymore. It partnered with authors, activists, scientists, and entrepreneurs to study the climate emergency—especially as it concerned carbon emissions—and to implement solutions. Partners—especially specialists in the nonprofit foundation sector—are critical, as we'll see in chapter seven, "Society." Interface and the coalition it co-founded realized we *can* reverse the climate emergency through sheer human ingenuity and some change of perspective—if everyone works together. In 2016, Interface launched a new sustainability mission called "Climate Take Back," to share research and encourage other companies to follow its roadmap. Since then, it's spearheaded an "Industrial Re-Revolution."[120] "The 'why' for Interface," Gould tells me, "is to lead the industry to love the world."[121] Reread that statement. Its purpose is the common good. Their purpose *is* to lead, and to *LEAD WITH WE*.

To *LEAD* the world—*WITH* all its stakeholders. And for many companies, that starts with keeping the public safe. Since 2019, Salesforce's policy has prohibited businesses that sell certain types of firearms from accessing its software. Amazon and eBay had previously banned the sale of guns on their platforms.[122] And Dick's, the largest sporting goods retailer in the US, fed up with the futility of the standard "thoughts and prayers," banned the sale of assault-style rifles, high-capacity magazines, and so-called bump stocks. In 2017, the company had lawfully sold the Parkland, Florida, high school shooter a rifle. "We have heard you. The nation has heard you," Dick's announced in a statement that also called for comprehensive gun legislation.[123] CEO Edward Stack told CNN he knew the company would face political backlash and see a drop in sales from its share of the $40 billion industry, but "as we sat and talked about it with our management team, it was—to a person—that this is what we need to do," he said. "These [March for Our Lives] kids talk about enough is enough. We concluded if these kids are brave enough to organize and do what they're doing, we should be brave enough to take this stand."[124]

What was the financial fallout? By the end of the first year after the ban, Dick's sales had declined $150 million (or 1.7 percent of annual revenue), which leaders attributed to the new policy. They defended their stance, insisting the temporary economic cost was "absolutely worth it" for the company's long-term reputation.[125] A year later, in 2019, the Pittsburgh-based retailer proved its decision to stop selling guns hadn't damaged its bottom line a jot.[126] Second-quarter sales rose 3.2 percent that year, outperforming the larger retail market by a hefty margin. The company enjoyed its highest single-quarter sales boost in three years, and its stock skewered skeptics' estimates.[127] This despite destroying $5 million in gun inventory post-ban, rather than return the weapons to their manufacturers.[128]

Dick's had followed Walmart, which ceased selling assault-style rifles in 2015, before seventeen people were shot and killed in Parkland. But after that seminal school assault, Walmart announced it would raise the minimum age to buy firearms to twenty-one, as Dick's and other retailers had. After two shootings at Walmart stores, the retailer then announced it would stop selling handgun and assault-style ammunition.[129] Kroger, America's largest supermarket chain by revenue, owns the forty-three-store Fred Meyer chain in the US Pacific Northwest and Alaska, which also banned the sale of assault-style weapons, calling it one of the "common sense steps we can take immediately."[130] Nevertheless, even as some local and state governments finally awaken with executive actions or other initiatives to the realities of gun violence, access to assault weapons, and mental health, others still dither.

While it's risky to skate out onto controversial ice, neutrality, like other forms of inaction, risks businesses getting frozen out anyway. Immigration is another hot button issue. In particular, consider Trump's 2017 executive order banning immigrants from seven Muslim-majority countries, his 2015 campaign-trail railing against caravans of "rapists" crossing our border from Mexico, his repeated attempts to revoke the status of "Dreamers," and his administration's incendiary week-long plan in 2020 to deport foreign students during the COVID-19 pandemic. Companies came out in droves with public statements. Netflix called the Muslim ban "un-American," while Ford Motor Company said, "We do not support this policy or any other that goes against our values as a company."[131] "Banning people of a particular faith or creed, race or identity, sexuality or ethnicity, from entering the US is antithetical to both Lyft's and our nation's core values," a statement from Uber's biggest competitor in the ridesharing space read. "We stand firmly against these actions, and will not be silent on issues that threaten the values of our community." The company ended the statement with a $1 million pledge to the American Civil Liberties Union.[132]

Still, not all business leaders are as outspoken. On one end of the spectrum is Coinbase CEO Brian Armstrong, who in 2020 offered severance packages to those employees choosing to leave the company after he discouraged staff activism and political discussions at work. "Internal strife" at Silicon Valley companies that "engage in a wide variety of social activism, even those unrelated to what the company does" is a serious threat to many businesses' long-term viability, Armstrong argues. "While I think these efforts are well intentioned, they have the potential to destroy a lot of value at most companies, both by being a distraction, and by creating internal division," Armstrong says.[133] Another CEO, Jason Fried, whose message to his staff that "societal and political discussions" were no longer welcome at work immediately prompted an exodus of about a third of the company's sixty employees—including its directors of design, marketing, and customer support—all of whom accepted a buyout.[134]

That's one reason Armstrong and Fried are in the minority. Political action by business is becoming more and more common. In July 2020, a coalition of nearly 150 companies and trade associations that represent half of US private-sector workers submitted a letter to President Trump, strongly urging him to leave the Deferred Action for Childhood Arrivals (DACA) program in place. Signatories, including Apple, Microsoft, Facebook, Google, Marriott, and Target, all belong to the Coalition for the American Dream.

Later, in opposition to Trump's attempted distortions of democracy prior to and just after the 2020 US presidential election, the BRT released no fewer than three statements. The first came in advance of Republican challenges to certifying legitimate election results already adjudicated in scores of courts. The second came during the unprecedented insurrection of January 6, 2021, and the third the next morning, when numerous CEO members also issued strongly worded messages on behalf of their respective companies. The National Association of Manufacturers, representing more than half of Fortune 500 companies in that sector, demanded the president be "deposed" for his acts of "sedition." The *Wall Street Journal* reported that dozens of CEOs—including leaders at Disney, Accenture, and Merck—had convened to confer over Trump and his followers' efforts to frustrate a peaceful transition of power—and "how it affects business and politics."[135] Twitter banned

Trump permanently, and Facebook at least through much of 2021,[136] for inciting violence in direct violation of the private companies' terms of service.

The January 2021 Capitol insurrection, when a violent mob sought to interrupt the peaceful transition of power, was a national story that provoked business to respond in unprecedented ways. And they did respond, right away, with major companies canceling contracts with President Trump, the Trump Organization, and his allies, or ceasing political contributions to those lawmakers who appeared to support his efforts by amplifying the false narrative of a stolen election. Soon after, hundreds of influential companies including Atlanta-based Coca-Cola and Delta, as well as American Express, Merck, Viacom, and Major League Baseball responded with strong statements, on their own and collectively, as well as state boycotts after Georgia enacted oppressive voting legislation. Companies such as American Airlines and Dell then began to actively lobby against similar restrictive voting laws popping up in other states, too. By April 2021, hundreds of major companies, CEOs, nonprofits, and law firms were reacting to hundreds of proposed restrictive measures across the US, by publicly rejecting "'any discriminatory legislation' that would restrict ballot access."[137]

Patagonia's CEO, Ryan Gellert, insists we must LEAD WITH WE now more than ever:

> We need more businesses to take a stand and we can use our business networks to expand our advocacy . . . Opting to stay silent while the constitutional rights of voters in Georgia and across our country are being threatened is tantamount to supporting these unjust laws. Our colleagues, clients and customers won't forget what we do in this moment.[138]

Patagonia knows that a business is the economic and cultural expression of its values. So, first, your business must *have* values. Then make sure they're *shared* values, with buy-in from as many stakeholders as possible—one in three of all staff surveyed by Deloitte in 2014 claimed their company's purpose is not clearly conveyed to all employees.[139] Next, *communicate* those values externally, whatever they are. And this is the big one: We must absolutely stand by our business's values during the various storms that will form around us and everyone else. *Exercise* them. Act on them. Use them as decision filters. Customers expect us to take a stand, and they respect us when we react accordingly to relevant contentious issues.

The most dangerous thing a company can do is try to play safe. We only alienate loyalists on both sides of any issue, and risk atrophying hard-won reputation capital that can take us years to recover. Take a stand. Deepen the commitment of brand loyalists. Shore up your relevance to the future.

We Must All LEAD WITH WE

We can't hide from all the changes confronting us. The possibilities are limitless. The time is now. The opportunities have never been greater for positive, optimistic vision and solutions. Exponential technology has reached its apogee; we've never found ourselves better equipped to provide solutions at scale. Our consciousness and capacity to address our planet and its social challenges has never been greater. But we need to (re)build organizations and cultures of purpose to achieve this. Smart, progressive companies today can turn poverty, inequality, and lack of economic access into new market opportunities, even as they drive up profits. This is a "prescription for a new, socially focused business model that reaches parts of the global economy previously left largely to public aid"[140] and other government intervention. We're already seeing massive new expressions of growth—a renewal and retooling of the concept of capitalism—and new measurement frameworks emerging. First movers who LEAD WITH WE will enjoy at least a five- to fifteen-year advantage over those who miss this boat.[141]

Even the stock markets and the mindset behind them—which have traditionally been one of the main obstacles to meaningful change toward our ability to LEAD WITH WE—are undergoing radical transformation. It's powerful to see Larry Fink of BlackRock announce in his 2020 annual letter (titled "A Fundamental Reshaping of Finance") that the climate emergency will force the capital markets to shift.[142] In 2021, Fink noted that the pandemic caused a surprising "tectonic shift" toward a more stakeholder-centered economic model, starting with a greater focus on the environment.[143]

Transformation is what we need, as a society, as a planet, and as individuals. We also know that change is inevitable—it's how life itself functions. But to create the kinds of impacts that these times demand, we need to work together to take charge of the transformation, to harness forces larger than ourselves and steer in a direction of our choosing.[144] We need to LEAD WITH WE.

What does that mean? Our starting point has to be a WE mentality (mindset focus). Our process must be focused on the WE, the collective benefit (practice focus). And our leadership mindset must put WE first (leadership focus). We can no longer claim we simply "can't afford" to act on global crises. We will spend *trillions* in response to COVID-19.[145] We will find success at the intersection of our businesses' core equity—what we do well, and only we can do—and consumers' concerns, born out of the realities of their lives on the ground.

This book provides that roadmap, in mindset and practice, with data and case studies and guidelines that my company, We First, has developed as a team and stress-tested over the past decade with some of the world's most prestigious, successful, and exciting companies. But this model is not a silver bullet. All our solutions must be systemic, shared, and collective. And therein lies the epic challenge. We're either *all* in—or we all fail together. If we're not all in, firing on all cylinders, our engine is doomed to seize, and we'll roll backward. And those who shirk will surely frustrate the efforts of others taking a more active role.

We also can't fool ourselves into believing that some permanent damage hasn't already been done. If we start today, we're already behind. Imagine if we had begun in earnest in 1970. Or even 1990. Biodiversity has suffered such great losses over the past century that we can't hope to restore their former levels for hundreds of years, if not longer, if ever.[146] But we can "reverse-reengineer" solutions at scale, preventing further damage. *We* as business leaders and consumers, as global citizens. Not to get caught in our own bubbles of self-congratulation instead of challenging ourselves to move far or fast enough, but as guardians of our shared well-being and future.

Key Takeaways

→ Business—meaning all its stakeholders, including consumers—is uniquely equipped to address compounding social and environmental crises now presenting an existential threat to humanity with speed and at an equal scale.

→ The twin crises of 2020–21—the global pandemic and the racial justice movement—have demonstrated how business must now respond in real time and with greater authenticity to better serve all stakeholders on other key crises, including the environmental emergency.

→ For humanity to survive and business to thrive, *We* must work *With* each other in new ways to restore the integrity and well-being of our social and natural ecosystems.

Action Items

---

1. *LEAD*—Collectively embrace a We First (versus Me First) mindset and then put it into action so we can all *LEAD WITH WE*.
2. *WITH*—Assume shared responsibility with other stakeholders in our future, then take collaborative action to address issues on which the well-being of business, society, and the planet depend.
3. *WE*—Adopt and amplify a new narrative for a collaborative stakeholder economy—We First Capitalism—in which all participants share the responsibilities as well as the rewards.

FIRST

MY RESPONSE

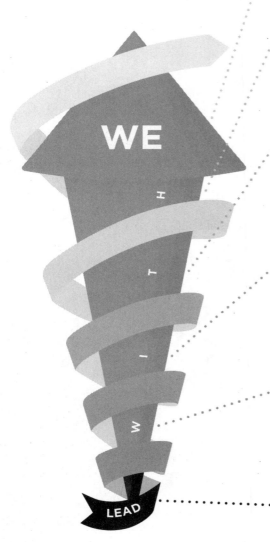

TRANSCENDENCE
FOSTER REGENERATIVE
& ABUNDANT FUTURE
Evolve principles & practices to
scale human & planetary health
Humanity & Planet

SOCIETY
COLLABORATE CROSS-
SECTOR & SHAPE CULTURE
Drive cultural conversations &
coalitions that improve society
Citizens, Collaborators & Sectors

COMMUNITY
MOBILIZE BRAND
COMMUNITIES &
BUILD MOVEMENTS
Engage external stakeholders
around purpose-led movements
Customers, Consumers & Partners

COMPANY
ACTIVATE PURPOSE
& ALIGN INTERNAL
STAKEHOLDERS
Integrate & apply purpose
throughout company
Execs, Employees & Supply Chain

LEADERS
DEFINE COMPANY
PURPOSE & GOALS
Conduct honest audit &
determine reason for being
Corporations, Businesses & Startups

ME
ADOPT *LEAD WITH WE*
MINDSET & BEHAVIOR
Recognize new reality, grasp
urgency & shift thinking

2

Urgency

A Confluence of Crises

Now Business Becomes a First Responder

What drives our initial motion up the Virtuous Spiral? First, the internalization of service to the *WE* as a primary function of business. Service in the best ways our particular position and business can offer it. This is often clearer to us in times of emergency. Consider the reputation of essential workers, such as paramedics, nurses, and EMTs, which received a long-overdue boost thanks to nonstop media coverage of COVID-19. Hospital, emergency, and critical care workers provide us with another way to extend the first responder mindset to include businesses and brands at the forefront. Businesses must create immediate, essential social value to ensure the long-term viability of their communities, the economy, and the "future-proofing" of society as a whole. That's a great way to jump-start your movement up the Spiral.

If the twin crises of the COVID-19 pandemic and the Black Lives Matter (BLM) protests taught us anything, it's that business often finds itself in the trenches and on the frontlines of social, cultural, and global challenges. The economy lives or dies on how responsibly, nimbly, and thoroughly business responds to the world outside its doors and domains, beyond its industry and customer base. Not only the public's *perception* of business responses, but also its real-world actions—its purpose put to work. As I say on my podcast all the time, a brand's crisis response is critical to its success.[1]

Corporate interests sit at the forefront of the solution as well as the problem. It's why many hundreds of brands over the past decade have sharply condemned the most disreputable forms of factory farming. More than one hundred global brands, from Walmart to McDonald's, have committed to phasing out battery cages for egg-laying hens. And big brands including Whole Foods, Aramark, and Compass have pledged humane (albeit a relative term, given their "products" still get butchered and eaten) conditions for their broiler chickens.[2] Meantime, millennials and others are choosing "meat analogs"—various vegetable protein substitutes for traditional meat—in unprecedented numbers, so much so that most big fast-food chains have introduced their own versions, generating good old-fashioned competition in the marketplace. Opportunity knocked, and these brands answered, providing a product that customers wanted. The brands are profiting and helping, as opposed to hurting, the planet. And these are everyone's problems—and everyone's responsibility to fix. WE must all work together to stop the accelerating destruction of our planet.

As a result of the economic shutdown in spring 2020, major environmental improvements were observed, mostly related to water and air quality,[3] along with resurgence of at-risk species populations such as sea turtles on temporarily empty beaches.[4] We've seen this before: Right after 9/11, no planes flew over the continental US for five days, during which the parts per million of atmospheric carbon dropped dramatically.

Finding ways to use the momentum of those unintended positive consequences to drive progress? That's a sane and sensible experiment that will yield real results. It's our choice. Pivot. Adapt. Revise. Learn lessons among the many corporate models from the COVID-19 crisis and beyond to uncover further solutions to our great challenges, even as we improve our bottom line. Not only can it be done—it must be done. It's time we all become "wartime" captains of industry, captains of our own future.

For example, when streaming giant Netflix recently shifted $100 million in deposits to bolster Black-owned banks,[5] it wasn't just giving anti-racist lip service, it was putting its money where its mouth is. Companies like Lego and Honeywell, which retooled their production facilities to make virus test kits, hand sanitizer, and personal protective equipment (PPE), managed and expanded their brands during the crisis. While responding to an emergency, they built their brands.

Make no mistake: Transitioning your business into a first responder will require getting involved in sensitive topics and, often, reexamining your own entrenched thinking. For example, leaders everywhere are interrogating their own assumptions and increasing the number of Black people, indigenous people, and people of color (BIPOC) on their boards. These recent cultural clashes are part of an ongoing series of movements—rights for lesbian, gay, bisexual, transgender, and queer (LGBTQ) people, the climate emergency, and #MeToo, to name but a few—that will continue to challenge businesses big and small for the foreseeable future. Those that survive and prosper will be the ones that have thought deeply about a first responder strategy, prepared it extensively, and rolled it out appropriately. Think of this as Crisis Management 2.0—the new and necessary, more urgent and proactive corporate response that meets our multiple challenges head on. But this form of crisis management is distinguished by a constant state of cultural flux punctuated by crisis flashpoints. We're no longer reacting to the occasional exception to the steady-state norm. Now we need to be ever ready: much more fluid, agile, and multifaceted. The stakes are no less than the survival of our businesses and the planet itself.

The events of today provide us an unprecedented opportunity wrapped in an ostensible burden. In considering our brands' crisis responses, let's remember emergency workers don't dread the 911 call. Instead, they rely on wide-ranging preparation and endless training for every scenario. They've anticipated likely and even *unlikely* circumstances, and they run drills to make sure they're ready for whatever happens in the field. Business leaders should do the same by speaking to all stakeholders throughout their value chain, researching relevant issues on which they have a material impact, and studying best practices—both real-time responses and systemic solutions. We need to base and templatize our first responder plans on successful past responses, so we can iterate and spin them up more quickly when needed. If your business survived the recent pandemic and economic crises, you've got the tools to plan for the next ones. This is the new normal for business, how brands should respond to challenging times—meaning all times. We all need to *Lead With We*.

Independent research undertaken by McKinsey & Company (no stranger itself to crisis management in light of nearly $641 million in total settlements related to its advice to opioid manufacturers[6]) found that in the midst of the 2020 pandemic, people who said they were "living their purpose" at work reported levels of well-being *five times higher* than those who weren't. And that same cohort was four times more likely to report higher engagement levels.[7]

Indeed, the facility for responding responsibly, empathetically, effectively, and authentically in the face of calamities is a necessary component in the "new normal" for companies of all types and sizes. For just one example, let's glance again at the corporate response to the BLM movement's sudden surge in 2020. BLM is instructive for all present and future crises of low probability but massive societal impact that inevitably will confront all businesses. The protests following George Floyd's murder caught many business leaders off guard. Companies large and small were left scrambling to communicate responsibly and effectively in real time—even as many shuddered with trepidation and shuttered their plate glass storefronts in fear.

Which businesses survived both the 2020 unrest and COVID-19? Those that were best at staying true to their core purpose and the ways their business was uniquely and authentically qualified to execute on those crises, and those that could redirect efforts to the immediate issues in substantive, defensible, common-sense ways. Of course, that required plenty of advanced planning. In any case, every company had a deeply meaningful role to play, whether it was a local restaurant donating meals to first responders during COVID-19, an online education platform providing free lessons to students, or employees volunteering to clean up local storefronts vandalized during protests. To do any less in fact courts costly backlash, as "all companies of all sizes must take action to address this systemic issue. In that sense, it is core to business outright and something every brand must address."[8]

That's likely going to be true for any future low-probability/high-impact crisis. Each and every one can become a "Green Swan" opportunity—meaning if we approach them with the right mindset, writes John Elkington, we'll find "solutions that take us exponentially toward breakthrough."[9] But only if we prioritize the collective—if we *Lead With We*.

To *Lead* our companies' training and prep to be first responders, our brands' crisis response strategies should encompass the following:

1. *Elevate over profit the health and wellness of people and the planet first.* We can't continue operating if our employees and customers are falling ill because their food, water, or air is tainted, or they can't afford the basics, or are otherwise shut out of commerce and society. Raise all boats while ensuring the health of the ocean, too. "The world is on fire . . . Wealth is rushing to the top," writes Harvard's Rebecca Henderson in *Reimaging Capitalism in a World on Fire*. "The institutions that have historically held the market in balance—families, local communities, the great faith traditions, government, and even our shared sense of ourselves as a human community—are crumbling or even vilified."[10] Now, "business must step up," Henderson argues. "It . . . has a strong *economic* case for action."[11] The case for action is that self-interest perforce includes the interest of others. This is the first principle of what we might think of as We First Capitalism as we begin to rebrand the old ways. America is a great experiment, and so are all countries reimagining their economic systems.

One US brand demonstrating such leadership is Vita Coco. The privately owned coconut water company was one of the few that experienced dramatically increased demand and sales as consumers—both panic-buyers and others—stocked up on shelf-stable beverages during the pandemic quarantines. Co-founder Michael Kirban didn't squirrel away those extra profits for an even rainier day. He gave them back to people in need—even as the company made contingencies for long-term lockdowns (during which the company could not receive the product—coconuts, which don't grow anywhere in the continental US—on which those profits depend). Vita Coco committed $1 million to Feeding America and No Kid Hungry. These efforts added to all the work the Vita Coco Project has done in the communities where the harvesting occurs, such as building schools and teaching intercropping techniques. "We have such commitment from the communities that we've supported . . . It goes a lot deeper than just a business and procurement relationship . . . Not only are we helping their children, we're offering them a market for this product that didn't exist before," Kirban tells me. Vita Coco didn't do all this for the credit. "It was about doing what felt right for these communities."[12] But Kirban didn't stop there. He took to Twitter to encourage other companies that were also benefiting from the crisis to donate *their* extra profits.[13]

The sock company Bombas, too, partnered with other direct-to-consumer brands to bring relief to those in need during the 2020–21 pandemic. Bombas was already well known for donating more than forty million pairs of socks to homeless people (one for every pair purchased) because "everyone deserves to put on clean clothes that make them feel good about themselves."[14] While these kinds of efforts provide much-needed help to society, they also result in considerable, measurable consumer goodwill for the corporate givers—consumers can't and won't unsee how brands respond to crises. The LEAD WITH WE methods also help to recruit and maintain top-shelf employees, according to Kirban. We'll study that in more detail in chapter five, "Culture."

2. ***Prepare to retool how our company works as necessary.*** If our business is closed completely because of a public health crisis, are we ready to switch to a virtual workspace? How about diversity, inclusion, and equity (DI&E): Does the makeup of our business personnel reflect the community where we operate, as well as our customer demographics? Continue this We First business strategy planning: Are all our suppliers and partners on board with our core values? We've all just experienced many literal, structural changes businesses had to make: moving tables outside, adding Plexiglas barriers, taking only online payment and credit cards. Now, how ready are we for the *next* challenge? And the next? They're inescapable.

3. ***Repurpose products and services to help however we can.*** How quickly and efficiently could we spool up significant changes to our business operations in response to an emergent need? Many companies rose to the COVID-19 occasion, marshalling resources to help the communities in which they work. SanMar had never made a mask before March 18, 2020, but by March 26, they were in mass production, and the company would soon churn out about ten million a month for the government's strategic stockpile.[15] They were not alone. Johnson & Johnson mobilized funds, medical supplies, and PPE across a spectrum of first responders and others on the front lines. Video conferencing company Zoom provided free access to schools across the country so teachers could continue instruction. "Luxury goods company LVMH . . . utilize[d] some of its perfume and cosmetics plants (think Dior, Guerlain, and Givenchy) to produce large

quantities of hand sanitizer and provide it for free to public hospitals."[16] Jack Ma, co-founder of China's Alibaba, donated half a million corona-virus testing units to the US. He also contributed a million face masks to the US and another two million across Europe. "We can't beat this virus unless we eliminate boundaries to resources and share our know-how and hard-earned lessons," the entrepreneur announced on Twitter.[17]

4. *Partner in new ways to scale our impact.* "Lineage Logistics, a cold storage, food transport and processing company, joined supply chain and nonprofit partners to create the 'Share a Meal' campaign." *Fast Company* reported about this movement toward "Smart Generosity": "Lineage will provide 100 million meals to Americans in need, guided by its purpose 'To Feed the World.'"[18] Cisco offered businesses free use of its Webex ser-vice to help brands transition—this was especially noticeable to hundreds of millions of consumers as the news media morphed into at-home report-ing. Most entities were more than willing to scale their impact by collab-orating strategically. "I sent an email to the Chief Sales Officer at UPS, who I'd met once before," SanMar's CEO, Jeremy Lott, tells me. "I asked if UPS would be willing to help. Thirty seconds later she said, 'UPS is here to support you.'" He says, "The biggest lesson I learned is that when you're in a crisis, it's time to leverage partnerships you've built during good times [when] businesses can think of the world as transactional. They'll move from one vendor to the next because it's 5 cents cheaper." Listen to Lott: "That comes back to bite you during tough times. When you treat people right, you build social capital that allows you to call on people when you need them most and they respond."[19]

With whom can we work to solve major problems, make money, and change the world? Think ingeniously and ambitiously. Take Tazo Tea, a Unilever brand based in Kent, Oregon, which in 2021 created an inno-vative partnership called the Tree Corps. The organization addresses the climate emergency and community well-being by planting trees; social inequity, by bolstering green spaces in BIPOC communities; and eco-nomic development, by providing forestry jobs with benefits in struggling inner cities. They call the movement "Tree Equity." This is a powerful demonstration of how the interconnectedness of crises that seem to be overwhelming us can be leveraged to work for us when we address multi-ple problems at once, and proactively.[20]

5. ***Innovate in real time to protect our business and help others.*** No matter how well they plan, and how creative their imaginations, emergency workers constantly encounter brand new thorny problems IRL. From a business and brand strategy standpoint, we can anticipate most problem *types*, from civil unrest to environmental catastrophes, and from infrastructure degradation to terrorism, and adapt our planned responses accordingly. By embracing an agility mindset and adapting to the fluid state of reality, we maintain relevance and business growth. Such examples from our recent crises include low-touch/no-touch restaurants; eBay helping businesses go online quickly; and Harry's (a men's shaving and personal grooming company) and other brands taking active steps to upgrade their own company cultures in response to the BLM movement. Leadership will increasingly be defined by such agility.

6. ***Think long term.*** No one knew how long it would take to get the coronavirus under control. We had to learn to live with extreme uncertainty, and to develop robust operations plans and communications strategies to continue business under this new reality—and others coming down the pike. Triage is no longer the exception, but the rule.

Planning for the future is key to business survival. We can all but "future-proof" our businesses by considering possible scenarios, and preemptively developing/testing plans. Remember a fact many civilians don't realize: First responders spend as much or more time proactively working on *preventing* future emergencies as they do reactively responding to the ones in front of them. Leading our businesses through the pandemic might have seemed at first like a burden, but it provided us all the training we needed to secure a better, stronger, and faster brand-crisis response that might just be the critical passkey to our future survival. Because the next pandemic (or its equivalent) is queued up and coming down the line. (More on crisis responses in chapter six, "Community.")

Now We Work from Wherever We Are on Our Impact Journeys

The country won't improve, John Adams wrote, until the people begin to "consider themselves as the fountain of power."[21] Historian Elizabeth Samet included this wisdom in her introduction to *Leadership: Essential Writings by Our Greatest*

Thinkers. "It can be dangerous to decide that you need to be led," writes Joshua Rothman, ideas editor for the *New Yorker*, in elucidating our culture of obsessively looking to our "leaders"—instead of ourselves—for solutions.[22] No volume of good intentions or critical need will persuade business to change course without the sanction of its leadership. The lack of such leadership has become so pronounced, it has been decried from the stage at the World Economic Forum to media around the world, and among business leaders when they correspond with each other.

We need to move beyond blind leadership and unthinking adherence to legacy thinking and behavior, to an enlightened mindset recognizing that the well-being of the whole turns on the health of the parts. This requires major shifts for corporations that have become household names. Organizations such as Coca-Cola, PepsiCo, and Nestlé, which have been named the world's biggest plastic polluters year after year, cannot withstand such critical scrutiny indefinitely as our natural environment deteriorates around us. Instead, they must embrace the challenge as an opportunity to reinvent their supply chains, products, and future. After many years of unmet environmental promises, they're finally on their way: With its 2021 paper bottle, Coke is experimenting with ways to replace the millions of tons of plastic waste it creates.[23] And Nestlé has committed to 100 percent recycled or reusable packaging by 2025.[24] Nestlé, with more than two thousand brands and a Godzilla-sized global footprint, first announced in 2018 its broad commitment to zero-waste packaging—including no plastics in landfills—and since then has undertaken a massive drive, working internally and with numerous partners to innovate creative solutions to that huge dilemma. CEO Mark Schneider says, "Plastic waste is one of the biggest sustainability issues the world is facing today. Tackling it requires a collective approach."[25]

The tenure of the CMO and the rise of new generations of leadership will pay little heed to, and show little patience with, any stewardship more limited than this. And all leaders will be tried in the court of public opinion, even as lagging products move from shopping aisles to dumpsters. The Virtuous Spiral demonstrates the new model of *LEAD WITH WE*, in which one can *LEAD* from wherever one sits, and in which traditional business "leaders" understand better who and what they're leading—and to what end. "It's hard to think of a time since World War II when the question of what makes a good leader was more central," writes Thomas Friedman in the *New York Times*.[26]

The good news is we can adopt and adapt this model starting today, regardless of where we find ourselves in our purpose process. This collectivized purpose will find different forms of expression, of course, relevant to our specific business. If, for instance, your business has already established a clear and motivating purpose, if you're already well into the purpose space and daily doing your bit to make the world better, that's great! You can measure your stated and practiced purpose against the LEAD WITH WE paradigm to expand as necessary and ensure it's consistent with best practices, given the greater need the world has right now, as well as the increased urgency. How exactly do you already LEAD WITH WE? Who and what entities comprise your WITH? How are you growing your WE? How are you sharing both the onuses and the bonuses of that process with all your partners, all the other stakeholders?

That could mean taking more responsibility—a leadership role—for embracing more immediate stakeholders in your local business system, your immediate community, and your brand's sphere of influence. Maybe it means jump-starting a movement, or your leadership, with a clear direction up the Spiral, like responding to a larger cultural need that aligns with your specific purpose, and participating in the way that society addresses it. Have you considered inflating your WE by working WITH a nonprofit foundation? Consider how veteran apparel maker Adidas has worked since 2017 with the nonprofit Parley Ocean Plastics to transform plastic waste into symbols of change by upcycling intercepted marine plastic debris for use in high-performance sports gear. And on the for-profit side, Adidas has partnered since May 2020 with a competitor, New Zealand/American footwear newbie Allbirds, to create the most carbon-neutral shoe on the planet. The idea is to LEAD their industry in ultimately reaching carbon neutrality.[27] Why? Because WITH. Because WE. *Through sport*, Adidas believes, *we have the power to change lives*.[28] Ideally, we all engage with, enrich, and guard the whole system. WE protect it. Contribute to it. Expand it exponentially in an ongoing feedback loop, wherein WE also receive tremendous abundance and security.

Now, let's say that, like Adidas, you're well aware that purpose is critical to success. But you're still not sure what precisely your company purpose should be or can be. Maybe this is because you assume purpose is tough to apply to what you do, make, or provide. Or you're lacking the deeper pockets of an international powerhouse like Adidas. Or perhaps your role in the system of stakeholders—say, payroll—seems to make no meaningful difference to the whole. Find ways that you can LEAD WITH WE wherever you are WITH whatever collaborators make the most sense. And work on expanding your influence beyond your present situation, energized further by a specific articulation of purpose by your company.

Finally, if you assume that you don't need a larger purpose beyond just staying in business, or to change any of your business behaviors, you will not escape the consequences of neglect, and no one will fix these problems for you. If you find yourself in this third group, adopt LEAD WITH WE in the way that's most applicable for you, then stretch yourself a little bit farther to do the things that need to be done for the collective. That could start as simply as more social responsibility or better environmental sustainability. Then get as enterprising and lofty as contributing to solving world hunger or homelessness in your corner of the world—whatever matters most to you and the communities you serve. The critical thing to remember is that everybody has the same purpose, which is to keep this Spiral going, by a communal effort to LEAD WITH WE, taking responsibility for the collective first. Every company has its individual purpose base, its context—what some business leaders think of as their "Come From"—that need to inform their unique expressions of the same We First mentality and practices. It takes different shapes, with the same motive/operating system. The purpose of US retailer Target is: *To help all families discover the joy of everyday life.* For SAP, the enterprise software leader headquartered in Germany, it's: *To help the world run simple and improve lives.* Brazilian steel producer Gerdau has: *Empowering people who build the future.* We all do our part to support the whole, each other, and ourselves, just as all species interact to serve the collective. We'll explore all this in detail in chapter four, "Purpose."

Now We Remember What We Forgot

Maybe when we think of "wealth," "profit," and "success"—even when we think of business in general—most of us don't immediately think of First Nations' traditions. This is to our peril. You see, it depends on how you define those terms. And most of us, of course, have consciously or not been inculcated in Western forms of Me First capitalism. The nightly newsroom diet of NASDAQ, Dow Jones, or S&P 500 performance is but one of countless sources of such indoctrination.

In this new narrative for business, we can learn much about who we are and what we need to do from a more aboriginal perspective. To do so necessitates our looking at the wisdom and thinking of indigenous peoples around the world as a guide for what we need to return to, especially in business. For example, Native American ideas about the cyclical nature of time, about respect for living things, the earning of wisdom from trials, and preservation of nature and traditions are all instructive. Most indigenous peoples understand themselves intergenerationally, some even considering themselves, for example, as "future ancestors." And native peoples' cultures have exhibited a greater ease and consistency in connecting the well-being of humans to the health of their surroundings. In fact, many indigenous peoples see the Western lack of connection as our fundamental—and terminal—illness.

For the most part, many indigenous people have historically framed their roles and responsibilities around the idea of interdependence with each other and the natural world:

> You have noticed that everything an Indian does is in a circle. That is because the power of the world always works in circles, and everything tries to be round. The sky is round, and I have heard that the earth is round like a ball, and so are all the stars. The wind, in its greatest power, whirls . . . Even the seasons form a great circle in their changing and always come back again to where they were. The life of a [person] is a circle, from childhood to childhood. And so it is in everything where the sacred power moves.[29]

These words from Hehaka Sapa ("Black Elk"), Holy Man of the Oglala Lakota tribe, remind us of these circles of interdependence.

What we need to remember is that our planet has finite resources but sufficiently supported, unlimited regenerative capacity. This is a big idea with enormous opportunities. The unlimited regenerative capacity of the planet, however, is currently hamstrung by humanity's unwillingness to reimagine its role in the world. Perhaps we could start by becoming symbiotic with our planet, instead of parasitic to it.[30] We must calibrate our practice of an adjusted kind of capitalism in accordance with the planet's capacity, while factoring in variables such as population, technology, and resources. We need to abandon the false presumptions of infinite resources and exponential growth to embrace concepts like responsible consumption and the kind of economy espoused by Patagonia, the radical transparency advocated by Everlane, or the generational responsibility embraced by eco-friendly Seventh Generation. By understanding the planet's regenerative capacities specific to resources that we need, we can retool what we make, how we make it, sell it, and consume it—and then grasp how optimizing those opportunities can and will improve the lives of all. This is where human ingenuity and Earth's capacity must combine to provide for all stakeholders and the planet. We can tie common indigenous peoples' mindsets back to our Spiral here, which provides a model for how business today can enlist and accelerate nature's regenerative capacity to restore our collective future.

Now We Use Nature as a Guide

"We human beings are the only species with the power to destroy the natural world," according to the Dalai Lama. As such, we share an "urgent responsibility" to protect wildlife and the planet.[31] "*WE*" is the operative word. And nature is the ultimate guide to understanding what *WE* means. Some have called it biomimicry. A philosophy in praxis for studying, absorbing lessons from, and imitating "the strategies found in nature to solve human design challenges—and find hope along the way."[32] As with the elders of our human family past—across thousands of years and countless cultures—the biomimicry frame reminds us of our interconnectedness. Researching it, then running our lives and business according to its principles, represents a return to the reverence of nature as wisdom. We look to the "forms and processes of nature"[33] for regenerative, rather than erosive, solutions. In so doing, we ensure our own survival.

There's recent thought leadership on "geomimicry," too—"the imitation of physical geological processes in the design and manufacture of products and services."[34] We've seen it in industry since a primitive human first fashioned a tool all the way to today, when mining, fractionation, energy extraction, and other industrial processes accelerate erosion and other natural progressions.[35] Of course, the vast majority of these industrial applications have been subtractive rather than additive. Nature provides a clear, viable model for ecosystem management readily adaptable for the business sphere. We can think of it as "corporate ecology," as business re-envisioned into a system nested within the larger systems of community, culture, humanity, and the physical environment.[36] That's a large part of what *LEAD WITH WE* means.

Each year scientists discover more details about the myriad ways that nature is sustainable because of the regenerative/circular dynamics that make that possible. There's no hoarding in nature, according to Lynne Twist, founder of the Soul of Money Institute, and co-founder of the Pachamama Alliance, both of which enable social justice and environmental sustainability, especially among biodiversity reserves such as the Amazon. Growth—personal, business, brand, cultural—must be considered similarly noncompetitive and reciprocal. Growth akin to hoarding, as happens in our culture of "Tycoon v. Homelessness," is simply not sustainable. Growth should be about achieving *sufficiency for all*. "Sufficiency isn't an amount at all," says Twist. "It is an experience, context we generate, a declaration, a knowing that there is enough, and that we are enough."[37]

How about mutualism? The birds and the bees complement each other's activities in a dance of balance and harmony. And trees secretly talk to each other underground. They're passing information and resources to and from each other through a network of mycorrhizal fungi that connect an estimated 90 percent of land plants,[38] and have operated this way for 450 million years in a "wood wide web."[39]

"How can business ecosystems emulate the vitality and longevity of their biological equivalents?" asks management educator David K. Hurst in a recent *strategy+business* article,[40] drawing from his book, *The New Ecology of Leadership: Business Mastery in a Chaotic World*. We can study interdependent life-support systems at the heart of the natural world. These include compassion, healing, solidarity, diversity, and resourcefulness. The infinite adaptive cycle[41] of birth, death, and renewal in dynamic loops. Nature, as outlined in detail by Janine Benyus, the architect of the nature-inspired innovation space, states, "When we look at what is truly sustainable, the only real model that has worked over long periods of time is the natural world."[42] She notes, "Animals, plants, and microbes are the consummate engineers. After billions of years of research and development, failures are fossils, and what surrounds us is the secret to survival."[43] Elsewhere Benyus writes:

> For designers, architects, engineers, and innovators of all stripes . . . Imagine discovering a catalog of sustainable ideas that are the product of 3.8 billion years of R&D—strategies from organisms that manufacture without "heat, beat, and treat" and ecosystems that circulate and upcycle materials, creating opportunities rather than waste."[44]

That's why it's not hokey to talk nature and the "Old Way" of humanity in a business book. For the same reason we all marveled at nature's reformative capacity as evidenced during COVID-19—rebirth of native species, cleaner air, quieter seismology—so, too, someday soon, we might adopt and adapt an analogous, more natural and organic species of capitalism that will drive exponential renewal if strategically directed to that end. Capitalism that puts "We First," as mentioned in the previous chapter. It's critical we realize that, without our intervention, "on a human timescale, ecosystems rarely recover completely"—in other words, we can't, as some suggest, "let nature heal itself."[45] We must take the *Lead*, together in an act of restorative ecology enabled by business. The business system we adopt must imitate more natural diversity across all our supply chains, as Benyus suggests. We saw this time and again during the pandemic, when companies great and small adapted on the fly in both production and organization, each fulfilling a different critical need based on its nature. What we haven't proven yet is whether we can stockpile in our corporate "seed bank" the necessary solutions to tomorrow's challenges and crises. Can we formalize attitudes and institute procedures for quicker, nimbler, and more efficient ramp-ups when the next iteration of COVID-19 inevitably hits? We certainly learned in 2020 that we can be efficient even while allowing for variation,[46] as Benyus says. Continuing to expose generative and regenerative forces in the natural world will allow us to imitate them, to leverage them for good in the business world. That's the secret to achieving a flourishing resilience. "Despite widespread consequences for human health, the economy and the environment, events leading to loss of resilience—from cascading failures in technological systems to mass extinctions in ecological networks—are rarely predictable and are often irreversible," according to a study in the journal *Nature*, which details new analytical tools and technologies for fixing that problem, and identifies tipping points—we're at one now, folks—so we can act as leaders.[47] Yes, becoming a well-prepared first responder business is essential to LEAD WITH WE. But it's not all about putting out fires in the urgent now. It's about tending now to a long-term future that's more imminent than we're pretending it is.

In the next chapter, we're going to get into the mindset of these vanguards. What story are they telling themselves to motivate the LEAD WITH WE movement? Then, we'll tackle each level up the Spiral one by one. Onward!

Key Takeaways

⟹ Recognize the urgency and responsibility to respond individually and collectively to the environmental challenges that threaten humanity, society, and your business.

⟹ Take a stand on social and environmental issues, even if and as they become politicized, to drive business relevance, growth, and impact.

⟹ Understand that our collaborative efforts—framed in the Virtuous Spiral—mimic the regenerative dynamics of nature that we must engage to increase the speed and scale of our response.

Action Items

1. *LEAD*—Adopt, execute, and iterate with a first responder mindset to best prepare your business to support all stakeholders in the face of ongoing crises—and inevitable future challenges.

2. *WITH*—Respond to polarizing or politicized social and environmental issues in alignment with your predetermined purpose and values, and in partnership with like-minded stakeholders and organizations.

3. *WE*—Seek to consistently expand the Breadth of Your *WITH* (all your partners) to increase your positive impact on the collective *WE*.

FIRST

OUR SHIFT

TRANSCENDENCE
FOSTER REGENERATIVE
& ABUNDANT FUTURE
Evolve principles & practices to
scale human & planetary health
Humanity & Planet

SOCIETY
COLLABORATE CROSS-
SECTOR & SHAPE CULTURE
Drive cultural conversations &
coalitions that improve society
Citizens, Collaborators & Sectors

COMMUNITY
MOBILIZE BRAND
COMMUNITIES &
BUILD MOVEMENTS
Engage external stakeholders
around purpose-led movements
Customers, Consumers & Partners

COMPANY
ACTIVATE PURPOSE
& ALIGN INTERNAL
STAKEHOLDERS
Integrate & apply purpose
throughout company
Execs, Employees & Supply Chain

LEADERS
DEFINE COMPANY
PURPOSE & GOALS
Conduct honest audit &
determine reason for being
Corporations, Businesses & Startups

ME
ADOPT *LEAD WITH WE*
MINDSET & BEHAVIOR
Recognize new reality, grasp
urgency & shift thinking

3

Paradigm

A Revolutionary New Narrative

Let's Tell a New Story About Business

As we continue our transformation from an individual "Me" into one equipped to LEAD a larger WE through a regenerative future, we must first craft a narrative that envisions restoration and renewal. Then we must stress-test, disrupt, and continuously iterate and adapt that narrative and associated practices. Revenues will come—and they *will* come—as a complementary benefit.

And there's plenty of precedent. Narratives throughout history have framed cultural shifts that have served a variety of interests and tipping/breaking points where culture needed to evolve. History provides many examples for the kind of new narrative language needed by a given moment, from the suffragists to Selma, Stonewall to *Silent Spring*. Here we need to overcome the presumption that capitalism and the role of business in society are somehow static and immutable, and instead realize it can be shaped through our collective thinking and behaviors— much more on that soon. We need a new narrative that prioritizes the interests of the collective WE. A reimagining and reengineering of global business practices for the sake of all stakeholders and the planet.

Critics complain that the language employed in LEAD WITH WE communications, of "changing the world" and "making the world a better place," contradicts the facts that business leaders continue to "hoard the overwhelming share of progress, the average American's life has scarcely improved,"[1] and trust in most institutions, business included, continues to erode. In the 2018 book *Winners Take All: The Elite Charade of Changing the World*, former *New York Times* columnist Anand Giridharadas[2] makes a compelling, if harsh, case for extreme caution when it comes to the kind of advocacy I'm encouraging from company leaders. Essentially, Giridharadas argues that a high-minded but ultimately misguided and "phony" "genre of elites believes and promotes the idea that social change" should be "pursued principally through the free market and voluntary action, not public life and the law and reform of the systems that people share in common"; that it is necessarily "supervised" by the "winners" of capitalism and their allies."[3]

"America's machine is broken," Giridharadas writes further in the *Guardian*. "The same could be said of others around the world. And now many of the people who broke the progress machine are trying to sell us their services as repairmen."[4]

I'm arguing that in the same way the US needs participatory democracy, the world needs participatory capitalism. So, when business leaders gather to do good, to hold their sphere accountable to the people, to self-police, that's a good thing. I'm arguing just the opposite of the "Winner Takes All" presumption of the greedy tycoons leading the world. The whole point of the LEAD WITH WE movement is that we do it—together. By us, for us. And WE—in common, not only the "elites"—engineer sensible solutions *for the good of all*. We should therefore empower, not undermine, business leaders—including CEOs and corporate boards—to cultivate, articulate, and activate their purpose. As long as their purpose is *our* purpose, WE operate together in answer to the public trust.

Let's aggregate agency across all stakeholders in our collective future. That's the entire philosophical basis for the advent of democracy in the first place. I'm not suggesting that business be the *only* driver of such positive social and environmental reform. I'm saying that because it *can* be, it *should* be—but only when it enlists the requisite stakeholders in our collective future. Because it possesses the means—and more, it bears the responsibility.

So, let's start our reimagining away from the idea of "winners" and "losers." Here are the top ten things to consider in reframing the business narrative toward LEAD WITH WE, to make the movement inescapably compelling to all of us:

1. Let's Remember This Is Not an Either/Or Equation

If WE are to LEAD by example in reframing the business world narrative, we need to see that, as more organizations and businesses join the call to serve people and the planet, we're witnessing significant victories these organizations have celebrated. Companies disrupting the paradigm in terms of environmental, social, and economic impact. There are some oft-cited examples, companies like Patagonia—fully committed to bettering the environment through net-positive carbon goals, renewable energy, recycling, and considerate sourcing—that have been reaping rewards in the form of an expanded customer base and healthier bottom line. Publicly traded companies such as Unilever and B2B companies like European research and biological solutions company Novozymes are also making huge strides in We First Capitalism. "Purpose-driven companies witness higher market share gains and grow on average three times faster than their competitors, all the while achieving higher employee and customer satisfaction," according to *Deloitte Insights*. A majority of consumers today decide where to spend their money based on "how brands treat their people, how they treat the environment, and how they support the communities in which they operate," according to a 2019 Deloitte study.[5] And Deloitte found in 2020 that such companies report 30 percent higher levels of innovation and 40 percent higher levels of workforce retention than their competitors.[6] Furthermore, about 55 percent of people believe businesses today have a greater responsibility to act on issues related to their purpose. Deloitte's consumer pulsing survey reveals that more than 80 percent of consumers would be willing to pay more if a brand raised its prices to be more environmentally and socially responsible. Out of these respondents, 15 percent said that they would be willing to pay 25 percent or more for a conscious brand's items.[7]

So, we clearly don't have to choose between win-lose ultimatums—people or the planet, profit versus people, product versus purpose. There is a new, inclusive way. The best news is that not only do conscientious businesses not lose, they accelerate their growth, as Timberland has (except during the pandemic)[8] by expanding its overall markets and product offerings. Such mindful companies not only do good things for the world, they reward their stakeholders with extraordinary returns.

A growing body of credible research and case studies[9] demonstrate that LEAD WITH WE businesses reliably outperform market averages and expand market share faster, usually with more profits. A 2020 Harvard–Columbia study[10] (revised from 2016 findings) estimated this annual "purpose premium" at 6 percent on average, equivalent to companies with "top-notch governance and innovation capacities."[11]

Many businesses continually outperform their counterparts on return on equity, with a 5.7 percent return premium between the top and bottom quintiles of the Russell 1000, an important stock market index, relative to LEAD WITH WE metrics. "Data continue to disprove the notion that balancing the needs of all stakeholders leads to lower returns," according to JUST Capital,[12] an independent nonprofit foundation (NPF) and a 501(c)(3)-registered charity founded in 2013 by concerned people from the worlds of business, finance, and civil society. Its sole mission is to track what "just" business behaviors US citizens consider important—and how companies align with those values. In fact, the corporations it ranks on its Just 100 List enjoyed a 56 percent higher total shareholder return over the past five years than other companies.[13] Since its inception in November 2016, JUST Capital's flagship index—the JUST US Large Cap Diversified Index—has returned 71.49 percent, or 6.43 percent more than the Russell 1000—equivalent to 1.10 percent annualized outperformance.[14]

Of course, any statistic for 2020–21 is going to reflect the reality of a global pandemic on certain consumer-spending sectors, down overall in 2020 on most measures.[15] But those companies that were prepared to adapt rapidly to dramatic shifts in consumer behavior dramatically outperformed those frozen out by the "unforeseen" circumstances of a novel virus loose in the world. And some businesses made up for loss of revenue with other, perhaps more valuable, forms of growth: increased loyalty, enhanced reputation, greater community engagement, and more influence over the cultural conversation—over society at large. They still managed to LEAD.

We need to live by a simple and fundamental creed: *In the expression of our responsibility for each other and the whole, WE will succeed together.* Now we must expand the purpose of leaders in this space and magnify their efforts with our own innovations. We're entering what David Cooperrider, impact investment strategist and professor of social entrepreneurship at Case Western Reserve University, and Audrey Selian of Rianta Capital, call a "decade of determination . . . And while . . . the speed of the transformation has caught many in business and industry off guard, there is no question . . . we are seeing the next episode in economic history unfolding. It will involve not a small step, but a giant leap."[16]

2. Let's Engage Our Emotions

Advertisers have long suspected that effective stories engage the listener on an *emotional* level. Research has now demonstrated that stories trigger a cascade of chemicals in the brain, all associated with an emotional and/or bodily response—with vicarious involvement *and* potential decision making. One can "change behavior by changing our brain chemistry."[17]

This represents an opportunity for us as businesses, by *telling a different story* about why we're in business in the first place, and what growth and success really mean. First, by becoming captivated ourselves by the new reality we find ourselves in, then by intriguing others with the newsworthiness of the new story.

We can tell our story with an emphasis on *empathy*. Emotional resonance and compassion for humanity and nature are the keys to a new beginning for business. By "putting yourself in someone else's shoes," to imagine what it would feel like to experience something from a perspective totally not one's own, we can rise with the central ascending arrow of *WE* in the Collectivized Purpose in Action Spiral.

Once we don the mantles of leadership, we shouldn't ignore our practice of Theory of Mind, our inbuilt facility for acknowledging and understanding others' plights and joys. When we *LEAD*, we must relate to all the diverse stakeholders in our enterprise. Do we know the real experience of our line workers? Our custodial staff? Our receptionists? Are we fully cognizant of the effects our schedules exert on childcare and education? Have we ever asked our staff what could improve their lives at work and beyond? How about our interview and onboarding process? What about identifying our potential customers' "pain points" and solving them? Do we regard the possible addictive, hazardous, or inefficient qualities of our products or services with adequate concern? Do we worry about the harmful effects our product, our shipping, or our waste has on the environment and in our communities?

As an example, in the US, there are more firearms than people. More than 389 million guns "are in the hands of everyday citizens, twice the number in the possession of every law enforcement and military in the world."[18] How could entrepreneurial innovation help with a viable solution? Enter Armory of Harmony (AOH), founded by musicians to support strong music programs in safe schools— and provide musical instruments *made from decommissioned firearms* that might otherwise wind up on the street and be involved in violent crimes.[19] Powerful. Multiple critical problems (school violence not the least of them) all innovatively addressed with one cool, simple plan that makes for a captivating story. AOH helps us understand the *whys* and *hows* of the problem and its process through compelling narrative and images. It has built coalitions, raised funds, and partnered with local communities, such as throughout Los Angeles, where it collects, smelts, upcycles, designs, and produces professional-grade instruments, some of which are used by pop stars,[20] who then act as influencers to expand the movement. What problems out there would you love to solve?

Let's start telling this new and different kind of story to ourselves and others about why our business is in business, what impact we desire, and why we deserve a leadership position. We don't have to solve all the world's problems. Let's try to make small improvements first. Then find an area we really care about and assimilate it into our profit-making purpose. *By pursuing purpose, we maximize profit.*

3. Let's Put People Before Plot

"We tell stories in conversation each and every day," says Steven Brown, associate professor and director of the NeuroArts Lab at McMaster University in Canada. "Very much like literary stories, we engage with the characters and are wired to make stories people-oriented."[21] Brown conducted a study, reported in the *Journal of Cognitive Neuroscience*, concluding that regardless of the type of narrative expression (words, gestures, illustrations), our brains relate best to the *characters*, focusing on the thoughts and feelings of a story's protagonist.[22]

We must *humanize* the corporate story among all stakeholders. Just as there is a product supply chain, there is also a *story supply chain* (see more in chapter six, "Community"), and our shared values and new vision for capitalism must be extended to all stakeholders through the entire life cycle of your products and all touchpoints of your brand. Not just to appropriately represent all parties, but also to recognize that the words and deeds of leadership, boards, and companies directly impact the lives of stakeholders from the top of the supply chain through to impact recipients. Think about telling the story from the perspective of suppliers' efforts, employees' contributions, customers' experiences, and the effect our business practices and behaviors have on real people in the real world. In *We First*, I talk about being the "chief celebrant, and not celebrity" of our stakeholder community to drive engagement, inspire advocacy, and scale impact as all stakeholders operationalize purpose together.

As we retool our narrative, we need to remember to share statistics, backed with tales of people and purpose. Stats are not abstract concepts for footnotes in a board report. We should instead individualize our impact. Just as we include people interacting with our product in our advertising—in order to hook new customers—we should do the same when we think about purpose, impact, and any improvements our business and the greater business world need to consider. When together *WE* retell this story, we'll be on our way to undoing the heinous damage of the past "'Me First,' and me at any cost" narrative.

4. Let's Start from Where We Are

As I've said before, anyone can contribute to the *LEAD WITH WE* business revolution and play a part in rewriting her business's narrative. Whether we're the CEO, a middle manager, or a team member, we get to contribute a compelling chapter to the story.

You represent the company in everything you do. Even if just for your *own sense of purpose*, your attitude, you can effect major change across your company. Your ethics in action. Your pride on display. Why do you love your company, what it stands for, and what you do for the collective? What specific outcomes make you most proud? Where can your institution improve most, and how can you help from where you're sitting? Wherever they are in the structure of an organization, everyone can *LEAD WITH WE*.

Similarly, it also doesn't matter what exactly your company *does*. Say you're making lamps. You might be thinking, "Well, I'm not providing clean water to the thirsty, or shipping food for the malnourished. I'm not transforming education. I'm not saving animals from immediate abuse." So what? You can treat your employees, coworkers, customers, and neighbors fairly. Wherever you are in your development, you can think about your manufacturing, your partners, your hiring, your footprint, your sourcing, your supply chain, the stands you take, the causes you support—the little and large ways you can exercise a positive impact on your business culture, your brand community, society, and the world at large. It's not only about making the best damn desk lamps your customers can find. It's about bringing light and truth to the world.

Finally, it would be naïve to assume that all products and services are well intended. But a sweeping tide of regulation, lawsuits, and employee, consumer, investor, and media activism are consistently course-correcting egregious business practices and the leadership behind them.

5. Let's Look Down the Longpath to "Downline Gen"

"A society grows great when old men plant trees in whose shade they know they shall never sit," goes the old Greek proverb. I think of this as "downline gen," meaning we consider in our decisions not only the immediate and longer-term future—but past even our own generation. Futurist and social systems strategist Ari Wallach calls this concept the *longpath*.[23] Don't think about gains and putting out fires today or even tomorrow. Focus on the *important* whenever you can—and try not to be distracted by that never-ending *urgent*.

Downline gen thinking requires us to assess the effects of our business products and processes beyond next quarter and next year, beyond even our tenure as a leader. And yes, let's think of future generations. We have clearly not been practicing the kind of "transgenerational empathy" needed to ensure we leave a better world for its future inhabitants. Again, let's look to the mindset of many indigenous peoples, such as the Native Americans who see their lives as custodians for the next seven generations. This idea inspired and animates the company Seventh Generation in its line of sustainable cleaning, paper, and personal care products.

As we regard our descendants with due compassion, writes Kim Polman, environmentalist author and founder of the Reboot the Future Foundation, we see that the Golden Rule is not applicable "just in the now, and it's not meant just for us. It's not just for *some* children or *select* species, either." We need to start "curating and sharing alternative roadmaps for a better future," Polman recommends. It's a call to intergenerational and interspecies compassion, "an idea which might suggest 'do unto your children as they would have you do unto them.'"[24] Our choices today have an absolute impact on our collective future.

And, unless we act decisively and quickly, we'll find "the future is no longer what it used to be," as French poet and philosopher Paul Valéry wrote.[25] It's why young climate activist Greta Thunberg condemned world leaders at the 2019 United Nations (UN) climate action summit in New York, declaring, "You have stolen my dreams and my childhood with your empty words," as she accused them of disregarding clear science regarding the climate emergency.[26]

So, let's not only *think* long term. Let's *act* in the long-term interests of all the players. Rewrite the story we tell, to make it about *potential*. Make the invisible, visible. Inspire with facts, probabilities, and even likelihoods. We can choose what we want our story to tell in the long run. If it's consistent with our intentions and our actions, *WE* can make it so.

"Too many organizations . . . still operate from assumptions about human potential and individual performance that are outdated, unexamined, and rooted more in folklore more than in science," writes Daniel H. Pink in *Drive: The Surprising Truth About What Motivates Us*. Pink uses multiple research studies to argue the performance alone of a meaningful task provides intrinsic reward. "Our innate need to direct our own lives, to learn and create new things, and to do better by ourselves and our world" holds the key to the real science of human motivation. In other words, our *purpose*.[27] Follow the counsel of author Gary Hamel, who told Pink that we "must find ways to infuse mundane business activities with deeper, soul-stirring ideals, such as honor, truth, love, justice, and beauty." Pink summarizes: "Humanize what people say and you may well humanize what they do."[28]

Downline gen thinking has begun to reach the mainstream—even the markets. The Long Term Stock Exchange (LTSE) was founded in 2019 on the principles of *LEAD WITH WE* by entrepreneur and author Eric Ries, after proposing the venture in his 2011 book *The Lean Startup*. "Our listing standards are designed to create a new public market experience that aligns modern companies and investors focused on creating value over generations," not just next year's returns, says exchange president Michelle Greene. Key to inclusion on the LTSE: "Long-term focused companies should consider a broader group of stakeholders and the critical role they play in one another's success."[29] Again, we're redefining "shareholders" as all those who share in our future. More in the investment side of *LEAD WITH WE* in chapter seven, "Society."

And take heed, business leaders: downline gen thinking and policies might soon become enshrined in law. In April 2021, a jury in Southwark, England, acquitted six activists who had damaged Shell's London headquarters two years earlier because they believed the company was directly contributing to the climate emergency, "thereby causing serious injury and death."[30] Because the jury had asked to see the pledge the defendants had signed before joining the environmental group that staged the attack, the ruling opens the door for further global legal defenses under the umbrella of "Earth Protector"[31] responsibility. Similar to common "Good Samaritan" laws that encourage bystanders to get involved in

emergency situations without fear of criminal or civil consequences, the idea of
Earth Protector or some similar status will likely be used, especially by the youngest generations, as both a banner and shield for taking action against businesses
they deem to not *LEAD WITH WE*.

6. Let's Invite All Stakeholders to Contribute

Let's look at UK coffee chain Costa's half-a-billion-cup recycling campaign, and
the necessity to engage all stakeholders. "The 21,000 baristas that we have here
in the UK are our front-line communicators to our customers and if there is a
disconnect between what our baristas are saying and what we are communicating
through all our other channels, we are very quickly going to lose consumer trust,"
Costa's communication and engagement officer, Jodi Wheatley, told a major Sustainability Communications event audience in 2018. "Therefore, great internal
communications are absolutely key to getting everything else right."[32] We're going
to cover such communication with our associates in chapter five, "Culture."

Since I wrote *We First*, the public—not business leadership—has taken the
reins of the business narrative. Because consumers make up the bulk of our community, it's *consumers* who get to tell the story of our brand. "Indeed, according
to a major study by Accenture Strategies, nearly two-thirds of US consumers surveyed believe their words and actions—from posting comments on social media
to participating in boycotts—can influence a brand's reaction to an event or
its stance on an issue of public concern." Fact is, "Brands are now community
property belonging to shareholders and employees, as well as customers who now
demand experiences on their terms, influence others to buy (or not), co-develop
products and services, and even act as sales channels." If not, one in five consumers
will "walk away forever."[33] This opportunity to differentiate our brand's authentic
self is created by customers. *LEAD WITH WE* businesspeople rely on the public to
become the ambassadors of their brands.

And *LEAD WITH WE* consumers take that responsibility gravely. Your
contribution—in dollars and cents, Yelp reviews, word of mouth, or collaboration
on impact initiatives—is the story writ large. Since I wrote my last book, a number
of potent tools, resources, and technologies, such as new carbon tracking labeling
across the footwear, apparel, and food categories, have emerged to empower consumers. But it's a mistake to limit communications to those outlets. Many business
entities are optimizing the ubiquity and variety of available online assets to expand

their impact on consumers.[34] Resonance is key here, because 58 percent of content created by the world's leading 1,800 brands is "poor," "irrelevant," and/or "fails to deliver."[35] Opportunities abound to rise above the noise with actions and content that are music to consumers' ears.

More and more consumers are taking actions in their own lives to support a more regenerative future. Yes, there remains an "intention-action gap" among many consumers, but still, in unprecedented numbers, people are rejecting single-use plastics, gas-guzzling transportation, and meat-eating lifestyles.[36] More people are shopping locally, composting, and recycling.[37] More people are bringing their own bags to the store.[38] More people are conserving water, reducing food waste, and choosing energy-efficient home appliances.[39] Brands, meanwhile, benefit from these trends. Recent research demonstrates that some categories of sustainable products enjoy *double* the growth rates of their conventional counterparts.[40]

7. Let's Rewrite the Story of the Successful CEO

New voices are telling a very different story about business leadership than we heard in J. P. Morgan's or J. P. Getty's time—or even just a decade ago. The future of CEO standings is now. The LEAD WITH WE movement is lately informing how leaders are graded in this emerging marketplace. *Harvard Business Review* (*HBR*), which rates the best-performing CEOs every year, has incorporated two LEAD WITH WE metrics in its ratings since 2015. Consider Pablo Isla Álvarez de Tejera, former CEO (now chairperson) of Inditex, a Spanish megacorporation and the world's largest fashion group, with flagships Zara and Massimo Dutti leading its portfolio. In 2017 and 2018, Isla was ranked number one (out of one hundred). Eighty percent of that's a function of *HBR*'s assessment of typical financial performance alone: "Since becoming CEO in 2005, Isla has led Inditex on a global expansion during which the company has opened, on average, one store a day."[41] But the other 20 percent derives from those two LEAD WITH WE metrics, Sustainalytics (the sustainability credentials of the company) and also a "CSRHub" ranking, measuring the positive work the company's doing for the world. Isla ranked 76 and 142 on those measures in 2017, and improved to 60 and 128 in 2018. But industry and media scrutiny, not to mention healthy leadership ambition, has since led the highly profitable, fast-fashion empire to retool aggressively around using sustainable raw materials and fibers, eliminating single-use plastics and bags, and declaring that 100 percent of the cotton, linen, and polyester used across all of its brands will be organic, sustainable, or recycled by 2025. In chapter seven, "Society," we'll more deeply study such benchmarking and how to leverage it. In 2019, *HBR* increased the weighting share of the Environmental, Social, and Governance (ESG) elements to a full 30 percent of the CEOs' final rankings. "The shift reflects the fact that a rapidly growing number of funds and individuals now focus on far more than bottom-line metrics when they make investment decisions."[42] Indeed, they do. And so should you.

JUST Capital and *Forbes*'s "JUST 100" list chronicles good "corporate citizens," too, calling them "Companies Doing Right By America" because "shareholder returns mean nothing if a company's workers, customers, communities and environments aren't considered, too."[43] "You can't expect people to embrace stakeholder capitalism if they have no stake in the economy," JUST Capital's CEO Martin Whittaker tells me.[44] Nearly 90 percent of business leaders agree that today offers an opportunity for large companies to hit "reset" and focus on doing right by their workers.[45] *Barron's* also considers ESG data in ranking CEOs for its legendary list, recently adding the once-"squishy" S for social factors such as treatment of employees.[46]

The plot of this story builds to the concept of an "anti-CEO." At the extreme—but attainable—end of leadership activism, this new figure on the corporate landscape looms, a kind of "antihero" shaking up what it means to run a company in the first place, and fostering a *Lead With We* culture there. Take Hamdi Ulukaya, the Kurdish American billionaire, philanthropist, and activist who is the founder, chairperson, and CEO of Chobani, the top-selling Greek yogurt brand in the US. Since his fabled 2019 TED talk[47] in Vancouver, British Columbia, he's been championing the idea of the "anti-CEO playbook." The rulebook that's guided CEOs for forty years is broken, Ulukaya declares. "Today's business book says business exists to maximize profit for the shareholders. I think that's the dumbest idea I've ever heard in my life." Instead, business should be about people over profits, gratitude over gratuitous accumulation of spoils. "This is the difference between profit and true *wealth*."[48]

Ulukaya knows a lot about wealth. In 2005, he scraped together enough money to buy a tumbledown factory in South Edmeston, New York, that Kraft Foods was shuttering. He hired some of its staff to rehab the building and engaged a "yogurt master" (cool job). He launched Chobani in 2007, when Greek-style yogurt accounted for just 1 percent of US market share.[49] Ten years later, it was 50 percent, thanks to Ulukaya's starting the trend—let's call it a movement.[50] And Chobani had overtaken Yoplait as second in overall yogurt sales in the US[51]—the top Greek style by 2018,[52] even as the company maintained clean sourcing, ingredients, and processing. In addition, Ulukaya plans to give his two thousand employees a 10 percent ownership stake in the company when it goes public[53] ("Now it's not just the yogurt that's rich," proclaimed the *NYT*[54]), which, assuming a $4 billion valuation, would make some early employees millionaires, and double, triple, or quadruple the average annual salaries on payout day. That's a great start in building a vibrant, loyal business culture.

What companies do with their profits will define the leaders of the future (and the future is now). Chobani's philanthropic, community-service, and incubator efforts in fulfillment of its purpose—*Better food for more people*[55]—are too voluminous to catalog. Lately, Chobani's undergone a minor rebranding, positioning itself cleverly as a "food-focused wellness company." In 2016, Chobani chided its rivals, General Mills and Dannon, in controversial ads insinuating their yogurts are rife with unsavory impurities.[56] The company brings in about $1.5 billion in annual revenue,[57] proving the "anti-CEO" is not averse to rules from the old playbook, such as Rule Number One: Make money. "I don't want more, I just want to *do* more," this anti-CEO says about his investment in people. "Whatever I see in the world that discourages me, I answer with Chobani."[58]

Ulukaya answered the fundamental question, "What is the purpose of business?" It is to serve the greater good. Then, in line with that, he determined the purpose of his individual company: I'll serve the commons with a healthy, delicious, lifestyle product, and use the proceeds to help the world, starting with my own people, in ever more expanding ways. And he employs that collective purpose as a lodestone that attracts aligned people, programs, and profits, magnetizing them all to perpetuate that purpose in movements that reach far beyond his original plant in upstate New York.

Forward-facing companies are now tying executive compensation (EC) to the achievement of *LEAD WITH WE* goals and impact milestones. "Executive remuneration should reflect stakeholder responsibility," declared the World Economic Forum at Davos 2020.[59] Still, short-termism tends to be the perennial disease of many boards and C-suites. Lisa Earle McLeod, the author of *Selling with Noble Purpose*, writes in *Forbes*:

> When a board overemphasizes backward-looking metrics like quarterly earnings, margin and revenue, company leaders cascade that overemphasis downward, often with disastrous consequences. It's been well

documented that overemphasizing short-term metrics has a chilling effect on long-term strategy. Often referred to as strategy surrogation, when a metric (like new accounts added) overrides a larger strategy (like creating a differentiated customer experience) employees wind up caring more about the metric than they do the customer.[60]

This is exactly what happened during the Wells Fargo account fraud scandal, for which the community bank agreed to pay US prosecutors $3 billion to settle criminal charges and a civil action for mistreatment of customers over a fourteen-year period from 2002 to 2016—and why the once-trusted brand suffered incalculable damages to its credibility. It's not that every employee will necessarily commit ethics violations in the mad dash toward sales and other commissions. But history has borne out that some will. Perhaps even many. The Wells Fargo case proves that it's no longer prudent to tie remuneration to traditional metrics. In fact, it's win-win-win when we consider reforming compensation—starting with EC—by tying it to the attainment of clear, transparent, and publicized impact goals that matter not only to the balance sheet, but also to balancing the needs of the planet. Such needs will be less sales driven and more purpose driven; less shareholder-centric and more stakeholder-centric;[61] less "Me" and more WE.

Even large, private company boards can hold themselves accountable to LEAD WITH WE metrics. Consider the Mars Compass, an enterprise tool developed by the Mars family, which adds to the traditional concerns over financially positioning some positive world impact goals, as well as becoming a trusted partner in society.[62]

Without such radical shifts in financial rewards and leadership strategies at the top, short-termism will win, and CEOs and other leaders won't be incentivized toward purpose. In 2019, Uber, which has a mostly White staff and a checkered history on some key social issues, tied executive pay to its DI&E 2022 goals.[63] McKinsey research determined that "organizations with a more diverse senior management team (gender and ethnicity) and an inclusive culture outperform their industry peers who are not as diverse."[64] That's one of the reasons why $100 billion[65] Johnson & Johnson does it. And German global drug giant, Bayer AG, which touts a purpose of "Science for a Better Life," is uniting its executive compensation with the focus on several Sustainable Development Goals (SDGs)—specifically food security, healthcare, and climate protection. Bayer pursues these key performance indicators (KPIs) with the same rigor as its financial goals.[66] Core to its brand now is the commitment to its vision of "Health for all, Hunger for none," and everything that purpose and goal entail.

Other companies have recently adopted this key LEAD WITH WE ESG strategy. Apple, Shell, Clorox, Alcoa, ING, Intel, Heineken, Allbirds, and others have incorporated fulfillment of these goals into their KPI-based EC plans.[67] In fact, such moves increased 50 percent over the two years between 2017 and 2019,[68] and they're still rising.

8. Let's Leverage Tech to Unlock Opportunities

Our access to the latest developments in innovative, efficacious technology is greater than at any time in history. Conceding some regional infrastructure and expertise obstacles, and some shaky trust issues (see the whole 5G debate), with the proper market incentives, tech will be a major partner in solutions going forward. With the best leadership and strategic collaborations, the institutional resources and reach of the business world will leverage extant and developing technology to exponentially increase the range of our potential impact into the realm of the truly transhuman: That's the essence of LEAD WITH WE. Consider these few examples:

→ **"Convergence 2.0,"** the juncture of biology and engineering, as outlined in former Massachusetts Institute of Technology president Susan Hockfield's 2019 book, *The Age of Living Machines*. The MIT professor of neurobiology argues in *Fast Company*:

> In terms of population growth and our food resources and our water resources and our healthcare resources, it's pretty clear that if we're going to go from our current 7.7 billion [people] to over 9.7 billion by 2050, we're going to need some new technologies in order to increase productivity without using up all the resources on earth.[69]

Hockfield elegantly argues that it's always been new technological advances put into the hands of the people that have saved humanity from multiple points of peril and potential extinction. The tech-heavy agricultural revolution of the nineteenth century is one prime example of stunning changes at scale. Electronics, genomics, robotics, nuclear science, and modern pharmaceuticals are others.[70] Watch this space—tech solutions to world problems advance daily. But it's important to remember that all tech advances are engineered by human hands and minds in response to human-recognized problems.

➠ **Omaze,** a global online fundraising platform that democratizes traditional auction-giving across 180 countries by offering everyone the chance to have once-in-a-lifetime experiences, be it lunch with George Clooney, pizza with Iron Man, or playing catch with Tom Brady. A powerful expression of a LEAD WITH WE strategy, it seamlessly empowers celebrities to rally support for causes they care about while promoting timely projects; nonprofits to benefit from the exponential donations and global exposure; and fans to contribute to a cause they and a celebrity care about while entering the drawing for unforgettable prizes. It's about leveraging ubiquitous technology to unlock greater potentiality, as CEO and co-founder Matt Pohlson shared with me in *Forbes*: "We want to make dreams come true. Optimism is a fuel for dreams and makes people realize what they thought was impossible is actually possible. We want to scale that."[71]

➠ **Charity: Water,** a model for a range of NPFs that have fully embraced innovative tech advancements and collaborations to deploy and maintain complex solutions for "simple" problems, such as water scarcity in Ethiopia. Water, human health, ecosystems, and the economy are obviously interlocked. Around 785 million people are living without clean water (not to mention that about two billion people who don't have a reliable toilet).[72] Tragic, and extra disturbing in light of the coronavirus pandemic, which has highlighted for the West the idea that hygiene is a life-and-death matter—something those in the developing world know all too well. But, as *Fast Company* reports, "Historically, humanitarian aid groups have wasted hundreds of millions of dollars on poorly planned or maintained projects that have broken down, according to the International Institute for Environment and Development, a global-sustainability research group."[73] Charity: Water, on the other hand, reports it is able to route 100 percent of all public donations toward project costs, avoiding such waste by employing tech solutions that map its wells and monitor flow rates from wells and gravity taps, while "sharing the continually updated information online publicly, which has endeared it to high-powered Silicon Valley donors past and present."[74] Its fundraising events are a thing of tech beauty, too, connecting donors to the real recipients of fresh water their dollars make possible.

➡ **Frontier 2030: Fourth Industrial Revolution for Global Goals Platform.** Aiming to solve in this decade most of the UN's immense SDGs—poverty, climate action, hunger, health, and well-being—by using innovative technological advancements akin to a "fourth industrial revolution," Frontier 2030 brings together tech companies, governments, civil society, and international leaders. The Internet of Things, AI, blockchain, 5G, CRISPR, and their ilk are radically changing the world at a rapidly accelerating, dizzying scale. "Big Data almost doubled in market size in three years with a total revenue of $49 billion in 2019," reveals the latest Frontier 2030 report. "Worldwide spending on artificial intelligence (AI) was approximately $35.8 billion in 2019, with a 44% increase from 2018; and for blockchain solutions nearly $2.9 billion was spent in 2019, an increase of 88.7% from 2018."[75] Most past industrial and technological revolutions have dramatically improved human life—but with two significant side effects: The benefits have been unevenly distributed to an extreme degree, based on economic tier (just as access to reliable internet service is today). And with every "advancement" comes predictable degradation either to human health, other species, or the climate.[76] Here's just one good example of this tech access and development disconnect from the *Guardian*:

> The more devastating impacts of pedal-to-the-metal digital capitalism fall on the environment and global poor. The manufacture of some of our computers and smartphones still uses networks of slave labor. These practices are so deeply entrenched that a company called Fairphone, founded from the ground up to make and market ethical phones, learned it was impossible. (The company's founder now sadly refers to their products as "fairer" phones.)[77]

9. Let's Share the Story of Our Impact

We are seeing more brands not only define their purpose (which we'll discuss in the next chapter) but also become action oriented and impactful through it.

As such, they are transcending their products, services, and categories to shape and improve society. Whether it's promoting women's rights, preventing the next school shooting, or shielding endangered species, more companies have humanized their brands through their leadership, engagement, and impact around key cultural issues.

Tim Cook of Apple wants to ensure equal inclusion of LGBTQ members of society in decision making and opportunity. Marc Benioff of Salesforce is working to expand economic prospects for the traditionally disadvantaged. Yvon Chouinard of Patagonia aims to realize a "responsible economy." Santa Monica–based Veggie Grill is committed to "make food matter more." Seattle-based MOD Pizza hires the formerly incarcerated, homeless people, and people with disabilities, calling it "impact hiring."[78] Let's join these companies that LEAD WITH WE in making money—and changing the world. They scale impact up and down the Spiral, always asking, "How will collaborating WITH others on this decision/application LEAD to positive impact on the world at large—on The Higher WE?" And the narratives of all those businesses—the stories they tell—are based on inspiring purpose and evidence of measurable impact.

Honest intent is not enough. We need reliability of impact—environmental, social, cultural—through consistent actions in pursuit thereof. When the buzz of freshly earned media wears off, brands survive not on what they want to do—but on what they actually do, and what, when the measurement is over, they have done (changed, affected, improved). Thus, our mindsets and methodology must be firmly grounded in the need to drive business growth *and* positive impact as twin turbines in the same engine.

Consider Disney. The company has weathered hardships from strikes, mass resignation, bankruptcy, and accusations of antisemitism, as well as recent mass layoffs during the pandemic. But as young Walt Disney, a Red Cross ambulance driver in World War I, developed a team of simpatico artists and business colleagues, collected strategic partners, listened to his audiences, learned from his missteps, and constantly innovated and modernized his industry with his profits from prior ventures, his business rose from his own discrete values up the Spiral into meaningful collective impact. In fact, for all intents and purposes, the Disney-Pixar brand owns the very concept of "magic." *That's* impact.

And that's the new story that LEAD WITH WE companies are telling.

10. Let's See This Challenge as an Opportunity, Not a Burden

For many, this story will climax in heroes finding treasure. In fact, there is no limit to the opportunities unleashed by solving for our future. According to the "Better Business, Better World" report by the Business & Sustainable Development Commission, achieving the UN's SDGs in just four economic systems (food and agriculture, cities, energy and materials, and health and well-being) could have already opened sixty market "hot spots" worth an estimated $12 trillion in market opportunities, business savings, and revenue. The total economic prize for implementing the Global Goals could be two to three times bigger.[79] Plus, "the long and difficult process of building and nurturing partnerships with concerned stakeholders could potentially result in an outcome that is more than just the sum of its parts," the UN reminds us, exactly on point.[80]

In dollars and cents for the individual business leader, a renewed focus on the SDGs helps the personal bottom line, too, as it aims to solve aspects of the climate crisis, according to *Bloomberg*:

> Four shareholders in China's giant supplier of electric-vehicle batteries have built a combined fortune of $17 billion. An Australian businessman has created a $7 billion net worth from recycling. A ten-figure stake in a hydrogen fuel cell trucking company has minted an American billionaire.[81]

Let's Commit to LEAD WITH WE

We've reviewed a new model of what it means to LEAD, primarily by embracing an urgent sense of collective responsibility, and telling ourselves and others a new story about the role business can play in creating a better world. Now, with these considerations in mind, let's explore the details of the *how*, the complexity of application, and the various forms LEAD WITH WE can take. We'll detail the actionable strategies, tactics, metrics, and potential partners and forms of collaboration required—what exactly WITH can and should entail. We'll review plenty of case studies for best practices and caveats/warnings about what not to do. But remember the basics: We always consider all stakeholders—the collective—as we continue to climb the Virtuous Spiral. We start with the people with whom we work, then loop in our partners and other collaborators, then expand out first to our customers, and then beyond into society. And we always use the broadest *WITH,* aiming for the widest *WE* as our decision-making filter. Let's get to our prescription for reengineering business.

Key Takeaways

➡ Initiate a new story of business, wherein *WE* all approach our shared responsibility for our future with optimism and hope, and employ our empathy and excitement to inspire others to join *WITH* us and this movement.

➡ Humanize your business by sharing people-focused stories that remind us all of our responsibility, agency, and incentives, while also securing and scaling engagement by all stakeholders and partners.

➡ Solve long-term issues while also addressing emergent crises with an expansive ambition to improve life for humanity and the planet.

Action Items

1. *LEAD*—Tell a new story about business. Cultivate a mindset and practice of business that finds and executes opportunities in challenges and crises.

2. *WITH*—Drive collaborative impact with nature as your model from wherever you are on your impact journey.

3. *WE*—Hold yourself consistently and transparently accountable to metrics that identify how you are benefiting all stakeholders through meaningful and measurable results.

PART
TWO

WITH

Think of *WITH* as a verb. *WITH* manufactures the collective noun *WE* through all our decisions and actions to cooperate as much as possible, to serve each other, to hold ourselves accountable to each other. *WITH* is the engine that drives the philosophy behind, and the actions of, our leadership. *WITH* describes the nature of the movement, the progress of our climb up the Collectivized Purpose in Action Spiral. We move, accelerate, and expand our compasses of impact in direct proportion to how many partners we win along the way. To put it simply, we're always stronger together than we are apart.

WITH means we gain impassioned, effective allies as we *LEAD*, appropriate for our enterprise. The more *WITH*s we accumulate, the closer we get to The Higher *WE* that we're meaning to serve. And *WITH* implies three main ways and several ancillary ways of working together on solving critical problems, thus ensuring long-term viability of brands and a more regenerative future for all of us. Each of these levels of collaboration represents a wider level of the Collectivized Purpose in Action Spiral at the top of the next chapter and the others.

➡ **WITH** *a powerful purpose,* which drives all our actions toward a desired impact. **WITH** *the company's own personnel,* **and within the** *internal* *culture* that collaboration forms. The company itself and all its key partners working together become a major change agent. This applies whether we're a big or small business, a public or private company, an entrepreneur or a global concern; B2B, B2C, B2G (government), or DTC (direct to consumer). And we can LEAD WITH WE from any point of entry. Founder, C-suite, board member, investor, marketer, HR/chief people officer, salesperson, middle manager, new hire. In fact, it's necessary for all stakeholders within the business to adopt the mindset and practices of LEAD WITH WE, company-wide, if we're to maximize impact. Working WITH each other, our company's internal constituents can exponentially increase impact to the point where we can build a brand community, shape culture, and better society, even as we drive growth and profits. We'll discuss internal company culture in chapter five, "Culture."

→ WITH *the company's customers (B2B) and consumers (B2C)—its community*, which we can evolve, mobilize, and expand. In chapter six, "Community," we'll cover becoming the chief celebrant of our customers and other ways to architect and build a community.

→ WITH *the larger society*, where we can change the world by leading a cultural conversation. WITH the people at large, now and in the future. This typically begins in local communities and expands upward and outward, eventually encompassing the physical infrastructures and environments in which people live and ought to thrive. This kind of cultural leadership is based on an idea I laid out in *We First*, that the best hope for business is to get itself quickly into the business of hope. To achieve that, we have to think big and divergently. "You never change things by fighting the existing reality," Buckminster Fuller writes. "To change something, build a new model that makes the existing model obsolete."[1] We'll discuss this new model, working at this level of WITH, including broad, cross-sector collaboration, in chapter seven, "Society."

→ WITH not only humans and our institutions—although we are, of course, important. WITH means all the entities with which we share the world: humans, animals, and the wider environment.

Ready to begin with this imperative? Come WITH me!

CORPORATIONS, BUSINESSES & STARTUPS

TRANSCENDENCE
FOSTER REGENERATIVE
& ABUNDANT FUTURE
Evolve principles & practices to
scale human & planetary health
Humanity & Planet

SOCIETY
COLLABORATE CROSS-
SECTOR & SHAPE CULTURE
Drive cultural conversations &
coalitions that improve society
Citizens, Collaborators & Sectors

COMMUNITY
MOBILIZE BRAND
COMMUNITIES &
BUILD MOVEMENTS
Engage external stakeholders
around purpose-led movements
Customers, Consumers & Partners

COMPANY
ACTIVATE PURPOSE
& ALIGN INTERNAL
STAKEHOLDERS
Integrate & apply purpose
throughout company
Execs, Employees & Supply Chain

LEADERS
DEFINE COMPANY
PURPOSE & GOALS
Conduct honest audit &
determine reason for being

ME
ADOPT *LEAD WITH WE*
MINDSET & BEHAVIOR
Recognize new reality, grasp
urgency & shift thinking
Every Individual

4

Purpose

The Leadership Mindset to Slingshot
Business Growth

With Purpose over Profiteering, Business Becomes Balanced

Having reset our thinking and retold the business and leadership story, we find ourselves more quickly and effectively able to climb the Virtuous Spiral toward success, up through collaboration en route to Transcendence. The motor that will propel us up and outward will be our business purpose. In LEAD WITH WE, we focus on the "*transcendent* purpose" over the "*transactional* purpose," as a recent Harvard study suggests.[1] This one step alone, this single change in the tone, tenor, and content of our narrative, can make a massive difference in outcomes. In other words, we aim high on the Spiral, and we ensure our purpose genesis and activations are maximally inclusive.

Today, I see most brand leadership increasingly viewing themselves as responsible to everyone—which is good—but then enlisting only their own corporate stakeholders to address the targeted issues, with increasing success and decreasing missteps. That approach doesn't go far enough. It limits inclusion and collaboration.

I'm arguing that *all* stakeholders—not just the company itself—have responsibilities here, and that includes helping define the company's reason for being. So, the real failure is *not* recognizing that there are heroes (I call them "leaders") everywhere, on every level of the Spiral. If we engage them in a fast-moving tornado of responsible, regenerative, LEAD WITH WE thinking, together WE can (literally) save the world. But, of course, much of the leadership, tone, and resources will derive from a few key influencers within each business. This information is for you, the leader among all those who LEAD. And, of course, the first collaborators are going to be your internal stakeholders.

Ask yourself where your company's real passions lie. Organizing metadata? Revolutionizing transport? Supporting troops? *What are you good at?* Don't just "do what you love." *What does the world need?* You might succeed in a given niche, but the more people your business can reach—and the more it can do for the collective—the better. *What are people willing to pay for?*[2] No one thought anyone would want to pay for these products and services: Drinking water from a bottle. Getting a ride in a stranger's car. Staying overnight in a stranger's home. Except someone *did* predict those things. And made hay while making a difference.

You might want to consider your company's origin story, its founding mythos. That's your—and *only* your—story. Your purpose put into words and symbols. Let's say your transactional purpose is to make money selling robots. But what's the real purpose behind what you do, why you exist as a company? Make a purpose statement out of your soul-searching inventory regarding the animating force that gets you out of bed in the morning. For optimal buy-in, ensure all your constituents are part of the building of your purpose, too. Write it out. Live it daily. Use the statement as a touchstone to avoid ego-driven battles and to make thorny policy decisions. Here's how Brian Chesky, Airbnb co-founder, CEO, and head of community, conceived his company's purpose:

> For so long, people thought Airbnb was about renting houses. But really, we're about home. You see, a house is just a space, but a home is where you belong. And what makes this global community so special is that for the very first time, you can belong anywhere. That is the idea at the core of our company: belonging.[3]

Then Chesky asks, "What is the purpose of a company?"

[I]ts purpose is to realize its vision . . . we must have the best interest of three stakeholders in mind: Airbnb the company (employees and share-holders), Airbnb the community (guests and hosts) and the world outside of Airbnb.[4]

With Cause-, Purpose- & "Woke"-Washing, Consumers' BS Detectors Will Go Off

Modern consumers and younger generations are hyper-sensitive to being "sold to." They want to believe a company's truly committed to something larger than itself. They want to understand the company's relevance and are distrustful of anything less than complete honesty. Exaggerating or outright lying about the eco-friendliness of our product is known as "greenwashing." Plant-based product innovator Quorn Foods experienced greenwashing accusations in 2020 with backlash over its disingenuous carbon footprint claims, and Nestlé was sued for claiming its cocoa is now sustainably sourced, even though accusers say it's in fact driving massive deforestation in West Africa. "Local-washing" is claiming local sourcing while ordering from outside one's country. "Cause-washing" is publicizing support for a cause while not actually committing resources, financial or human. All these have caused significant problems for corporate America and Europe,[5] even before a few false COVID-19-related business moves. Along with disproportionate, scattershot, and uninvolved "window dressing" corporate social responsibility (CSR) efforts, these insincere activities have rightly stung many a business in the butt in the age of ubiquitous social media. Beginning with the "cancel culture" that came to a head in 2020, those stings can be deadly.

Now enter "purpose-washing." Remember Pepsi's "Jump In" campaign that starred spokesperson Kendall Jenner, and missed the mark on purposeful advertising in 2017? When "hashtag-Resistance" could first be commoditized, Pepsi was the first brand that attempted to cash in on it.[6] A widely derided example of purpose-washing, the soda maker effectively trivialized the Black Lives Matter (BLM) movement without showing *how* the brand was substantively addressing the issue, let alone offering consumers a means to get involved. The company pulled the ad. Jenner, in tears, apologized to the public. Pepsi apologized to Jenner. Everyone lost.

Has external business communication about purpose progressed since those cringe-worthy days of yore? Nordstrom, Marvel Studios, Viacom,[7] and countless other companies, mighty and minuscule, came out with direct, purposeful, sincere, and highly sensitive statements in the wake of the killing of George Floyd in 2020. But the public didn't regard all efforts equally. Some companies took major reputational hits and merciless mocking—with stock drops for many—after missing the mark. COVID-19 and the social injustice protests have exacerbated the burden on brands to walk the talk. Brands are judged more than ever on authenticity and tone—and held more accountable than ever.

What's the preventive for this problem? We should simply *do right* in a multi-stakeholder way, in a *We* First way, with sincerity—and relevance (and make sure we can back it up with our proof of purpose, or POP). Because younger people in particular choose brands with the consideration, "If you're not with us on fixing the future, you are against us." How can business help them achieve *their* purpose—help them be their best selves? By definition, a company's purpose defines the meaningful role it will play in bettering all lives, directly or indirectly, irrespective of age. And as such, the company and its purpose serve as an inspiring platform through which all stakeholders of every age can engage and co-create that desired impact as an expression of their personal purpose.

With This Shift in Perspective, Everything Changes

All our purpose journeys must be sincere, organic, bottom-up, all-inclusive processes that provide all our stakeholders agency in whatever necessary changes top our collective list. And what each company contributes must be relevant to its industry and its stakeholders' values, arising out of its clear and activated particular form of the universal *Lead With We* purpose.

➡ ***Purpose Genesis.*** Today's purpose imperative is driven by the intersection of three megatrends: social and cultural evolution, transformative social technologies, and significant shifts in demographics. They all coalesce to increase awareness of the multiple challenges we face as a species, as well as the heightened expectation on business to answer those calls.

➡ ***Purpose Differentiation.*** Purpose, mission, goals, positioning, vision, and story—each a mainstay of business and brand strategy—are six different though closely associated concepts. A *purpose* statement is why you exist as a company. A *mission* statement is how you achieve that purpose and the actions you take to that end. *Goals* are the measurable milestones along the way. *A positioning* statement is how you define your space of opportunity and the unique value you offer your target audiences. A *vision* statement is where you are headed, the ideal end state toward which you're working. Finally, your *story* is the external encapsulation of all the above—the simple, emotional, and innately shareable narrative you circulate, the distillation of the *why* behind your business. But a *purpose*—and this is critical—is *why you do it all in the first place*. As such, purpose is the main driver we'll focus on, as it is the animating force for each of us as individuals and as companies holding sway in the world. Our purpose is going to be our story, and our story is going to bring our community together in a movement. That movement will change the world. For example, Dove: *To make beauty a source of confidence, not anxiety*. UPS: *To move the world forward by delivering what matters*. Unilever: *To make sustainable living commonplace*. These are not missions. They are purpose statements.

➡ ***Purpose Process.*** Purpose is a starting point and process-aligner. It's not an end point. You ask *why* before you unspool *how*. Too many brands simply tick the box by defining some ad hoc purpose, then fail to ever put it to work collaboratively with all stakeholders. It's also a continuous process, not a static stage. Along the way, you use it a touchstone, a decision filter, an ego eraser, a tie breaker.

➡ ***Purpose Alignment.*** If your personal and business purposes don't seem allied with the collective good, it's high time to reevaluate and reengineer. If it's time to change companies or even your industry—if there's little hope you can contribute meaningfully to shifting things from the inside—muster the courage and find your tribe. Quoting former US president Barack Obama's eulogy for civil rights pioneer and congressman John Lewis, "That's where real courage comes from . . . in our beloved community, we do not walk alone."[8]

➡ ***Purpose Unification.*** Remember that *all purpose is the same in this new conception*. We all do the same thing, but in different ways. We all *LEAD WITH WE*, one way or another. Define your unique purpose; share with all stakeholders; engage employees to co-create how to activate it; mobilize customers to collaborate with you to bring it to life; and partner across your industry and beyond with like-minded leaders and brands to scale your impact and transform the industry.

With New Generations Come Fresh Evolutions in Purpose

Let's look at some recent demographic trends that are especially relevant to the *LEAD WITH WE* revolution. We've already begun experiencing what business strategist Glenn Llopis calls "The Cultural Demographic Shift," or major changes in the dynamics of the workforce and consumer base, which is crashing squarely into our "Age of Personalization,"[9] in which younger generations reject the cookie-cutter treatment of organizations, ideas, and advancement. Also, the US Census projects the country will by 2045 become for the first time "minority white."[10] Given these factors, Llopis argues, "every generation is more diverse than the next. Gen Z is nearly half non-White, and they've just started entering the workforce.[11] Both millennials and Generation Z embody individuality above all—as opposed to toeing some company line foisted on them from on high or through the ages. They don't simply follow policy, nor jump through prescribed hoops just because "that's how it's always been done." If you are not ready for the inclusivity and sustainability these new generations demand, "they will leave you behind, quickly—as employees and as customers."[12]

New generations are daily remolding capitalism. Wealthy millennials are already taking control of vast family fortunes (a $30 trillion transfer in the next decades),[13] which is changing purchasing and investing alike, both depending more heavily on brands' *impact*[14] as much as traditional factors. As just two examples, "Generation Z is generation green," according to Ad Age. Up to 73 percent of younger shoppers (under the age of twenty-two) are willing to pay more for eco-friendly products.[15] And millennials' investments in sustainable companies are two times higher than the average.[16] The appetite for private impact investing tops $5 trillion,[17] with $71 billion in extant socially responsible private investment assets managed (and $462 billion in public markets).[18] By the way, the average return rate on the top third of such impact investments is a whopping 34 percent (10 percent on the median).[19]

New generations reaching their prime spending and working years come not only with new demographics, but new psychographics—new expectations based on new ways of looking at the world. There's a definite age gap on social and environmental/energy issues—especially among GOP voters.[20] Across the political spectrum, about 63 percent of millennials choose "improve society" over "generate profit" when asked what businesses should aim to achieve.[21] While 66 percent of consumers in general would switch from a product they buy to a new product from a *LEAD WITH WE* company, this statistic increases dramatically, to 91 percent, for millennials.[22]

"Purpose is the new digital," according to *Deloitte Insights*.[23] To the next generation of customers, a company activating and expressing an authentic purpose is now as important as a digital presence has been for extending your retail brand.[24] Brands that have a purpose activated with a significant *WITH* have more meaning in the eyes of consumers—especially younger ones. As retailers and other kinds of companies start putting a *LEAD WITH WE* purpose at the core of their strategies, they find themselves fundamentally rethinking, rebranding, and repurposing their businesses: What do they stand for? How are they helping to keep the world spinning? How can they redefine the commercial model required to deliver such promise and capture new generations of consumers who care about such things as never before?

Younger people are not only digital natives who came of age during a time of greater globalization and economic disruption than ever before, most simply *care* a lot more about diversity, inclusion, and equity (DI&E), healthful environments, personal wellness, and sustainable sourcing, among other things, than many of their baby boomer and even their Generation X—my generation's—forebears. Yes, they put off traditional family milestones such as getting married and having children. But they do so in order to make a difference in the world. And they concentrate on the *WITH* in most decisions, even economic ones, where Me First had been the traditional metric. They're more about access than ownership, per se.[25] Of course, there are plenty in the older generations who are mindful and leading the way—it just seems to come more naturally to younger people. "The Millennial generation has seen a lot of natural disasters, political disasters, and corporate disasters. They feel personally responsible, and they feel empowered to create change,"[26] says Kelly McElhaney of the Haas Center for Responsible Business at UC Berkeley. A full 94 percent of millennials intend to use their skills to benefit a good cause,[27] numbers the world hasn't seen since perhaps members of the "Greatest Generation" defeated fascism in the 1940s.

Just how do millennials spark so much innovation? asks *Triple Pundit*. "The old-fashioned way: by speaking up and leading the way." For example, millennial employees at As You Sow,[28] a nonprofit foundation (NPF) leader in shareholder advocacy, discovered their company was invested in fossil fuel, even as the organization advised others about environmental and social corporate responsibility, including oil divestment. In response, these young stakeholders innovated and launched a tool for like-minded employees to research their own retirement plans for fossil fuel contributions.[29] Revelatory moments help to define purpose that leads to transformative movements. As I wrote in *We First*, life's necessities must generate the necessities of life.

The B2B landscape is no less influenced by new millennial values. This is because, according to *Brand Quarterly*:

> Millennials do not "silo" their concerns between personal and business lives. Multiple studies indicate that the big-picture, emotional rewards millennials feel (and seek) when buying TOMS or Warby Parker glasses, are the same rewards they're looking for as B2B buyers. Appealing to personal values with this new generation in B2B can make them up to twice as likely to do business with you, versus appealing only to standard business values such as price or performance.[30]

International business thought leaders, David Cooperrider and Audrey Selian, add:

> Millennials place huge importance on the social good ideals of The Triple Bottom Line . . . so much so that they're transforming workplaces at companies large and small. In fact, according to Bentley [University]'s PreparedU Project, 86 percent of millennials agree that it's a priority for them to work for companies that are socially responsible and ethical.[31]

This is significant because there are seventy-plus million millennials making up the workforce majority.[32] And the generation following millennials will exercise no less impact on the economy, the workplace, and the larger culture. Gen Z is best described as "hyper-aware"[33] and concerned about human impact on the planet. Gen Z members are 85 percent more likely to support a brand after learning it supports a social cause or demonstrates social responsibility; 84 percent are more likely to buy such a product; and 82 percent are more likely to recommend it.[34] We can slow disasters and reverse inequities, but only if we work *WITH* each other against them. A 2019 report, "The State of Consumer Spending: Gen Z Shoppers Demand Sustainable Retail," indicates that 62 percent of Generation Z, who started entering the workforce that year, favor purchasing sustainable brands, similar to the millennials who came before them.[35]

It would be wise for your business and its impact to listen to young people like Greta Thunberg, as some have; those young people who took part in 2017's

Climate March; and those who organized the National School Walkout and other anti–gun violence activities in 2018. Gen Z is already entering and influencing the workforce—and decisively shaping the economy. A wide and international coalition of well-coordinated, politically motivated, algorithm-savvy youths—"TikTok Teens"—were likely responsible for sinking attendance at President Trump's July 2020 Tulsa, Oklahoma, rally.[36] Young voters were critical in the 2021 Georgia Senate runoffs, which turned the balance of the US Senate.[37] Tomorrow these people will make policy. "In 2020, for the first time, the youngest generations (both millennial and iGen—born in or after 1997) are projected to make up the largest proportion of registered voters," the Yale Program on Climate Change Communication reminds us.[38] And this younger demographic can become partners who help spread our messages, or adversaries who call us out and punish us if they don't think we're acting in their best interest—if they think we're not *WITH* them and their values. Younger demos want to lead change. They're not waiting for brands to make the first moves. In fact, brands need to be invited into their movements—or face the consequences of getting on their bad side (see chapter seven, "Society"). As the adage goes, while youth accounts for only about 30 percent of the population, it represents 100 percent of our future.

WITH Is the Way: Five Stages in a Purpose Journey

Where are you in the *LEAD WITH WE* process? I mean not only where do you sit within your company, but where are you and your company in terms of readiness to *LEAD* in this purposeful manner? In particular, to what extent are you leading *WITH*, and *WITH* whom? Where are you in terms of inclusiveness, that Breadth of Our *WITH* introduced in previous chapters? Where is your business, and where are *you*, mentally and financially?

There exists a sliding scale of awareness of the *LEAD WITH WE* imperatives— and a continuum of preparedness and/or processes already underway. In other words, what's your relative level of awareness as to the limits of capitalism as it's been practiced for the past few centuries? And what are your ideas for solving the problem(s) rather than continuing to fan the crises? To help assess where we are in the journey of becoming a purpose-led brand, let's explore five distinct stages, and how they manifest themselves within a company as it evolves from a Me First to We First way of being.

Stage 1: *We Lead with Me First*

Our company is living and operating in the past, employing an outdated mindset and legacy strategies unengaged with facts on the ground. We're oblivious to long-term purpose metrics. For example, in this era of exponentially iterating technology, we're not aware of how our products or services—cloud-based, AI, drone, and so on—could ultimately be used. Will they bring harm to some segment of society or the environment? This world we live in, especially when we partner cross-sector or with government entities, necessitates a thorough review. Do we want our tech to be used to recognize faces for the purposes of, say, rounding up undocumented people at their schools, workplaces, or healthcare facilities? Do we want our company's steel used to build prison infrastructure if incarcerations and the overall justice system continue as is? Are we okay pushing to the legal limit of gas-guzzling combustion-engine specs to maximize profits? I declare it *should*, but *could* the business turn down a massive contract if we knew our expertise ("Dow Know-How in Every Drop of Napalm"[39]) would be ultimately used for a purpose that competes with our values? Right now, we lack the right mindset to make that kind of decision. Where's our line? We don't have one. We don't really care. We're like Domino's in 2009. It took just two of its employees posting a stomach-churning video on YouTube to nearly cause the massive company—which didn't react to the crisis for two days—to suffer extreme damage. United Airlines suffered similar (possibly irreparable) reputation damage in 2017 when a video of a screaming, bloody passenger getting dragged off a plane went viral. The tepid apology that followed didn't help[40]—and next came a spate of videos of disgruntled United customers shredding their loyalty cards.

> *Example:*
> In 2019, Purdue Pharma reached a $270 million settlement, because the opioids it had been hawking contributed to the deaths of thousands of people in Oklahoma. Two years later, Purdue and the Sackler family that owns it faced a further payment of $8.3 billion.[41] *LEAD WITH WE* purpose activation can ensure such egregious and tragic corporate behavior never occurs in the first place.

Stage 2: *We Lead with Me (Prioritized)*

We're still clinging to old purpose paradigms. We'd still like to maintain some semblance of the status quo—or to pretend that today's the same as yesterday. We're a company with basic or peripheral awareness of social issues, some philanthropy, and marginal efforts toward purpose-based people-management, accomplishing the minimum by industry standards and customer/employee expectations. Lots of "lip service" masking limited interest. We might communicate purpose externally through press releases, blogs, and the like, but we're really still a Me First operator. When our purpose is enacted, we're more likely motivated by how it can benefit ourselves and the company than how it can shape the greater good.

Example:

CrossFit, the branded fitness regimen, found itself called out for such attitudes after its founder and CEO, Greg Glassman, appeared to make light of the BLM movement in a glib June 2020 tweet. Despite Glassman's next-day apology—he had earlier fired an executive for homophobic communications on social media—the brand, till then famous for intense, near militaristic consumer devotion, quickly suffered a slew of sponsor, gym affiliate, and customer defections—along with volumes of terrible press. "It will cost CrossFit millions, in royalties, in its Reebok deal, in licensing fees, in sponsorships,"[42] writes Justin LoFranco, editor of *Morning Chalk Up*, a newsletter covering CrossFit. But the more profound damage was reputational, LoFranco writes. One month later, Glassman was forced to leave the company, which was soon put up for sale.

Stage 3: *We Lead with a Me/We Hybrid*

We're a company that's aware of and awake to many of the new expectations, and the potential for purpose to serve as a growth driver. We're trying to integrate LEAD WITH WE elements on certain levels. We're in the middle of the pack with other companies, more than occasionally inputting WE First factors into important calculations.

Example:

The two hundred or so companies in the US Business Roundtable (BRT) encompass a wide spectrum of progress, ranging from those in the hybrid Me/We category to those that comprehensively LEAD WITH WE. But as signatories of the new Statement on the Purpose of a Corporation that calls for stakeholder over shareholder primacy, they know the right thing to do and they're on their way, publicly committing to do better. A 2020 survey by JUST Capital, the NPF that tracks corporations' effect on the social order, found that firms whose

CEOs signed the BRT pledge a year before—people like Jeff Bezos of Amazon and Doug McMillon of Walmart—outperformed their non-BRT counterparts in delivering paid sick leave, financial assistance, and other socially beneficial perks during the COVID-19 crisis.[43] Yet the global pandemic proved a critical stress test: "In the first four weeks after the coronavirus hit the US, businesses that signed were" far more "prone to announce layoffs or furloughs" than similar companies that didn't join the pledge. Signers were also "less likely to donate to relief efforts, less likely to offer customer discounts, and less likely to shift production to pandemic-related goods."[44] Extraordinary circumstances, no doubt, but other studies covering more than just the pandemic era show the "revolutionary pledge" of the BRT has yet to translate into sufficient and consistent revolutionary *action*, per se, by all members.[45] Yet coalescing market forces that reward such decisions, and effective examples within the BRT that inspire replication, bode well not just for the members themselves, but for the wider cohort of CEOs and companies that follow their lead.

Stage 4: *We (Prioritized)*
Our company actively and intentionally strives to make a difference within its industry and beyond by setting an example. We're convinced that a LEAD WITH WE purpose can be an effective strategic growth driver. We listen carefully to current and potential consumers and others, then retool all aspects of our business to prioritize people and planet. We often partner with other experts, and we lend our expertise where it can do the most good. WE LEAD WITH, and for, as many stakeholders as we can.

Example:
In the consumer packaged goods (CPG) arena, Grove Collaborative, founded by Stuart Landesberg in 2012, is disrupting the status quo in an established industry. Grove is a quickly growing, sustainability-focused online retailer. It became the world's first zero-waste and net-positive CPG. Just one of its many initiatives saved more than a million pounds of plastic in its first few years. "I wanted to save the world. [And] if I'm going to work a hundred hours a week, I want to leave the world better than I found it," Landesberg told me for a *Forbes* article. "We never sell out our values in terms of curation. I'm talking about health, safety, and sustainability but also efficacy. Natural products need to work—or consumers are not going to come back."[46]

Stage 5: *We* LEAD WITH WE

We've transcended our product, service, and category to shape culture. Ours is an exemplar company, constantly innovating and redefining what it means to be a brand that positively influences its industry and exercises a measurable impact on the wider culture. All aspects of the company are committed to realizing its stated purpose, in line with the betterment of the whole collective. We know our role in the world extends far beyond our workplace—and our purpose goes beyond just making money. Our purpose is fundamental to the entire organization, from supply chain to value chain. We know we can make money and change the world for the better. We're one of those companies that "are breaking the mold," writes Rosabeth Moss Kanter, the Ernest L. Arbuckle professor of business at Harvard Business School. "They view community needs as opportunities to develop ideas and demonstrate business technologies, to find and serve new markets, and to solve long-standing business problems."[47]

> *Leadership.* We've established and honed a well-defined purpose, leading a cultural conversation that propels our movement, which in turn shapes both our industry and the greater culture. Our CEO, board, and other leaders actively advocate, provoking and inspiring change based on profound insights into societal trends and consumer needs. Our operations are nimble enough to act quickly as a first responder to inevitable crises. Our company has gone beyond a mostly net-positive role in the world, and established through strategic collaboration an exponentially regenerative enterprise, contributing substantively to improving people's lives and the planet, even as we increase our brand's profile and profits. More specifically, all the internal people who *LEAD* the efforts are not only resident experts on our business, its industry, sector, and competitors, but are also trained in effective movement-making strategy and history. They have extensive experience with financial modeling within the recent business world, where strategic funding, partnership development, stakeholder engagement, and right-minded mergers and acquisitions accelerate capabilities and increase impact.

> *Products.* Transparent and public materiality assessments, consistent and purposeful, industry-leading innovation/R&D. Products become enablers of impact, serving as material expressions of purpose (POP) with net positive impact in closed-loop, regenerative ecosystems (return on purpose, or ROP), all acting as an engine up the Virtuous Spiral.

Partners & supply chain. Responsible, transparent, accountable, highly vetted suppliers and collaborators. Together we drive industry upgrades, challenging competitors to do better, holding ourselves publicly accountable through transparent Environmental, Social, and Governance (ESG) goals, benchmarks, and metrics.

HR. Collaborative and co-creative culture in which the company empowers employee impact. A high sense of employee agency in driving internal evolution and external (societal, cultural) influence. Employees are the active face of our internal, DI&E-driven culture and brand out in the world. We've created a beloved company to work for, and we can attract and retain the cream of the crop in terms of talented crew.

Marketing. Seamless purpose/product storytelling. Consistent, meaningful, and resonant storytelling across the whole supply chain and all channels. Our staff and—better yet—our consumers—have become our chief storytellers. Our product is "selling itself" because we've become the chief *celebrant* of our consumer. We are not the celebrity—*they* are.

Impact. Comprehensive impact across key pillars beyond traditional sustainability milestones, reflecting recent crises, and authentic support of social and environmental issues relevant to our purpose and values. Purpose brought to life at global, national, regional, community, local, and internal (company-wide) levels. We're leading with our legacy. We're not at all perfect, and our efforts are always going to be a work in progress—but we're well on our way.

Example:

Founded 137 years ago, Marks & Spencer (M&S) is a leading British retailer of food, clothing, and homeware, with a global customer reach and seventy-eight thousand "colleagues" on the payroll. Along with longstanding purpose and sustainability leaders that include Patagonia, Unilever, Nike, Ben & Jerry's, Starbucks, Lego, IKEA, Danone, P&G, Seventh Generation, Eileen Fisher, Salesforce, VF Corp, Target, and Natura, it's one of the most obvious examples of a company with a clear, purpose-based *Lead With We*–like statement at the heart of its operations, driving its goals, actions, and impact. One key pillar of the M&S purpose is called "Plan A"—because there is no Plan B—launched in 2007 with a hundred commitments to achieve in five years. M&S extended this goal in 2012 to 150 commitments to be met by 2015 with the aim of becoming the world's most sustainable major retailer. They further expanded this program in 2014 with a hundred new, revised, and exciting commitments to be achieved by 2020, focused on three target areas: People, Product, and Planet, all related to relevant Sustainable Development Goals.

Plan A includes extensive opportunities in a necessarily "evolving framework" for M&S consumers, colleagues, and supply chain partners to co-create a better world while unlocking new revenue-generating opportunities. Community projects, volunteerism, and waste and energy reduction are some of the hallmarks, along with targeted political activities, around such pressing issues as human trafficking, all integrated with its other broad purpose initiatives beyond sustainability. The company appears 99 percent committed to complete transparency in reporting its results. Importantly, all its environmental benchmarking is science based. We don't have to reinvent the wheel when we work as M&S did with benchmarking partners like the London Benchmarking Group protocols for community investment, the World Resources Institute Greenhouse Gas Reporting Protocols, and On-pack Recycling Label definitions of recyclability.[48]

M&S was on track to completely embed Plan A throughout all its operations—rather than a series of separate programs that worked in parallel—when the novel coronavirus slammed the UK and the rest of the world. Profits took a £52 million nosedive in March 2020 alone, and costs and stock write-downs hit about £212 million by that month owing to the virus. But M&S leadership took advantage of the unprecedented opportunity to reengineer from the ground up, according to a *Forbes* profile, and stuck to its Plan A guns:

> For years [M&S] has had a heavy, unwieldy culture and generally regarded for its tortuous bureaucracy. None of which are suited to being a swift and responsive retailer in the best of times, let alone in the completely new normal which we now face.
>
> However, overnight, it has had to do something it failed to do for years—transform itself into a far more digital, leaner, and agile business. Chief executive [Steve] Rowe said: "Most importantly working habits have been transformed and we have discovered we can work in a faster, leaner, more effective way. I am determined to act now to capture this and deliver a renewed, more agile business in a world that will never be the same again."[49]

In fact, "Never the Same Again" became the philosophy that drove all of M&S's pandemic efforts, helping evolve its initial Plan A of "mere" sustainability into far more regenerative realms. The company put Plan A at the center of much of its customer storytelling, not as a sideline or secondary consideration. Long before there was competitive or investor pressure to do so, it has continually upgraded itself to address evolving and emerging environmental and social challenges. Now it's even embedding ESG concerns at the board level by creating an ESG subcommittee.[50] M&S's early, consistent, and boldly innovative trajectory, along with its recommitment to Plan A and redoubled sustainability commitment at a challenging time for the company, positions it as a standout *LEAD WITH WE* company.

Example:

Here in the US, our largest retailer, Walmart, daily demonstrates similar paradigm-shifting leadership. In September 2020, the company, along with its Walmart Foundation, committed to become the world's first fully regenerative company. It is addressing the growing climate crisis by targeting zero emissions across the company's global operations by 2040, and by protecting, managing, and restoring at least fifty million acres of land and one million square miles of ocean by 2030. All this is an urgent response to our escalating loss of soil health, species, and biodiversity. To achieve this, Walmart is adopting new regenerative practices across its global supply chain, such as decarbonizing operations, eliminating waste, advancing equity for all stakeholders, and otherwise effectively transforming both *how* and *why* the corporate behemoth does business. As president and CEO Doug McMillon stated at the plan's announcement, Walmart's "path to becoming a regenerative company . . . works to restore, renew and replenish in addition to preserving our planet, and encourages others to do the same."[51]

On that last point, the scale and daily reach of Walmart into countless customers' lives makes its vow significant in its own right, but the signal it sends to other retailers worldwide that seek to stay relevant—and how that in turn shapes global supply chains, market forces, and consumer buying habits—cannot be overstated. Walmart's example will trigger a cascading effect that will accelerate understanding, adoption, integration, and, importantly, competition in the context of business practices that embody an enduring commitment to the well-being of all, through the equally expansive collaboration of suppliers, employees, customers, consumers, investors, and nongovernmental organizations (NGOs). As such, Walmart is a force multiplier empowering global business to LEAD WITH WE.

Of course, past practice is no guarantee of future leadership. Every brand must continue to challenge themselves and hold themselves accountable. Anyone who pays attention to this business revolution will understand former US president Bill Clinton's assertion that "the perception that business must choose between turning a profit and improving the communities where they operate is outdated and irrelevant in our interdependent world."[52] In fact, we must continue to redefine the idea of "self-interest" so that it encompasses the greater good, because the self and The Higher WE are not meaningfully distinguishable.

So, what's your business purpose that can form the basis of that level of enlightened self-interest? Better to address the question long before you're faced with a specific decision—and especially before inevitable crises ensue. What do you stand for? What are you trying to achieve? How do you want to change the world? If you've clarified these questions in advance, you won't struggle with a difficult decision on the spot. Your ego won't get in the way of your purpose. You won't see infighting among your leadership. The answer will be obvious and conflict-free. Consider:

> Rana el Kaliouby, a co-founder of Affectiva, an "artificial emotional intelligence" start-up . . . whose software uses A.I. to track human emotions, had several early offers from government agencies, including a venture fund backed by the Central Intelligence Agency [CIA], that wanted to use the product to improve their surveillance capabilities.[53]
>
> Even though the company needed the money at the time, it turned down the deals. Affectiva has since raised more than $50 million from other, nongovernmental sources, and has made ethical A.I. use a core part of its brand. "We wanted to be trusted," el Kaliouby told the *New York Times*. "We used the core value of integrity and respecting people's privacy as a way to weed out use cases."[54]

We LEAD by living our legacy every day. In chapters six ("Community") and seven ("Society"), we'll take deeper dives into this kind of cultural leadership. For now, we must understand that both the internal culture of our business, and our later, external communication of our *raison d'être*, are wholly driven by purpose and measured repeatedly by our impact. A *LEAD WITH WE* purpose allows us to inspire our investors, attract and retain excellent employees, woo new customers, and keep them not only coming, but themselves "selling" our brands. Constituents want more than shiny widgets. They want to do good in the world *WE* share, one where, ultimately, we together exert real, positive impact. All of which starts with purpose.

With Purpose Comes Self-Auditing & Assessment

For managers, the purpose-building process works by gathering key stakeholders and carefully listening to them. Seek continuous feedback. Ask questions that help externalize ourselves with the ultimate aim of devising a purpose statement that defines us—all of us—in a way we can express authentically to all stakeholders. And if we are a stakeholder at any level, we must advocate to be heard, take the process seriously, and helpfully contribute. The process must be cooperative and curious. We're going to perform together an honest, thorough, and often quite painful self-inventory of where the company stands now—and where we want to be, given practical limitations and a good measure of optimism for what's possible with a real commitment. When we set our ambitions extra high, we unlock the possibility of expanding and augmenting growth by innovating to capture the greater potential opportunity in ways that wouldn't otherwise happen via incremental planning from where we are now. Think Elon Musk.

Our self-inspection process therefore must be open, inclusive, nonjudgmental, and developmental. Whatever we do, we shouldn't forget the people in the trenches—our team. And we must continuously remember our consumers. How do they see us? What matters most to them? Where and how can we do better? What do they love most about working with us, about the products or services we deliver? When we feel ourselves flailing, we must assess ourselves from all sides and angles of our operations and keep using our core strengths and most intense passions as a touchstone.

Investors, institutional and retail, no doubt also exert a powerful influence on the decisions and behaviors of our companies. We will examine their impact in chapter seven, "Society," as they increasingly play a determinative role in enabling new market forces that drive and scale a reengineered role for business.

Below are several examples of self-analysis questions to determine where you and your company stand in the *LEAD WITH WE* process journey, and where you might want to focus more attention. All of these questions precede a deeper analysis of your company's purpose, which we'll look into through a number of lenses next.

Ambitions & Impact

- **What** are our grand ambitions? What impact do we want to have in the world?
- **What** issues are we uniquely equipped to address, contribute to, or solve?
- **How well** are the stories and outcomes of these efforts being communicated today?

Business

- **To whom** does the company answer? Founder, investors, parent company, some other entity?
- **What** trends in the space or market forces hold greatest potential value for the business to leverage? Do we see the company engaging with those trends? How and why/why not?
- **What** prize would our company most want to compete for?

Internal Culture

- **What** is the current internal culture like? Enthusiastic? Uncertain? Toxic? What's driving it, positively or negatively?
- **What** are some unique traits we see in our staff that seem particular to our company? In other words, what kinds of people are self-selecting into our employ?
- **What** tools would most help us communicate to employees and customers what our company stands for? What tools do we already have at hand?

"Marketing"

- **How** defined is our customer/consumer target? How has that target evolved over time? How do we see the target and their expectations shifting now or expanding in the future?
- **What** are the company's social and environmental initiatives pointing toward, ultimately? To what end are we doing this?
- **How** are we inspiring the rest of the world to care about what we're saying and doing?

Competitors
- *Who's* doing a good job? Who isn't? Why and how?
- *Who* else stands for the type of change we want to see in the world?
- *Where* are we vulnerable? How could we be disrupted?

Purpose Barometer
- *To what extent* has the company articulated or shared a defined purpose in the past?
- *What* education is needed around the business case for purpose?
- *To what degree* is purpose understood and activated within the company?

Purpose Storytelling Barometer
- *How* is the brand purpose activated throughout the company?
- *What* is the current unifying rally cry for the company and its stakeholders, if any?
- *How well* do the purpose and its storytelling positively shape culture?

With Awareness of Where We Are, We Can Define Where to Go

Having completed a self-audit to generate an honest assessment of where you are on the *LEAD WITH WE* journey, you can then define, evolve, or upgrade your purpose with confidence. As the adage goes, this process is essential because it's hard for any company to read the label from inside the jar. In our work with clients, many of whom are referenced in this book, we define purpose as the intersection of three discrete areas of inquiry. We'll list the three, then take a deeper dive into each.

⟳ *LEAD: We Alone as a Company*
- *Why* was our company/brand started? Not how—*why*. What are the most timeless aspects of the company's heritage story? How might they carry the brand into the future and remain relevant over time?
- *What* does our brand *stand for*? Not crafted marketing speak. What do we value most highly?

- *What* is our brand's enemy? What do we stand *against*—and what are we fighting for, trying to prevent, or attempting to lessen?
- *What* are we the only one of? As a function of our unique heritage, team, moment in time?
- *When* we are at our best, what are we doing? What superpower capabilities do we, as a team, possess?

⇒ *WITH: The Company & Others*
- *What* values do we hold most dear? What other stakeholders, competitors, partners might share them?
- *Where* are we making the most *difference*? How do we best cooperate and collaborate to get that done?
- *How* do we best *differentiate* ourselves from the competition in meaningful and measurable ways?
- *What* emotional attribute do we want our company to be known for (joy, curiosity, honesty, care, etc.)?
- *When* someone thinks of our brand, consciously or not, what do we want them to feel?

⇒ *WE: The Company & the World*
- *What* specific *needs* does the company address? What *problems* does it solve?
- *What* impact would be most authentic to the company and meaningful to the world?
- *How* is the world (or how will it become) better because we are in it?
- *What* legacy do we want to own? How can we more effectively live it each day?
- *What* should our brand be known for in ten, twenty, fifty years?

Because these three areas focus on the ascending levels of the Virtuous Spiral, your animating purpose has the depth and dimension to ensure your company can LEAD WITH WE. The trick is to answer these questions honestly and observe the themes, key words, and impact intentions that reveal themselves through the answers. Then, distill those authentic and differentiating elements down into a simple, emotional, and sharable purpose statement.

With a Defined Purpose, We Can Create Meaningful Impact

The anatomy of a purpose statement follows this formula: "*Our company purpose is* [the difference our company will make in the world] *by* [how we will achieve it] *in order to* [why it will be meaningful to us, our company, the collective *WE*]."

That said, purpose statements vary in length depending on the preference and tone of each brand. Here are some great examples that demonstrate different ways to express various intents. Note that growth and performance in LEAD WITH WE companies always derive from the confluence of purpose and specific initiatives and goals. Success doesn't happen by accident.

⇒ **Impossible Foods**, the Silicon Valley, plant-based meat alternative company is most concerned that all human-made structures occupy less than 1 percent of Earth's land surface, while grazing or growing feed crops for livestock takes up almost half of the rest.[55] "Our use of animals as a food-production technology has brought us to the verge of environmental catastrophe," the company declares. "The destructive impact of animal agriculture on the global environment far exceeds that of any other technology on Earth."[56] With this firmly in mind, the company expresses its role in the world simply: *To save meat. And the Earth.*

⇒ **Airbnb.** No less ambitiously, the online accommodation marketplace embodies the articulation of Douglas John Atkin, author of *The Culting of Brands*, when he described the ideal purpose statement as "grounded in something that's universally experienced so that it's recognized to be true. Done this way, it will resonate, be 'bought' into, and not rejected as corporate or brand-overreach. And if the Purpose is derived from an experienced truth, then it increases the chances that you land on something that is yours and yours alone. It's differentiating and true to you."[57] Airbnb articulates its purpose as: *To create a world where anyone can belong anywhere.*

⇒ **Kellogg's** purpose statement is a little longer. The immense multinational food company's purpose is: *To nourish families so they can flourish and thrive, by enriching and delighting the world through foods and brands that matter, in order to bring us all together.*

⇒ **Amgen**, one of the world's leading biotech firms, has as its purpose: *To serve patients by transforming the promise of science and biotechnology into* *therapies that have the power to restore health or save lives.* Simple, right? Yet it animates a complex system of interwoven initiatives that, taken together, all push the company far beyond making drugs. For example, Amgen is working to scale science literacy by supporting youth science education.[58] The company's Biotech Experience has reached nearly a million high school students.[59] It also runs the Amgen Scholars program for college students. Each year, 360 students from across the globe are offered a sponsored research-lab internship opportunity. With $75 million invested in the project, it's become one of the most competitive summer science programs. To make science accessible to more people, Amgen funded a set of biology modules with partner Khan Academy. It also recently partnered with Harvard University to develop the LabXchange project, including extensive resources for teachers to bring more experimental science into their classrooms. Notice the words in Amgen's purpose statement: "serve," "transform," "power"—not "formulate biopharmaceuticals."[60]

➠ **Hershey.** The classic US chocolate company has a history of empowering youth. In 2019, Hershey launched the "Makers of Good" Teen Summit[61] to address youth social isolation, bullying, suicide, and social media pressures. Hershey also started the Heartwarming Project Action Grants program to fund local acts of kindness via micro-grants for youth.[62] What's Hershey's role in the world? Is it making tasty chocolate? No. It's: *Creating connection.* "From the beginning, Milton Hershey believed that if you do good, you'll do well. By doing what we do best—from our delicious snacks to spreading goodness in our communities—we bring people together."[63]

➠ **Nike**, a preeminent marketer but equally astute impact creator, has as its purpose: *To unite the world through sport, to create a healthy planet, active communities, and an equal playing field for all.* The leading global apparel brand's extensive efforts started early and range widely, from diversity and inclusion ("Until We All Win" investment program and National Coming Out Day support); to equality ("Common Thread Series"); to community (Nike N7 Ambassadors); to extensive supply chain, sustainability, environmental, climate, and net zero initiatives (e.g., "Move to Zero," which encompasses the Converse, Jordan, and Nike brands' joint efforts). As president and CEO John Donahoe declares: "Nike exists to progress sport. But in recent years we face an even broader challenge: to protect sport itself," by protecting the planet.[64]

In all these companies' cases, leaders consciously chose to define the higher-order role the company would play in the world. The results are deceptively simple, yet each is the result of an intentional process. Let's explore such a process here.

Mammut, the prestigious Swiss mountaineering brand founded in 1862, enjoys a long, proud heritage. Its leaders wanted to define the company purpose in a way that would make their company relevant for the *next* 160 years. The brand was already synonymous with the Swiss Alps and outdoor adventurers of every stripe. But it had ambitions to expand past the limited toeholds it had established in the Asian and urban markets. It needed not only to maintain its existing legacy and longstanding credibility regarding its reliability, safety, and reputation for expertise, but also to stretch and connect with future consumers who were not (yet) extreme mountaineers, and to reach into metropolitan markets and regions around the world that aren't as synonymous with rocky summits as Switzerland is. Its new purpose statement did just that: *To create a world moved by mountains.*

Each word in that phrase is active, relevant, and resonant. "Create" speaks to the company's products through the lens of innovation made possible by the collective efforts of employees, and via the wider collaboration between the mountaineering communities and loyal fans of the brand worldwide. "World" has all that associated dimension to it—my world, your world, the inner city, from Hong Kong to the Snowy Mountain range of New South Wales, Australia. It's the entire planet, which the company seeks to infiltrate. Then "moved" speaks on several levels to the *emotion* that mountains inspire—from fear to joy to awe—and the proactive, progressive nature of the brand and its adherents. If you're a traditional Mammut customer, you're not wearing outdoor gear to sit still on your sofa, right? You *move* physically and *are moved* emotionally and spiritually. The mountains, wherever they are, have moved Mammut's founders, leaders, and devotees since before cars came on the market. Mountains were and still are the hallmark, the soul, of the brand. There may be no more apt symbol of bountiful nature, of pristine environments that demand our awe, appreciation, and protection. And this extends to folks who are "moved" to wear Mammut only as a fashion choice.

So, Mammut's purpose statement, *To create a world moved by mountains*, along with its associated digital storytelling, allows the re-energized brand to speak both to its diehard, extreme athletes, climbing the world's most rugged peaks in the toughest conditions, through to folks who have a deep appreciation of the style, functionality, and "cool" factor of its products, who might or might not aspire to such feats—as long as they can get a little bit of the mountain life in their wardrobe. Along the way, the purpose statement captures new, environmentally conscious consumers, and others who want to make a difference on a planet where cities sprawl, glaciers melt, and massive swaths of continents burn out of control. Best of all, Mammut's purpose statement is consistent with its actions and ambitions, whether phasing out perfluorinated compounds in its waterproofing process, repairing worn-out products, supporting athletes with disabilities, or protecting animal rights. At Mammut, they say, "We have a strong drive to preserve what is worth preserving and to improve what is not yet perfect."[65] *Perfect*.

Let's look at how Emeryville, California's Clif Bar & Company models the architecture of an authentically purposeful brand. Its origin story includes a crucible moment that ultimately led to an exemplar brand, born to be purposeful, and daily walking the walk. Nearly thirty years old, the privately held company, owned by family and its thousand employees, began its LEAD WITH WE journey with its core purpose—*To serve athletes with "nutrition for sustained energy."*[66] Clif has lived this purpose through its commitment to "make decisions for our business that prioritize our people, communities and the planet," according to founder Gary Erickson.[67] Its biggest test came when the company turned down a $120 million buyout offer:

> The . . . profound "why" came [and t]here was tremendous relief in that defining moment of turning down the buyout. Not giving in to the "expected" finish line of a big payout gave us freedom to rethink the game—so we created a new five bottom line business model focused on sustaining our business, brands, people, community and the planet, which we call our Five Aspirations.[68]

It then offered 20 percent of the company to its employees through an Employee Stock Ownership Plan, which fostered an ownership mindset and increased employee engagement, performance, and retention. "We're working to run a different kind of company," says Clif's CEO, Kit Crawford, whom I wrote about in *Forbes*: "The kind of place where we'd want to work, that makes the kind of food we'd like to eat, and that strives for a healthier, more sustainable world—the kind of world we'd like to pass on to our children. And those aren't just words."[69]

With Guidelines & Guardrails, We Can Activate Our Company Purpose

The idea here is to reposition the company, products, and services as proof points of a higher-order commitment to our purpose (POP). *We must become a purpose with a company, rather than a company with a purpose.* We will infuse our purpose throughout our organization, rather than leaving it an addendum to a core motive of generating profit, only after which we shave off contribution in the form of corporate citizenship, CSR, or philanthropic efforts.

To achieve this, our company purpose must meet several criteria, all of which will ensure it is authentic, actionable, and sustained. These serve both as guidelines for how we frame our purpose and a filter by which to assess its execution. Use this extensive checklist to ask, "Do our company purpose efforts . . ."

⟼ *Inform* all lines of business (LOBs), brands, or sub-brands, as well as all departments and functional roles within our company? A full understanding and practice of our purpose should extend through R&D, product/service development, strategy, HR, day-to-day culture, partnerships, communications, community engagement, and so on. Our purpose should be the lungs or bellows of our organization, breathing in and out each day what matters most to us.

⟼ *Ensure* different departments and employees don't balk at a company purpose that feels prescriptive or limiting because it is perceived as a top-down edict? Our purpose must be conceived and executed as a bottom-up platform on which all LOBs, brands, and employees are enabled, supported, and empowered to bring the shared company purpose to life.

⟼ *Unlock* the value of the network effect across all business units, tapping synergies and combined impact through all stakeholders to accelerate and scale the company's purposeful impact?

⟼ *Serve* as a unifying context that aligns, organizes, and amplifies the various impact efforts within our enterprise or company, so every effort is understood as a function of that singular, unifying, and inspiring purpose?

⟼ *Express* clearly the need our company is solving for, and by extension the true business we are in, with differentiated, emotional resonance?

➡ *Connect* the head, heart, and hands of all stakeholders so that the purpose isn't experienced as a sleepy statement in an annual report or hollow words painted on a boardroom wall? It should be active, muscular, and visceral, a living thing that drives thinking and behavior across the company.

➡ *Share* the impact on the lives of our employees, customers, and the world at large? The most important step any purposeful brand can make today is from *integrity of intent to integrity of impact*. Without meaningful, measurable, and defensible results, there is no ROP.

➡ *Calibrate* our tone? The voice of our purpose will arise out of listening intently. We listen first to our personal purpose, then to our team members, 86 percent of whom, according to *Conscious Company*, believe it's important that their own employer be responsible to society and the environment.[70] We listen to the community. To society.

➡ *Balance* motivations? Are we heeding the words of Daniel Lamarre, CEO of Cirque du Soleil? "At the end of the day, you want to be profitable, but that's not the meaning of life."[71]

➡ *Represent* real meaning to all our stakeholders? We're meant to inspire through our purpose, as they do at Starbucks: "When you're surrounded by people who share a passionate commitment around a common purpose," says former chairperson and CEO, Howard Schultz, "anything is possible."[72] Our purpose should relate to all core audiences within our diverse and extensive stakeholder set.

➡ *Sustain* our purpose, which must be an "inside job" that both originates and is championed and maintained from within the company, driven by all employees? Contrast this with an outside, optics-management strategy that exposes an organization—quite rightly—to accusations of purpose-washing.

➡ *Support* long-term, sustainable growth that leads to abundance and regeneration, rather than scarcity and depletion?

➡ *Inspire* a culture and practice of innovation? Companies with a strong sense of purpose are able to transform and innovate better than their counterparts, according to a Harvard study.[73]

➡ *Evince* authenticity? Defining our company's purpose is not about coming up with something new or changing who we are. It is simply codifying what's already there. It just reveals who we are, even to internal stakeholders.

➠ *Think* big? It's called a higher purpose for a reason. The purpose must be greater than the company itself, its leadership, employees, or products in order to play a meaningful and transformative role in the world.

➠ *Adapt* over time? Today's cultural reckonings continue to evolve in sweeping, disruptive, and revolutionary ways that are actively reshaping the business and social landscapes for all our companies' key audiences. Effective navigation requires us to regularly reconsider how best to bring our purpose to life. Filter all initiatives, established and new, through this lens. Be prepared to sacrifice our pet projects, if necessary, and evolve to meet new needs as timely ways to execute against our timeless purpose.

➠ *Quantify* clear metrics and targets for purpose-led impact and leadership? Have we determined toward what are we aiming, and how will we know when we've gotten there?

➠ *Aspire* to improve? Have we positioned the company for improved leadership and increasing relevance, specific to our industry and the challenges we seek to address, using our best forecast of five or ten years down the track? Then, have we framed our purpose to solve rapidly approaching challenges? Given the pace of disruptive technology and the escalation of social and environmental crises, the past has less to do with the future than ever. So, let's set our sights on solving for a future that will be here far sooner than any of us expect. Can we see and appreciate what's coming down the pike?

With Purpose Comes Opportunities

By pursuing a *Lead With We* purpose, we maximize profit. That is, of course, as long as our businesses are efficient and sensible in other realms. Remember Traditional Medicinals (TM), the responsible tea company we met in an earlier chapter? It set a mandate not to increase prices for ten years. This forced the company to assess where it was spending money and search for more efficient ways to cut costs and scale growth. CEO Blair Kellison made key operational changes like IT integration and high-speed tea processors, an increased marketing budget, and more. It took time, but the company's profits exploded. TM is a powerful reminder that if you aren't running an efficient business, it will be ever more challenging to execute on purpose, and scale your impact, let alone raise your bottom line.[74]

Brands that have managed this feat have increased their valuation 175 percent over the last twelve years, more than double their nonpurposeful counterparts.[75] The Edelman-affiliated Zeno Group, which operates in twenty-plus markets worldwide, confirmed in its 2020 Zeno Strength of Purpose Study that consumers are much more likely to engage with companies that have a clearly defined, LEAD WITH WE–like purpose. Zeno looked at metrics such as fair treatment of employees, product/services that reflect the needs of people, ethical and sustainable business practices, support for important social causes, creation of new job opportunities, diverse/inclusive culture, issue advocacy, and a strong set of values. Here are their findings:

➠ *94 percent* of consumers said it is important that companies they engage with have a strong purpose akin to LEAD WITH WE.

➠ *76 percent* of consumers have taken action in response to a brand doing something with which they disagree.

In addition, they found that customers are

➠ *4 times more likely* to purchase from a brand following LEAD WITH WE principles,

➠ *4.1 times more likely* to trust the brand,

➠ *4.5 times more likely* to champion the brand to friends and family, and

➠ *6 times more likely* to protect the brand in a challenging moment, yet only

➠ *37 percent* of consumers believe companies today have a clear sense of purpose[76]—which puts the onus on all of us to clearly communicate our purpose in our quest to shape culture.

This is why and how global giant Unilever's portfolio of fully integrated purposeful brands (Seventh Generation, Ben & Jerry's, Breyer's, Hellmann's, etc.) grew 69 percent faster than the rest of its business in 2018,[77] with 75 percent of the company's growth deriving from said sustainable brands.[78] Unilever's Sustainable Living Plan, launched in 2010 as a blueprint for sustainable growth, saves costs company-wide, drives more profitable growth, mitigates risk, and increases trust among all its stakeholders—building a movement of movements, which ultimately impacts the 2.5 billion people a day who use Unilever products. "With change," Unilever reminds us, "comes opportunity,"[79] all unleashed at the confluence of meaningful brands and consumer concerns. Unilever's been divesting itself of the nonpurposeful brands in its portfolio, owing both to inconsistency with its values—and to their inferior growth. "We will dispose of brands that we feel are not able to stand for something more important than just making your hair shiny, your skin soft, your clothes whiter or your food tastier," says CEO Alan Jope.[80]

That's credible evidence driving the belief of 87 percent of business leaders that business whose purpose goes beyond profit will outperform their counterparts.[81] The growth rate for B Corps in the UK is 28 percent faster than other companies.[82] According to a survey in *Fortune*, a mere 7 percent of Fortune 500 CEOs believe their companies should "mainly focus on making profits and not be distracted by social goals"[83]—and those stats reflect realities *before* COVID-19 radically altered the business terrain.

Across the board, "Meaningful Brands outperform the stock market by 134 percent," according to the 2019 Havas Global Meaningful Brands study, which analyzed 1,800 brands in thirty-one countries, with 350,000 respondents. A staggering 77 percent of all brands could literally drop off the face of the Earth—and no one would care. If we want to be included among the top ten performing Meaningful Brands (Google, PayPal, Mercedes-Benz, WhatsApp, YouTube, Johnson & Johnson, Gillette, BMW, Microsoft, and Danone), we'd best get cracking on rising above the noise of the bazaar. To stand out, we must stand up. "Respondents indicated that content is falling massively short of consumer expectations."[84] That content should focus on how our business can and does *LEAD WITH WE*—with an emphasis on collaboration *WITH* consumers and *WITH* the purpose of bettering the world.

Half of all consumers across fourteen major markets define themselves as "belief-driven" buyers.[85] While 90 percent of consumers expect brands to provide clear, relevant, and meaningful content connecting the values of the company with their own, such content is either missing—or drowned out.[86] This is a potentially catastrophic problem for businesses. Because 48 percent of consumers disappointed with a brand's words or actions on a social issue complain, 42 percent walk away from the brand—and 21 percent *never come back*.[87]

With Purpose as Our Guide, Impact Evolves

A leader of social entrepreneurship, TOMS was founded by Blake Mycoskie, whose travels to South America in the early 2000s acquainted him with a surfeit of shoeless children. He later learned (allegedly from Bill Gates) that bare feet are a significant contributor to disease. The absence of proper shoes also makes schooling a challenge in the developing world. So Mycoskie decided to manufacture and sell in the US a popular and inexpensive type of Argentine walking shoe—and for every pair he sold, to give away one pair to a needy person in the developing world.

Mycoskie's scheme literally led the rise of the "social impact" space—companies formed or re-formed by conscious entrepreneurs *in order to solve a key problem*, even while making money along the way. This "one for one" giving model that Mycoskie pioneered was later adopted by the likes of Warby Parker, launched in 2010, which donates a pair of glasses to someone in need for every pair it sells (more than five million pairs as of 2019, prior to the pandemic);[88] and by the apparel company Bombas, launched in 2013, which gives away a pair of socks or a T-shirt to a homeless person for every pair it sells (nearly 20 million to date).[89] Another in-kind-giving company that picked up the TOMS mantle is THINX. Whenever anyone purchases its high-tech, environmentally friendly "period-proof" panties, the company donates menstrual pads and education to girls in Uganda, whose "weeks of shame" often interrupt schooling.[90]

As the proliferation of one-for-one brands attests, impact inspires meaningful replication.[91] This example is important to relate as we undertake our own company's self-assessment, leading to our unique purpose statement, because it illustrates the compressed complexity that master brand builders consciously fold into seemingly simple purpose statements. They embed nuances of meaning in ostensibly uncomplicated language, all based in an authentic idea that truly represents the company's ethos: why we do what we do, why we wake up in the morning and stay up late, and what we accomplish when we're at our best. "Simple can be harder than complex," Steve Jobs famously said. "But it's worth it in the end, because once you get there, you can move mountains."[92]

The goal is a single purpose statement to unify all efforts across the entire company, all its products and services, all the regions around the world in which they operate. It can and should speak meaningfully to all stakeholders in one sentence (sometimes two—but there better be a damn good reason). It speaks to each one of those stakeholders through the *Lead With We* lens, rooted in a simple, concise, consistent, and scalable story that resonates on multiple levels. It literally *re*-presents, "stands for" the essence of us and what we believe in. Think of Uber's *To evolve how the world moves.* Uber's purpose is not "to provide rideshare services to people," any more than Airbnb's is "to provide temp housing for travelers."

That's *what* those companies do, not their purpose, the higher-order *why* behind it all—why they do what they do.

Let's break down TOMS's stated reason for being: *We're in business to improve lives.* Just because some accident of birth and lucky geography enables you to afford a pair of (pricey) shoes does not mean you should ignore those who aren't as fortunate. Its prior one-for-one model, and now its direct granting (see hereafter), allows people to "mind the gap" in economic strata. Its purpose permeates TOMS's leadership philosophy, with the whole company's team acting on behalf of each other and the world to realize a better future for all. It applies to its staff and collaborators in the US—and those around the world, because in the new global marketplace, we really are living and working both *WITH* and *for* one another, wherever we are. It applies to the company and its longtime giving partners, such as World Vision, teaming up to raise awareness, give shoes, and improve life circumstances for the underserved. And it applies more broadly to the public and private sectors living and working for one another. So, it's a big, expansive, multidimensional idea, which speaks to all stakeholders, internal and external.

From the beginning, TOMS's evolving purpose has allowed the company to better grow and adapt to new realities on the ground, as the humble social impact company strengthened into a thriving global business. The new purpose led the company to take tentative, then audacious steps past its one-for-one ideology and practical program, to address gun violence, homelessness, mental health, equality, women's rights, and beyond. And it helped the company quickly adapt to the pandemic, too, evolving its purpose consistent with its core. Through the TOMS COVID-19 Global Giving Fund, the company generated more than $2 million by mid-2020 in support of global relief efforts for frontline workers, delivering supplies and building hygiene stations.[93]

"Everything from the issues our communities are facing, to the savviness of consumers, to the next generation who will be the major consumers over the next five to ten years" is changing rapidly, Amy Smith, TOMS's chief giving officer, tells us. The company's purpose evolved with the wider society, and now that commitment is directed toward a vision of *an equitable tomorrow, where all people have a chance to thrive*:

> Our commitment to helping humanity to thrive won't change—it never will change. But we are expanding how we're delivering impact . . . because we started to ask, "Are we having as much impact as we can? Do

we have the opportunity, or even obligation, to really think about what we're doing, how we're doing it, and is it everything we could be doing?"[94]

Smith expresses that authenticity is paramount—and here's where the right purpose really matters. "If you tell a story that doesn't feel true to the brand, savvy consumers are going to see right through it," Smith told me for a *Forbes* article. "You really have to take the time to think through 'What is your DNA as a company? And what's sustainable? What can you continue to invest in and contribute to?' You don't want to do something one-off, just to join the bandwagon."[95]

Yes, TOMS has suffered its share of challenges, financial and structural.[96] And the in-kind model of charity has spawned its share of detractors[97]—skeptics, especially those doing nothing themselves, are quick to criticize the defects in others' specific methods. "TOMS is committed to progress, not perfection," Smith reminds us. It embraces a "Build, Learn, Adjust" model of doing business.[98]

With the World as Our Market, We Need a Unifying Purpose Statement

One company that understood ROP exceptionally well, and retooled accordingly, was Timberland, the New Hampshire–based footwear and apparel brand. Despite enormous efforts to better the world through *Lead With We* business practices, it had found itself lost in the noise and clutter of other brands touting similar language, all citing sustainability claims about the impact they were having on issues ranging from their supply chains to the world at large. Timberland, a leading brand within the VF Corporation portfolio (which also includes Vans, The North Face, and Dickies), intended to redefine its purpose with a statement that stood out, that effectively straddled all its stakeholders, regions, and products. It needed to unify a brand that comprised multiple product lines coming to life in different ways around the world.

For example, in the US, extensive market research uncovered that Timberland's iconic tan boot was very much understood as an outdoor work product associated with individuals, companies, and partners in the "natural environment"/"nurturing the planet" space. You found it in the mountains, in forests, and in the desert, among folks at work or amidst adventurers outdoors. At the same time, it had also become deeply wedded to urban hip-hop culture and iconography—a fact the company capitalized on to enlist new generations of consumers. In Europe, however, the brand and its tan boot in particular was understood more as a fashion item, loved as much for its style statement as its practical utility for steep terrain. At the same time, its associations with rap culture certainly carried over into that market, heavily informed by US- and London-based pop culture influencers. But generally speaking, in Europe you'd be more likely to find the boots worn in trendy, upmarket coffee bars, social events, and so on. Last, in the Asia-Pacific region, the boot was understood not so much as a work shoe, an "urban" expression brand, or a strictly hiking/outdoor exploit product. Instead, this region—which encompasses a wide variety of countries and cultures—thinks of "Tims" as a weekend shoe designed to empower them to escape the heavy toll of the working week.

That's a tough, multifarious heritage to collate and combine into one concise, consistent, and scalable message. Yet the company had to consider Timberland's passions, expertise, and actions, especially its efforts to leverage its business to catalyze positive impact. That latter goal is part and parcel of the VF group of companies, which are all engaged in environmental sustainability, human rights, and many other concerns.

Together with the Timberland leadership from North America, their Europe, Middle East, and Africa group, and the Asia-Pacific, the brand defined its purpose this way: *To inspire and equip a new generation of adventurous doers to step outside and move the world forward.* There's an empowerment message in stepping outside, getting going, getting moving, becoming proactive, and taking—*leading*—the first "steps" toward the world we want to create for ourselves. The brand, its parent company, and its corporate siblings were living by that standard. And for the Timberland consumer, the collaborative nature of what we do, whether it's running ops in a manufacturing facility in Costa Rica, busking with a band on the streets of Edinburgh, scaling Kilimanjaro in midwinter, or just hanging out in a Tokyo café, means we're likely not alone. We're part of a tribe, a community. And it's that togetherness that *moves the world forward.*

Timberland quickly got to work activating its purpose. In 2019, the company announced it would plant fifty million trees across the globe within the following five years, building on the massive tree-planting efforts it's led since 2001. Part of that "Plant the Change" initiative is to help build what the brand calls "The Great Green Wall" with partner organizations like TreeAid, Smallholder Farmers Alliance, and JustDiggIt. The Wall will span more than eight thousand kilometers across Africa. The reforestation project aims to act as a carbon sink and will also increase economic opportunities for members of local communities while fostering biodiversity, now rapidly declining in that region.[99]

With Practice, We Can Consistently Put Purpose to Work

To LEAD WITH WE is simply necessary—as when Intel proactively disrupted and reengineered its whole supply chain to put the kibosh on three conflict minerals—tungsten, tantalum, and gold. Each is a necessary component in the manufacture of consumer electronics, and all are often tied to various atrocities, such as mines controlled by armed militias that commit human-rights abuses such as child labor in Central Africa. Intel demands of all its suppliers complete transparency and compliance with existing government guidelines, among other assurances. It partners with customers, NGOs, intergovernmental alliances such as the Organisation for Economic Co-operation and Development,[100] and other bodies such as the Responsible Minerals Initiative[101] to develop longer-term strategies to end the brutalities associated with its industry—even when it's not participating directly or indirectly somewhere in its supply chain.[102] The issue is bigger than the company. Yet Intel is big enough to exert an influence over smaller companies, so the whole effort exceeds the sum of the parts. Intel's then-CEO Brian Krzanich went so far as to call out his entire industry from the stage at the Consumer Electronics Show in 2014,[103] exhorting it to follow Intel's lead and create a cascading impact on the industry.[104] And that's the point, that first step we take. No matter how large or small, our company can create a ripple effect that, combined with others' efforts, can drive industry change and positive impact that would be unimaginable on our own.

The more of us who do this, the more market and competitive forces will then reorient and reward these new behaviors more quickly, and the financial rewards for doing so will follow accordingly. If you're a small business leader, here's where you can take some comfort. The weight and influence of a lot of small businesses can reach or exceed the power of the few corporate behemoths that seem to be doing the right thing. The whole—the WE—benefits (and in turn, the parts WITH which the whole is made) when we aggregate all our individual leadership movements.

With Healthy Competition, Purpose Gets Sharpened

Beyond the basics of striving for the competitive edge—say, Nike and Adidas vying for the top spot as disruptors of their industry—we see the likes of KIND Bar challenging Clif Bar and vice versa over each other's sustainability and the wholesomeness of their ingredients. I find the public argument to be a heartening example of progress in the right direction. The spat's not over who has greater market share. It's not an "I drink your milkshake!"[105] threat by either side against the other's right to operate or access necessary resources. Instead, it's all about who can dominate the LEAD WITH WE space through more healthful ingredients for consumers, more long-term viability of the WE.[106] On and on they sparred, with each company pushing the other to do better, to double down on its integrity of intent and actions. This constructive one-upping can be exercised across any industry, with one or more of your competitors, for any length of time to help the entire community become more aware and start making better choices in their brand selection and overall consumption.

A similar battle had simmered, then raged in 2019 between Coors and Bud Light brand beers. MillerCoors, the US subsidiary of Molson Coors, sued the Anheuser-Busch company, parent of Bud Light beers, in response to its rival's Super Bowl ad that blatantly "shamed" Miller Lite and Coors Light for their dependence on corn syrup. What ensued was an epic fray, replete with accusations of trade-secret hijacking, all in service of making a healthier, more sustainable, and responsible product.[107]

Along those lines, the BRT and B Corps have been in dynamic dialogue for a few years now, challenging words over actions:

> In the *New York Times* on August 25 [2019], 33 B Corp CEOs called for the business leaders . . . to put their words into action by adopting benefit corporation governance structures . . . and spread . . . into a more purpose-driven future [because] the purpose of capitalism is to work for everyone and for the long term.[108]

With an Enterprise Purpose, Sub-brands Thrive

When Mahindra Finance, the financial services arm of the Mahindra Group, a $20 billion Indian conglomerate, wanted to define its value proposition [*Harvard Business Review* reports], it looked to its parent company's longtime purpose-driven strategy of improving . . . lives—encapsulated . . . by the simple motto "Rise." It's a word that the company's third-generation leader, Anand Mahindra, expects will inspire employees to accept no limits, think alternatively, and drive positive change.[109]

But unifying a purpose across an extensive portfolio comes with unique challenges. Consider VSP Global, the extensive enterprise brand (both B2B and B2C). It's one of the largest eyewear and eye care providers on the planet—and the US's biggest vision benefits provider.[110] Headquartered in Rancho Cordova, California, it encompasses five different affiliated LOBs and multiple, well-known, long-independent brands in its portfolio: eye care insurance, frame brands, lens enhancements, ophthalmic technology, retail optical locations, and connected experiences. The complex and multifaceted organization sought to unite its allied entities under a single, strong enterprise purpose; then, on the strength of that purpose, empower each of the affiliates to develop its own concomitant purpose, unique to each form and function—a movement of movements.

The question was, how could VSP differentiate itself from large competitors such as the EssilorLuxottica and GrandVision Groups, which vie for industry leadership, by communicating actions and aspirations well above and beyond the basic products that it made and services it provided? To differentiate, VSP laddered up past the limits of the industry standard, declaring a purpose commitment *to empower human potential through sight*. This reframed what business VSP Global is actually in: not human eyes, per se, but human *potential*. So, the tool of the VSP trade is sight, represented by all the products and services it brings to market. But its purpose is potential, which makes intuitive sense, because sight is one of our most fundamental faculties, from which so much of our limitless potential derives. The company was already well established in empowering human potential by enhancing people's capacities through better vision. This ran the gamut from innovating more sustainable frames, lenses, and software for doctor–patient and doctor–corporate software; through greater access to vision insurance; to distribution of free frames and vision clinics after disasters like Superstorm Sandy in 2012. In fact, the company's "Eyes of Hope" program provided care to more than three million people in need, with 8,500 of VSP Global's network doctors participating annually. Its Mobile Eyes buses covered 621,000 miles to provide access to care in rural and inner-city neighborhoods.[111]

One Eyes of Hope initiative was the "We See," A Child Eye Health Project launched in Soweto, South Africa. The foundation partnered with the Brien Holden Vision Institute, an Australian nonprofit, as well as local government agencies, to create a program aimed at integrating kids' eye care into school health and education policies. This included creating an optical health clinic within Soweto's Nike Football Training Centre, which, in addition to training and coaching, also provides HIV/AIDS testing and education in the regional community. The results: 95,000 local children received eye screenings within the first three years; 2,500 life-changing prescription glasses were allocated; and the program was successfully integrated into an existing healthcare infrastructure run by the Gauteng Department of Health—representing the country's most populous province, including Johannesburg and Pretoria—thus bolstering the program's impact and sustainability.[112]

Such a stated purpose also drives innovation, as evidenced by VSP Global's "Level Smart" glasses rollout. Embedded in stylish frames, sensors track physical activity such as steps walked, calories burned, and distance traveled. What's more, users are awarded points for meeting daily activity goals, which can be used to trigger a charitable donation from VSP Global on the wearer's behalf. The eyewear company is essentially incentivizing people to get more exercise by motivating them with the possibility of making a positive contribution in areas they care most about.[113]

To LEAD WITH WE is an unending process—not a final destination. No company gets it all right all of the time, and how a company practices its purpose is an ongoing and thoughtful experiment, both internally and externally. One thing is clear, however: Deceptive or disingenuous practices such as those exposed in recent, much-publicized scandals, such as falsifying revolutionary technology at Theranos, faking diesel emissions data at VW, and setting up fraudulent accounts at Wells Fargo, will not fly. Greed and dishonesty will be exposed at great cost to a company's reputation, leadership, culture, and sales—and only a few companies will survive and emerge stronger for a second act. Barring such self-destructive extremes, however, no company needs to be perfect for this work to start. We must simply begin and continuously improve. Purpose done right will drive desired profits without the need for duplicity. And if we slip up, we need to be honest about it, and work to redeem our own name and the reputation of business in general. We, individually, become better when we begin to become WE, collectively. As Amanda Gorman, former US National Youth Poet Laureate, reminded the world at the 2021 presidential inauguration, we're "not broken but simply unfinished."[114] We will likely never find our desired impact "finished." But a strong, defensible, meaningful purpose around which all stakeholders can rally provides a solid start. Purpose continually fuels the engine of our business like a perpetual forward-motion machine.

Key Takeaways

➡ Upgrade your business ambitions to drive growth through purpose, as they are two sides of the same coin.

➡ Enterprises, companies, and startups can each leverage purpose to enhance their supply chains, build a productive culture, drive sales, and scale impact in partnership with all stakeholders.

➡ Purpose must be activated in authentic and collaborative ways to inspire the trust, especially among younger generations, that drives engagement and scales impact.

Action Items

1. *LEAD*—Identify where you are on your purpose journey through an honest self-audit, then take appropriate and persistent steps to upgrade your leadership.

2. *WITH*—Use the *LEAD WITH WE* methodology to define an authentic and differentiating purpose that serves as an animating force for your company and its stakeholders to co-create its activation with you.

3. *WE*—Leverage your purpose as a company-wide decision-making filter to ensure that all aspects of your company are consistently working, evolving, and innovating to unlock solutions that benefit society and the planet.

EXECS, EMPLOYEES & SUPPLY CHAIN

TRANSCENDENCE
FOSTER REGENERATIVE & ABUNDANT FUTURE
Evolve principles & practices to scale human & planetary health
Humanity & Planet

SOCIETY
COLLABORATE CROSS-SECTOR & SHAPE CULTURE
Drive cultural conversations & coalitions that improve society
Citizens, Collaborators & Sectors

COMMUNITY
MOBILIZE BRAND COMMUNITIES & BUILD MOVEMENTS
Engage external stakeholders around purpose-led movements
Customers, Consumers & Partners

COMPANY
ACTIVATE PURPOSE & ALIGN INTERNAL STAKEHOLDERS
Integrate & apply purpose throughout company

LEADERS
DEFINE COMPANY PURPOSE & GOALS
Conduct honest audit & determine reason for being
Corporations, Businesses & Startups

ME
ADOPT *LEAD WITH WE* MINDSET & BEHAVIOR
Recognize new reality, grasp urgency & shift thinking
Every Individual

5

Culture

Guiding an Internal Transformation of Your Business

Together *WE* Activate Purpose

By defining our business purpose, we can start to move up the Collectivized Purpose in Action Spiral. We've already begun to interact with cohorts within our company, gathering our first significant partners *WITH* whom we developed and began to pursue our purpose. We recognized the crucial step of aligning this first team of internal players, integrating, communicating, and executing on a shared purpose. In this chapter, I will lay out details and practical steps for execution. Because purpose is the nucleus of the *LEAD WITH WE* paradigm's power, we're going to explore how to specifically apply it within each company. And as we do so, we'll work on ways to increase the Breadth of Our *WITH,* by engaging as many internal stakeholders as possible at all times around our collectivized purpose activation, guided by the right kind of leadership. We're aiming for maximum buy-in and full engagement. In particular, we'll focus on maximizing the opportunity to engage our employees in the definition, integration, and activation of our company's purpose to deepen advocacy, productivity, and retention.

The result of all this internal orientation and alignment work will be an effective, cohesive, and purposeful company culture. We do that with proper planning, training, and tools. I won't dwell on the general idea of culture per se, because, like purpose, it's been exhaustively examined in business literature for a decade. Here, I just want to distinguish the difference between any old random culture—or worse, various forms of toxic culture, such as the Old Boys' Club—and the kind of LEAD WITH WE culture we need to solve major crises, saving business itself and the world at large. Culture is the water in which our company swims. Our crew constitute the purposeful fish. We must clarify and purify our company culture the same way we ensured our purpose was authentic and life sustaining. In the same way that purpose reaches every corner of the business, so, too, must culture. From hiring to alumni programs, culture permeates every decision we make.

Culture—both the underpinnings and expressions of how we think about our environments and act within them—is the basis for making a difference in the world. Internal culture is the platform on which all our efforts will stand and take flight. Think of culture as *purpose, entrenched and galvanized into action when shared by many.* To be effective and ring true, every activation element must serve a clear function, grounded in the purpose strategy, arising out of a sincere interest in solving a significant problem, and commensurate with our company's unique skills and strengths. And all that begins with leadership at the top. We want to win today's talent wars by dramatically improving our business's reputation within and beyond our industry. And that hinges on the fulcrum of a fully articulated and activated LEAD WITH WE purpose. Remember, 76 percent of all employees expect their leader to take the first steps, and 71 percent believe it's critically important for their CEO or other leader to respond to challenging times.[1]

The unique expression of our LEAD WITH WE purpose becomes a slingshot that will propel a movement, driven by the cultural conversation the brand will lead, sustained by its effective storytelling. That's what ultimately changes the world. We'll detail those further stages up the Virtuous Spiral in the remaining chapters. Here, we need only understand that our movement gathers momentum as we assemble teammates in our own initial compass of impact WITH our own workmates and staff. Knowing the movement must eventually reach beyond our walls or website into communities and society at large reminds us it must be carefully plotted, field-tested, tweaked, and solidified long before it's conveyed externally.

The moment we articulated our purpose, we loaded the slingshot. Now when we communicate about it with and to our internal stakeholders, we're pulling back the projectile. Later, we'll impart our impact to the public, and we'll be aiming for a bull's-eye.

Together *WE* Innovate

Purpose, innovation, and culture are all intertwined. They're all why we exist, and they all should inform all departments of our company, our product and service development, partnerships, strategy, R&D—everything. They're all filters for all aspects of our business. Internal cultures must be liberated from oppressive leadership styles and motivate all of us to think long and hard about, then respond creatively to, real-world problems. As Bill McDermott, former CEO of SAP, says:

> If the team has a good experience . . . our people have the freedom and the ability to voice ideas and concerns. Continuous innovation provides real, tangible freedom. People are empowered to think and act creatively. That creates trust and offers personal confidence.[2]

And all that leads to new innovation. These pivots and other business transformations typically occur for one of three reasons, or a combination of the three, all of which affect company culture:

1. *Visionary leadership* and top-down mandates. GM's Mary Barra. Unilever's Paul Polman. The kind of vision Indra Nooyi, PepsiCo's former leader, showed repeatedly. When Nooyi took over as CEO in 2006, three-quarters of the company's goods landed squarely in the "*fun* for you" foods category—in other words, they were sugary and bad for you. During Nooyi's tenure, she contracted "a globally renowned endocrinologist and obesity expert to help revolutionize the nutritional base of the company's old and new products." By the time she departed her role in 2018, the company's "*good* for you" (i.e., somewhat more healthful, less sugary) snacks comprised half the company's product portfolio.[3] During PepsiCo's signature "Performance with Purpose" rollout:

    > Nooyi proved that the presumed tradeoff between short-term financial returns and long-term investing is a false choice [according to her alma mater, Yale] . . . She has led

the industry in responsible water use, ended the use of trans
fats and dramatically reduced sugar in PepsiCo's products,
introduced recyclable packaging, and achieved other inspiring sustainable and nutritional milestones aimed at helping
communities and customers.[4]

PepsiCo is just being practical with its activism. Its previous products
not only posed a serious risk to the health of its customers (without whom
the company would have no business), but they also threatened the economic health of the company through reputation damage and risk exposure.

Interestingly, visionary leadership sometimes works the other way
around. For example, at Mammut, its CEO, Oliver Pabst, tells me he had
no choice but to begin to innovate along *LEAD WITH WE* lines because his
employees insisted on it in a "grassroots push . . . to make me wake up."[5]
It might be a given to assume that large organizations in particular are
designed to resist change, not to make it, creating structures and systems
rarely designed to evolve. But the past two decades have proven beyond
a shadow of doubt that those who *LEAD WITH WE*—like long trains with
powerful engines—can relatively easily and quickly change tracks to
avoid crashing.

2. ***Response to consumer or media activism***, as when we or our industry
   is called out for bad behavior, or cultural shifts overtake our stuck-in-the-
   mud mindset. In response to intense public pressure, Mattel has launched
   new iterations of its iconic, rail-thin, heavy-chested Barbie doll[6] with new
   skin tones and body shapes. Mattel's response reflects the diversity and
   body types of real people in the real world. As much as Mattel tried tirelessly over the years to brand Barbie a feminist (e.g., astronaut, business-
   woman, surgeon), sales had begun to plummet after 2012.[7] Critics argued
   it was because her inhuman morphology never evolved with the times.
   Slumber Party Barbie in 1963 came with a diet book for girls that contained only two words, all caps: "DON'T EAT!"[8] Since the initial rollout
   of the more diverse Barbies, the company has taken its efforts further.
   As of 2020, you can get a Barbie in a wheelchair, one with no hair, even
   one with vitiligo.[9] Sales of the doll have risen since the advent of the new
   Barbies.[10] Though the changes have been long overdue, this new legacy
   of thinking—not to mention the enormous and complex undertaking

of a major redesign and rebrand—is no small challenge. Mattel deserves major accolades for the move, and for recognizing how to unlock huge opportunities from cultural criticism. Its new marketing mantra—"You can be anything"—is a message of empowerment to children everywhere and a way to usher in endless new expressions of its product. More on companies responding proactively and reactively to consumer demands in chapter six, "Community."

3. *An obvious threat looms on the horizon.* San Francisco–based Levi Strauss & Co. models this kind of proactive innovation, sensing the zeitgeist and realities on the ground. For more than a decade, its recycled denim Levi's and Water<Less Dockers managed to innovate inside the $40 billion global jeans market the company practically invented and still dominates.[11] Along with carbon-negative wool sweaters from Sheep, Inc., replete with complete supply chain transparency,[12] Levi's fits into a huge trend in the garment industry and other sectors toward regenerative methods. On the one hand, all of this innovation is driven by new market opportunities unlocked and supported by the shared public- and corporate quest to solve world problems. But on the other hand, and more critically, Levi's acted in response to anticipated public pushback—even before any massive outcry put direct pressure on it around the costly use of precious water and chemical dyes in the labor-intensive finishing process. More recently, Levi's Eureka Innovation Lab's (EIL) team of designers, developers, engineers, and scientists (including MIT) created its "Future Finish" line, a century and a half after the company invented blue jeans. EIL's laser-powered tech digitizes the design and development of denim, even as it personalizes it for each consumer: "By going digital, we're able to use fewer chemicals in the finishing process and reduce our environmental impact."[13] The new initiative helped the company maintain a 5 percent net revenue increase in the first quarter after launching Future Finish, and aided its hedging against the onslaught of the coronavirus lockdowns, which at that point had already closed almost all of its substantial China operations.[14] Innovating from the inside, in advance of specific consumer pressure, might have kept Levi's at the top.

Again, innovation drivers are inseparable from healthy internal business ecosystems. Therefore, they must go hand in hand with taking care of workers. In

2016, Levi's announced it would aggressively expand its worker well-being initiatives begun in 2011. Its ongoing goal is to extend its several well-being programs to more than three hundred thousand workers worldwide—its whole supply chain—by 2025—all the more necessary since the 2020 pandemic. And it's encouraging competitors to join the effort by sharing best practices,[15] a lesson of industry collaboration up the Spiral that we'll uncover in chapter seven, "Society."

Isn't all this costly? Yes—but so is going out of business. Is it risky? Yes. But as I often share with We First's clients, if you don't like risk, you're really going to hate irrelevance. By aiming for maximum "collateral good" in our efforts to innovate—while remembering that it will require a healthy, engaged, and excited internal team—we likely won't go wrong, either ethically or financially.

PayPal, for example, tends to include multiple stakeholders in its decisions. Daniel Schulman, president and CEO, "is arguably the most comfortable of his Fortune 500 peers with discussing abstract questions of corporate governance in human-scale moral terms," according to *Fast Company*. "He shares PayPal's wealth with a range of stakeholders because it's the right thing to do—or, as he likes to say, because it's in keeping with 'red, white, and blue values.' Over the past two decades, he has become a leading advocate for what he calls 'reverse Friedmanism.'"[16] For example, in 2019, the company, seeking to foster more passionate staff, "slashed by more than half the costs those employees pay for benefits like health insurance."[17] Moves like this engender increased loyalty, productivity, and goodwill among the internal crew and build a healthier corporate culture.

Similar to MOD Pizza's and Dave's Killer Bread's practice of hiring formerly incarcerated people, Greyston Bakery of Riverdale, New York, is another great example of a business existing to solve the same social problem through its "Open Hiring"/"Radical Inclusion"[18] policy. They're not alone. The Second Chance Business Coalition, comprising twenty-nine large corporations, including household names as well as Eaton, Schnitzer, and Vistra, is working to expand opportunities for employment and greater upward mobility for people with criminal records, even including re-entry policies in its Racial Equity Tracker.[19] WE must extend to those reentering society.

Not all businesses are even close to changing their cultures for the more inclusive and otherwise better in ways like these. In the US, "up to $3.8 billion per year is spent on outdated and demeaning HR practices such as background checks and credit checks, filtering capable candidates out of the workforce based on their past actions, rather than the potential for success."[20] By investing in human potential, companies receive big dividends. Greyston is a for-profit entity, a certified B Company, but all its profits go to its nonprofit foundation (NPF) parent, which in turn serves the community. "We don't hire people to bake brownies," the company states. "We bake brownies to hire people."[21]

Recently valued at $1.4 billion,[22] Harry's is a US consumer packaged goods company. In addition to revolutionizing the shaving industry with a successful subscription model—famously acquiring a million customers in just two years,[23] which was mostly responsible for its 35 percent year-over-year growth, or three times the industry's average[24]—it simultaneously continues to shake things up internally. In response to the Black Lives Matter (BLM) movement's progression in 2020, for example, the ten-year-old company further expanded the definitions of diversity among men, including multiplying its BIPOC representation, boosting retention. It empowered success across the company and its leadership through its model "share, learn, practice" program.[25] It partners with multiple NPFs and donates 1 percent of its profits, mostly to mental health programs. Aiming to help half a million men by 2021,[26] Harry's is right on track.

Over in Battle Creek, Michigan, equally enlightened work is underway, with innovations related to diversity and new product lines rolling out together regularly at the Kellogg Company. Kellogg's culture is already 100 percent compliant on the Human Rights Campaign's (HRC) Corporate Equality Index (the national benchmarking tool for corporate policies, practices, and benefits pertinent to LGBTQ employees);[27] and it secured the thirty-fourth spot on DiversityInc's Top 50 list, which measures companies' talent pipelines, talent development, leadership accountability, and suppliers, all related to diversity, inclusion, and equity (DI&E).[28] "Closing the racial equity gap means creating $8 trillion in additional gross domestic output by 2050," according to the Kellogg Foundation, citing US Chamber of Commerce stats.[29] The company is growing more diverse and inclusive, and as a result, related innovation is at an all-time high. Kellogg's marked innovations and impact, along with its unusual employee retention rate, are, I contend, direct results of its culture of diversity—leading to its $13 billion annual revenue.[30]

Together WE Evolve the Idea of Leadership

More and more universities and academics are driving a major transformation of business. So much great work is getting done at various California state universities, Texas A&M, Cornell, Oxford, Helsinki, Presidio, and Bainbridge—some looking at regenerative agriculture and circular economics, others creating new tools, but most really looking hard at the root causes of systemic problems and how to solve them. I've been honored to engage with members of the Harvard Business School Association of Boston and elsewhere along these lines. All of this transformation at progressive B-schools is great cause for optimism, especially as nearly all focus on creating a new breed of more responsible, ethical, and collaborative leader.

That's going to be necessary. For the process of LEAD WITH WE purpose onboarding to work, there's often a need for significant leadership changes. What are some necessary new attitudes and activities to ensure purpose will stick and grow internally as the foundation of a thriving company culture? We know that buy-in across the gamut of our company's constituents is one trademark. So, how do we get that? We start by cultivating empathy: a realization that our business exerts an influence on real people in the real world, beginning with our staff and partners. So, we put WE first in all our calculations:

- ➡ *Incorporate* humanity at the core of every decision, action, innovation, and stance. Think people and their collective best interests, first.

- ➡ *Reframe* every response and decision through the LEAD WITH WE lens. This constant and consistent commitment to our purpose will help ensure its authenticity, credibility, commonality, and constancy. Repetition leads to automation. We're fostering the development of habits here.

- ➡ *Share* a painstakingly constructed, carefully vetted, collective-input-heavy *brand purpose handbook* and other tools, tailored to the business. Get everybody inside the company to sing from this same hymnbook, a guide that makes clear how the company's purpose can manifest in the ways that everyone involved thinks about it, acts on it, and speaks of it.

- ➡ *Utilize* the purpose to continually innovate ways to stay efficient, effective, inclusive, and immediate in our real-time responses to challenges, both internal and external. Stay nimble and ready—outside influences will inevitably force reactions and changes. Predict responses.

- ➡ *Guarantee* lasting, transformative adoption of LEAD WITH WE thinking by ensuring initiatives are all Co-owned, Co-created, and Co-authored through Collaboration. (See chapter six, "Community," for more details on "The Four C's.") Purpose can be employed in service of business objectives only with nonstop and comprehensive stakeholder engagement.

➡️   ***Sustain*** long-term energy and momentum through consistent *cadence.*
Purpose is a dynamic process, living, breathing, and evolving all the
time. So, establish regular traditions, routine opportunities to contribute and advance purpose, and dependable reporting to keep this fully
inflated balloon in the air.

At the top, when trying to inspire commitment from a board/investors/
CEO, we always start with what they're willing to listen to—and where they
are philosophically. (Maybe *we* are that person at the top of the hierarchy.) As
leaders, we're not leading a company or a brand—we're leading only people.
So, our job is not to command a ship per se, but to hold the rudder and help
the crew navigate together in the right direction, through whatever seas might
come. In short, we're culture conductors. And if we're not in an obvious position
of leadership, we can still provide some simple reminders to the decision makers at our companies of every leading indicator pointing toward the propulsive
progress of this *LEAD WITH WE* movement of movements. Reminding them that
business culture creation, though collaboration, begins and ends with us all—
the *WE*—as leaders:

➡️   ***Purpose-Based Cultural Leadership***
Unilever, which GlobeScan research (with 700 business leaders
interviewed) rates as the number one company for *LEAD WITH WE*–style
sustainability,[31] is so successful precisely because it has fully integrated a
LEAD WITH WE purpose into its company culture, its movement of movements among its beloved brands, and its growth strategy. Everyone's on
board. As Unilever's CEO, Alan Jope, puts it: "Our company is guided
by three deeply held beliefs: that brands with purpose grow, companies
with purpose last, and people with purpose thrive . . . So we will not
waver one iota in our commitment to purpose-led business."[32]
Jope and Keith Weed, Unilever's chief marketing and communications officer and another thought leader in this space, are hardly alone.
Industry and mass-market media have dedicated millions of column
inches to the subject. JPMorgan's Jamie Dimon recently joined Bridge-
water's Ray Dalio, Mark Cuban, and other billionaire business leaders shouting from their corporate rooftops about (among other things)
stark societal inequality in the US, partly in response to obvious societal
conditions, but more so in response to their own staffs' concerns. In a

May 2020 memo to stakeholders, Dimon declared "a call to action for business and government to think, act, and invest for the common good and confront the structural obstacles that have inhibited inclusive economic growth for years."[33] The more diverse and inclusive our employees are, the easier we often find it to get unity of purpose that aligns with societal needs.

In activating a LEAD WITH WE purpose in the culture of our company, we need appetite and aptitude in equal measure. In fact, nine out of ten business leaders have both, believing the purpose of business is to LEAD WITH WE, to create value for *all* stakeholders, to (quoting GlobeScan) "partner with all stakeholders to create wealth, tackle climate change and inequality and to do so fairly and inclusively." Only 8 percent of the leaders in that survey feel that the purpose of business is to merely make a profit and deliver returns to shareholders.[34] Seems 92 percent of global business leaders understand that profit for profit's sake comes at a much higher cost than mere money.

Transformational Change Leadership Dynamics

Marshall Ganz, the Rita T. Hauser senior lecturer in leadership, organizing, and civil society at Harvard's Kennedy School of Government, has categorized four essential leadership skills—motivational (telling the story), relational (building affiliations based on trust), strategic (developing plans), and action-oriented (catalyzing ideas into reality)[35]—that all assist us in climbing the Collectivized Purpose in Action Spiral. To LEAD WITH WE requires "accepting responsibility for enabling others to achieve purpose under conditions of uncertainty."[36] In other words, there's an *adaptive* imperative. Part of instilling this kind of culture within a company is training individuals to work together on overcoming constantly shifting challenges, and activating shared purpose to achieve real impact. How does everyone keep sailing in the same direction despite the winds and waves? The answer lies in the rudder of purpose: "Leaders . . . need to be able to practice what Walter Brueggemann has called 'the prophetic imagination'—which involves balancing the tension between 'criticality' (articulating the problem and the pain) and 'hope' (avoiding both despair and being over-optimistic)."[37] We create a culture that both recognizes how bad things are—and how much we can do together to improve potential outcomes.

Together *WE* Can Revolutionize "CEO Activism"

Unrealistic over-optimism is not the same as audacious ambition. Of course, we leaders must not only consider the collective good, the social purpose of business, but also respond to our real fiduciary responsibility to weather the gathering storms that will threaten the business landscape. Taking responsibility. Mitigating risks. Building resilience. Engaging with team members, present and potential. Reporting our progress to our own people and the public beyond. Asking for help and collaboration. Most importantly, acting, and acting now, before it's too late. The cost of waiting will far exceed any expenses we undertake to transform right now. Inaction might cost us our reputation, our competitiveness, our relevance, our job, or even our whole business (not to mention the world). We've become, like it or not, a kind of Fifth Estate in our culture—an influential "CEO Party" as some have described it—calling out the other institutions for their inaction or shortcomings.

A wave of CEO activists began rising in the past decade or so, concurrently with employee activism as a major driver of corporate, political, economic, environmental, and social change, sometimes from the bottom up, and others from the top down. Facebook's staff revolt over hate speech, Amazon's over the climate crisis, Uber's over driver mistreatment, and Google's over inequitable pay scales all created inside cultures that encouraged taking strong stands on important issues. On the CEO front, Howard Schultz embargoed weapons at his Starbucks locations in 2013 (well, he "respectfully requested" his customers don't come in packing heat). Tim Cook in 2015 confronted his home state of Alabama for its lagging LGBTQ protections.[38] "America's business community recognized a long time ago that discrimination, in all its forms, is bad for business," Cook writes in a *Washington Post* opinion.[39] A year later, CEOs of a hundred companies (e.g., TD Bank, Hilton, Starwood) signed an open letter to the government of North Carolina, strongly urging the state to repeal a transphobic law.[40]

And here's what billionaire Salesforce founder, Marc Benioff—he who sounded capitalism's death knell at Davos 2020[41]—tells the *Harvard Business Review* (*HBR*):

> CEOs have an obligation to use their leadership to create that change of the world . . . It could be around LGBTQ, it could be about schools, it could be about the environment. These are things where CEOs can take very simple and concrete actions, and I'm encouraging them to do that.[42]

Company culture moved the political needle.

To advance a cause at your company, ensure your activism is warranted, aligned with your purpose and a reasonable degree of public sentiment, enjoys wide enough buy-in (with reasonable opt-out options for employees who don't agree), won't come as a surprise to your board or investors, and is articulated to the public with the utmost caution and clarity.[43]

In 2013, Starbucks' Schultz took a strong public stance for gay marriage. The company announced its support for the state of Washington's referendum backing gay marriage. In response, the National Organization for Marriage launched a boycott of the coffee chain, and some blamed that response for lower sales.[44] Schultz found himself challenged in the boardroom by a conservative shareholder over "disappointing" returns allegedly related to that boycott by traditional-marriage advocates. Schultz's response was a *LEAD WITH WE* triumph, drawing applause from the attendees as the board meeting:

> Not every decision is an economic decision . . . The lens in which we are making that decision is through . . . our people. We employ over 200,000 people in this company, and we want to embrace diversity. Of all kinds. If you feel, respectfully, that you can get a higher return than the 38 percent you got last year, it's a free country. You can sell your shares in Starbucks and buy shares in another company. Thank you very much.[45]

Perhaps we, too, could start at home, considering our internal stakeholders first. According to research of more than six hundred US businesses with fifty to five hundred employees, 63.3 percent of companies say retaining employees is actually harder than hiring them. And 71 percent of executives recognize that employee engagement is critical to their company's success. Companies with high employee engagement are 21 percent more profitable. However, it costs about $5,000 every time an employee leaves your company—and eight out of ten of all employees are seeking another job right now.[46]

Our people are a vast, untapped, overlooked brand-advocate mass. They live and breathe our business purpose every day. Yet, how often are they included in co-writing the purpose, the plan of action to get there, the how and why—not just the *what* for which we employ them—of the brand? Are they part of a broader governance, members of a multi-stakeholder board?[47] Are we thinking about them as long-term assets? A trailblazing study from the *HBR* showed that companies with strong labor policies (among others) enjoyed double the market cap eighteen years later.[48]

Best practices for ensuring stakeholder capitalism and reducing shareholder primacy include the International Business Council's leadership initiatives on long-term investment; common Environmental, Social, and Governance (ESG) metrics; lighthouse public–private partnerships projects and targets for combating the climate emergency; board toolkits created by World Economic Forum (WEF) communities in the areas of cybersecurity, AI, and climate governance; and the WEF's 2020 Stakeholder Principles in the COVID-19 era and related Workforce Principles for the pandemic.[49]

Another huge challenge is diversity and inclusion. Are we aware, for example, of the "staggering" wealth gap between Blacks and Whites? "The net worth of a typical white family in 2016—including home, retirement accounts, and all assets—was nearly 10 times greater than that of a Black family"—$171,000 versus $17,600—regardless of education level, according to *The Week*.[50] As of spring 2021, White people in the US now have median earnings 42 percent higher than Black people here, and 45 percent higher than what Hispanic Americans earn, *Axios* reports.[51]

The global pandemic hammered Black and Brown people far more piteously than Whites. Further, "wealth begets wealth through generations, and African Americans have missed out on that transfer for centuries."[52] So, too, poverty begets poverty. Where do our employees and partners (not to mention our consumers) fall on that super-tipped scale? What are we doing about it? In what ways might our business be perpetuating a stunningly unfair and unnecessary inequality?[53] We have enormous power to influence that internally. Overwhelmingly, "across many demographics—liberal, conservative, high-income, low-income, men, women, millennials, and boomers—Americans want companies to put workers at the heart of fair business practices," according to JUST Capital 2020 research. Their number one issue? That companies should pay a fair, livable wage.[54] Pay equity has become a hallmark of a happy and productive company culture, but in the US and elsewhere, there's still widespread resistance (most notably in Congress) to the prospect of raising the minimum wage, with some exceptions among corporate leadership, such as at PayPal, Chobani, Chipotle, and Costco.

The head of the world's most financially and culturally prominent sportswear brand took a stand against racial inequality in the US. In 2016, Mark Parker, chairperson, president, and CEO of Nike, issued a manifesto to the company's thirty-two thousand staff in response to the killings of Philando Castile and Alton Sterling. Citing Nike's long history of fostering equality, Parker wrote, "I am proud that Nike stands against discrimination in any form. We stand against bigotry. We stand for racial justice. We firmly believe the world can improve." Then, critically, he implored all stakeholders to discuss the issue and brainstorm practical ways to work on that improvement: "This is your company and we want you to be heard."[55] Like discussions that took place at Starbucks' eight thousand locations, shut for one day in 2018 for its 175,000 team members to discuss racial bias after an unacceptable incident at one of its Philadelphia stores,[56] such conversations are a necessity for transforming a company's culture.

With the advent of COVID-19 and the increasing visibility of the BLM movement in 2020, business leaders, most of them White men, came out in droves to make a salient point: "We need to start with acknowledging that racism is also a pandemic," wrote Steve Rendle of the VF Corp to his employees in summer 2020—"and one that has been an immensely debilitating factor in our society and abhorrent to our professed values of inclusion and equality."[57]

It's also worth noting that only 6.4 percent of CEOs in the S&P 500 list are women. That's only thirty-two out of five hundred.[58] And, as of June 2020—at the time of George Floyd's killing by a police officer in Minneapolis—there were only four Black CEOs in the S&P 500. Less than 1 percent.[59] Further, a third of S&P 500 companies do not have any Black board members whatsoever.[60]

Despite Richard Branson's colossal wealth—he founded more than four hundred companies and employs about seventy thousand people[61]—the Virgin tycoon is one of the good guys who LEAD WITH WE. He tells Business Insider that companies must "adopt responsible practices to eliminate the risks that often lie at the root of inequality and poverty."[62] For Branson, this means, among other things, that his fellow 1 percenters ought to LEAD by paying more taxes into the collective WE.[63] It means universal healthcare and empathy and opportunities for immigrants. Branson walks the walk, too. In 2018, he scuttled a deal with Saudi Arabia after Washington Post reporter and Saudi dissident Jamal Khashoggi disappeared after entering the Saudi consulate in Istanbul to get divorce papers.[64] Branson's suspicions turned out to be correct: Khashoggi was indeed assassinated (drugged, then dismembered) by Saudi Arabian agents.[65] The findings "would clearly change the ability of any of us in the West to do business with the Saudi Government," Branson says.[66] The Higher WE needs to uninvite people from the group until they reform. So Branson killed his partnership deal with Saudi Arabia's Public Invest-ment Fund, costing Virgin Galactic a promised $1 billion investment toward its interplanetary adventure plans. Branson has continued this kind of advocacy by taking a stand against the death penalty in the US.[67]

In contrast to Branson, Patagonia's Yvon Chouinard questions interplanetary travel when we have our own planet to save.[68] Chouinard founded and operates his half-century-old, billion-dollar global brand as a purpose with a company attached: *Patagonia is in business to save our home planet*.[69] A "political power" in his own right, he's taken on US presidents, outed and ousted climate deniers, championed the B Corp and regenerative agriculture crusades, and steered major environmental and social campaigns such as "1% for the Planet," a cooperative of companies that pledged to bequeath 1 percent of proceeds (more than $225 mil-lion since 2002) to environmental groups. "We're in a triage situation. Things are so grim," he told *Fast Company* in 2019. "It's World War III."[70]

Chouinard has always been careful in his selection of generals, those who best carried out the mission in the field. That lineage is in good hands with the new CEO, Ryan Gellert, who in September 2020 told *Fast Company*:

> I want to create an environment where people really feel like the hard work they're putting in is worth it. They see what it's contributing to . . . We don't want to work in a hierarchy. We know good ideas come from all over the organization, and inspiration and passion oozes from everyone here. That magic happens when we all work together . . . Our strategy here is, yes, we're a business, but it's a means for us to pursue our mis-sion. . . . the new mission statement . . . [isn't] the equivalent of a bumper sticker or T-shirt slogan.[71]

This is all the more important, according to Gellert, as the "world is chang-ing," and it's unlikely business leaders will ever again be "dealing with one big issue at a time. We're now in one where, unfortunately, we're going to be dealing with a lot of challenges stacking up at the same time."[72]

Together *WE* Are Reconsidering DI&E

A diverse, inclusive, and equitable internal culture is essential to expressions of *LEAD WITH WE*, and it must precede any external activations and communication. A full 61 percent of people report experiencing discrimination in the past.[73] *WE* doesn't mean only "us over here." It means all of us. There are a few key things to remember here:

1. ***Proactiveness.*** Let's tie DI&E efforts to tangible investment, strategically positioned around upstream, preventive interventions. Build a diverse and inclusive infrastructure from the ground up. Conduct an honest and searching internal audit: On the strength of what we hear, do a thorough assessment of what's working and what needs improvement. Then start getting our house in order, from onboarding to pay scales to promotions and more, while prioritizing DI&E. NASDAQ now says it will kick out brands without diverse boards of directors,[74] and Goldman Sachs won't take a company public without at least one board member from a non-majority background.[75] Among NASDAQ's 3,249 listed companies, 85 percent of their boards already have either at least one woman or person from an underrepresented group.[76] A record forty-one female CEOs are either running or slated to run Fortune 500 companies in 2021.[77] Four of NASDAQ's top five biggest companies—Apple, Microsoft, Alphabet, and Facebook—already "have boards on which straight white men are the minority," according to CNN.com, but as companies get smaller and farther from the public eye, DI&E diminishes precipitously.[78]

   Although it's not strictly her department, Lisa Boyd, Lyft's director of social impact, takes ownership of the company-wide efforts toward DI&E. "We have a huge mentorship and sponsorship program internally to support communities of color who work at Lyft, and to help their growth and development within the company," Boyd told me for a *Forbes* piece:

   > For four years, there's been a pay equity program, which starts with an audit of everyone's compensation, to make sure that there are no discrepancies. There were none found in 2020. "We do that every year to make sure that we're being thoughtful, and everybody is being paid fairly," Boyd says. 'We have diversity hiring goals around both at all levels. We have an internship program that was our most diverse cohort.
   >
   > At the leadership level, the company has adapted the National Football League's "Rooney Rule," which requires league teams to interview ethnic-minority candidates for head

coaching and senior football operation jobs. "Here," says Boyd, "we have what's called the Rooney Rule 2.0, which basically means that for any director level or above, you need to have a woman and an individual [of] color on the final candidate list in the final round of reviews."[79]

2. **Entrenchment.** Evidence proves that diversity does not necessarily equate to inclusion. And neither ensures equity. True equity must live and breathe, institutionalized inside the company DNA as Lyft is working on, activated horizontally and vertically, across departments, and in all territories around the world. It must include the whole supply chain. This means confronting some hard questions, admitting to unconscious biases, and absorbing the fact that some people in society as now structured are simply privileged. Among the entrenched hurdles and enduring biases: Historically disadvantaged groups (e.g., the BIPOC community, regardless of skill and educational attainment) are less likely to get hired, endure stricter scrutiny after hiring, and are far less likely to get promoted to management or professional positions—an even lower proportion in upper management.

3. **Improvement.** Embed end-to-end data sets, from stakeholder insights informing all strategy and tactics, through to benchmarking, tracking, and rewarding DI&E outcomes. For example:

> BlackRock has for the first time linked the cost of tapping bank lending to three metrics: how many women are in senior roles, Black and Latino employment, and how much it invests in assets that benefit society and the environment. The interest rate and fee that BlackRock pays lenders on any amounts it draws from its primary credit facility, worth $4.4 billion, will rise or fall annually from 2022 depending on the number of targets it meets.[80]

We should strive to get to the point where we can inspire others on this metric, setting the bar high. The rewards will expand proportionally. The more inclusive of stakeholders and diverse in thinking (and staffing) our company is, the more ideas and ingenuity we'll unlock as we shift from a culture of individualism to an "open source" approach that incorporates different thinking, perspectives, voices, understanding, and, ultimately, potential.

4. ***Transparency.*** Publicly declare short- and long-term commitments. Share your plan, priorities, and resources for addressing internal issues. Brands need to learn how to talk in straight lines instead of angles. Keep the evolution of the current state and the aspirations real, raw, and forward thinking by candidly appreciating the nuances, challenges, and useful tension points implicit in the process. Transparency, as we'll see later in this chapter and in chapter six, "Community," is a function of where we start and stop our impact storytelling. And if the current state of our DI&E isn't ideal—and it's likely not—let's call that out, holding our own company's feet to the fire—and by extension keeping both the industry and business at large accountable. We can and should include these "warts and all" in our public storytelling. Be like Citi: "They are not shying away from difficult and uncomfortable conversations, and when they do fall short, they strive not to sweep their failings under the carpet."[81]

What does DI&E look like in real-world practice? It looks like Aetna, Staples, and Activision Blizzard offering health insurance to their part-timers.[82] It looks like 150 CEOs writing Congress to support President Biden's $1.9 trillion coronavirus bill that all Republican members rejected.[83] It looks like job search engine and employer review site Glassdoor introducing a feature that unlocks employee-provided company ratings and salary reports based on demographics broken out by gender, race, and ethnicity.[84] It looks like ratings monster Nielsen announcing that it will begin tracking diversity and inclusion on TV.[85] It looks like McDonalds' aim for at least 35 percent of its US senior management to come from underrepresented groups by 2025—and tying executive pay to reaching those goals.[86]

For benchmarking and other ideas, the Corporate Racial Equity Tracker, a JUST Capital tool launched in 2021, provides a transparent picture of disclosure on twenty-two key measures of DI&E, from workforce demographics to education and training programs, among 100 of America's largest employers. It reveals, for example, that 100 percent of companies tracked employ anti-discrimination policies, but only 31 percent are addressing pay equity problems.[87] More in chapter six, "Community" on how DI&E relates to communities outside our business.

Together *WE* Are Getting More Engaged

When Daniel Martínez-Valle, CEO of Orbia (formerly Mexichem), took over in 2017, he inherited a company with $7 billion in revenue and its fingers in several disparate industries and sectors, including building and infrastructure, data communications, irrigation, plastics, and chemicals. It operated in an astonishing one-half of the world's countries.[88] Its purpose? Who knew? He therefore undertook to transform the Mexican behemoth into a global *LEAD WITH WE* front-runner. What was the overarching post-profit purpose of Orbia? That question launched him on a years-long transformation expedition, inclusive of the company's twenty-two thousand employees, who he engaged, surveyed, workshopped, and consulted on the plan. Orbia's is a story not only of clear and ambitious sustainability goals, but an exemplar of eventual *WE First* priorities. Orbia's purpose, the company ultimately discovered, is: *To advance life around the world.* Martínez-Valle told *Forbes* in 2019:

> At the core of what we do, we keep things moving forward . . . ensuring food security, reducing water scarcity, reinventing the future of cities and homes, connecting communities around the world to global data infrastructure, and expanding access to health and wellness with advanced materials.[89]

LEAD WITH WE companies like Orbia are daily discovering more and more ingenious and effective ways to engage their crews in the unique expression of their collectivized purpose. Reinforcing it. Allowing people to constantly invent it. "Ignite and co-create," as I like to say. When it's fully realized, it's a self-efficacious, kinetic feedback loop of ROP. As we co-create with internal stakeholders all the content across the infrastructure of our business, we foster exponential impact on their performance, loyalty, and inspiration. This increases the meaningful, dynamic understanding of the enterprise's purpose, which in turn serves as a self-perpetuating, long-term, internal culture builder. And such momentum further solidifies earnest adoption that propels widespread, organic engagement with the company purpose (continued co-creation). Congratulations—we've officially started to *LEAD, WITH* the first level of *WE*: our own workers.

For our internal *LEAD WITH WE* culture rollout, there are several key ways we can lead the start of this movement, all of which are adaptable and scalable depending on our business size, type, and organizational structure. First of all, we best nurture the company culture and expand our scope of impact by ensuring our C-suite leads by example, as I've just detailed. In terms of our employees, we do the following:

➤ **_Empower them._** We give employees input and ownership of the company purpose, and opportunities for them to express their personal purpose through it. We interview them regularly (though not annoyingly, to avoid that dread disorder I call "Survey Fatigue Syndrome"). We ask how our brand should speak to them. How we can best reaffirm our purpose and keep investing in our people. How we unlock creative collaboration inside the company. How we help our people think and act in new ways, on their own and in teams. How we grow and adapt to ensure our culture is resilient and productive. We establish a purpose and impact council with representatives from all internal constituencies, and give them license to take action. We offer employees a role in planning how to make the most meaningful difference. What's the point in thwarting manifestations of purpose, a natural personal motivator? There's a lot of research in and around the effects of purpose on employee satisfaction and productivity. For example, *HBR* and the Energy Project found that employees with this kind of clear sense of purpose are three times more likely to stay with a company.[90] They also report about twice as much job satisfaction[91]—or, as another reputable study reports, they are 66 percent more likely to feel "fulfilled."[92] Because of the enormous investment in recruiting, onboarding, training, salary, and benefits, it's wise to include staff in the process. Doing so helps develop institutional knowledge— one of the most valuable assets for moving our business forward. So, let's give them opportunities beyond pushing papers, counting beans, or monitoring a line. We'll foster much better, more loyal, more vocal spokespeople for our brand. And they will be more adaptable and resilient when the chips are down. This is in stark contrast to the findings of a PWC study called *Putting Purpose to Work*, which revealed that less than a third of business leaders help employees connect to their own purpose through their work.[93] There's a huge disconnect there, because almost 80 percent of business leaders think of purpose as central to their business success.[94] Walk the walk, together.

➡ ***Protect them.*** We protect workers' health and financial security above all. We adopt practices to minimize overhead and job loss. We put workers first, and partner with government to support them. We support local communities, suppliers, and customers. We express care and commitment to help address crises, both internally, and those external that nevertheless affect our workers, and we offer compassion and support. We ask what we can we do to prevent, prepare for, and "pre-mitigate" negative consequences of future crises. We ask ourselves: How do we address the preexisting and continuing inequalities that put so many of our community stakeholders at risk in the first place?

➡ ***Educate them.*** We offer as much immersion training—practical, tactical—as we can so they fully understand, safeguard, and eventually personify the purpose, and embody the brand. Train-the-trainer workshops. Weekly check-ins. Designated purpose and impact ambassadors. Leadership training within their realms—how can they activate the company purpose in their roles? What are they deputized to do, solve, create on their own? (A food server, for example, ought to be able to make the decision to offer a free meal for legitimate reasons without having to consult a manager. A customer service rep should be empowered to reimburse up to a certain amount for good reason.) Provide them with a clear decision-making filter based on the company's purpose, to ensure that purpose informs all their actions. An effective rollout will ensure individuals and teams will rally around our LEAD WITH WE purpose, co-creating a high-growth, high-energy, high-impact, culture-forward organization.

➡ ***Give them tools.*** Offer clear, simple, consistent, unimpeachable tools, such as a "purpose placemat"—a one-sheet each employee can post and consult—as they do at Disney and elsewhere. Give everyone an evergreen purpose handbook, too, with guidelines, guardrails, and more details, outlining the company's LEAD WITH WE principles and proactive things they can do/say/create to activate and maintain it. We curate, synchronize, and consistently deliver our purpose messaging internally. Consider offering a kickoff keynote introducing the retooled LEAD WITH WE purpose to all stakeholders. And let everyone hear from *them*, too—not just the CEO. Keep education, learning, and development an ongoing priority through regularly updated, relevant, well-thought-out, well-organized, and well-run resources such as off-site purpose retreats for senior execs and/or departments. Listen, learn, and *LEAD*.

➡ ***Make them comfortable.*** Apple, Amazon, and Facebook might have started this trend with their spaceship-shaped buildings and treehouse conference rooms. But many *LEAD WITH WE* companies have followed, understanding that in hot job markets, and given new generational anticipations, employees need inspiration—and a sense of community at work. The physical environment ought to be employed as just another level of connecting tissue, linking the brand's core values to its team. Like many companies in the San Francisco Bay Area, Clif Bar provides some welcome amenities for its employees, from an in-house gym and a yoga room to daycare. The physical environment of the company feels like a community. What else can we offer our crew? How about streaming services, meal-kit delivery, virtual exercise apps, or other at-home "fringe benefits"? Teleconference services? Standing desks, gaming chairs, blue-light-blocking glasses? Laptops and ergonomic workstations? Online classes? Telemedicine memberships? Home workout equipment? Books, live plants, games?

➡ ***Share stories internally.*** Provide numerous multimedia avenues for employees to share their firsthand, inspirational stories of themselves and their colleagues as they *LEAD WITH WE* at work and beyond. NPF boards call these "Mission Moments." These stories work best when shared in an engaging, lo-fi way. Exceptional drivers braving adverse conditions. Workers who sideline as EMTs or volunteer firefighters. Possibilities abound here. Then, collaborate on a company-wide manifesto narrative and/or video, detailing how the business is transforming, and the purpose and values behind that. Make it compelling and emotional, and suitable for publication internally and beyond. It's doable with a phone camera. We can show Fatima from Accounting, who modernized some reporting tool; Juan from Customer Service, who brought the plight of a particular customer to management; Amber from the plant, who organized other workers to volunteer as mentors in the community. Do this spontaneously. It's a new take on the old management adages to "catch people doing good," and "praise in public—counsel in private."

➡ ***Synchronize our identity.*** Let's lock up our brand logo and other design elements so they all speak to a consistent, easy-to-grasp purpose, reflecting the company culture, too (for extra points!). At We First, our tagline is "Growth through purpose." For Novozymes, "Rethink Tomorrow." Or we can feature the B Corp Certified insignia (or whatever accreditation we've earned) on our products. Danone, a leading global food company with no fewer than twenty-seven B Corp Certified brands, sports its credentials to leverage its impact throughout shopping aisles around the world.

Having said that, we could go the exact opposite way, as Orbia has. Instead of creating a purpose-focused tagline, it's created what it's calling an ImpactMark, which "puts our long-term commitment to people, planet and profit front and center." Radically committed to the power of transparency, Orbia's insignia is constantly in flux. "We want to highlight the organization we want to be and mark our progress towards this aspiration. To quote Max Planck, the renowned physicist: 'When you change the way you look at things, the things you look at change.'" So Orbia's ImpactMark is updated every year, reflecting its performance in key areas. Go ahead, Google it. Initially, it looks odd, right? However, there's so much integrity, humility, and awesome aspiration in that mess. Its ragged three loops indicate its three most recent years. And as the company does better in the future, the lines will progress outward, smoothing into stable shapes. "We're constantly striving, trying to make a perfect circle, knowing we'll never achieve perfection."[95] Isn't that inspiring?

➡ *Create traditions & celebrate efforts.* Share the load—and share the credit. Create rituals, traditions, and micro-incentives, especially those that recognize, reward, and reinforce unity. LEAD WITH WE activities and achievements in crew members' day-to-day roles are an essential ignition source for purpose integration and healthy culture. It's a modern take on the Employee of the Month programs of yesteryear, except these typically celebrate victories beyond traditional metrics. Now we need to celebrate individual stakeholder efforts and company impact, including heroes we recognize among ourselves. When it comes to our employees, we remember to reward not only their financial successes. Imagine a business world where the public leaderboards honor nontraditional metrics beyond sales quotas. For instance, research from GlobeScan shows that 85 percent of Gen Z "are interested in sharing ideas and experiences with companies to help them develop better solutions to social and environmental problems."[96]

Volunteer and community service efforts are a great opportunity to not only build more solid and loyal teams, but also to keep purpose and impact fires burning beyond employee roles at the company. Since 1992, Timberland employees have been able to follow its Path to Service program—and get forty guilt-free paid hours off per year[97] to pursue a community service passion. And regarding the whole supply chain, German multinational athletic equipment company, Puma—the third largest sportswear manufacturer in the world[98]—rewards its suppliers for sustainability practices by offering desirable financing through partners.[99]

By establishing various timeline arcs from monthly to annual (as opposed to that spontaneous "catching out"), we demonstrate that employees are committed to the impact platform in an authentic and ongoing way. Merit-based awards, spot bonuses, or cash/gift-card mini-incentives can work, but they're not necessary. Peer-to-peer nominations/recognition go a long way here, too, maybe even further than money. This process won't be achieved overnight, but rather is a journey that starts with small wins that build momentum inside our company. Think of inspiration for purpose as a balloon inside our business: To stay aloft, it needs to be filled continuously—lest it drop.

Together *WE* Become More Transparent

Performance, profitability, purpose, and impact—how will anyone know what they are, how well we're doing, or where we still have room to improve? We'll tell them—that's how. Transparency reaches into three interconnected realms:

1. *Our internal communications,* where building this active culture requires us to maximize across-the-board awareness of, and support for, any and all of our purpose-grounded initiatives and progress—and be clear, warts and all, about our relative progress.
2. *Our marketing to consumers,* where we shouldn't lie ("take the BS out of business"[100]), and we shouldn't "wash" or "bandwagon" our *LEAD WITH WE* efforts. We'll talk more about storytelling in chapter six,

"Community," because a brand is not only in the marketing business, but also the movement-making business.

3. ***Our reporting & accountability,*** where we publicly report on LEAD WITH WE metrics that matter to the world. We've witnessed that beyond the purely emotional argument for LEAD WITH WE management—*the world is burning and we must douse it right away!*—the rational, fully defensible bottom-line argument is critical motivation to most people, not the least of whom are your board and the public: 22 percent greater market expansion for most LEAD WITH WE companies, according to *HBR* and EY, and 23 percent more product innovations.[101] Brands that LEAD WITH WE have the ability to charge up to a 20 percent price premium for their purpose-based assets, tangible and intangible.[102] COVID-19 seems to have actually accelerated this willingness. "Notwithstanding the high premiums"—lately 39 percent—according to NYU Stern Center for Sustainable Business and IRI research, "sustainability-marketed products grew over seven times faster than conventional products" during the peak of the pandemic, "demonstrating consumers' strong preference for these products and their willingness to pay higher prices."[103] And there's a lot less churn—89 percent of consumers report they're likely to switch brands to one associated with a good cause.[104] Conscious brands, even when they humbly report on their own demerits, build in social capital for a rainy day, or for when the market is tough—even during recessions.[105] As for A+ talent, a LEAD WITH WE reputation magnetizes a business. Younger workers—90 percent of them—will even take a pay cut to work for one.[106] We will discuss the specifics of corporate reporting in chapter seven, "Society."

Together, *WE* Can Build an Enterprise from Aligned Brands

Under Steve Rendle, VF Corp's new chairperson, president, and CEO, and Letitia Webster, its former global vice president, corporate sustainability and head of purpose, the enterprise shifted to become purpose led and performance driven. Now the company could more effectively respond to the coming climate apocalypse, emerging economic trends, and consumer demographics, as well as the evolving marketplace demands we've been discussing. The $14 billion apparel, footwear, and accessories powerhouse has been around since 1899. By 2017, this global leader, comprising twenty-plus brands including The North Face, Vans, Timberland, and JanSport, was operating in more than 170 countries with in excess of seventy thousand employees. Of particular import, the companies within the VF portfolio—active lifestyle brands, all—could no longer take for granted a captive customer base: The world population is growing steadily more sedentary, thanks in large part to "advances" in technology.[107] The company needed to inspire people, to enable them to get more active, and to tie that effort to a deep meaning beyond personal health, important as that is. The process started at home, with VF's own people.

To build this culture, Rendle and the senior leadership team committed to making VF a company that would drive positive change across the globe, and in doing so, bring critical relevance to the firm and its lines of business at a time when consumers are rewarding responsible brands—including the company's toughest competitors. In so doing, VF had to go beyond retooling its own organization (what it makes, how it makes it, and how it communicates its brands' stories both internally, and to the world). It also had to challenge the entire footwear and apparel industry by reimagining its role in the world and leveraging its relationships with loyal customers and consumers to better our shared future. To start, they had to drive "buy-in" and inspire advocacy among employees around their purpose statement:

We power movements of sustainable and active lifestyles for the betterment of people and our planet.

VF's powerful purpose statement summed up the ambitious goals for all the brands in its holdings. The key strategic insight was to create a movement of movements among the enterprise and its portfolio of brands. Critical to this effort was a mindfulness that the process must be inclusive, collaborative, and respectful of the equity already built by each of its leading brands (Timberland, The North Face, Vans, etc.). This way they would achieve the sort of delicate balance any enterprise must strike between a parent company and its portfolio.

This new enterprise-wide commitment has quickly translated into bold and unprecedented *LEAD WITH WE* initiatives, such as VF Corp leading the boycott of leather from Brazil, and The North Face leading the boycott of Facebook to protest hate speech. And such purpose-led efforts helped VF respond compassionately to the COVID-19 crisis and the BLM movement. Reggie Miller, former VP of global inclusion and diversity, shared with me that the week after the killing of George Floyd, a number of VF's brands responded to it, and then the entire company made a decision to "take the organization through this journey from grief to healing." They started with a moment of silence, expecting only three hundred or four hundred of their associates would show up. Twelve hundred people participated. The next day, they conducted a listening session, so associates could just get things off their chest and share what they were feeling. Another twelve hundred people showed up. At the next one, nineteen hundred people joined. "And there were tears . . . there was pain . . . raw emotion . . . people shared stories about . . . their own fears for their children or fears for their husband or their spouse," Miller said, representing "a real cathartic moment for the organization." The following week, VF conducted a session focused on advocacy and "allyship," supplying more details as to how associates could respond and take steps forward. More than two thousand people took part in that. Overall, the company reached more than seven thousand of its associates (or about 10 percent of the total) through all of those scenarios. "And the first thing that people asked afterward, was, when can we do this again?"[108]

We can't use our brand to create such societal movements that build our businesses, move product, and scale impact, if we don't *move our own people first*. Empathize with them. Understand their humanity—not their utility—as the touchstone of all interactions. Discover and amplify, as VF did, what everyone shares in terms of fears, hopes, and goals. And we'll have swept our purpose higher up the Virtuous Spiral toward greater impact. We'll have mastered our internal culture. And now we're ready to rise one level further up, into the communities outside our walls and our supply chains, to loop in our customers and consumers. Always remember—anyone can copy our company's *strategy*—but nobody can copy our culture.

Key Takeaways

➡ Recognize and rise to the new expectations of leadership to build, strengthen, and reward a productive culture of purpose, starting with your own employees, whose expectations and demands have changed with incoming generations.

➡ Examine collaboratively what issues your company can address together, and what it means to *Lead* authentic, collaborative action on what you all care about most.

➡ Build a culture that recognizes, elevates, and celebrates the humanity of its employees and their passion for addressing social and environmental issues.

Action Items

1. *Lead*—Align around integrating purpose into business goals and internal communications so that culture starts at the top and is built bottom up.

2. *With*—Use planning, training, and tools to consistently integrate purpose among internal stakeholders who then co-create its activation and advancement.

3. *We*—Consistently review, and transparently communicate, progress across the breadth of internal activations, including sustainability, ESG, and DI&E efforts.

FIRST

CUSTOMERS, CONSUMERS & PARTNERS

TRANSCENDENCE
FOSTER REGENERATIVE
& ABUNDANT FUTURE
Evolve principles & practices to
scale human & planetary health
Humanity & Planet

SOCIETY
COLLABORATE CROSS-
SECTOR & SHAPE CULTURE
Drive cultural conversations &
coalitions that improve society
Citizens, Collaborators & Sectors

COMMUNITY
MOBILIZE BRAND
COMMUNITIES &
BUILD MOVEMENTS
Engage external stakeholders
around purpose-led movements

COMPANY
ACTIVATE PURPOSE
& ALIGN INTERNAL
STAKEHOLDERS
Integrate & apply purpose
throughout company
Execs, Employees & Supply Chain

LEADERS
DEFINE COMPANY
PURPOSE & GOALS
Conduct honest audit &
determine reason for being
Corporations, Businesses & Startups

ME
ADOPT *LEAD WITH WE*
MINDSET & BEHAVIOR
Recognize new reality, grasp
urgency & shift thinking
Every Individual

6

Community
Inspiring Customers to Scale Growth & Impact

Move from Transactional to Transformative

In 2011, I introduced the "We First Social Contract Between Brands and Consumers" in the first edition of my book, *We First*. It's an adaptable template that businesses can use for engagement with the public, based on the premise that companies and customers should become partners in social change to build a better world. It assumes that companies have a right to innovation, entrepreneurship, and profit-making, while consumers have a right to a healthy society and planet.[1] I thought it was high time the idea of a (literal) social contract was implemented for the business world. Business must coexist in balanced, harmonious, and homeostatic ways with its consumers as key stakeholders in the ecosystem.

This idea serves as an instructive backdrop to the next level up on the Spiral seen at the top of this chapter, representing the first "community" beyond your own business associates—the customers (if you're a B2B company) or consumers (if you're B2C). It's time to examine how—and how well—your company executes against that social contract. Before we could reach this point, we needed to talk about the power of purpose and narrative to empower business to remake our world. Then we outlined how to stress-test that purpose by building a strong internal culture among our employees. Now we're going to use collaborative engagement and storytelling strategies to activate our purpose outside our walls, launching legitimate and meaningful movements with maximum and measurable impact, thus changing our communities for the better. *LEAD WITH WE* is both business for good—and good business. This key stage of building a high-growth and high-impact movement is the co-creation of a brand community. And the keyword there is *co-create* through that social contract. We make a commitment in which the brand and its internal stakeholders participate with others—starting with its customers—on an equal footing.

In our work at We First, we've noticed over the years a tendency toward DIY, especially with smaller brands that are under-resourced and always punching high above their weight. They feel an onus to do it all themselves. On top of every other outsized burden they experience, including competing demands on their time and resources, these organizations believe that if they only 10X their marketing department, the customers will come.

That's the wrong way to think about it, no matter your brand's reach or your company's size. We need to think instead about ways to mobilize all stakeholders associated with our brands. While "company" refers to the organization that makes the products and/or services, "brand" is the image or personality it projects outwardly. We must consider building a community that willingly and voluntarily acts as an extension of our marketing department in the same way that everyone from leadership, employees, and partners promoted and extended the brand on the previous level of the Virtuous Spiral. Now customers, consumers, and the media can contribute to creating and expanding our brand community. And our brand loyalists will become key ambassadors for our products, services, and impact because they fully understand—and, with our help, believe in, subscribe to, and embody—the greater purpose we share with them, and the impact we create together.

We as corporate executives and other leaders in a business of any size are constantly challenged to keep our companies alive—even in the absence of a global challenge such as a tragic pandemic. How will we meet payroll? How can we grow our customer base to keep up with rising labor, supply, and distribution costs? How do we beat out our competitors who are constantly nipping at our heels?

How do we squeeze the most out of the precious dollars of our marketing spend in a highly complex and constantly shifting minefield of polarizing social media?

We're probably also asking—and this might well be the most important question nowadays—how do we make our business heard in the world when there's so much noise out there? How do we attract, excite, retain, and grow our customer and consumer base? Who isn't at least *talking* about their purpose? About all the good work they're doing, the impact they're having. How do we challenge the status quo, rise above the clutter, and leverage our authentic purpose to attract an expansive new audience, forge new partnerships, and inspire new public conversations?

When it comes to this external brand-building level, we're simply not going to unlock the power of the dynamics driving today's marketplace unless we alter our whole way of thinking about the potential solutions to the larger questions challenging how business is done. It's only when we radically shift our mindset to a *LEAD WITH WE* framework that the full range of organic, adaptive, and advanced resolutions naturally click into place. That new mindset is the key, and the only way in, to access them.

When starting a movement with consumers, what's the limiting, conventional mindset to which I'm referring? The purely transactional attitude. *This is our product or service. This is what it does, and this is what it costs.* Even when we include its unique selling proposition ("This is the only one of its kind"), we're still severely stymieing our growth potential in today's world.

We have to set that trajectory much higher, from economically *transactional* to culturally *transformative*. We want to transform our business, yes. But in order to do that, we'll have to transform our thinking, our relationships, and our business practices. We have to win the trust of consumers using the authenticity of our commitments. A worldwide study revealed consumers are five times more likely to "purchase, protect, and champion" real purpose-driven brands.[2] We want to fully leverage our purpose to drive profit in a virtuous cycle of doing good in this first level of the outside "real world," with our customers, consumers, or users. This way, we can do well in the marketplace, then keep serving the community and beyond.

At that point, we can conduct an entirely different type of conversation with customers, consumers, and citizens at large, which will allow us to position our product or service not as a mere "thing," but as *social proof of our brand's purpose.* It's the proof of purpose (POP), our business purpose manifested into a necessary and highly desired product, service, and *story.* With properly activated *LEAD WITH*

WE purpose, especially once it's rolled out effectively *inside* the business first, every aspect of a company becomes a story *WE* can and will tell to the outside world. That's because purpose informs every aspect of a company, integrated and activated consistently using internal communications, and the resulting efforts and culture serve as social proof of authenticity. So, it's not about the specifics of what customers have contracted for (fro-yo, software, accounting, sculpting, gutter cleaning), nor what consumers will receive in concrete form (a snow shovel, a mug, palazzo pants). It's not even about what consumers *think* they specifically want, or for which they initially go shopping. Instead, what we offer them is a compelling *story* they can believe in because it's an authentic, measurable, and transparent activation of our purpose. Something they want to be a part of. And the product or service is but a *re-presentation* (proof) of what we and the consumer mutually believe in, literal evidence of what we stand for.

Move the Needle Meaningfully & Measurably

Moment by moment, brands build movements. A brand movement is an active, dynamic, and evolving joint effort by stakeholders aligned around shared values and common goals to address unmet social or environmental needs. It inspires emotion on the strength of our brand's higher purpose and shared values with stakeholders, motivating them to act and become part of a community experience. That shared experience becomes a source of pride, infusing a brand and its products with "badge value"[3] on the strength of what the company stands for—as long as the brand is authentically committed and transparent in its collaborative efforts. As such, a brand movement is clearly distinguished from an advertising campaign or one-off sales tactic, because those lack a higher-order purpose directed toward some impact goal. A brand movement persists, inspiring long-term engagement through a commitment to something higher than itself. That commitment may find expression in brand storytelling through periodic campaigns, but these must be seen by consumers as *"chapters" in a longer story arc*, or vertebrae in the spine of the long-term brand commitment, which we'll detail later in this chapter.

Let's think of a brand-fueled movement as a long-term outreach strategy that speaks to some societal issue and aims to exert a positive impact on a large number of people and/or ameliorate a substantive problem.

If any of us is still thinking all this "movement-making" stuff might not apply to our line of business (LOB), read on. Every brand ultimately seeks to shift consumer thinking and behavior in some way, most notably by buying their product or service. How far a brand goes beyond those conventional, transactional goals is unique to each business, its leadership team, and the brand community it manages to bring along. LEAD WITH WE businesses aim much higher, to drive growth, *to make money while changing the world*. As for whether all companies are "qualified" to become movements, it's important to remember that a brand movement can range in scope and intention from the local and humble to the global and profound.

On one end of the continuum, our business might not even have a "Big Picture" cultural, environmental, or social problem it cares about enough to address. It could instead be an economic problem, one that can ultimately revolutionize an industry or sector. For example, building on the origins of modern craft beer in the 1960s, and the rising popularity of home brewing in the 1970s, a voluble and influential movement of microbreweries bloomed in the 1990s, seeding more entrants for the next three decades. Their specific purposes were as many and wide ranging as the small businesses founded, but the gross *movement* was rooted in joint ambitions, beginning with both the fierce independence of the DIY and crafting cultures, and the resistance to corporate monopolizing that inevitably precedes the "watering down" of quality, variety, and freedom of choice. By 2018, the number of independent craft breweries in the US had reached about seven thousand.[4] Along the way, this movement of movements came together for collective action: for example, forming a coalition to rally WITH each other to lower excise taxes for breweries, in order to free up monies to reinvest in their businesses and employees, and to better serve a growing body of consumers and customers (the WE) who value the movement.[5]

Farther along the continuum, a business might simply aim to get more people to buy products that are truly good for them. Here, health and wellness is the value proposition. One example is Jessica Alba's and Christopher Gavigan's wide-ranging wellness brand, The Honest Company, which in May 2021 raised $412.8 million for its IPO.[6] It was founded on standards of safety, transparency, and promising peace of mind. In Alba's words, "I created The Honest Company because you shouldn't have to choose between what works and what's good for you."[7] Despite establishing such strong standards for itself, the company faced some media challenges and consumer criticism about its ingredients, and used the opportunity to upgrade its supply chain and products. Likewise, in the case of Kate Farms of Santa Barbara, California, and Waltham, Massachusetts, the company has so well defined its space, purpose, and goals, it stands head and (healthful) shoulders above its competitors. On the strength of its purpose, the company has successfully educated, engaged, and inspired consumers, the media, and investors around the transformative power of plant-based nutrition, specifically among people with chronic conditions who require tube feeding. Its efforts dovetail, of course, with the massive, general plant-based movement and the even larger movement of lifestyle health and medicine. Its commercial success and appeal with funders (it recently raised $23 million,[8] then a further $51 million Series B[9]) has allowed Kate Farms to donate thousands of vegan meal replacements—up to $1 million worth—to hard-hit tribal communities, among other community services. That's the Virtuous Spiral in action.

The next segment of purpose as a driver of community engagement shows how brands take stands on social, cultural, political, and/or environmental issues (migrants' rights, human trafficking, mine worker safety, polar bear habitats, "blood" diamonds, etc.); issues that genuinely reverberate in the hearts and minds—the *values*—of the brand community. Individual businesses and brands can exert major influence, yes. But when a consortium of like-minded individuals and organizations (such as the US Business Roundtable or B Corps) hops on board the movement—even better, when they start driving it—real change can and likely will occur.

For the past few years, a comprehensive suite of Lyft initiatives under the banner of "LyftUp: Transportation for all" has sought to solve a critical challenge: that "millions of people lack access to basic needs because they can't get a ride." The LyftUp program, and indeed, the company itself, grew out of "the core insight and thought that our most authentic and unique value-add to the world is transportation," says Lisa Boyd, director of social impact:

> "We try to stay as focused as possible on transportation." When considering any new proposal, collaboration, or action, its leadership asks, "Is there a core reason why transportation is a problem here? And do we have a unique value-add in this circumstance?" With voting, for example, Lyft and its partners uncovered "disturbing, but interesting" data: "In 2016, it's estimated that 15 million people did not show up to the polls because they did not have a way to get there. That is a clear way that we could make a difference."[10]

Beyond voting, Lyft is trying to ensure everyone has access to affordable, reliable transportation to get wherever they need to go—no matter their age, income, or postal code. They need transportation to jobs, to the grocery store, and to get vaccines and other healthcare. The world is on the move, and Lyft doesn't think it's fair that some should remain stationary.

Because a "movement" simply means that we inspire and mobilize (*Lead*) people inside and outside our company to work alongside (*With*) us on making that kind of difference, to make things better for everybody (*We*). Much more on large-scale collaborations in the next chapter.

Move Consumers (to Vote with Their Wallets)

Any substantive, controversial sociopolitical issue playing out publicly among citizens necessarily includes consumers (just as it does employees), because it affects their everyday lives and livelihoods. Where our brand stands—or doesn't stand—on such issues will drive our sales growth,[11] plain and simple. Our brand movement *moves* humans on an emotional level. Yes, ideally, one of those "movements" occurs when they eventually open their wallets, swipe their cards, and "check out" everything in their shopping carts. But that's not what *Lead With We* businesses aim for, or even focus on. The "sale" that occurs is an emotional transaction: When we move consumers' feelings on some issue that matters to them, we don't manipulate them—we join with them.

"At a time of profound challenges and new possibilities," GlobeScan/BBMG writes in its 2020 *Radically Better Future* report, younger generations especially are seeking the kind of "transformative brand leadership" we're talking about here: "co-created solutions and systemic change to realize a radically better future."[12] Generations X and Z are seeking brands that are part of the solutions they care most about, not contributing to the problems. Smart, progressive brands are getting ahead of this opportunity, articulating clear movements based on their values. These businesses are being clear with consumers about *what* they're saying, thoughtful and deliberate about *how* they're saying it, and certain first *why* they're saying it. These companies are leveraging highly sophisticated and fully integrated new communication campaigns, on digital, social, and traditional channels, aiming for multiple audiences.

But—and this is critical—they're doing so with extraordinarily uncomplicated messaging, distilling that complexity down to simple, consistent, and scalable storytelling that is easily shared. Fishpeople Seafood in Ilwaco, Washington,
aims to revolutionize its industry to become more regenerative through responsible, totally transparent, socioeconomically sustainable, small-scale fishing. "The
industry needs a new story for the twenty-first century," co-founder Kipp Baratoff
told me for a *Forbes* interview. "How do you write that story? You need an alliance
of individuals and stakeholders from the consumer all the way down the supply
chain. We asked ourselves, 'How can we work together with others to create it?'"[13]
Ultimately, Fishpeople decided on a pretty simple but utterly transformative and
profound philosophy: *Do good stuff for fish and do good stuff for people.* That's a small
business (though not small for long), which learned that LEAD WITH WE generates
its own narrative (and financial) momentum—a great way to grow.

At the start of the 2010s, we were still seeing brands talking solely about
themselves and their products and services. Now we see them talking about issues
far larger than themselves; genuine, well-considered stances that make them more
relevant, meaningful, and impactful on the everyday lives and future of a wider
spectrum of consumers and other stakeholders. It's important to note, for example,
that the Fishpeople story is really about something greater and more relatable to
the average consumer. It's about justice and fairness, doing "good stuff for people."
"When there's a collapse [of capitalism]," according to Baratoff, "tragedy of the
commons occurs." And it's about nature, like keeping fish stocks and water sources
healthy and thriving: "do good stuff for fish." After the company discovered its
intended and differentiated impact, and developed its authentic story to match,
its story had to "catch" on with consumers nationwide, the community at large.

In the long run, says Baratoff, "when you have a purpose-driven brand that's
delivering great products and adding wonderful storytelling, you begin to disrupt
categories."[14]

As we launch externally with expanded and aligned storytelling, we're simply
mobilizing a wider WE, working WITH more stakeholders to create meaningful and
measurable impact. Here's the short course:

- ➡ *Focus* on authenticity.
- ➡ *Develop* products that embody the purpose.
- ➡ *Tell* an authentic and meaningful story that resonates with people's lives.
- ➡ *Create* for consumers strong *calls to activism*—not mere "calls to action."

➡ *Recognize* and reward customers, retailers, and consumers for their participation, just as we did internally for employee engagement.

➡ *Strengthen* our impact platform by looping in partners as Fishpeople did—nonprofit foundations (NPFs), government, influencers, other brands—and scale activations and influence (more on this in chapter seven, "Society").

Then scale by the following:

➡ *Encourage* collecting, co-creating, and sharing stories of enduring impact on consumers' lives, perhaps even more specific to our brand when appropriate. *LEAD* strategies, channels, and tactics that support a more inclusive *WITH*, and a wider *WE*.

➡ *Codify* the plan with consumers in a content and channel rollout plan that aligns with all other marketing touchpoints, such as our website(s).

➡ *Build*, amplify, and otherwise constantly support our brand community by consistently incorporating all stakeholders into our messaging.

Move to a "Community-First" Mindset & Methodology

All this begins by deliberately *elevating the humanity of our brand*—focusing first on the people involved, not the product or service itself. Moving from *advertising to advocacy*. Nike isn't in the shoe and apparel business—not strictly. Acme isn't in the grocery business. Chevrolet isn't in the car business. All these companies—and our businesses, too—serve people. People first. *WE* First. This one simple shift in focus accounts for a great percentage of the difference between today's most successful and relevant businesses, and those that have withered on the vine—or will soon.

All of this falls under the rubric of what I call "community architecture" (as opposed to what is traditionally described as advertising). It's purpose and people centered, rather than transactional or self-serving like straight sales or conventional marketing. It's *WE* First. It's about impact on real problems beyond the P&L and communicating that through effective storytelling. We can engineer our company's place in the community while we improve said community along the way. It's ultimately about The Higher *WE*, but typically expressed through a more specific sector of society ("In the particular is contained the universal," James Joyce reminds us).[15] These efforts arise organically out of expressions of an acknowledgment of our interdependence, namely the presumption of Co-ownership, Co-authorship, Co-creation, and Collaboration, "The Four C's" of *LEAD WITH WE*.

1. ***The Presumption of Co-ownership.*** *WITH* presupposes *WE* are all in this together. We all own all the problems—and we share the responsibilities and rewards of our impact on the world. From a business standpoint, Co-ownership is a radical shift from legacy presumptions. It means all stakeholders—including consumers—co-own all brands, and thereby enable their success. So, it's not the major investors, not the board, not the CEO, not even the market alone at the helm. Any and all stakeholders can and should therefore *LEAD* within their realms of influence. As an extension of its social license to operate, everyone owns the brand. *WE* all own it.

2. ***The Opportunity for Co-authorship.*** *WITH* means that all business stakeholders—from CEO to consumers—get to define, align, and create the overall role and specific impact each brand and business can exercise. Basically, this means everyone gets a "Co-writer" credit on the story of the brand's impact. Together *WE* leverage brands as platforms for change and communicate that story in a positive feedback loop.

3. ***The Practice of Co-creation.*** *WITH* entails all stakeholders *together* creating the actual content and driving its impact. Whereas Co-authorship focuses on impact, Co-creation has more to do with the specific storytelling content, the "marketing materials" that aim to amplify and expand that impact, along with growing sales and loyalty. Think about Dove's "Real Beauty" and Always's #LikeAGirl campaigns, which continue to invest in transformative social programs that address and support those brands' core issues of women's identity and girls' self-esteem, by writing and revising *with consumers* the definition of female beauty and girls' empowerment. In both cases, the brands approached their award-winning marketing campaigns as Co-created social experiments that exposed limiting beliefs and cultural stereotypes around women's beauty. So, neither Dove nor Always sought just to hawk soap, shampoo, and feminine hygiene products, but to mitigate a significant challenge in the culture—not only sexism, but self-esteem. Especially as some of Dove's storytelling

featured women discussing their concepts of beauty, about "choosing beautiful," its campaigns are a great example of a truly *humanized* brand. Of course, it's Marketing 101 to make customers feel better about themselves. But these brands did so in communications with people that were not strictly transactional (you'll *be* beautiful—if you use our product), but transformational, authentically—you *are* beautiful, whether you buy our stuff or not. We all know that brands have traditionally bristled at the idea of employees or consumers kneecapping them (through Glassdoor, Yelp, and Amazon reviews, for example). And indeed:

> Digital platforms are powerful amplifiers. As historian Niall Ferguson warns in a recent *McKinsey Quarterly* interview, "If your company has not been on the receiving end of a Twitter storm, then don't worry, it soon will be."[16]

We need to reframe that fear. Those same tools can work in our favor, if our business is working *WITH*—and not without (or worse, *against*)— all stakeholders.

4. ***Extension Through Continual, Effective Collaboration.*** *WITH* requires creative and effectual strategic partnerships and co-branding efforts with others, with influencers, even with competitors, to scale the reach and resonance of our company's efforts. We'll cover this extensively in chapter seven, "Society," but for now think GoPro and Red Bull; BMW and Louis Vuitton; Starbucks and Spotify; Cover Girl and Lucasfilm; Taco Bell and Doritos[17]—even rabid foes, Burger King and McDonald's, partnered in 2019 for a children's charity in Argentina.[18] Why not? When the goal is to enhance impact, the more, the merrier.

Campaigns are neither limited nor siloed, but fully ingrained and interpenetrative. Authentic, carefully considered, and meaningful movements tend to alienate fewer stakeholders (though we can never please all the people all the time), and achieve greater overall engagement—and impact. Success hinges on engaging and mobilizing a full ecosystem of stakeholders. Think of this as ongoing and internal validation, as opposed to campaigns justified only externally by some real problem in the world on which the disingenuous company purpose-washes for its own gain. Again, the *LEAD WITH WE* company is largely driven by enduring impact-outcomes. It's looking for evidence of having made a meaningful and measurable difference in the world, not just hitting sales or market share benchmarks for profit's sake, then telling *that* story. In fact, its purpose and profit motives are seamlessly and consistently interwoven. Its supply chain management; its employees; its culture, products, and innovations; and, yes, its impact initiatives all serve to generate measurable results, which, in turn, build reputation, productivity, and sales. Its goal is to drive business growth by authentically solving social issues relevant to its purpose, and to wield bona fide, lasting benefits on the world—and, in turn, the business—in a win-win-win. Movement-making is not a method of marketing, but a way of being; not a tactical construct, but a foundational perspective.

Move to Values-Based Brand Campaigns

Ideally, our customers share our content—which is much, much easier now because of the near-universal reliance on social media over the past two decades. People talk about our business with their friends. They post free advertising for our brand—or free criticism, often more willingly. In either case, they expand our reach. When those friends walk down the street—proverbial or actual—and encounter ten different brands on which they *could* spend their money, they're going to be more inclined, consciously or not, to support the brand our customers lauded, based on what we've clearly communicated we stand for, and the impact we've demonstrated in some compelling way. And they appreciate and support what we stand for. Because we stand for them, and by them. At the least, they've *seen* us out there, and generally associate our brand with doing good. They spot, say, the Wild Planet brand in a supermarket's "Sustainable Seafood" sign, and snatch a couple of cans. They know the company's committed to not fishing in proposed high-seas sanctuaries, instead using other sustainable fishing techniques, such as pole-and-line and trolling, which greatly reduces "bycatch" of other marine creatures (e.g., dolphins).[19] Fact is, many shoppers won't even look to see if there's a cost difference between Wild Planet and other brands.

Like most conscious consumers, I strongly prefer businesses that don't just talk at me or merely sell to me. The ones that scream "Eat at Joe's!"—with no cultural context, no meaning for me in my life, no good, contemporary reason for me to choose them from among the bevy of competitors. Because all the data shows that few people trust traditional advertising anymore[20]—84 percent of younger consumers no longer do.[21] People are turned off by companies that "sell at" them.[22] As today's leaders, we must now be transparent about what we stand for, because younger consumers—92 percent of millennials, for example—are more likely to buy products from ethical companies. And 82 percent of those consumers believe ethical brands outperform similar companies that lack a commitment to ethical principles.[23]

So, *Lead With We* brands are scaling their impact by shifting their mindsets from *advertising* to *advocacy*, from *marketing* to *movement-making*, and from making *themselves* the celebrity, to *celebrating their community*, the people who are actually using their product or services.

Move Through the Stages of Movement-Making: Part I

Community architecture isn't necessarily any easier than traditional marketing, and will, for the reasons just mentioned, require more of a long-term perspective. Ben & Jerry's didn't just do a brief marketing campaign for the environment or social justice, or against White supremacy; the company has been engaging in those issues for well over a decade as part of a collaborative social movement. As a result, the company's impact on society—like that of Patagonia, among others— has been enormous. "There's no doubt that Ben & Jerry's has influenced capitalism more than capitalism influenced Ben & Jerry's," co-founder Ben Cohen tells the *New York Times Magazine*.[24] Jay Curley, its global head of integrated marketing, calls what his company does "Brand Activism." While this level of engagement increases sales and brand equity, it's not about that.[25] Movements are made in three main stages:

➡ ***Build.*** We define and activate our company-wide purpose, developed in collaboration *With* stakeholders, first internal and now external. We design and create purpose-led products, programs, and partnerships that activate our purpose. We identify current and effective efforts already underway by other stakeholders and organizations, and we partner and collaborate with them. We apply brand resources and offer people clear roles to play toward the desired, shared outcome(s). And we measure and share progress toward outcomes regularly, then prepare to adjust, adapt, and refine. Brands themselves don't really run the movement show. They *LEAD WITH* others to achieve them.

➠ **Launch.** We leverage brand storytelling to inspire action, then recognize and celebrate participation and achievements. We strive to demonstrably improve real people's lives throughout the value chain of our company and the communities it serves—showing our brand story in action. We focus our storytelling on stakeholders (rather than the company or its leadership) as the heroes. We consistently communicate and clarify the connection between our product/services, participation by all stakeholders, and the social issues or pain point(s) we're all addressing together. We create content that captures the process, and we share it in feedback loops with stakeholders to show the results of their participation.

➠ **Scale.** We create, support, and grow community engagement through The Four C's to drive purposeful behavioral/cultural change. We innovate, incubate, and experiment nonstop, including *WITH* partners. We use compelling storytelling around people, participation, and impact to grow community engagement, aspiring to make our business part of the social fabric. We keep driving toward cultural shift(s) and major system change to expand our brand relevancy even as we scale societal impact. We further boost business performance by offering more and diverse choices to address social and environment needs. Ideas—not brands nor products—can *LEAD* movements. By focusing on the big idea and not the product or even the company itself, we humanize our brand, motivate consumers, and scale impact. Tesla started with the big idea, as Elon Musk wrote in his now famous 2006 "masterplan" blog post:

> The overarching purpose of Tesla Motors (and the reason I am funding the company) is to help expedite the move from a mine-and-burn hydrocarbon economy towards a solar electric economy, which I believe to be the primary, but not exclusive, sustainable solution.[26]

The masterplan was deceptively simple:

1. Build sports car
2. Use that money to build an affordable car
3. Use that money to build an even more affordable car

4. While doing above, also provide zero emission electric power generation options

5. Don't tell anyone

All this began with Tesla's clear articulation, and commitment, to Musk's original purpose. Tesla's socially conscious philosophy has proven vital to both its growth as a brand, and the explosive success of the Model 3. It's also why "Step 5" in his plan is only half meant in jest—why would Musk need to tell anyone about what he is doing when his army of brand loyalists will do it for him? The movement self-evangelized.[27]

Move Through the Stages of Movement-Making: Part II

There are three key features to remember about movement-making, as opposed to traditional marketing. The first feature is that we must not think of a "movement" as a passive noun, but rather as an active verb. It's a living progression of people taking action around their shared values. A dynamic and evolving joint effort by all stakeholders.

The second feature is that movements can survive only when propelled by continuous stakeholder engagement. So, we constantly leverage and reapply the Four C activations to keep the momentum going, with a broad *WITH* and a wide *WE*. This is best accomplished through people who can *LEAD* through a variety of circumstances complicated by changing industries, societal trends, consumer pains, sector issues and opportunities, competitors' efforts and attacks, and effective partnerships. Keep in mind, there will be obstacles. We need that friction to get traction around existing thinking and behavior. We need people who can *LEAD* using an über-entrepreneurial approach to business (i.e., the ability and willingness to recognize and seize opportunities beyond the scope of the traditional business lens).

The third feature is that movement-making as a function of our business purpose must be, like purpose itself, embedded, then radiated through the entire community, horizontally and vertically, with every stakeholder deputized to *LEAD*.

In terms of process, we can further break down movement-making into six key components that allow movements to thrive. The same dynamics apply to startups, individual brands, and complex, global enterprises, which build a movement of movements. The process also applies to any and all of a company's purpose-based goals:

1. **The Stand.** This is the *what*. The social, political, environmental, or cultural change our movement is "for" or "against." Sadly, there is no shortage of need in multiple areas, but a bulk of recently effective LEAD WITH WE businesses have chosen from among some obvious realms: climate and the environment (e.g., promoting sustainable agriculture, enabling carbon sequestration, protecting biodiversity and wildlife); diversity, inclusion, and equity (DI&E; e.g., addressing racial inequality and social injustice, supporting people across all expressions of love and life); the workplace and wages (e.g., providing a fair and living wage, supporting and elevating the trades, and advocating for fair labor practices); culture and the arts (e.g., expanding engagement and access to music, museums, and arts education); and/or the law and justice (e.g., championing fairness and equality in housing, policing, and jurisprudence; reducing gun violence).

How about addressing cultural stereotypes, as Always does through its #LikeAGirl empowerment storytelling? Challenging industry norms, like Beyond Meat, Impossible Foods, Meati Foods, Alpha Foods, and Eat The Change, all of which have committed to enabling a sustainable food system through their plant-based products, and all of which have seen interest, adoption, and sales soar as the movements they have co-created have grown? (Though greater collaboration is still needed, given that plant-based meat represents only 1 percent of the overall US meat market.)[28] And the industry-wide movement around responsible packaging launched by the "clothing for positive change" maker, prAna? Or the small UK brand, Project Blu, disrupting the pet product industry by sharing with consumers the fact that manufacturing and logistics of traditional pet beds exerts an outsized impact on the environment? Did you know the industry is a major contributor to global warming? The answer to this problem: sustainable dog beds![29] The possibilities are, of course, limitless. Not incidentally, the number one issue across all political, economic, gender, and generational demographics, according to the latest data from a JUST 100 survey: "Americans want companies to put workers at the heart of just business practices."[30]

2. ***The Ask.*** More *what*. What we want people to do. So, this focuses on the specific beliefs and behaviors our movement is advocating to alter. What does participation in this movement entail? (Hint: It's not becoming our customer.) Do I need to get my head around spending more money on a responsible brand or product? Spending less time at something wasteful? Giving something up? Adopting something? Thinking differently about some aspect of my daily life? Educating myself?

    Recreational Equipment, Inc. (REI), the Kent, Washington–based upscale outdoor-gear company, defied industry norms in 2015 when it announced it would lock the doors at 143 of its stores on Black Friday, traditionally the busiest retail shopping day of the year, so that its employees "can do what they love most—be outside." It paid all twelve thousand of them. As a result, REI started a movement across the whole retail landscape. Called #OptOutside, it took on a life of its own. In its first year, more than 1.4 million people and 170 organizations[31] chose to #OptOutside. By its fifth year, more than fifteen million people and seven hundred organizations[32] now join REI by closing their stores, allowing their staff (and now shoppers) to spend time with their families or outside, maybe cleaning up litter or helping restore parks. Participants post pictures online of themselves avoiding the typical Black Friday mayhem. The attitudes and actions of our companies can and do change society.

3. ***The Stakes.*** This is the *why*. It focuses on the implications of our movement's success or failure. What's the worst that can happen? The best? It's where we share stats. Show outcomes. Demonstrate impact. Narrate scenarios. Premium women's fashion shoe brand Tieks of Los Angeles provides a remarkable example of how a brand can mobilize its community to do good during a crisis. After learning of the shortage of face masks in the early days of the COVID-19 pandemic, the company's leaders told that story in a compelling way and launched a challenge to their brand community to #SewTOGETHER, a campaign that went viral and helped to generate four hundred thousand face masks for frontline medical workers. In return, Tieks rewarded the contributors with gift cards.[33]

4. ***The Goal.*** This is more *why*, and is about the potential and real impact of our movement's target outcomes. What does the world look like when our purpose drives consistent, collaborative action, when we *LEAD* a wave

of individuals to take action toward solving some problem? Tieks, along with its partner, the Gavrieli Foundation, aimed to support disadvantaged women in business by becoming the largest single lender on microloan site Kiva, contributing more than $10 million to thousands of women entrepreneurs in seventy countries.[34]

5. ***The Path.*** This is the *how*. The strategy and structure of collective actions that mobilize our movement. Members of our community must understand the replicable instructions and motivations for clear, desirable actions beyond clicking "Buy." The French food service and facilities management company Sodexo serves more than nine thousand sites in North America. When it decided to flex its muscle for good several years ago, it was to influence behaviors among its millions of customers: *to waste less*. It adopted the "Save the Food" mantle from the national public service campaign developed by the Ad Council and the Natural Resources Defense Council. Then, simply, methodically, logically, and emotionally, Sodexo engaged its customers to reduce, reuse, and recycle instead of contributing to the "nearly $165 billion in wasted food that Americans throw out annually."[35] UpChoose, a recent San Francisco startup, focuses on unnecessary and costly waste, too, in the baby clothes market. The "sustainable consumption" company "sells new parents a full set of organic cotton clothes." As their kids grow, the parents return the clothes and get a discount for the next size up; "the old clothes are resold on the same platform to other parents."[36] Simple and meaningful, right? So, what's the specific activation we're asking for? Donating? Volunteering? Uploading? Sharing? Joining? Sewing?

6. ***The Players.*** This is the *who* in our community. The proponents, detractors, and audience of our movement and for our brand. Who? *We*. Beginning locally, with our own consumers, then expanding up and outward on the Spiral. In this way, the players—not the business world—control the table today, a point that activist business leaders Jeremy Heimans and Henry Timms stress in their seminal 2018 book, *New Power: How Power Works in Our Hyperconnected World—and How to Make It Work for You*. People today carry in their pockets "the means of participation" in a "vast, decentralized army," and our future will hinge on a "battle over mobilization," wherein "everyday people, leaders, and organizations who flourish will be those best able to channel the participatory energy." "New power"

models, at their best, reinforce the human instinct to cooperate (rather than compete) by rewarding those who share their own assets or ideas, spread those of others, or build on existing ideas to make them better. This new power is more like an open, active, fluctuating "current" than a closed, static, elite-owned, "currency," the authors argue.[37] Businesses looking to LEAD WITH WE must learn to map with the dynamics of citizen-led, "New Power" movements—especially when facilitating "surges" of activity in that power, and thus impact.

I'm thinking here about Ben & Jerry's leaders again, who always make the point that brands should first consider collaborating WITH existing movements rather than launching and leading their own from scratch. Brands can look to their purpose to identify the most relevant and pressing issues, then scan society to find the most like-minded, equipped collaborators, and/or partners within an existing movement—but in need of help—then focus and apply their own expertise and other resources where they (the companies) are best suited to slot in. This is a key point and a pure expression of LEAD WITH WE.

Move the Movement Lever with Clear Business Goals

If purpose is the plan, then goals are the bricks in our great community architecture project. Like the unique expressions of a company's purpose, LEAD WITH WE goals must boldly back out of the future, rather than look back to the past or incrementally improve on the present. We can't move people unless we know where we want them to go. So, our goals and those movement directions derive from the stark realities of both the worst- and best-case scenarios, given our collective action/inaction. On the strength of specific goals are movements made. Goals should be simple, meaningful, measurable, inspiring, and sharable.

➡ ***Impossible Foods (IF).*** The average US citizen devours three hamburgers a week.[38] That's fifty billion burgers a year, which harms the environment in exponential ways. IF set a grand goal of getting rid of cattle as a food source, a movement designed to turn back the clock on the climate emergency and stop the global collapse of biodiversity.[39] IF's name might be a nod to the audacity of its goal: to innovate tasty plant-based replacements for meat products and massively displace market demand for same. "By replacing animal products, consumers have enormous power to spare land for biodiversity and carbon capture, halt greenhouse gas emissions at the source, and alleviate demand on fresh water needed for healthy ecosystems."[40] Yet its goals, and those of its chief competitor, Beyond Meat, turned out to be entirely *possible* to achieve. As Kellogg's learned in its recent meat-analog launch, market demand and brand expansion for plant-based burgers and other foods have increased dramatically, as we discussed in chapter four, "Purpose"—even more so as the 2020 pandemic disrupted the traditional meat industry.[41] IF is already considered a top environmental startup. But it also feeds hungry kids, advances civil rights through education, and has a major goal:

> to make [IF] the world's best place to work, too. Our Employee Resource Groups (ERGs)—employee-led, executive-sponsored advocacy teams—help us do that by working with People, Communications, Finance, Supply Chain and other functions to consistently improve our workplace. They accomplished a lot in 2020: from executing a self-audit of the Human Rights Campaign Corporate Equality Index, to founding a women-led mentorship program, to making our recruiting process more inclusive.[42]

➡ *Avery Dennison.* This global leader in materials science and manufacturing in 2019 set ambitious sustainability goals for 2025, including responsible sourcing, corporate transparency, and internal ethics, that are not only transformative for the company itself, but—because it's one of the largest packaging companies in the US—enormously impactful across multiple industries as well. As a company uniquely positioned to transform industries and communities, it's leading a movement of materials science innovation dubbed *Making a material difference.*[43] For its ongoing commitment to operate a more LEAD WITH WE company both socially and environmentally, Avery reported in 2020 on substantial progress toward those 2025 sustainability goals, such as having reached 94 percent landfill freedom, 92 percent certified paper, and 34 percent women in management positions.[44] It also publicized three new goals for 2030, one of which includes innovations that advance the circular economy. The metrics on that goal include 100 percent of its core product categories meeting the third-party ClearIntent Standard, and 100 percent of its standard label products containing recycled or renewable content—and all its regions enabling circularity of plastics.[45]

➠ **Warby Parker (WP).** The rising, eleven-year-old eyewear company was founded by Wharton Business School students who discovered that almost a billion people worldwide lack access to glasses that help them learn and work. So, the company launched a movement with partners such as the NPF VisionSpring to ensure people maintained *the right to sight*. As their website says, "There's nothing complicated about it. Good eyewear, good outcome."[46] WP's products are high quality yet much more affordable than average eyewear—another key problem the founders were trying to solve. For every pair of glasses sold, the company distributes a pair to someone in need. Despite having donated more than eight million pairs of glasses,[47] the company was recently valued at $3 billion by *Fortune*, proof of concept for LEAD WITH WE.

"We view our investment in our social mission as having an incredibly high ROI over a long time frame," Dave Gilboa, co-CEO and co-founder, shared with me for *Forbes*. Its movement is built on the Breadth of its WITH. WP immerses its employees in its impact programs. Team members who have worked for the brand for at least three years are offered an all-expense-paid trip "out in the field" to places such as Guatemala or El Salvador, where they work with NPF partners to facilitate eye exams and deliver glasses. It's a major reason the brand enjoys an esteemed place in the public consciousness. "When customers connect to our values they want to talk about us. They develop loyalty to the brand," Gilboa says. "It would be penny wise and pound foolish to cut these efforts."[48]

➠ **Farmacy Beauty.** On the smaller business front, think of the indie brand Farmacy. The New York–based personal care company began with the goal "to share the potent power of natural ingredients and support small farmers" while ensuring farm soil's facility to recycle nutrients. Its vertically integrated, clean-beauty network now includes the gradual goals-based acquisitions it achieved along the way: a second-generation, family-owned Indian drumstick tree farm in Southern California, and an acerola cherry farm in Northeast Brazil. After some smart growth, in September 2020 it unveiled the fruition of its former goal, its "very own certified organic, non-GMO, regenerative" operation in partnership with regenerative farming pioneers in the Hudson Hemp farm network. The nascent movement is in its name and its slogan, *farm-to-face* skincare. The company maintains a list of nine hundred "no-no's" that includes practices and ingredients the company avoids. For example, David Chung, founder and CEO, tells me, "Our 2021 agenda is to assess each product['s packaging] and ask, 'is it 80 percent or 90 percent carbon-free?' If not, how can we change the packaging?"[49]

Move People Through Effective Storytelling

Motivating humans, especially by business, requires intentional and considerate strategies and tactics. We could study for advanced degree after advanced degree (psychology, sociology, marketing, etc.) and still fall short of understanding the awesome power of story. But Marshall Ganz at Harvard University's Kennedy School of Government is insightful at explaining the reality of what's required now to effectively influence consumer behavior—and the critical role of brand (public) storytelling to trigger the necessary levers in the right order, which ultimately can and will change the world.

Yes, as a business, we can and to some extent must stand for ourselves. But that's never enough—in fact, it's ultimately counterproductive. We must instead stand—then act—*WITH* our brothers and sisters, together as a community. The *WE* will always be more powerful than the mere "Me." But we don't necessarily come together spontaneously—we need a compelling invitation, a good reason, a sense that we belong because of shared values with those people standing over there. *WE* come, in short, because of some public story that convinces us, that figuratively and literally *moves* us.

That takes a certain kind of leadership. Crafting a compelling public narrative the way successful brands do, Ganz believes, represents the confluence of three core elements of what it means to *LEAD* today:

1. **Story.** Hearing why we must act, and why now. This comes from the leader's heart, aiming for the public's heart.
2. **Strategy.** Seeing how specifically we can act now, which is all about the leader's head connecting with the heads of the people tuned in.
3. **Stages.** "Stepping Through the Stages" is my term for knowing *what* we then do—because we know we must—to act on our convictions. This is the practical "hands" part of the equation.[50]

Luckily, story is not only great for codifying the past; it does an equally powerful job in defining the future. Here are two of many inspiring examples. David Heath, co-founder and CEO of Bombas, used to give socks to the homeless people he encountered on the way to work in New York City. "I saw one guy take his shoes off and . . . he had . . . a bandana around one foot and he'd literally wrapped the other foot into a plastic bag to stop the boot from rubbing against it," Heath says. He wondered: "How can I solve this problem at scale?"[51] On the other side of the world in Australia, a father, Nik Robinson, and his sons, Harry (eight) and Archie (six) were having dinner one night, and the kids, who were learning in class about the environment, shared real distress about how much plastic waste was piling up in the world: "Is there anything we can do about this?" Their question led to the launch of their company, Good Citizens, a brand of sunglasses whose frames are made from 100 percent recycled plastic bottles, mostly formerly seaborne ("one bottle makes one pair"[52])—another heart-led, super-compelling story.

Move Consumers to Activate More Regenerative Lifestyles

We can parlay all our experience in purpose and movement planning, activation, and impact into a rich source of narrative elements. This will allow us to focus our new "marketing" on real people's lives, and to examine our company's role in solving real problems those people are most anxious about. In so doing, we bolster our brand reputation by expressing our values and imbuing our products with meaningful value as a result. We can start with moving people toward regenerative practices.

Forrester, a research consultancy focused on "customer-obsessed" approaches to doing business, reinforces other findings that consumers desire real partnerships with favored brands. Consumers see themselves as activists, and play a huge role in convincing other consumers where to shop.[53] This activism can take various forms: as affiliates, influencers, instigators, advocates, ambassadors, or amplifiers. Our customers are not a means to financial ends; they are co-creators. But they will often need business led by co-building coalitions of the willing, which we'll discuss in detail in chapter seven, "Society." When brands inspire consumers to participate in movements, but also remind them to embrace greater agency in their own lives as coequal stakeholders in the future, there's a lot we can do. According to InSites Consulting:

Trends like "flipside shopping" (i.e., obsessively checking the back of packaging for provenance and artificial additives) will continue to grow. Apps such as Yuka and Think Dirty, allowing users to separate the wheat from the chaff by just scanning bar codes on products, already have millions of users.

In a global InSites study conducted before COVID-19, 80 percent of consumers already reported sustainability as "important" to "very important."[54] Many people had already received, read, and implemented the memo about the environmental emergency, and had begun to take action in their lifestyles and consumer behavior. They eat differently, deal differently with waste, and travel smarter. They also buy more durable, circular, nature-friendly, equitably and fairly made, sustainable products, often by looking for certifications or accreditations on labels. And it's about much more than the climate catastrophe: As we saw in earlier chapters, they also base who they work for on their perceptions of wider purpose. They look where their pension fund is invested, and choose where they invest in the markets, which we'll look at in chapter seven, "Society." In fact, that old standby—voting—ranks *fourth* as a way young people believe they drive change, according to other research.[55] And they stick by the brands that have earned their trust and loyalty, which, you'll recall, are harder commodities to come by than ever.

Move Beyond Common Mistakes in Leading a Movement

We've covered several missteps in thinking and execution already, demonstrating that neither purpose nor movement-making works flawlessly every time. With an agile and creative attitude in mind, here are the things to avoid when rolling our movement-making pursuits out to the public:

➡ ***Self-Directed Messaging.*** The company fails to embrace the most critical marketing consideration: that an authentic commitment to meaningful impact cannot be communicated in a self-centered way. The brand must celebrate all stakeholders, from suppliers to employees to customers and partners. It's about the W*ITH* and the W*E*. If we can't answer quickly, "*Who's this* W*ITH*?" we're doing it wrong. Solution: Employ any and all of The Four C's.

➡ *Stasis & Inertia in Messaging.* Earlier I mentioned that repetition leads to automation. That's true of logos, taglines, and brand devices that stick in one's mind. But brands can fail to change up the way they're sharing their purpose; when they do, they risk their various stakeholder audiences shutting down, tuning out, or looking elsewhere. The good news is that because purpose is infused throughout our entire organization, all aspects of our company become opportunities for meaningful storytelling. When a new initiative, impact data point, or other newsworthy effort that fits into the larger purpose happens, we can tell that story. On responsible supply chain management, take Swedish packaging company Tetra Pak, which now requires third-party verification that its paperboard suppliers "do not use wood from any form of deforestation that breaks the natural forestry cycle."[56] On internal company culture, how about Under Armour's "three statements" method that makes sure people's voices are heard? "Everyone must have a voice, and everyone deserves clarity. Those things increase performance, satisfaction, and speed."[57] Women-owned Blume Honey Water's product innovation story starts thousands of years ago in the distant lands of ancient Greece and the homes of India's Ayurvedic practitioners and continues through ultramodern biological preservation and sustainable beekeeping.[58] When we're feeling uninspired and noncreative, we need only employ The Four C's: Commit to the WE.

➡ *Failing to Connect Purpose & Product(s).* The company forgets, is too humble to, or otherwise fails to tie its product, service, or program to its purpose and the authentic impact it's generating. Provocative and political as its movements are sometimes perceived, Ben & Jerry's does not divest its ice cream from its social purpose; the two are intertwined like peanut butter and chocolate. It puts many of its products—including, famously, their names ("Save Our Swirled," "Empower Mint," and even a Colin Kaepernick–inspired flavor called "Change The Whirled")—to work for its purpose. It also uses its "Flavors on a Mission" to spotlight and amplify key issues its community cares about. In 2018, French fashion legend Lacoste altered its iconic crocodile logo—the third-most recognized in the world—for the first time in its ninety-year history, to depict ten endangered species on its polos. For every shirt someone bought, the company donated to a wildlife conservation partner. What a cool way to engage consumers, prove social value (POP) through a product, and encourage collecting (limited editions, of course, which quickly sold out, several times over—return on purpose).[59] Consumers could show by wearing Lacoste shirts how and why they supported a worthy cause. The shirt itself was a story-starter.

➡ *Fractured, Ad Hoc Actions & Marketing.* Disparate, siloed, or competing efforts by individuals and departments or LOBs acting autonomously are not optimizing the story, and are likely countering success and growth. Mixed messaging across myriad channels? All these conflicts obfuscate authentic and aligned expressions of purpose. There's no *Lead*, no *With*, and no *We* there—not even internally with our own associates—until we connect the dots. Solution: *Lead*. Note: There are always different audiences for our storytelling, at different stages in their journey as discussed, and each requires tailored storytelling arising from a unifying purpose. Consider:

- *Government agencies & NGOs* adept at calling out false claims and hollow promises—literally their job.
- *Corporate watchdogs* such as consumer and media activists—again, that's what they're there for.
- *Employees* who seek fulfillment in their work but will as readily expose wrongdoing (think of the challenges from employees of Amazon, Google, and Apple)—this is their life.
- *Investors*, individual and institutional, who determine a company's literal value and long-term prospects—with so much on the line, it's serious business.
- *Customers* or retailers who will expose or disavow suppliers who put their own reputation at risk—lots at stake.
- *Consumers* who are increasingly conscious of how and where products are made, and vote with their dollars—let's not mess with their hard-won money.
- *Competitors* ever ready to expose rivals' shortcomings.

➡ *Ignoring Generational Differences.* It has never been more important for us to understand and embrace our various audiences. As the media landscape has fractured, so, too, has how we reach the varied cohorts on which our business growth depends. In 2020, millennials account for one-third of the adult population, and Generation Z owns 40 percent of the consumer power.[60] If there's one force with sufficient power and momentum to turn the business tide toward LEAD WITH WE, it's this "economic youth boom,"[61] which is why I keep mentioning them in various contexts. GlobeScan's research is really clear, pointing to young people reporting actual and desired personal lifestyle changes undertaken during 2020 far exceeding their older counterparts'.[62] Companies must respond to these younger people, who have the kinds of disposable incomes brands require, because, GlobeScan's Chris Coulter tells me, that cohort will expect the businesses it engages with to be just as willing to change, grow, and learn as they are.[63]

➡ ***Failing to Include Impact Outcomes in the Story.*** As I introduced briefly in chapter three, "Paradigm," there exists a story supply chain, in the same way we need materials supply chains to bring final products to market. I'm talking about taking the final step in communicating a brand's story to the public, that "last mile" where a brand reports back on the measurable impact that was created, so consumers (along with all stakeholders and, notably, employees) know that their participation led to something—and will be willing to participate again. What effect has our purpose and movement had on real people in the real world? We start with our employees and include recipients of any assistance our business has offered. And we never leave out the at-large members of our brand community. We must close the story loop. If we're promising to help the inadequately housed by donating a dollar with each sale of honey, and we've already given away hundreds of thousands, and that money was used to build a new shelter, then we should share the story of that positive impact on people's lives! Whereas we might have begun with a story about the problem we were trying to fix and how much everyone cares, this story is about the fix itself—what in the NPF world they call the Impact Report. It has an outbound, positive focus—and is not about *us*, but the brand community's efforts and impact. It's about The Four C's. About working WITH each other, and what WE together built. In this way, momentum persists, participation in movements grows, and impact efforts continue to amplify and compound.

➡ ***Pedantic & Didactic Lecturing.*** Someone high up at the firm has chosen to "lead" by edict, proclamation, or diktat—or the company plays that foolhardy game with the public. To communicate purpose properly, launching long-term, effective movements, we have to LEAD in three different ways at the same time, each requiring some finesse: ***Top-Down***, in the same way we consider our organizational structure, P&L, and supply chain management; ***Bottom-Up***, where the driving purpose of the organization bubbles up from the base of the organizational pyramid, as the foundation from which everyone does their work and contributes their own ideas, values, stories, and leadership; and ***Over Time.*** (Note these are just as important when communicating internally to build the company culture.)

Over Time is worth further analysis. We must regularly honor and celebrate members of our community. Through our storytelling, we have to show our purpose coming to life via the movement ("motion," "emotion," and "motivation" all share a root)—we must highlight the humanity to really excite, grow, and sustain a community of like-minded members. We have already adopted rituals to regularly mark achievements and participation of our employees, partners, and supply chain. Now we redouble those efforts for the external players in our brand community. The US Bureau of Labor Statistics reports that ninety million Americans self-identify as "conscious consumers." There is a $3.2 trillion conscious consumer market in the US.[64] Best to loop them into our WITH and include them among the WE that we serve. Invite them frequently, habitually, not only to partake, but to take part. This will keep the lifeblood flowing in a movement and help mitigate inklings of elitism related to the part of our necessary Top-Down endeavors. And speaking of those, this Over Time necessity feeds back into the Top-Down imperatives for us as we LEAD. Key higher-ups likely will need to ensure over time the consistency and potency of the purpose, even as the movement evolves with the masses, with all stakeholders playing various and interconnected roles.

The Top-Down, Bottom-Up, and Over Time prescriptions apply not only to the leadership style in our organization, but also to our storytelling for the sake of growing a movement. We don't want to be didactic, but rather allow people to literally and figuratively see themselves as the heroes in the brand's storytelling, the way Nike does in most of its wildly successful ads. Let's not re-create the P&G brand Gillette's misdirected attempt—"Razor burned,"[65] claims one critic—at combatting toxic masculinity by dictating what consumers should believe because "We Believe" here at Gillette.[66] It was a hard-won lesson that nevertheless bore fruit, as evidenced by the company's powerful, provocative, and on-point global campaign that followed. Titled "The Choice," it presented consumers with the resources, insights, and partners to work to end racism. Again, a collective effort whose success turns on *WE*.

Two main approaches avoid purpose-washing and other key mistakes so you can deliver and grow a credible *LEAD WITH WE* brand movement:

1. ***Evince Authenticity.*** We don't automatically expect trust from a skeptical marketplace. We have to earn it—and we can lose it in a heartbeat. Nearly half of Americans find brands *less* honest today than they were twenty years ago,[67] even as transparency in labeling, social media attention, and stricter regulations have swelled. But more than 80 percent believe that right-minded, *LEAD WITH WE* brands *can* transform the world for the better.[68] For evidence of such a truly authentic and effective crusade, look at Always's 2015 Emmy Award–winning #LikeAGirl campaign,[69] which was strategically first aired during Super Bowl XLIX. In the spot, the P&G women's hygiene brand featured real conversations with women and girls about what they thought it meant to act (run, fight, throw, etc.) "like a girl," underscoring a transformational shift in generational perceptions about women's role in society. It came from the bottom up *WITH* real people. The Always brand demonstrated its products added real and meaningful value to a real and meaningful movement larger than itself. It focused on pertinent societal issues. Last, it still managed to fulfill advertising rules numbers one and two: It sparked an authentic emotional connection with consumers, and it paid for itself many times over with reputational goodwill and an expanded share of the market. In turn, the company started to give back even

more. In 2018, for example, Always launched its End Period Poverty campaign, and donated one menstrual pad to a person in need for every package sold.[70]

2. ***Create Simple Ways for People to Be Part of the Solution.*** Endless coverage of urgent, compounding global crises—disease, hunger, inequality, environmental degradation—tends to overwhelm people. *What can I do? Can I do* anything—or is it too late? Our brand can and should extend to consumers a clear, inspiring, effective route to making a difference on an issue they care about. Every month when I buy my pads, some girl somewhere gets a free pad. Every time I buy this *reposado paloma*, a new tree takes root nearby. Everywhere Greenbar liquor is sold, menus and servers tell customers that whenever you drink a Greenbar product, you become carbon negative for a day. "I know that makes them feel like they've done something good. It makes them feel like they're part of the solution," says that company's leadership."[71]

For another example of a company inviting consumers to join them in more actively building a better world, let's look at State Farm. In a campaign begun in 2017, the insurance company told a story about a man who felt inundated by the state of the world and helpless to effect any meaningful difference. At the end of the spot, State Farm ("Like a good neighbor, State Farm is there") suggested a viable solution for the guy to take action, by participating in its community outreach program, Neighborhood of Good, which matches volunteers to local causes they care about. People can donate their blood, time, money, or other resources, help solve a problem, and soften their existential frustration or ennui by proactive involvement.[72] The program *turns caring into doing.*[73] State Farm, like other companies offering similar avenues, has been rewarded with goodwill, good press (earned media), word-of-mouth advertising, and ultimately, more business. These companies are succeeding at LEAD WITH WE by not just *talking* about problems, but becoming problem solvers, by proving to a skeptical public how their brand serves a higher purpose—and inviting them to join WITH their purpose-driven ranks. It's notable that in 2021, State Farm began (along with Intuit's TurboTax, Colgate, AT&T, Valvoline, and other brands) widely running TV ads on English language stations *in Spanish*. This takes WE to a whole new level.

Move Your Portfolio Brands into a Movement of Movements

At huge enterprise companies like Procter & Gamble (P&G), the parent company has to work WITH many offspring and acquired brands. As any wise and experienced parent knows, this means they have to articulate a clear and definite enterprise purpose, along with right-minded values that they live daily, then lay out a proposed path for their brand progeny. But, importantly, they can't be prescriptive with their portfolio brands. Instead, the parent company must serve as a foundation on which the portfolio brands stand. Unconstrained. Empowered. Aided by respectful guidance and necessary resources, yet independent (each in their own way) nonetheless. At P&G—"Force for Good, Force for Growth"—the rollout of unique purpose happened separately at each of its brands. The impetus for movements happened locally, too, with individual brands. But all these efforts aligned around the foundational enterprise purpose. For example, Always's "Like a Girl." Secret, which focused on equal pay for women. Head & Shoulders, which is all about its innovative commitment to reducing waste and responsible packaging. All nuanced expressions of the unifying enterprise purpose.

At Unilever, there have been some extra challenges creating an enterprise movement of movements, wherein unlikely bedfellows had to start working WITH each other. The planet's third-largest consumer goods company, this corporate giant acquired Ben & Jerry's in 2000, distressing many in the business-for-social-good movement. Practically, it meant that a fierce and fiery activist brand had to wrangle its singular mission, insights, and past promises into a deal with a parent company that calibrated purpose and profit differently, at least according to the (many) critics of the deal. In the end, there were compromises on both sides.

Later, in 2016, Unilever bought known conscious company leader Seventh Generation, the largest eco-friendly cleaning-supplies seller in the US. By this time the enterprise, under the new leadership of Paul Polman, was already well underway in its LEAD WITH WE evolution, itself a global leader of sustainable and transformative business ("I see us as a co-creator, with the consumer, of mainstream sustainable living," says Polman).[74] Once again, two different but purposeful cultures had to integrate their missions, mindsets, and methodologies. As Seventh Generation CEO Joey Bergstein says, "Unilever is not only committed to boosting our shared social and environmental mission, they're giving us new power to achieve it." To further integrate purposeful leadership, Seventh Generation created a Social Mission Board. This senior leadership committee ensures the brand implements, measures, and meets its purpose goals[75]—and that its parent understands and respects its distinct role. After all, its sustainability leadership is what attracted Unilever to it in the first place. Just at Unilever, its enterprise Sustainable Living Plan translates as "Dirt is Good" for its Persil brand; handwashing for LifeBuoy; "Real Beauty" for Dove; decreasing poverty at Vaseline; "Food Forward" at Knorr; and unity through DI&E at Lynx (Axe in the US). And, of course, over at its "wholly owned subsidiary," Ben & Jerry's, they're still working hard on the climate emergency, social justice, and more.

There was a similar dynamic at VF Corporation and its many footwear and apparel brands. For this movement-making process, the community architecture component, it was again critical to differentiate the individual entities. Each brand—Timberland, Vans, The North Face, and more among them—brings their unique purpose to life as an expression of the enterprise purpose. All of these efforts were unified through some singular, signature identifications in various visuals and styles. This kind of enterprise consistency ensures that the independent efforts of the brands all ladder up to the collective effort of the VF Corporation parent.

And just as occurred with the internal rollout that built the company cultures, VF Corporation provided further guidance to the brand portfolio by identifying the key territories in which its purpose would come to life through its community architecture. Those three areas—Outside Matters (The North Face, Eagle Creek, Timberland, et al.); Free to Be (Vans, JanSport, et al.), and Worthy Work (Williamson-Dickie, Wrangler, et al.)—were all consciously designed to accommodate its wide portfolio of brands, as well as the enormous variety of impact efforts that VF brands support across the globe. At any one time, a brand could lead movements focused on one of these three territories, or all of them; or their focus could change over time. The only critical requirement was that all brands, all their movements, and all their impact efforts fall within these three territories that, again, fit comfortably with VF's touchstone enterprise purpose.

The strategic rigor exhibited by P&G, Unilever, and VF, especially during the pandemic, epitomize how a LEAD WITH WE trajectory can not only organize and align disparate brands across wide portfolios, but also catalyze a multidimensional, synergized movement of movements, whose impact is thereby greatly compounded.

Move *WITH* the Times

In a single month, June 2020, major brands, franchises, and industries found themselves forced to respond to massive cultural shifts, led by social justice movements and widespread consumer and citizen outrage, to change brand names, alter team monikers, and transform trade terminologies that were in some cases centuries old. Here, consumers were often the ones in the *LEAD*, and brands followed *WITH* them.

➡ *PepsiCo's Quaker Foods* announced it would let go of its stereotypical "Aunt Jemima" brand name and logo, after 130 years of consistent sales; the new name is Pearl Milling Company, after the brand's original owners.

➡ *Mars Foods* followed suit by preparing to "evolve" its "Uncle Ben's" brand identity, a staple in America's groceries since 1946, likewise because many consumers perceived the brand as a racist trope. It settled in May 2021 with "Ben's Original."[76]

➡ *Conagra Brands* says it's pensioning its intended "loving grandmother" brand, "Mrs. Butterworth's," as some might interpret the sixty-year-old shape and image in a way that's inconsistent with the company's egalitarian values and its full support of Black and Brown communities.[77]

➡ *Nestlé USA* is rethinking its racially derogatory "Eskimo Pie" label for its iconic ice cream bar brand in its ninety-ninth year on the market.[78] At the same time, it's rebranding its Australian subsidiary Allen's "Chicos" and "Red Skins" candy brand names and packaging in line with more cultural sensitivity.[79]

➡ *Sports teams*, such as the Washington Football Team (formerly the Washington Redskins),[80] Cleveland Indians (currently in the process of renaming),[81] and other professional franchises and academic teams have recognized the potentially culturally insensitive histories of their names and mascots (e.g., Chief Blackjack at St. John's University). These moves have been driven in no small part by advertising boycotts, real or threatened.

➡ *Legacy jargon* is changing, too, perhaps out of an abundance of caution—and some say extreme political correctness. Even the real estate term "master suite" is falling by the wayside in that industry, in favor of less racially evocative (and gendered) terms such as "primary bedroom." Terminology in other sectors is sure to follow.[82]

Words come preloaded with history, prejudicial connotations, and sometimes overtly hateful intent. And business names are no exception. Many companies are undergoing careful inventories around their business and brand monikers. We're not talking about trademark issues here, or even effective marketing taglines. We're talking about ensuring an absence of offense. Here's how we do that effectively:

1. ***Rebranding hurts.*** We have to understand that it is neither easy nor cheap to rebrand midstream. But it just might be necessary. We shouldn't jump on the bandwagon reflexively, the way many brand dominoes fell in June and July 2020. This is a big decision. Make it wisely. Take swift but considered steps. Don't hesitate or reject the notion of the change out of hand the way the founders of the Sambo's restaurant chain did for decades, in open defiance of public sentiment—and what's simply right.

2. ***Don't follow here.*** LEAD. We shouldn't wait for public outrage, because by then, it might be too late. Proceed proactively, anticipating it might simply be time to retire names and terms that might be construed as culturally insensitive to today's sensibilities.

3. ***Think long & hard.*** We ought to consider carefully whether our name contains any unintended baggage in the reckoning of the public. It must not only be a response to active social movements such as Black Lives Matter (BLM), but also in anticipation of much wider and necessary cultural awareness and sensitivity. Could our name be simply out of touch with today's marketplace? How inclusive—or exclusive—is it? Remember, WE does not mean just "us over here." It means all of us. Let's ask around, conduct surveys, inquire widely, and not just rely on our own POV. Terms some segments of the population (or some regions) consider perfectly palatable might rankle others.

4. ***Recognize that times change.*** What might have once been acceptable might not be anymore. Think of Stroh's short-lived "Crazy Horse" malt liquor brand. Or Pillsbury's "Funny Face" drink mix product, intended to compete with Kool-Aid. Its flavors, such as "Injun Orange" and "Chinese Cherry," came accompanied by ethnic stereotype images.[83] Tolerated, unfortunately, in the 1960s. But now? Definitely not okay.

5. ***Put purpose center stage.*** If and when we find we must rebrand, let's think of joining the trend in business naming that puts company purpose and values front and center in the name itself. We can be subtle like

"Tesla" or "Nike," or more direct, along the lines of "KIND Bars," "Just Water," "True Car," "Innocent Smoothies," and so on.

6. **Walk the walk.** Let's remember that a name alone is no substitute or shield for the truth of our business practices. The substance behind our name is what really matters. That is, it's not enough just to ensure our business name does not offend, but also our products and partnerships, our business expenditures, our supply chain. But our business or brand name is not trivial. "Never mind that Sambo's hired a much higher percentage of Blacks than most other companies and restaurant firms," writes the company's biographer, Charles Bernstein.[84] Between the negative connotations of its ill-advised name, and their resistance to changing it, the business was doomed.

Move Along a Spectrum of Roles & Tones of Voice

In terms of roles, it's important to remember that, for all our talk of taking controversial stances, there is a critical difference between *politics* and *values*. The greatest opportunity for brands is to compound their value by doubling down on their values. So, movements don't need to be political—only positive and values based. We don't have to pick fights. We don't have to demonize or even go negative on our competitors, other industries, or political administrations. But that doesn't mean we deny our own values. It doesn't mean we capitulate to Senate minority leader Mitch McConnell, who warns corporate America to "stay out of politics" (except for donations).[85] We do need to take a stand on behalf of the well-being of the WE, and ideally, we all work together to do that.

The research firm Global Strategy Group finds public awareness of corporate stances on political events hitting all-time highs, and doubling about every two years.[86] It's likely our business-led movements, whatever they are, will spark some naysayers just as government policy does. Many people inherently distrust corporations, with good reason, especially as they've become increasingly entwined with government. This is especially true since *Citizens United v. Federal Election Commission*, a landmark 2010 US Supreme Court decision, which many argue likens the rights of corporations to those of people. But it's largely because all of this growing cross-sector collaboration that *LEAD WITH WE* is taking off.

Having said that, the actual people who make up the WE are, unfortunately, experiencing "cause fatigue" of late.[87] This is because media has given every brand, from corporations to celebrities to TikTok kids, global reach and potential impact. There are so many competing voices, so much to care about. It's up to the brand itself to decide how it will position itself in the marketplace, in terms of tone, attitude, overall brand "personality," and "voice." Different brands choose to play different roles, ranging from persistently positive (think KIND Bars) to positively provocative (Ben & Jerry's). Some are outright confrontational against public institutions, politicians, competitors, or industries at large—even to consumers they perceive need reeducation and reminders. There is a spectrum of choice for how our brand will show up to inspire, enable, and drive the change we seek by taking others—and the WE—with us.

Some businesses decide they will remain in a relatively safe role, yet still manage to wield huge impact. Companies that quietly, steadfastly work with regulators and government agencies to change things for the better. Brands, large and small, from global consumer goods leader Unilever, to eco-conscious, fair-trade lingerie brand Naja, which celebrates regenerative business and a circular economy.

Next, there's a middle ground, in the form of holding one's own industry accountable for responsible sourcing, transparency, worker safety, and other key measures. For thirty years, members of the chemical manufacturing industry have subscribed to the Responsible Care program it founded with a nonprofit partner regarding health and safety.[88] More and more often, individual companies take things one step further, seeking to change government policies and laws. Beauty-counter, leveraging the larger Clean Products Movement, sent a hundred of its advocates to personally lobby on the Hill for the passage of the Personal Care Products Safety Act, which would fortify the US Food and Drug Administration's authority to regulate ingredients in beauty and hygiene products. The Santa Monica–based company also rallied thirty thousand political activists—members of its brand community—to demand these safer product ingredients.[89] Or take US fashion brand and American Sustainable Business Council member Eileen Fisher, which has established itself as a mostly noncontroversial leader for decades in terms of sustainability, equal opportunity, and rights—especially women's empowerment[90]—all grounded in constant innovation:

> Our vision is to make clothes in a way that actually makes things better. It will require systemic change, moving away from the linear take-make-waste model to a circular one that reuses or replenishes the resources involved. That means working with farmers who are regenerating

damaged landscapes. It means adopting a manufacturing process that eliminates waste by using old clothes as the raw material for new ones. And it means doing business in a way that improves the lives of the people who make our clothes . . . [for a] future where we make and consume the right things, not everything. Where benefits for some don't mean sacrifices for others. Where our actions have a positive impact on the planet.[91]

Of late, the certified B Corp brand's Vision 2020 initiative, launched in 2015, lays out the role Eileen Fisher plays in helping consumers understand that they are equally responsible—and excitingly, can exert real impact—with their decisions at the end of a garment's lifecycle. It was part of a larger goal to become "100 percent sustainable" over five years. Spoiler: It was able to do a lot—and still has a distance to travel. That didn't stop the company from debuting its Horizon 2030 program, building on its legacy of success to set ambitious goals, which it communicates transparently to consumers in key areas such as "Future Fibers," "Climate Correction," and "Thriving Communities" (where it is today, where it wants to be tomorrow, and where it intends to wind up next year).[92]

Last, there's the vigilant, often aggressive "protagonist" role that some of the pioneers and paragons of LEAD WITH WE engage in. Patagonia confronted President Trump about his 2017 reduction of Utah's Bears Ears National Monument by 85 percent and handing over more than a million acres of the ecosystem—thousands of archaeological sites, sacred cultural landscape—to "extractive industries and development."[93] The company's uncompromising and assertive stance was right in line with the attitudes of its brand community. Patagonia is mostly unbothered by the "loss" of those it antagonizes by its stridency—trying to reach nonbelievers simply wouldn't work. On the other hand, Sam Murch, Patagonia's Action Work's program manager, tells me, "Somewhere on that ladder of engagement is a place for everyone, and it might be . . . that [we just] need to find the correct conversation."[94] Further context is provided by Patagonia's former CEO, Rose Marcario: "People are saying that we're really politically active, when the reality is that it's proportional to what's happened," she says of the threat to millions of acres of public land. "We've never seen anything like it. We felt like we needed to get involved."[95]

Again, consumers do like to be part of the solution of some of the large-scale problems that daunt their thoughts—and they'll pay for the privilege to do so, either by supporting our brand with their money and/or spending their time working *With* us on our movement. Or they're just as likely to employ those same resources actively working *against* us for not assuming greater responsibility. They deleted Uber en masse over its treatment of drivers; they "canceled" many a previously solid CEO and beloved celebrity in the #MeToo movement and its offshoots. BLM protestors assailed certain brands for their hollow DI&E claims. Even people's shopping decisions "turned into acts of protest for the millions of people in pro- and anti-Trump camps. L.L. Bean, T.J. Maxx, and many other companies have already been pulled into a sort of ideological tug of war,"[96] the *New York Times* reports.

To segue into the next chapter, we're attempting to change something critical in society through our movement(s). Movements make history. Our impact will derive from our purpose and the buy-in we earn through the authenticity of our motivation, activation, and inspiration. The more traction the movement gets, the more likely it climbs up the Virtuous Spiral, widening our *We*.

Key Takeaways

➠ Shift from "marketing" to "movement-making" in ways that inspire all stakeholders to build your business and its impact *With* you.

➠ Use your purpose to launch brand movements, building momentum through storytelling, partnerships, and impact.

➠ Determine the appropriate tone of your brand voice and engage consistently with selected social and environmental issues on this basis.

Action Items

1. *Lead*—Determine what issues or impact are most authentic to your brand, aligned with your purpose, and relevant to your future.

2. *With*—Leverage The Four C's to ensure your brand becomes an effective community architect: Co-ownership, Co-authorship, Co-creation, and multiple forms of Collaboration.

3. *We*—Create new movements, or join existing ones that most effectively solve challenges that are meaningful and motivating for all your stakeholders.

we

FIRST

CITIZENS, COLLABORATORS & SECTORS

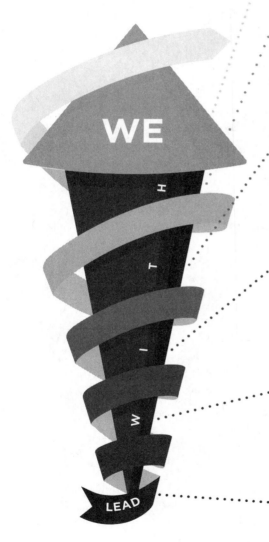

TRANSCENDENCE
FOSTER REGENERATIVE
& ABUNDANT FUTURE
Evolve principles & practices to
scale human & planetary health
Humanity & Planet

SOCIETY
COLLABORATE CROSS-
SECTOR & SHAPE CULTURE
Drive cultural conversations &
coalitions that improve society

COMMUNITY
MOBILIZE BRAND
COMMUNITIES &
BUILD MOVEMENTS
Engage external stakeholders
around purpose-led movements
Customers, Consumers & Partners

COMPANY
ACTIVATE PURPOSE
& ALIGN INTERNAL
STAKEHOLDERS
Integrate & apply purpose
throughout company
Execs, Employees & Supply Chain

LEADERS
DEFINE COMPANY
PURPOSE & GOALS
Conduct honest audit &
determine reason for being
Corporations, Businesses & Startups

ME
ADOPT *LEAD WITH WE*
MINDSET & BEHAVIOR
Recognize new reality, grasp
urgency & shift thinking
Every Individual

7

Society

Collaborating to Reinvent Business

Transform Leadership by Influencing Society

Lead With We businesses can instigate, leverage, and grow social movements around specific issues and social challenges that consumers and citizens care about. These brands share an ongoing, compelling, humanizing story containing clear calls to participation and inclusion, through which people can express their own agency to drive change. Our companies educate, inspire, and motivate people in the spirit of authentic collaboration, thus influencing individual thinking and behavior on the moral/ethical plane—not just the commercial.

We've been *Lead*-ing our way up the Virtuous Spiral, starting as individuals, through our companies, into communities, from the inside out. The realm of Society, far up the Spiral, becomes activated when we members of the business world are able to *Lead large-scale cultural conversations* based on our authentic purpose, conversations that transform not only our own companies and our conscious consumers, but the whole of society. The propulsive purpose with which we began, now having gained mass and momentum by attracting a vigorous and vocal community both inside and outside the company, reaches its impact apogee when the community works *WITH* us and each other en masse. Now big things can change, with lasting effect for the better.

When our companies *LEAD* by accumulating along their way a wide Breadth of *WITH* partnerships in pursuit of their purpose, we eclipse our products and services and even our own individual brands. We transcend our categories entirely, and, together *WITH* wide and novel coalitions, start to solve meaningful social, environmental, or economic problems (e.g., the SDGs) on a global scale. In short, *WE shape culture*. In this manner, we gain an incalculable competitive advantage—even as the primary focus necessarily remains on growing our business. There is only one limit to the lengths *WE* can go to solve formidable challenges when we *LEAD* this way, at scale—and that's the extent to which we are willing and set up to collaborate and practice The Four C's introduced in chapter six, "Community." Every decision across all efforts at this Society level of doing business is all about *WE* in its many forms. *WE* is the touchstone we reach for if and when we get uncomfortable, lost, challenged, disheartened, or otherwise knocked off our leadership path. The collective is the alpha and the omega. Now instead of asking merely *WITH* whom we are undertaking initiative X or drive Y, we ask, "How large a *WE* will we reach through this plan? What problem are we trying to solve? How big is the tent to which we're inviting stakeholders, communities, and sectors—and how do we hope to specifically benefit everyone who comes?"

And that conversation, that conception of *WE*, needs to loop in the funders, and recognize the more recent broader influence of the investor class, both institutional and retail, as a powerful "external" force affecting our impact. For example, the coming "fundamental restructuring of capital markets" that BlackRock's Larry Fink presaged in his 2020 annual letter will be based in part on the universal acceptance that "climate risk is investment risk," and a more "inclusive capitalism"[1] should be our mutual goal. One year later, Fink doubled down, noting that not only did COVID-19 not distract companies from climate risk, but "the reallocation of capital accelerated even faster" than he'd predicted in 2020. Again, he framed the transition to more *LEAD WITH WE* business thinking on the climate as a "historic investment opportunity."[2] It's already spawning collaboration on an unprecedented scale.

But none of these high-level collaborations will work without us having first established unshakable trust in the minds of our potential partners and the public. GlobeScan has been studying public trust in business, starting with the release of key findings as early as 2016. It uncovered some disturbing facts. The trust capital of global business was roughly one-fiftieth that of scientific and academic institutions. "Given the low levels of trust in business," it concluded, "it is critical that companies work to build alliances, partnerships and collaborations with the most trusted institutions in society, especially scientific/academic institutions and NGOs [nongovernmental organizations]." Importantly, the old model of traditional public–private partnerships might not be sufficient any longer, GlobeScan says, because of equally low levels of public trust in government. The new model looks more like PepsiCo's Mountain Dew brand partnering with Historically Black Colleges and Universities, such as Howard and Hampton, to sponsor a $1 million prize to bolster the upcoming generation of Black entrepreneurs.[3] We've also witnessed a significant gap between trust in national companies and trust in global companies, meaning that communicating a strong commitment to the *local* market is likely to increase trust with the brand community and other area citizens.[4] Trust is a key to transcendence.

The Polish American scholar and rabbi Abraham Joshua Heschel writes that a person's "true fulfillment depends upon communion with that which transcends him."[5] Similarly, the influential psychologist Abraham Maslow eventually revised his thinking about his famous hierarchy of needs. At some point late in his life, he adjusted that pyramid to include above the previously highest level (of Self-Actualization) a territory he thought of as "Transcendence":

> the very highest and most inclusive or holistic levels of human consciousness, behaving and relating, as ends rather than means, to oneself, to significant others, to human beings in general, to other species, to nature, and to the cosmos.[6]

This is simply the presupposition of the existence of, and responsibility for, others beyond ourselves. Even those we don't see, we don't necessarily know, and might not (probably won't) ever even meet. Those far away in distance, time, or economic strata. The *WE* that transcends the "Us–Them polarity." It transcends ostensible limitations, expected boundaries, and conventional assumptions. And it transcends the past, fear, space, and the false dichotomy between people and nature.[7] "The word transcend also means 'surpass' in the sense simply of being able to do more than one thought one could do, or more than one had done in the past," according to Maslow.[8] To truly *LEAD WITH WE*, we must transform not only the world by our actions, but our entire understanding and posture first. Our experience of responsibility and "work"; our ideas of progress, success, and value; our concept of our own future and that of everyone and everything else. Our way of "being" in the world. We're going to elaborate on the larger idea of transcendence—what The Higher WE could mean—in chapter eight, "Transcendence." Here, suffice to say that, especially during the launch, growth, and evolutionary stages of our business, it will benefit us as individuals, our businesses, the business world in general, *and* the greater WE beyond if we transcend business as usual and *LEAD WITH WE*.

For example, if we follow the *LEAD* of the likes of Prince Charles, who's working to raise $10 billion for his Earth Charter, the *Terra Carta*, we'll be on the right track. The prince, following his late father as a veteran champion of environmental health, says he "can only encourage, in particular, those in industry and finance to provide practical leadership to this common project, as only they are able to mobilize the innovation, scale and resources that are required to transform our global economy."[9] Or follow the leadership of President Joe Biden's administration, which on May 20, 2021, issued an executive order to ultimately assess "climate-related financial risk," urging federal agencies to determine the vulnerability of financial systems, pensions and savings, and US competitiveness to climate change, and enact needed regulations.[10]

Transcend Limited Notions of Whom We're Doing All This For

In the past two years, business has fueled the motors of societal change perhaps more than any other time in history (and surely more than any other sector). The year 2020, in particular, was a watershed period. A year when Microsoft once again ranked first among the "JUST 100" companies of the world, because of CEO Satya Nadella's attitude that we need "to essentially have a referendum on capitalism . . . I always go back to that social contract of our company with the world around us. Because that to me is at the core of the license to operate," he says. "You can't exist if all you're doing is benefiting yourself . . . Profit [comes] because of the larger surplus you're creating around you."[11] And at the heart of Microsoft's assumptions about that abundant "surplus" is the idea that protecting the natural environment ought to rank at or near the top of a *LEAD WITH WE* company's purpose, along with safeguarding democracy. Democracy, which like We First Capitalism, is consciously designed to protect and serve collective interests and promote resilience. Again, we're not talking here about any other

"-ism" besides a more sustainable form of the capitalism on which the West was founded and business best thrives, but rather one based on We First thinking. We achieve this through the monumental but feasible shifts we've been reviewing, from extractive to regenerative, from short term to long term, from self-centered to circular-systems oriented.

There's no time to waste. *WE* who *LEAD* in business must act urgently and follow through thoroughly if we're to recover quickly from the turbulence of the early 2020s. Forum for the Future's latest Future of Sustainability report, "From System Shock to System Change—Time to Transform," explores key dynamics that lie at the heart of the momentous global transitions already underway. It deems that our human and planetary destinies are unavoidably interlocked. The report outlines how, of the several potential futures we're facing, only one will lead to the "just transition" immediately needed "if we are to avert the worst of the social, climate and biodiversity crises we all face."[12] While we're all busy "competing and retreating," we're rapidly *depleting* the resources upon which our survival depends. "The decisions we make in the next six to 18 months will determine the future of our society, our economy, and the planet," the report warns. We must steer toward a "transform trajectory," rallying and racing to fully and deeply change society, with business in the pole position—and "we can't go back to 'before' COVID." More specifically, we must exploit the recovery from the pandemic as a "reset" to fast-track a just, equitable, environmentally responsible society rooted in resilience and "regenerative thinking,"[13] which we call We First Capitalism.

It's pretty easy and inspiring to say "Build Back Better," as Joe Biden did during his 2020 presidential run. It's far more challenging to design a regenerative system that effects measurable change across industries and society—such as through progressive infrastructure engineering—not to mention the global economic, environmental, and social terrain. To do so, *WE* who *LEAD* need to transcend old mindsets and old power brokers (monopolies/duopolies, etc.) to transcend our own complacency. We must transcend gross misinformation serving selfish interests. How do "resilient" and "regenerative" translate into practical business methods based on shared values and a common higher purpose? Without The Four C's—Co-ownership, Co-creation, Co-authorship, and Collaboration—they don't.

Here are two good examples. First, on the environmental front, Andrei Cherny is the co-founder and CEO of Aspiration, a truly disruptive financial services company that turns every transaction into a positive action. When you deposit your money with an Aspiration Spend & Save account, your deposits are guaranteed fossil fuel (and firearm) investment free, "as opposed to any of the top twenty or thirty banks where most people are banking," Cherny tells me. He can think of one well-known behemoth bank that "spends more in terms of financing of fossil fuel exploration and exploitation on an annual basis than the combined market capitalization of ExxonMobil and BP." But because "American consumers spend $36 billion a day . . . *where* they spend that money and *how* they spend that money and the decisions that drive them to do so matters a great deal . . . those are enormous levers for change and impact." So Cherny and his partner, Joe Sandberg, launched the alternative bank, committed to "clean money," helping customers do well while doing good. Its model is based on impact, conscience, and sustainability. It allows customers to pay whatever they want for its cash management services, based on "fairness." Even if it's zero, the company still gives to charity 10 percent of what it earns. Its Aspiration Impact Measurement tool displays your own personal sustainability score as you're shopping on the Aspiration card, monitoring your choices and suggesting better ones when necessary.[14]

I deliberately mention these environmental and economic initiatives together—they're inextricably linked, a fact that was clear in the Biden administration's transition initiatives. Emerging from profound twin public health and economic crises, Biden launched several national efforts to avoid us ever getting "caught flat-footed again," the White House posted.[15] On day one of his tenure, Biden signed an executive order recommitting the US to the Paris Climate Accord, and rolled back Trump's Keystone XL Pipeline efforts. In April 2021, coinciding with Earth Day, the new administration vowed to make the US a clean energy leader, pledging to cut the country's carbon emissions by half (of 2005 levels) by 2030—and promising that would lead to "good paying union jobs." That target nearly doubles the US's prior commitment, and will demand the kind of "dramatic changes in the power, transportation and other sectors"[16] that Biden intends to address through his multiple infrastructure initiatives.

But it's important to mention that the president is not acting without extreme pressure from the business world. In fact, the move to make the environmental pledge was spurred by an open letter written by a coalition of 408 business leaders and investors[17] representing, respectively, seven million US workers and $1 trillion in assets under management.[18] Seems many businesses know how to *Lead With We*.

Of course, doing so isn't always so easy, especially when circumstances beyond our control limit cash flow. Take, as the second example, Unilever's latest

Sustainable Living Plan initiative with consumers as collaborators—its three-year-old, nature-based, ethically resourced beauty brand called "Love Beauty and Planet." Says Sonika Malhotra, co-founder and global brand director, "Our purpose came from a combination of logic and magic." When it became clear to the brand that younger consumers were worried about how much unnecessary time they were spending in the shower—and how much water they were therefore wasting—the brand decided to develop the world's first quick-rinsing hair conditioner. That's smart—especially given its potential impact. Love Beauty and Planet's R&D, PR comms, and rollouts rapidly became something of a benchmark for Unilever's whole portfolio.[19]

The world already belongs to younger leaders with new ideals and ideas for their future. Separately, they fight to end gun violence, stop deportations, end incarcerations and murders of Black and Brown people, and reverse the climate crisis. "They may seem like disparate goals," say the watchwords of the coalition called #CountOnUs—comprising members of the Sunrise Movement, March for Our Lives, Dream Defenders, and United We Dream, among others—"but we really have one task: to bring an end to a society that cares more for profits than people." Together, they represent a potent, unstoppable force. "We are coming together to deal with the systemic problems of our generation."[20] The continuance of the WE requires us to LEAD regeneration efforts—lest we all die off in just a few generations. And we do this first by leading, not ignoring, the cultural conversations about these issues.

Transform Agency Through Inspiration

No matter where we sit at the table, one word can't be stressed enough: *agency*. The key is to encourage stakeholders in every capacity, and inspire consumer and citizen action by empowering them in their process of achieving the change they—especially the youngest among them—want to see. Our brands effectively join the "influencer" class this way. Yes, the celebrity brands young citizens follow do so by inspiration—but also by *continuous and emotional engagement in conversations about meaningful things*. Their influence has sparked and continued to fuel multi-stakeholder cultural conversations, all about inclusion, agency, and empowerment. The topics are varied and all important, and have stellar advocates: Lady Gaga (bullying, mental health), Julia Louis-Dreyfus (oceans and parks preservation), Russell Brand (social justice, wealth redistribution), Peter Dinklage (animal rights, vegan advocacy), Justin Timberlake (children's health, cancer treatment), Beyoncé (disaster assistance, racial equity), Neal Patrick Harris (LGBTQ family issues, hunger), Julianne Moore (gun control), Leonardo DiCaprio (climate emergency), and Robert Downey Jr. (climate-crisis coalition) all *LEAD* major movements for global change—*WITH* their hundreds of millions of followers. Our brands can, too.

Consciousness is contagious. For example, "If a billion people around the world were to take a few small steps and make them into permanent lifestyle changes," according to the *Guardian*, "global greenhouse gas emissions [GGEs] could be significantly reduced, a new campaign [Count Us In] argues." Tiny—but mighty—steps. Eat local. Less meat. Buy clothes that last. Drive and fly less. Walk more. The campaign, supported by businesses including IKEA, HSBC, BT, and Reckitt Benckiser (Gaviscon, Durex, etc.), urges people to sign up and vow to take at least *one simple step* that will reduce GGEs.[21]

The true challenge for business leaders is this: We must get all of these steps right or we risk none of it working. The steps I've outlined so far are all interconnected and interdependent. They build exponentially. Yes, every "tiny" step counts. But each step is not in and of itself enough. If we break any important link in the *LEAD WITH WE* chain, we eliminate the ability to compound our efforts, especially necessary once we're working at this level of driving major cultural change.

Transform Citizen Power Through Technology

The advent of new, powerful tools makes it easier to take part in cultural conversations. Companies, agencies, organizations, and citizen innovators, from the bottom up, are providing effective, fun, and simple tools for consumers to make conscious, future-facing decisions in real time:

- ⇒ *Aspiration.* Plants a tree for every purchase made by depositors via its "Plant Your Change" program.[22]
- ⇒ *OpenInvest.* Lets consumers invest only in companies that share their values.[23]
- ⇒ *Adopt-a-Meter.* Allows you to adopt a plot of soil in order to draw down carbon.[24]
- ⇒ *WePledge.* Enables people to spend 1 percent of their time in service.[25]

⇒ **Pawprint.** Presents an online tool through which people can track their carbon footprint.[26]

⇒ **Joro.** Reveals ways to improve our carbon footprint through different spending habits.[27]

⇒ **Sustainably.** Empowers employees and consumers to round up their purchases, and companies to match donations to their favorite charities.[28]

⇒ **Deed.** Empowers employees to share time, skills, and money among a global network of two million people serving countless causes, doing various good "deeds."[29]

There are far too many new tools to recount here. We as consumers need only open our eyes and browsers. And companies that don't remove their own blindfolds to new consumer behaviors will wind up plunging off the cliff.

Transform Traditional Diversity, Inclusion & Equity

As we've seen, every level of the Spiral requires our careful attention to diversity, inclusion, and equity (DI&E). But here, especially, as we're crafting alliances for societal changes, we ought to ask, "How wide is this *WE* we're working *WITH* here? How representative is it?" This watershed moment carries a vast opportunity for a new breed of corporate-guided societal leadership, starting with a higher bar for DI&E efforts.

This is not about adding a human rainbow to the cover of our annual report. We don't need more commercials or Facebook ads. We need social movements, cultural conversions, and systemic change. Whether huge or humble, *LEAD WITH WE* companies possess every aspect of what next-generation leaders of inclusion and equity require. Edelman's special report, *Brand Trust in 2020*, informs us that 82 percent of US respondents say brands would earn their trust by taking a stand against racism. Fifty-four percent say companies need to invest in addressing the root causes of racial inequality to earn or retain their trust.[30] Racial equity is an economic imperative, with $2.6 trillion of additional spending waiting to get unlocked by closing the racial earnings gap.[31]

Within days of George Floyd's killing by police in 2020, Target CEO Brian Cornell communicated the company's commitment to "stand with Black families and fight against racism," including investing $10 million in funding social justice programs in local communities, such as in Minneapolis, where its flagship store was looted and nearly destroyed in the wake of the killing. "Target then launched a Racial Equity Action and Change committee (REACH)—made up of six senior company leaders—to create an action plan," focused on four areas: Team, Guests, Communities, and Civic Engagement and Public Policy[32] (the four central levels of our Virtuous Spiral). REACH was baked into laudable efforts Target had been undertaking since 2018 to combat public perception post-settlement of a class-action lawsuit that accused the retailer of racial discrimination in hiring. The company had continued to fall short of its own goals to retain minority workers, and at the time of the Floyd killing, only two of its fifty-one top executives were Black.[33]

So, this is not just about an internally diverse and inclusive company culture, as discussed in chapter five, "Culture." There's also the wide array of potential consumers to consider—the world at large. We mustn't be caught out by inadvertently insensitive actions like the release of H&M's "monkey" sweatshirt. The Swedish fashion retailer appointed a global diversity leader in 2018, following the public backlash and loss of strategic influencer partnerships over its ad that showed a Black child wearing a hoodie proclaiming, "Coolest Monkey in the Jungle."[34] Despite its generally progressive leadership, it was not the company's first scandal. Global fashion brands have suffered severe accusations of racism in the past after such scandals as Gucci's blackface-reminiscent knitwear, Prada's "Little Black Sambo" bag charm, and Dolce & Gabbana's anti-Asian comments.[35] So, when such companies jumped headlong (and presumably with good intentions) into social media support for Black Lives Matter (BLM) during 2020, that only amplified the backlash, now focused on perceived hypocrisy—public-facing "activism," without inclusion at board and company-wide levels. Of course, it's good to publicly denounce racism, as long as there's no disconnect between our words and actions, which seriously erodes trust in our business and the business world.

Rather that rush to address some *au courant* DI&E issue, understand that we are likely in some way complicit, consciously or not. Before we rush to market with a message, or even try to fix an issue internally, we ought to take the time to look inward. Listen first, then lead. Move all stakeholders beyond head-nod agreement, into energized and demonstrated alignment. We must do the hard, costly, and uncomfortable private work first. You can hire a diverse staff, but if you're not actually creating an inclusive and equitable environment, you will lose it.

To pioneer a paradigm shift in the role corporate entities play in advancing meaningful racial equity and social justice, we clarify what constitutes impact with ownable and durable key performance indicators. Global business case studies demonstrate clear increases in market share, innovation, productivity, and reputation when companies accelerate DI&E outcomes as active stimulants. Highly diverse companies are 35 percent more likely than less diverse ones to financially outperform the industry median.[36]

The Gap enterprise and its subsidiaries (e.g., Banana Republic, Old Navy, Janie & Jack, Athleta) faced a major DI&E challenge a few years back. Employee turnover—a substantial cost to a large employer—was mostly caused by its conventional hiring, training, and HR policies, which were failing to account for the challenges prevalent among entry-level employees—often disproportionately BIPOC. In response, the company instituted training courses and a ten-week internship and mentoring program to address obstacles in hiring and retaining BIPOC employees. By providing skills, mentoring, and support, the Gap program created a talent pipeline with *double* the average retention rates. This is an excellent example of how a specific department (HR in this case) can make an overall difference to a brand—and the world.

Cascade Engineering, based in Grand Rapids, Michigan, and comprising nine strategic business units with a core competency in large-scale plastic injection molding, was also seeing high turnover in employees of color and employees in financial crisis. In response, it provided wrap-around services to staff previously engaging government social service programs. Half of these employees tended to be BIPOC. The impact of Cascade's Welfare to Career program dramatically decreased turnover from 65 percent to 5 percent. Meanwhile, French multinational retailer Sephora's US division is dedicating 15 percent of its shelf space to Black-owned brands, becoming the first retailer to accept the challenge initiated by a Brooklyn-based creative director in the wake of 2020's BLM protests.[37]

You're not on your own in retooling DI&E. Intel's chief diversity officer, Dawn Jones, told JUST Capital: "No one company will be able to do it alone."[38] That's why Intel, along with Dell, Nasdaq, Snap, and NTT Data, formed the Alliance for Global Inclusion to open-source ideas with each other regarding goals, metrics, and best practices in DI&E, including leadership representation and inclusive product development.[39]

None of these companies' leaders achieved such successes on their own. They considered the *WE*, then embraced cooperation with other stakeholders to implement meaningful impact. Every brand needs the support of those best equipped to help them navigate this sensitive and complex issue.

Transform Departments, Products, Markets, Supply Chains & Industries

Core to trust among all consumers, of course, is the quality of our products or services. Is our business the one best equipped to provide such solutions? A KPMG/ *Forbes* study engaged a group of top CMOs who confirmed this LEAD WITH WE truism: "The best actions are those that leverage the strengths and capabilities a company already has." Although it might not instantly be obvious where our purpose and business specialty meet important actual needs in our customers' lives.[40] Let's remember that most consumers, especially in younger demographics, have already made major lifestyle and spending changes, adopted new tools—or claimed they wish to. Our business might be able to adapt fairly easily to slot into one of these new markets, especially around the huge and growing Lifestyles of Health and Sustainability (LOHAS) movement.

The $355 billion US LOHAS market segment focuses on optimal human health, both mental and physical; the environment; personal development; sustainable living; and social justice.[41] About three-quarters of US adults, for example, believe the country should do "whatever it takes to protect the environment."[42] More than half rank the environment as a top policy issue the government should tackle this year.[43] Plus, it's a *$546 billion international market.*[44] The industries, corporate activities, products, and services that fall under the LOHAS umbrella tend to be environmentally conscious, sustainable, socially responsible, and healthful—both for the planet and its inhabitants. About 20 percent of all US adults (forty-one million people) are *active* LOHAS consumers, and those attracted to this thriving market represent one of the largest and most affluent and educated groups in the country.[45]

Now that more customers demand more responsible, more ethical, more sustainable, and even *regenerative* companies and products, suppliers simply need to provide them, or risk insignificance. When it comes to products across the supply chain, we must transform the remedial into the preventive and LEAD product innovations that are net positive. Moonshot, a startup food brand committed to "climate friendly" snacks, does this. Timberland vowed to transform into a 100 percent net-positive company by 2030,[46] including working with partners on the ground in Thailand to help scale a dynamic agroforestry system for growing its natural rubber.[47] The similarly eco-minded Modern Meadow (purpose: *Transforming the material world*) chose a different route, by pioneering its groundbreaking product line in its lab. Their ZOA is made from "a bio-alloy and assembled with engineered proteins and bio-based polymers."[48] Its premium material looks and feels like high-quality, designer leather. The applications are legion. No cow had to suffer and die, and no widespread environmental devastation had to be reined in. Meanwhile, the Brooklyn-based "cellular agriculture" company is transforming not only the fashion space, but the whole manufacturing industry.

Other companies are awakening, too, to animal-less fur and fabrics constructed out of various recycled waste. Salvatore Ferragamo sells scarves created from orange fibers. Cariuma creates sneakers from bamboo, sugarcane, and cork while restoring rainforests in Brazil.[49] For Adidas, Stella McCartney and her partner, California's Bolt Threads, are perfecting faux silk outfits made from proteins inspired by spider-web DNA.[50] In addition to its "eco-canvas" and "eco-suede" lines made from recycled materials, Vivobarefoot's X Bloom Collaboration created the first ever pair of shoes—the Ultra III—made from harvested algal biomass, which greatly damages the ecology of waterways worldwide. "Every pair helps recirculate fifty-seven gallons of filtered water back into natural habitats, even as it *prevents* the equivalent of forty balloons full of CO_2 getting released into the Earth's atmosphere."[51]

Every industry can be transformed through a *LEAD WITH WE* mindset and methods. To achieve this, we need to completely reboot the system by transforming not just products themselves but the prevailing mindsets that create and consume them. The Arkansas-based B2B/B2C firm Cooks Venture is reinventing the entire poultry industry. At the start of 2020, the regenerative agriculture startup, co-founded by Blue Apron COO Matt Wadiak, raised $4 million to expand national distribution of its pasture-raised, "slow-growth" heirloom chickens.[52] Just six months earlier, the company had raised $10 million to breed healthier, chemical-free poultry and improve the environment. Since a key 2019 partnership with FoodID, Cooks has become the first US company to test for adulterants, and the "only company that can independently validate that it never uses antibiotics and provides verified Non-GMO feed to its birds."[53] Says Wadiak:

> We are working hard to drive the agricultural industry toward greater biodiversity and breed diversity. We want to provide our customers with a truly transparent and better choice that they can feel good about and that's healthier for them, for the planet, and the animals that we're growing for food.[54]

Now other meat suppliers are starting to follow suit, scrambling to compete for who's responding more effectively to new consumer demands and environmental imperatives.

Or consider the industry disruption of Ripple Foods, a midsize San Francisco company, whose pea-protein dairy alternatives are turning the dairy industry on its ear the same way its founder, Adam Lowry, disrupted the cleaning product category at his former company, Method. Lowry has begun to ripple the sugar and diabetes industries, too, through his new company, Sugarbreak. "It's pointless to make green products for green people," Lowry told me for a *Forbes* interview. "We need to make green products for *everybody*." Lowry realized a couple of defining *LEAD WITH WE* lessons for his leadership, some rather early, others along the way:

1. ***Commit.*** "If you have to trade off between your financial and environmental bottom line, you haven't found the right solution."[55]

2. ***Limit.*** Don't overextend. "There's a difference between smart growth and growth for growth's sake," Lowry shared of his experience at Method. "We had a successful formula of how we were bringing consumers in. Retailers were excited about how we were reinventing categories. They asked us to reinvent lots of different categories across the store. We did too many of them and we had to lay off about a third of our staff."

3. ***Share.*** Continuously communicate your impact outcomes with the world. Ripplefoods.com features a real-time counter displaying the amounts of savings in water and GGE, increased protein intake, and reduced sugar consumption and plastic use that results from people buying Ripple. "We're giving credit to our consumers, for their ripple effect."

If your company is just starting out on its *LEAD WITH WE* journey, you can use a platform like HowGood.com to plan and track your progress. It allows brands to discover the Environmental, Social, and Governance (ESG) impact in every ingredient of their formulations; retailers to align their product offerings to the ESG issues of most concern to consumers; and investors to develop impact metrics and build a sustainable portfolio.[56]

Transcend "Competition" Through Radical Collaboration

An exhilarating area in industry transformation has been dubbed "pre-competitive collaboration." "We need to build strong, multi-stakeholder collaboration around pressing global challenges that can only be addressed at the industry level," Harvard's Rebecca Henderson advises in her lectures on reimagining capitalism. "Let's make them pre-competitive."[57] The Pre-Competitive Collaboration (PCC) movement, well underway now, was arguably born out of the greater Open Innovation (OI) model as first investigated by Henry Chesbrough of the Haas School of Business at the University of California, Berkeley.[58] Chesbrough proposes that seeking competitors' assistance ("purposive inflows and outflows"[59]) provides a viable path, both cognitive and practical, to accelerating advancements in tech-dependent industries. "A centralized approach to [R&D] has become obsolete," writes Chesbrough, citing a central tenet of the OI community.[60] "Useful knowledge has become widespread and ideas must be used with alacrity." The OI drive was itself a natural offshoot of the once-radical 1998 Open Source Initiative of Palo Alto, California, fame. Netscape first offered up its entire code, some eight years after Linux—"open to the point of promiscuity"[61]—developed into a world-class operating system from a wholly decentralized throng, much like Wikipedia or the internet itself.

Along similar lines, IBM's Call for Code (CFC) Global Challenge was created by David Clark Cause and supported by charitable partner, UN Human Rights. It's one of the most impressive of a series of businesses inviting developers and other problem-solving techies around the world to build innovative solutions to combat the most pressing, interconnected problems of our time, such as the climate emergency. Together with the Linux Foundation, top solutions are open-sourced—AI, the cloud, and the Internet of Things—and deployed quickly for everyone to use at scale across the world. The 2019 grand prize went to a team that developed health-monitored applications for firefighters. In 2020, CFC unleashed the mental muscle of its considerable crowd—a third of a million participants from 165 countries—on solving the difficulties occasioned by the advent of COVID-19, offering a $200,000 grand prize and substantial sub-prizes for the most disruptive and feasible solutions, which would then be immediately implemented in communities in greatest need.[62] In 2021, IBM's fourth CFC is tackling the climate emergency. It comprises more than four hundred thousand developers, data scientists, and other problem solvers from 179 countries, who together have created more than fifteen thousand apps.[63]

Great corporate precedents for PCC include Honest Tea and Safeway; UPS and DHL; Google and Yahoo!; Ford and GM; and Apple and Samsung.[64] At its simplest, the PCC concept is analogous to crowdsourcing. But in this case, the "crowd" consists not of multitudinous masses of web wizards, but of competing corporations or other business entities. And they "open" coveted, deeply protected trade secrets and other valuable intellectual property (IP) to that crowd of other businesses. If a pharmaceutical giant wants to get to market quickly, then it might consider taking the minor risk of PCC[65] by working not with just one academic partner (which has been the norm), but *WITH* an open consortium of other companies, too. Each company would share its knowledge and experience, rather than hoarding patents on molecules in the hopes of someday maybe developing a breakthrough drug.[66]

When each collaborating partner is invested first in the *purpose* of the undertaking (in this case, solving some scientific conundrum) rather than its commercial potential, then the group (the *WE*) can go further, faster. And everyone, ideally, can share a piece of the crowd-completed pie. *WE* share the burden. *WE* share the benefits. *WE* share the credit and reputation enhancement for achieving something higher than ourselves. We hold ourselves and each other to a higher standard. Yes, there's a critical balance of the interests of individuals and the community. But along the way, we wind up mitigating our individual business and/or industry risks by *sharing* the responsibility. John Fullerton, a regenerative capitalism expert, writes, "Consequently, individual and community needs are not only inseparable, but their unique contributions are mutually beneficial."[67]

That's the secret behind how several wildly effective COVID-19 vaccines came to fruition in astoundingly record-breaking time in 2020 and 2021, with many more in the pipeline. All these collaborative efforts were accelerated by the Chinese–Australian release of the genetic sequence of the virus even before there was proof of human-to-human spread.[68] In fact, Moderna's vaccine had already been made and shipped to the National Institutes of Health (NIH) to start clinical trials a full month before the first US citizen died of the coronavirus.[69] Big Pharma was suddenly a host of heroines and heroes riding in on white horses, rather than a greedy dragon as previously perceived. This is how whole industries become transformed and how the world transcends old paradigms. Business and society engaged in an imperative cultural conversation—"How do we save human lives from this virus?"—and a consortium of business, science, and citizens rose to the occasion. So, not only did these advancements, propelled by collective purpose, save humanity from the coronavirus, but they also will potentially save us from various cancers and other ailments that wouldn't have received this level of scientific activity had it not been for this big step forward.

The higher the stakes, the more rational and judicious collaboration on this scale seems. Consumers and citizens judge brands in stark terms: We're either complicit in the problem or critical to the solution. For this reason, "a growing share of business competitors are also scaling impact by connecting their proprietary data—rising from 7 percent to 17 percent" between 2017 and 2019, according to McKinsey research.[70]

There are two essential ways to practice PCC. The first is to simply open up our IP to a competitor, industry-wide, or to the entire market. Full transparency. Faced with the fact that many more than a hundred million people across the globe are homeless,[71] with no access to everyday services—including showers—San Francisco–based startup Lava Mae partnered with nonprofit foundation (NPF) The Right to Shower to provide mobile showers, which transform local California communities on the ground. Then, by open-sourcing its Mobile Hygiene Toolkit, Lava Mae invited a network of service providers to deliver their own brands of "radical hospitality" to homeless people across the globe.[72]

Citing Elon Musk again, as part of his leadership of the "popular uprising" against "the biggest industry in the world"—fossil fuel—in 2014 Tesla released all the IP for its electric vehicle technology. "If we clear a path to the creation of compelling electric vehicles, but then lay intellectual property landmines [he means lawsuits] behind us to inhibit others, we are acting in a manner contrary to that goal," Musk announced.

> Technology leadership is not defined by patents, which history has repeatedly shown to be small protection indeed against a determined competitor, but rather by the ability of a company to attract and motivate the world's most talented engineers. We believe that applying the open-source philosophy to our patents will strengthen rather than diminish Tesla's position in this regard.[73]

Toyota took another, though equally consequential, approach to sharing its IP, demonstrating the second method of PCC. In 2010, it was leading its own alternative energy revolution. After open-sourcing some of its tech, and allowing royalty-free use of thousands of its gasoline-electric hybrid patents, Toyota *licensed* its signature Hybrid Synergy Drive technology so other automakers could use it: "Selling hybrid components and complete drivetrains to competitors could help finance . . . future electric car development."[74] Indeed, the moves extended the life and influence of hybrid vehicle tech across the whole auto industry and scaled up Toyota's overall impact. Meanwhile, Toyota is shaking up its industry in other innovative ways, too, on its quest to become a "mobility company." It unveiled in 2020 a line of potential future products such as "an autonomous vanlike transportation module" that aims to reach people underserved by conventional transportation options.[75] And with a partner, it's developing self-driving "robotaxis."[76]

Tim Brown, New Zealand professional soccer player and co-founder of the radically sustainable Allbirds footwear brand, a certified B Corp, led the drive to become the first—but not at all the last—fashion brand to label its carbon footprint "like calories." He told me that petroleum-based ethylene-vinyl acetate (EVA) is ubiquitous in the twenty billion pairs of shoes manufactured each year. To counter this reliance on fossil materials, "we found that we could make it from a waste stream of ethanol from sugarcane—and it's carbon negative . . . We made it open sourced. Not because we're good guys, but because if more people use it, the costs come down." The Allbirds process became a *Time* magazine "innovation of the year,"[77] and set a new standard for the industry. Says Brown, "There [are] now a hundred companies globally in the process of using it. It's an example of when business and purpose come together to actually make the sum greater than the individual parts."[78]

As of this writing, multiple governments are considering pressuring pharmaceutical companies into "technology transfer" deals, wherein patent holders would "license rival companies to produce their vaccines for a small cut of the revenues. AstraZeneca has already made such deals to facilitate large-scale production in India and Japan."[79]

Still other companies license their patents beyond direct competitors and into adjacent industries. Interface, the carbon-capturing floor company we met in the earliest chapter, is considering, among other ideas for spurring more collaboration to enable faster progress, such a licensing model for its proprietary formula and processes. This would allow other businesses, including in Europe and Asia, to scale their own sustainability efforts—the core purpose of Interface—and provide a revenue stream for the company.[80]

Let's look at a summary of the logical, extensive process for LEAD WITH WE industry disruption occasioned by PCC, as seen through the experience of Interface's process thus far. We can adopt and adapt these steps to suit our unique circumstances:

1. ***Buy-in.*** First, Interface's purpose—reducing excess CO_2 in the environment—needed to gain wide awareness: that this *matters* in the big picture, and to real people. That every sector has to do its part, and the building and construction industry in particular, as the world's single largest emitter of GGEs (about 35 percent of total global emissions), has a lot to do.[81] That Interface first—starting with its own employees and customers—needed to take responsibility for changing. Because Interface is, after all, the world's leading carpet tile manufacturer. The company guided this stakeholder alignment with onboarding training modules that covered its history, purpose, and sustainable-to-regenerative evolutionary efforts, as well as education on environmental issues it could meaningfully influence.

2. ***Innovation.*** Then, of course, it had to get creative. It looked across the board for new, needed products, and revised or discontinued those complicit in the carbon crisis. Its flagship, carbon-neutral, carpet tile product provided a primary proof of purpose (POP). It brought that innovation to life in its sales training, labeling, and storytelling. It had to prove there was a viable market for carbon-neutral flooring materials.

3. ***Adaptation.*** Interface needed to adjust and/or create internal policies to make the proposed collaborations possible, and to ensure that the widespread adoption (and potential licensing) of its tech would not cause any untenable risk to the company's financial future. It would have to win in any new deals. Its competitors would have to win. Winners had to include customers/consumers, the industry, and, ultimately, the environment.

4. ***Continuing education.*** The company had to study market forces and trends to scale its PCC commitment. Amid other data, it discovered that, according to Bloomberg, among the ten leaders (including Musk) whose fortunes resulted mainly from the business of innovating solutions to the climate emergency, there was "a combined green net worth of $61 billion

at the end of 2019—about three times the market capitalization of oil services firm Halliburton." There was an emerging "superrich vanguard in the fight against global warming."[82] Interface could build its business and change the world.

5. *Invention.* It needed to help develop specific tools, processes, and partnerships to enable its whole industry to adopt its tech, not to mention innovate its own products to solve the greater environmental problem. For example, it worked with allies in industry and academia as a critical early partner, funder, and supporter of an environmental labeling tool for Microsoft called the Embodied Carbon in Construction Calculator (EC3). Built by Skanska and the Carbon Leadership Forum, EC3 was the first free, open-source tool of its kind.[83] Such progress inspires similar efforts in adjacent industries as evidenced by electronic design company Logitech's "Total Carbon Transparency" pledge, which commits the company to label all its products with a footprint number and universally readable symbols across its entire portfolio by 2025.[84]

6. *Collaboration.* Interface had to scale by building and leading a coalition of partners. For example, it co-founded the Materials Carbon Action Network (materialsCAN) with collaborators Gensler, Skanska, Armstrong, CertainTeed, and USG. The new group convened its industry to discuss solutions for reducing embodied carbon in the materials it employed.[85] By this point, a legitimate movement was underway.

7. *Operationalization.* The company had to get this coalition working and moving, by mutual education, and by defining a unifying story for the whole industry to use. It had to keep sustainability and net-positive efforts exciting—and profitable—to maintain the partners' engagement. That started with Interface moving on from its successful "Mission Zero" story, and adjusting that mission to the scale and speed of the accelerating environmental emergency.

8. *Execution.* Interface collaborated around factories, production methods, and new product development. It worked with Janine Benyus's Biomimicry 3.8 to develop a radical approach by which it and other companies could transform facilities from the old "zero footprint" modes that once seemed sufficient by Ecological Performance Standards, so that there was

no functional distinction between the factory and "the wildland next door."[86] It called the high-performing, nature-mimicking, regenerative ecosystem methodology "Factory as a Forest" (FaaF).[87] It had to demonstrate viability and share that story. In fact, the multi-year FaaF pilot produced positive performance outcomes for Interface and the ecosystem along with a framework and methodology to scale its application and vision.[88] Now the movement extended beyond the initial industry, offering profoundly disruptive opportunities in other sectors—and the potential for significant worldwide impact. Industry competitors are collaborating using several models, including Benyus's Project Positive—"Generous Design for an Abundant World."[89]

All of this is scalable. You can use a tool like Salesforce's Sustainability Cloud, a carbon accounting product for businesses to drive climate action at your company.[90] In fact, the size and age of your company should never be a barrier to shifting industry paradigms. Contrasted to mega-player Interface's fifty-year legacy, BrewDog is a relatively new startup, but it's been a catalyst for industry-wide change for some time. The midsize multinational craft brewery and pub-chain owner has run its Scottish plant on wind power and biomethane fuel it makes out of spent malted barley. It's transferring its vehicles to electric. For a few years, it's been successfully trying to reduce its carbon footprint.

Then came a great reckoning. "We thought we were doing our bit when it came to sustainability," CEO James Watt tells *Fast Company*.[91] But after the company leaders met with nature historian David Attenborough, they started digging deeper. "And then it hit us, the blindingly stark realisation that we were not doing anything like enough. And in fact we were massively contributing to the current existential problem that our planet and our species are facing."[92] Things were never the same again at BrewDog. Now the company is carbon *negative*, removing twice as much carbon from the atmosphere as it emits, including all the pollution in its supply chain. How did BrewDog double its carbon offset? It bought a forest. Well, it's restoring a two-thousand-acre native forest in the Scottish Highlands that had been used for cattle grazing. And it will plant a million trees there by 2022 to help sequester carbon. "Our carbon. Our problem," says BrewDog.[93] Quoting its first sustainability report, "F*ck You, CO_2."[94]

Transform Business Through Cross-Sector Collaborations

We can also surprise society with unexpected but no less organically sound collaborations. Skeptics might wonder how much impact these companies and collaborations are *really* having on entire industries. At this point, we're only so far into the practice of LEAD WITH WE at this societal level. All the examples here are legible signposts for a mindset and practice that has to go much further to fully express the potential of this movement of movements. But these companies and consortiums can and will change their industries as more and more come onboard, fortify new market forces, and accelerate adoption.

In spring 2020, tech monsters Apple and Google began a partnership for COVID-19 contact-tracing technology. The rivals enabled interoperability between Android and iOS devices—a significant shift in practice, in the interest of public health.[95] Olivela, an upscale UK fashion-brand platform (*Luxury shopping—with a purpose*) launched in order to literally change girls' lives through education: "You: Shop your favorite designer fashion and beauty brands. We: Give twenty percent of the proceeds of anything you purchase directly to one of our partner children's charities."[96] This is an interesting model because Olivela's platform serves as a rally point for other brands in its industry, a significant enabler of impact.

Many large, entrenched companies have huge costs to consider, not to mention unwieldy bureaucracies. Our small business might be able to lead an initiative with these juggernauts as a credited partner. We take them along and bridge them into this brave new world. This is a really important expression of LEAD WITH WE. Australia-based social enterprise Thankyou reached out to consumers around the world in late 2020 to show the collective power of the WE by challenging consumer products behemoths Unilever and P&G to sell their products through its aptly named "No Small Plan" initiative, wherein the collaboration could help ameliorate extreme poverty. And Vita Coco, introduced earlier, took to Twitter to challenge larger companies with outsized pandemic profits (e.g., Nestlé Waters NA, Netflix, and Charmin) to follow its lead and help food-insecure kids. By challenging larger laggards, small companies can move mountains.[97]

On an even larger scale, several coalitions of companies have emerged over the past decade, all around collectivized purpose and shared cultural conversations. Some work industry-wide. Like Interface's materialsCAN, Tea 2030 is a global project focusing on a number of innovative platforms intended to deliver a sustainable global tea industry. The Sustainable Apparel Coalition (SAC), a pioneering industry collaboration that includes the Higg Co.'s index and the Apparel Impact Institute, has developed a suite of tools to standardize value chain sustainability measurement and accountability for all participants. Likewise, The Fashion Pact, a global coalition of clothing companies WITH their suppliers and distributors, is committed to a common core of three key environmental goals: stopping global warming, restoring biodiversity, and protecting the oceans.[98] Cotton 2040 is another multi-stakeholder collaboration designed to accelerate the mainstreaming of sustainable cotton, which anticipates major climate adaptation. Cultivated in more than eighty countries, including many of the world's neediest economies, cotton production supports the livelihoods of more than 350 million people. Yet, unless it's grown sustainably, cotton production often causes significant social, environmental, and economic impacts.[99] Fair Wear is a coalition of 131 clothing brands (e.g., Mammut, Tricorp, Sandqvist) established to improve garment workers' lives and the industry's reputation through political action and education on living wages, necessary changes on the factory floor, and worker empowerment. Fair Wear's Brand Performance Check metrics are an impact-benchmarking tool that works across members' entire supply chain.[100]

Also on the supply-chain front, global brands Mars, PepsiCo, and Unilever are among the founders of the six-hundred-member SourceUp, a collaborative online platform powered by the Sustainable Trade Initiative, with the goal of increasing environmental and social conditions in commodity-producing regions of Africa, Asia, and Latin America.[101] While blockchain-built cryptocurrencies face rising scrutiny over unconscionable fossil fuel energy use for currency mining and its environmental fallout (the reason behind Elon Musk's swift retraction of Bitcoin as a payment method for Tesla[102] and the newly formed, UN-backed Crypto Climate Accord), it also enables powerful transparency tools like BanQu software that enables distributors, processors, buyers, and recyclers to track and trace raw materials and goods from source to shelf to salvage.

Some coalitions work across industries to address specific global challenges. OneTen is a coalition of thirty-five leading employers from different domains (e.g., Lilly, Whirlpool, the Cleveland Clinic) to create a meaningful and measurable impact on racial and economic injustice (specifically, to upskill, hire, and advance one million Black Americans over the next ten years into "family-sustaining" jobs with opportunities for advancement).[103] The Ocean Plastic Leadership Network/ Ocean Cleanup Partnership/The Plastic Bank all drive accelerated and collaborative action to solve the ocean plastics crisis. The Fintech Equality Coalition, which includes Betterment, Credit Karma, SoFi, and others, focuses on redesigning a financial ecosystem that's more inclusive and equitable for Black employees, investors, and business leaders.[104] And the US Plastic Pact brings together businesses, government entities, NGO researchers, and myriad stakeholders committed to a common vision of a circular economy. Led by the Recycling Partnership and World Wildlife Fund and launched as part of the Ellen MacArthur Foundation's global Plastics Pact network, its signatories include Walmart, Target, the Coca-Cola Company, Colgate Palmolive, Kimberly-Clark, Molson Coors, and Mondelez, among others.[105]

Many NPF and NGO platforms are finding other ways to leverage corporate partners, and vice versa. Researchers discovered in 2018 that partnerships with NGOs for social investment, when executed well, can deliver up to a 6 percent increase in share price, a 20 percent surge in sales, a 13 percent increase in productivity, a 50 percent decline in employee turnover, "and a boost to reputation worth up to 11 percent of a company's market cap."[106] For example, the X Prize promotes radical innovation through corporate partnerships that have delivered significant impact—not to mention truly important ideas, like how to end hunger in our lifetimes. Not Impossible is an innovation platform leveraging corporate partners to solve seemingly impossible challenges, such as seeing the world through sound, writing with our eyes, restoring voice to those with amyotrophic lateral sclerosis, and providing prosthetic limbs to child victims of war. Parley for the Oceans is a large-scale plan led by corporate and government partners to increase awareness of the beauty and fragility of the oceans—and to collaborate on projects that prevent its further destruction.[107] And Carbon Vault, launched in 2020, uses public and corporate donations to buy and retire permits from the world's remaining carbon cap and trade markets.[108] It then allows investors and companies to pay for them, both preventing emissions now and reducing current carbon from the atmosphere—*LEAD WITH WE* at its best.

Such cross-sector collaborations are not new, of course, but they've certainly been on the rise since the 2010s. This is owing to the increasing severity and urgency of the crises we face, and, more pragmatically, because philanthropic and US federal government grants are more often requiring recipients to work across sectors to solve problems. It's even the explicit focus of one of the United Nations' (UN's) SDGs.[109] Plus it just makes sense.

These partnerships—and there are way too many to enumerate here—all presage the sort of collaborative leadership that I believe will become the first and best solvers of the world's worst problems. Its ultimate aim will be to LEAD vital cultural conversations WITH the collective—not just to turn a profit. It's not that the legacy business, economic, and social systems aren't working. They're working exactly as they were designed, built, and maintained to work—and thus imperiling us all. We need a new system. Better goals. Solutions enabled by and serving both business stakeholders and the planet. As Alex Edmans argues in *Grow the Pie*, repurposing capitalism in this way is not only possible, it can be done in a way that creates value for society and for the business and its investors that populate it, thereby expanding the total value created.[110]

Transcend Legacy Systems Through Regenerative Coalitions

Established in 2017, the Regenerative Organic Certified (ROC) label is a revolutionary new endorsement for food and personal care ingredients. ROC farms and products meet strict standards for soil health, animal welfare, and farmworker fairness. Corporate partners include Dr. Bronner's, Navitas Organics, and the carbon-offsetting PUR Project.[111]

With members spanning the Fortune 500 (Novo Nordisk), major cooperatives (Organic Valley), and startups and small businesses (Whole Health Marketing), ReGenFriends is a coalition of companies and organizations working in consumer packaged goods, finance, regulatory, tech, food, agriculture, fashion, logistics, renewables, and more. The idea is to work WITH each other to promote regenerative business practices. The goal is to "fundamentally shift global production and consumption to reverse climate change and create a thriving future for all."[112] One major initiative in this direction is its Billion Person Movement, which aims to gather through various activations one billion (#BillionPersonMovement) consumer mentions by Earth Day 2025.[113] To that end, ReGenFriends is looping in consumers and citizens to form the bulk of its constituency. The coalition's own Emerging Regenerative Consumer reports of 2019 and 2020 detail some thrilling findings, indicating, for example, vigorous support on the part of the average consumer for regenerative business practices. "Whether you're a B2B or B2C, the customer owns your company, so it's best to understand and delight them every day in every way."[114]

Along those same lines, Regeneration International consists of about 250 global partners—in concert *WITH* a wide body of consumer activists—all co-creating a growing number of "regeneration alliances" throughout the world. The group works *WITH* multiple stakeholders in key regions (e.g., South Africa, India, Mexico, Guatemala, Belize, Canada, and the US) who are committed to building alternative food and farming systems "for the purpose of restoring climate stability, ending world hunger and rebuilding deteriorated social, ecological and economic systems."[115]

The message here is that we can and will find the right partners to scale our purpose activations and our impact. None of us is alone.

Transform Society Through Cultural Conversations

Consider the symmetry and simplicity of Airbnb's *universal belonging*, Everlane's *radical transparency*, and Sweetgreen's *healthier communities*. These curated, mini-purpose statements differ from cultural conversations, which animate the brand's purpose in the real world. We structure cultural conversations around several pillars, or interconnected themes and rollouts of the overall purpose/story, which activate in myriad ways around key issues, such as the Farm Bill, National Park preservation, voting rights, or access to education. Each pillar must quickly and clearly establish guidelines and guardrails for where the brand can "play" with legitimacy, and how it can be understood and embraced by the community. This structure defines what to do and what not to do. Each pillar needs to include "Reasons to Believe"; that is, why the brand has a right to work in these areas, or its defense of and main proof(s) of purpose. And, finally, it includes some individual talking points, including more proofs for each pillar. Take for example, Sweetgreen of Culver City, California.

The company had five pillars, five interrelated "issues" it was tackling, all rooted in the company's overall "passion and purpose" (i.e., *To inspire healthier communities by connecting people to real food, To be a critical link between growers and consumers, To protect the future of real food*).[116] The pillars were Scratch Cooking, Transparency, Local Sourcing, Sustainability, and Animal Welfare. As an example, for Animal Welfare, its Reason to Believe—its proof—was its productive partnership with the American Society for the Prevention of Cruelty to Animals. The more detailed talking points included: "We believe the food journey begins with caring for ingredients and animals. That's why we put just as much care into how an animal is raised and treated as we do into the soil our kale sprouts from. We have a dedicated team who continuously seeks and researches the latest welfare standards."

Sweetgreen started in 2007 with one location in the upmarket Dupont Circle neighborhood of Washington, DC. It happened to be directly across the street from the city's most successful Starbucks location, and the company ingeniously positioned itself as "Starbucks for salad." From its cultural conversation around real food and healthful eating, the company has grown steadily by 2020 to more than one hundred locations in eight states, still maintaining "intimacy at scale." It did this by shifting the conversation around fast food, gradually convincing people that real, local, healthful food could be had in a fast-casual setting. It hasn't concerned itself with competition, because, as co-founder Nathaniel Ru told me for a *Forbes* interview, "All tides rise when people are getting healthier."[117]

Sweetgreen has integrated its purposeful social impact into every initiative it's undertaken. Purpose was never a side dish to its business model, but rather the main course—or at least the recipe's signature sweet sauce. Its journey goes beyond quality food products, bridging wholesome food and culture. For a time, the centerpiece of its public outreach was its annual Sweetlife music and cultural festival, which began as a backyard block party in its home city, but soon swelled to a major, pricey, two-day megastar-studded bacchanal. It's lately contracted back down—by Sweetgreen's conscious choice—to a series of free neighborhood shows around several of its locations. The company hopes to become an official sponsor of the Olympics someday soon. By contrast, the longstanding Olympic partnership with McDonald's mostly ended in 2018 after an onslaught of terrible press and criticism from public health advocates. The International Olympic Committee had been "undermining its own emphasis on health and athleticism by taking money from companies that sell junk food."[118] Imagine, says Ru, "instead of McDonald's, it's Sweetgreen . . . that's really going to change the conversation [to] make it more mainstream."[119]

From the beginning, Sweetgreen has favored creative, effective collaborations. It launched a significant partnership with the American NPF FoodCorps, whose mission is to work with communities to hook up school kids with healthy food. It turned its stores' general managers into "head coaches" to educate these local school kids through the FoodCorps program and beyond. It also collaborates in "win-win-win" partnerships with celebrity chefs, music influencers, sustainability experts, and, importantly, its own thirty-five hundred associates in developing its menu items and holding public conversations about issues such as the climate. In 2021, it announced that it would cut its carbon footprint in half over the next six years.[120]

Sweetgreen measures its impact not by sales growth but by increasing access to, and education about, real food. For example, it served hundreds of thousands of free meals during the pandemic and partnered with Chef José Andrés's World Central Kitchen, which works directly with restaurants to get meals to those who need them most while also uplifting an industry that needs help keeping its doors open. "COVID has taught us that we can change much faster. I think we all need to change on so many levels within our industries and beyond for climate, for bio-diversity, for all of these reasons," Ru says. His best counsel for those entrepreneurs and established businesses that wish to *Lead With We*? "[T]rust is earned in drops and lost in buckets. And if you can just start small and focus on the small things that are at the core of who you are and what your business you're building, the opportunities will find you."[121]

This is how Sweetgreen, started more or less in a B-school dorm room, fifteen years later sits squarely in unicorn territory with a $1.6 billion valuation.[122] How Bombas, in half that time, grew through its commitment to helping homeless people, making a more comfortable world through its charitable giving while growing to a $100 million company[123] and expanding into wholesale. How Nike's stock—even in the face of strong opposition to its support of Colin Kaepernick—grew 18 percent over the following fourteen months[124] through its activism, by uniting the world through sport. How startup Cooks Venture grew through industry disruption, by embracing regenerative agriculture, raising $26 million[125] in two years to shake up the poultry industry's coop. If we want to lead a cultural conversation like these and other *Lead With We* vanguards, we'll need to:

- **align** our purpose and the cultural conversation we seek to lead.
- **clarify** our unique point of view on the social change we hope to enable.
- **listen** intently to our community and beyond.
- **reconsider** everything—especially because, after 2020, all bets are off.
- **find** our role in the changes. How and where can we help?
- **partner** with like-minded organizations. Who can help? Or who can we help?

⟶ *act* short and long term. What needs to happen now, tomorrow, and later?

⟶ *ensure* our responses are sincere and purposeful. Is this merely performative?

⟶ *share* simple, consistent, scalable stories focused on our community, over time.

Regarding that last point, remember each campaign/initiative/collaboration should be a logical progression from the last, or at least a piece of the same puzzle. We activate the cultural conversation through bold, *integrated* campaigns. We can study the almost twenty-year sweep of Dove's Real Beauty messaging, with each piece acting as another strategically released chapter in a long-term story arc, and each milestone responsible for major upticks in sales. This owes largely to earned media, a huge part of the return on purpose and value of driving cultural change. Importantly, real change is found at the edges of issues, where the most advanced and potentially heated dialogue is. The media, the industry, and the public will pay particular attention around the fringes. There's little safety in the middle of the road. Little differentiation, authenticity, consistency. No motivation to join a movement.

Transform Cultural Engagement Through Strategic Activations

Through that systematic, gradual release of chapters in the business purpose and impact narrative, in upward phases, we launch our global change movement. Think of this as an integrated multiyear storytelling sequence:

1. **Announce.** We share our ambition and commitment. Educate on issues and strategies for solutions.
2. **Engage.** We formulate and strengthen emotional connection. Collaborate and co-create solutions.
3. **Inspire.** We identify new obstacles and broaden our scope. Amplify others' efforts and stories.
4. **Expand.** We unite others in action and encourage new partners to join in the mission. Build and adapt accordingly to new facts on the ground.
5. **Evolve.** We explore new approaches with partners and the community. Identify new ambitions while celebrating progress.

These phases are flexible, so adapt the order accordingly. If we investigate Patagonia's responsible-economy stewardship purpose, for example, we'll see such chapter activations released over time as cultural conversation leadership starters. Ads. Documentaries. Tours. Park openings. Funding. Partnerships. Political action. Various factors will contribute to the sequence of how we roll out each chapter of our business's ongoing purpose storytelling: availability of resources, regional specificity, cultural relevance, market maturity, and relative emergence of the issue(s) we're taking on. Ideas and sub-campaigns can flex over multiple sequences, or one idea per sequence.

Building on our discussion around the tone of our community-building in chapter six, "Community," the tenor of our cultural conversation—and the constituency, energy, and outcomes of the resultant movement—will depend on our self-selected roles. How do we see ourselves in this movement? We can range among the following roles:

- **_Activists_** (driving action). Activist businesses stand up and speak out, proactively pursuing change, acting as catalysts of transformative action, and prioritizing the endgame for substantive impact. They bring issues to people's attention, often sparking first actions, instigating change, and launching movements. Activism works, like Patagonia Action Works (PAW; see hereafter) confronting the misuse of public lands.

- **_Advocates_** (supporting action). Advocate brands are champions (sponsors, donors, suppliers, and organizers) of others. They listen carefully. To address social issues, brands must first _seek to understand_ so their role can _then_ be understood. They amplify and otherwise bolster existing movements, but usually stay one step back from the front lines. Advocacy works, like Ben & Jerry's Advancement Project tackling racism and criminal justice. Or Lyft offsetting the carbon footprints for all its rides,[126] and partnering with organizations like Goodwill, Dream Corps, and Year Up to get low-income individuals, the formerly incarcerated, and immigrants to job interviews and maintain their new employment.[127]

- **_Allies_** (elevating action). Allies are businesses that act as literal accomplices, helping in the trenches. Taking cues from the thought leaders in the thick of the fight—and sometimes supplying their own thought-leadership weapons in the field—they also help elevate relevant and related ideas through their storytelling. Allyship works, like Maybelline's ongoing "Brave Together" initiative, in partnership with Crisis Text Line, a texting-based hotline for seeking mental health interventions.[128] Or the industry-wide Ad Net Zero initiative launched by the Advertising Association, its members, and partners, which mobilizes collective action across the UK's advertising, client, production, and media companies to address the climate emergency caused by CO_2 emissions.[129]

We each get to choose how to proceed—but proceed we must. If our business is resource rich, like Starbucks, we likely can take on multiple issues at once—and probably have to in order to stay relevant in ever-changing markets. In Starbucks' case, all the issues coalesce in the overarching mission (i.e., *To inspire and nurture the human spirit—one person, one cup, one neighborhood at a time*), which becomes the unifying and organizing principle around all activations. That carefully curated and brand-appropriate mission has allowed Starbucks to address issues as wide-ranging as political donations, same-sex marriage, post-traumatic stress disorder, refugees, employee education, job creation, sustainability, and more. It's about the compounding of purpose, programs, and partnerships. We can scale that approach to the size of our business in order to meet the new normal, in which "genuinely 'purpose-led' brands stand to grow at twice the rate of those without any higher-order societal aim," according to Kantar Consulting's Purpose 2020 research.[130]

So, how can companies drive cultural conversations, including in times of crisis? They can do so in three ways. *Lead With We* brands can be:

1. **Proactive.** Paid media and traditional marketing opportunities set the foundational tone and articulate messaging in advance via a clear, decisive purpose. This continuous campaign of releasing storytelling chapters will take place on paid media channels, across the social media landscape, at point of sale and in-store marketing, and through other strategic communications and experiences. We can tell that brand, purpose, and impact story through the lens of ESGs, the SDGs, our B Corp or other credentialing organization status, or our efforts toward regeneration in all its forms. Better yet, let's do it through *Lead With We*. Great example: UPS's "committed to more" mantra and associated global activations.

2. **Responsive.** The business responds thoughtfully and proactively using neither traditional advertising nor marketing to events and concerns

uncovered in culture or society. It presses "issues" larger than the company itself, yet aligned with its values and established purpose. Storytelling activations position the brand with a perspective on real people's lives and their meaningful concerns. Here the business demonstrates more depth and range of relevance, more respect for people, and more responsibility for solving the world's problems. These activations often show POP and/or social impact. This can be achieved through new product/service developments, provocative partnerships, published opinions, advertorials, white papers, or lifestyle and pop-up events. Great examples of responses to ongoing cultural shifts: Airbnb's "Open Homes Program" for Syrian refugees or firefighters in Australia, among others. Or, since 2010, the company formerly known as DONG Energy ("Danish Oil and Natural Gas") has blazed trails. Facing rising opposition to harmful energy practices, the company successfully transformed itself into Ørsted, a renewables-led utility, with "offshore wind the flag-bearer for its new identity, but biomass conversions and acquisitions" also playing a part.[131] The formerly bedraggled old energy company reimagined and reengineered itself, boosting its net profits by $3 billion annually.[132]

3. **Reactive.** Brands reply in real time to emergent crises and flashpoints, usually handling them with more radical actions such as website takeovers, mission-aligned rapid funding, active advocacy platforms, CEO remarks/announcements, and strategic collaborations with like-minded partners. While foresight and planning are critical, here it's the speed of our response that is determinative, on several levels. First, by definition, the issue at hand demands an immediate response, given our values. Second, by doing so, our brand most effectively communicates and, ideally, doubles down on its stated purpose, mission, and commitments. Third, by doing so with alacrity, we give the brand the greatest chance of capturing the enormously valuable earned media that raises awareness and response to the issue, as well as the title of a brand leading the charge. As noted in chapter six, "Community," when President Trump announced in December 2017 his National Monument shrinking plans, Patagonia executed an unprecedented website repurposing within hours, declaring "The President Stole Your Land." Specific actions included leading the Utah Outdoor Retailer Show to choose a different location for its conference, removing about $50 million in revenue from the state. Then

Patagonia partnered with Google to launch a VR storytelling campaign to share a conversation with the public about the efforts to preserve the monuments. And, by joining lawsuits filed by a coalition of Native American and grassroots environmental groups, Patagonia thrust the issue onto the national stage, receiving nationwide coverage way ahead of other outdoor apparel brands, which scrambled to respond. It was praised for its leadership. As Patagonia's general counsel, Hilary Dessouky, explains, "It took exactly one email to the Board and the response was instant. 'Yes. Absolutely. Go for it.'" Within the short few weeks that followed, Patagonia launched its PAW platform to pair concerned individuals with grantee organizations working on environmental issues in the same communities. In a crisis, speed is always of the essence, and self-assuredness of purpose and leadership generate impact and scale that also benefit a business.[133]

Note that these three activation types interpenetrate and heavily overlap. And, obviously, the more self-assured we were in our earliest stages (the lower levels of our Virtuous Spiral)—establishing our purpose story, integrating it within our company culture, and mobilizing it with our brand community—the better positioned we are to capitalize now, so far up the Spiral, for example, on earned media, and respond appropriately and with haste to any potential cultural flashpoints.

Transform Investments & Returns

As we consider our partners, we must remember the investor set, without whose trust and financial support most businesses would be out of business. Investors complete the necessary coalition of stakeholders to drive substantive change that represents an authentic alternative to the persistent Me First mindset of traditional capitalism. This new generation of investors demands purpose *and* profit. They need to ensure that capital continues flowing into the industries of the future, and less—preferably none—into the interests and industries of yesterday. And as investors and shareholder activists exert influence over the markets with their views on marketplace opportunities in solving crises, more companies are incentivized and rewarded for their *LEAD WITH WE* activities, which create growth and bring competitive advantages. The whole system is shifting, from board oversight to capital markets. The problems the world faces are not a burden for business, but an enormous opportunity for innovation and impact. Especially when *WE* pool purpose and resources. This is where we are in the Virtuous Spiral.

A 2020 Harris/JUST Capital poll found that 89 percent of Americans agree that the COVID-19 crisis provided an opportunity for corporations to hit a "Great Reset" button, and to start focusing on doing right by workers, customers, and communities.[134] But that doesn't mean nearly 90 percent of the buying populace spends its money on purposeful brands, anywhere near 90 percent of the time. Turns out, investors are way ahead of consumers at large in terms of grasping and even demanding companies serve and operationalize a collective purpose. Today, nearly 80 percent of retail investors, for example, believe that companies making a positive difference in society are more profitable than their less purposeful, more self-centered competition, according to 2020 GlobeScan research.[135] And institutional investors are seeking a seat at the same table: 10 percent of all new funds are socially responsible,[136] and that ratio is likely rising.

Trace the money, says Sunny Vanderbeck, co-founder and managing partner of Satori Capital, and author of 2019's *Selling Without Selling Out: How to Sell Your Business Without Selling Your Soul*. While some corporate leadership might remain opposed to change, when the funding partners push for it, leadership listens. And it works the other way around, too. "The original source of capital behind most investment firms is a family, a foundation, an endowment, a pension or a similar entity," Vanderbeck says. "When those groups change their priorities, the investment firms will reflect those priorities." So by influencing the primary investors, we can catalyze this process by selling folks on social good.[137] This will often require rethinking investment timelines, Vanderbeck tells me. "If, as an investor, I only plan to be there for a year or two, I might not care about the environmental impact whatsoever. I'll be gone before it matters, right? But if my time horizon is indefinite, permanent, or even twenty years, all of these things become exceedingly important."[138]

Such longer-term investing in companies through a *LEAD WITH WE* lens has become more than the minimum entry requirement over the past few years to participate in the market. European investors are better at recognizing the financial value of future-forward companies; US short-termism on ESG investing will continue to stunt growth, according to the *Financial Times*.[139] In general, though, the tactic has been swaying substantial capital while simultaneously helping position savvy companies to rise above the noise as sound investments (both fiscally and socio-environmentally). In turn, such financing helps business entice further funding, ultimately bettering financial performance and transforming the overall markets. Timothy Nixon, managing editor for sustainability at Thomson Reuters, puts it this way:

> The managing director of banking at Barclays . . . is not alone in his views that investors increasingly see carbon risk specifically—and environmental, social and governance risk generally—as material to mainstream investing and asset management. This hidden hand is deploying huge pools of capital to reduce risk and promote economic growth in the long term. Retirement funds, college endowments, insurance companies, hedge funds and retail investors are all integrating sustainability or ESG risk into their approaches.[140]

This authentic sustainability precludes companies blathering about being left behind by a fast-moving megatrend.[141] And both the coronavirus pandemic and the 2020 protests over racial equality "have brought social factors to the fore, with investors and other stakeholders viewing sustainability more in terms of a company's ability to withstand the financial shocks from social upheaval as well as its ability to address some of these issues, both internally and externally," according to the *Wall Street Journal*.[142]

The purpose-focused, socially conscious young adults making up the largest percentage of the US population aren't the only ones aligning their money with their purposes. Prescient impact investors who risk their financial futures on these *Lead With We* trends comprise shareholder vanguards at long-resistant companies like ExxonMobil, where investors are locked in an epic battle with the company management over GGE targets;[143] at P&G, where investors are piling on the pressure to comply with stricter environmental standards;[144] and at DuPont, where 81 percent of investors have demanded the company address its plastic problem.[145] It's why Satya Nadella, CEO of Microsoft says we need a referendum on capitalism. "The measure of corporate success lies not in the surplus companies create in their own enterprise, but in the surplus they create around them."[146]

Again, that level of abundance relies on the cornerstone of thinking longer term, for both company roadmap planning and investor timeline horizons. "Capitalism is at a crossroads," says Sarah Keohane Williamson, CEO of FCLTGlobal. "The next few years will surely shape its trajectory for the next few decades. A narrow spotlight on shareholders has given way to a renewed focus on all stakeholders— employees, customers, suppliers, communities, and shareholders alike."[147] We're also seeing legacy financial institutions, unions, and philanthropic and political dynasties getting onboard with these longer-term actions and backings. For example, in 2015, the Rockefeller Brothers Fund—a fortune born and steeped in Big Oil—shockingly nixed all fossil fuels from its $850 million portfolio, yet beat its financial benchmarks anyway, thanks largely to the hammering the gas and oil sector suffered soon after (ExxonMobil, "long-term climate change deniers and obstructionists to the clean energy revolution,"[148] lost billions in value in 2020[149]). "We are able to show it can be done," fund president Stephen Heintz says, "without causing harm to the overall performance of your investment portfolio"[150]—not to mention causing less harm to the planet and its inhabitants. No surprise, either, that the term "impact investment" was coined at a meeting of the Rockefeller Foundation in 2007.[151] Rigorous inquiry indicates that *purpose promotes profit*, and at this level up the Spiral, such purpose must be supported by society, perhaps starting with financial abetting:

> Research from the Deutsche Bank and the University of Hamburg[152] reviewed over 2,000 empirical studies to assess the correlation between . . . ESG . . . metrics and Corporate Financial Performance (CFP) and found that in 90% of cases studied, ESG showed a non-negative relationship with CFP. Further, a recent Legg Mason survey found that over 43% of high net-worth individuals and 56% of millennials would like to invest more in ESG assets. Additionally, 82% and 88% of each group respectively would like to learn more about them.[153]

So, if we're looking to raise capital for our business, be it from individuals, venture capitalists, or institutions, we should endeavor to take full advantage of the storytelling potential of our purpose to entice investor interest by showcasing our brand's ability to scale profits and impact. Project ROI, a comprehensive research endeavor demonstrating the positive ROI of well-run sustainability programs, finds that for large, publicly traded companies, corporate responsibility can increase their market value about 5 percent, reduce systemic risk by 4 percent, and over a fifteen-year period, increase shareholder value by $1.28 billion.[154]

The aforementioned Ørsted transformation, from coal-fired power plants to a mostly "pure-play renewable energy" company (according to the Corporate Knights Global 100 Ranking for 2020) proves there's no trade-off between a sustainable business model and a lucrative business. The formula for this evolution was simple: Ørsted saw the harm it was contributing to, the shifting market forces, and the need to slow the rising environmental emergency. It decided to embrace a new role and narrative for its future. Powerful proof that such shifts are not only possible for legacy brands within largely harmful sectors, but provide a potentially dramatic financial upside, especially for first movers who set new standards. Since the company shifted its focus in 2016, its market value has quadrupled. Its return on capital is 300 to 400 basis points higher than the European average. And it's become one of the most successful stocks not only in Denmark, but in the entire European energy industry. Global Knights named it the world's most sustainable company for 2020.[155] Great story.

For more recent (albeit extraordinary) evidence of the benefits of LEAD WITH WE, consider that Pfizer and Moderna will generate about $32 billion[156] in COVID-19 vaccine revenue in 2021—Pfizer alone brought in $3.5 billion in the first three months of 2021—all while saving millions of humans from almost certain death.

And it's not just the LEAD WITH WE companies that benefit from this financing; investors also gain. Several new and emerging platforms provide ease and transparency around impact investing. Nearly 90 percent of the impact investors surveyed by the Global Investing Impact Network (GINN) in 2020 said they met or exceeded their financial expectations on their investments.[157] That partly explains the fact that impact investing was a $715 billion market in 2020—up from about $500 billion in 2019, according to the GINN.[158] This represents a $12 trillion opportunity[159] in unlocking responses to the SDGs and wider ESG needs (or one in four dollars of the $46.6 trillion in total assets under professional management in the US) and a dramatic 38 percent increase over 2016.[160]

At last reckoning, four in ten private equity investors collaborate with partners regarding the SDGs,[161] and that rate's likely to reach half by the end of 2021. The space is huge, with plenty of room to grow exponentially. There's blue ocean out there—even if the seas are sometimes stormy. This Spiral is both virtuous and valuable.

Transform Capital Markets

While "change agent" stakeholders self-select to reengineer and evolve business to innovate meaningful change and scale their companies' impact, they are not enough. We also need regulations to keep pace with compounding needs.

Politicians and investors most of all must get on board, incentivizing and reward-ing *LEAD WITH WE* practices. "The right data . . . drive[s] decisions to deploy capital in support of sustainability," according to a 2019 World Economic Forum (WEF) report on unlocking capital markets to support the SDGs. The outstanding value of the global bond markets is estimated to exceed $100 trillion, and the global equity market capitalization, $85 trillion.[162] That's a helluva lot of horsepower to fuel the *LEAD WITH WE* engine.

Again quoting Larry Fink's letter to CEOs in January 2020, in discussing BlackRock's allocation of more than $10 billion[163] of those dollars: "Climate change has become a defining factor in companies' long-term prospects . . . But awareness is rapidly changing, and I believe we are on the edge of a fundamental reshaping of finance."[164] By this year, we had, indeed, begun that great reshaping. Later, in 2021, Fink wrote:

> [T]he pandemic has presented such an existential crisis—such a stark reminder of our fragility—that it has driven us to confront the global threat of climate change more forcefully and to consider how, like the pandemic, it will alter our lives. It has reminded us how the biggest cri-ses, whether medical or environmental, demand a global and ambitious response.[165]

Concurring with other capital experts, Fink continued, "From Europe to Austra-lia, South America to China, Florida to Oregon, investors are asking how they should modify their portfolios,"[166] because investments that are unsustainable over the long haul are simply no good.

BlackRock, of course, faces its own credibility challenges, still holding some $85 billion in coal investments as of this writing.[167] Nevertheless, Fink's warning bell is "both a recognition that capital markets are changing to address the climate crisis and a clarion call to companies, other investors and policymakers every-where," writes Mindy Lubber, CEO and president of Ceres, a nonprofit sustain-ability organization, in *Forbes*. "Every capital market actor has a fiduciary duty to scale action on the greatest challenge of our time."[168]

Bart Houlahan, along with his partners, Jay Coen Gilbert and Andrew Kassoy, co-founded B Lab—the NPF organization focused on leveraging the talent, resources, and impact of business to resolve social and environmental challenges—in 2006. The consortium propels systemic transformation via three interrelated initiatives:

1. ***Global Impact Investing Ratings & Analytics.*** A rigorous, comprehensive, and comparable rating platform that drives capital to impact investments by assessing the social and environmental performance of companies and funds—including how companies treat their employees.

2. ***Benefit (B) Corporations.*** A relatively new, legally recognized corporate form that shifts the idea of fiduciary duty, permitting companies to create shareholder value *and* simultaneous social value.[169] The benefit corporation is a legal structure for a business, analogous to an LLC—but fundamentally different. Until recently, the global ecosystem of B Corps primarily comprised small and midsize companies like Lemonade Insurance (offering values-based, real-time insurance), Revolution Foods (providing healthy school meals), and Sundial (a Unilever health and wellness brand). The B Movement Builders Program is now enlisting the might and reach of publicly traded companies with at least $1 billion in revenue, including Natura & Co, Gerdau across Latin America, and the French food giants Danone and Bonduelle,[170] the former of which is leading the global charge as author of an influential brand strategy manifesto, its triple-regenerative "One Planet. One Health" initiative.[171] In 2020 Danone announced its commitment to become a global B Corp by 2025.[172] Athleta (part of Gap) transformed and is now leading with its B Corp status. Amalgamated Bank, an old familiar face in the industry, is now also a transformed B Corp. These companies are working *WITH* their own subsidiaries, *WITH* each other, and *WITH* the coalition of B Movement Builders companies.

3. ***Certified B Corporations.*** Subtle but meaningful distinction here: This is a third-party certification based in part on a company's verified performance on the B Lab's B Impact Assessment. Some companies are both Certified B Corporations and benefit corporations, sustainable businesses or social enterprises that meet higher standards of social and environmental performance and legal accountability.

At the 2019 B Corp Champions Retreat in Hollywood, Houlahan spoke about how companies and campaigners can get the capital markets to evolve more rapidly, more precipitously, to keep pace with the need occasioned by a world in multidimensional collapse. We can vote recalcitrant politicians out of office. We can all change how we go about running a business from the ground up, from inside out. But the vitality of business still depends largely on the lifeblood of capital, infused into various business arteries mostly by large capital investment firms and individuals. Investors' motivations, despite recent swings toward the impact investment we've explored, are still often less than lofty. And such thinking can be institutionalized. We can talk good optics and exalted rhetoric all day, but how are we really going to get these markets to fundamentally bend toward a *LEAD WITH WE* agenda?

Houlahan was followed onstage by former Massachusetts governor Deval Patrick, who was running a new impact-investment arm delivering "outsized returns" at Bain Capital, before he stepped away to run for US president. Patrick reminded us that large private equity firms of institutional investors tend to focus on the alpha level of their portfolio (i.e., to what degree it's outpacing the market), where they're financing all kinds of companies in multiple sectors. And they're finally feeling the pain of externalities in their own portfolios—the confluence of crises we've been discussing in this book. They can no longer enjoy their profits on one hand, or in certain sectors of their portfolio, when it comes at a cost to other sectors, or the beta side of their portfolio, owing to the world at large falling apart.

So, we're finally at a point where the capital markets are waking up. The issues that we're dealing with are sufficiently acute. And they exert real, negative consequences on companies in the intermediate and long terms. We just need to be practical and get to work. As we've seen with Fink and the BRT CEOs, other forces have begun to coalesce in the form of new regulations and increased consumer demand to incentivize, enable, and reward capital markets to invest in *LEAD WITH WE* ways, gradually shifting their focus toward portfolios that better serve the collective.

The future is now. Global sustainable investments rose 34 percent from 2016 to 2019, to $30.7 trillion, bolstered by Japanese pension funds, global retail investors, and widespread worry over the climate crisis, according to the biennial report from the Global Sustainable Investment Alliance, a sustainable investment group aggregator.[173] Europe tops the list for sustainable investment regions, with approximately $14 trillion tied up in *LEAD WITH WE* companies, up 11 percent from 2016.[174] Japan's been the fastest-growing region in sustainable investing over the past few years. The trend hit 63 percent of all professionally managed assets in Australia and New Zealand by 2018, the highest share of any region in the world. In Canada, it was 50 percent.[175] This trend continued upward, according to the Forum for Sustainable and Responsible Investment, which reported US sustainable investing assets topping $17 trillion in 2020, 42 percent higher than 2018. "A tidal wave of growth is poised to follow in the retail sector," a Morgan Stanley survey predicts.[176]

So far, it's mostly large pension fund managers who have shifted their focus in line with new investor, consumer, and employer expectations and demands, especially owing to the exponential commercialization of ESG-focused companies. These managers are abandoning in droves climate/carbon risk—particularly after COVID-19—for more sustainable (ESG-friendly) investments, as such conscious, LEAD WITH WE funds differentiate them from lagging competitors. Who wants stranded assets on their books? For example, the Government Pension Fund of Norway, known, unfortunately, as the "Oil Fund," has demanded its portfolio companies share detailed plans to shift to a low-carbon economy.[177]

CNBC reports that more than 2,250 money managers, who oversee a collective $80 trillion in assets and a majority of the world's professionally managed investments, had by the start of 2019 become signatories to the six "voluntary and aspirational" UN-backed Principles for Responsible Investment—strategies that take a company's ESG factors into consideration.[178] They are all about ownership, responsibility, collaboration, and transparency/disclosure.

Now, a key concession I have to make here is that some recent, controversial research suggests that the "ESG outperformance narrative is flawed," as the *Financial Times* summarizes. The flaw is largely because of analytical vagaries arising from trying to measure nonfinancial factors empirically and to interpret them as financial information—even if we can all find a way to agree on the metrics themselves. So, critics argue, the sector only appears "alpha" versus the market because the terms, such as "profitability," and the factors rated are both vague.[179] Without a doubt, ESG reporting can and must evolve (a process well underway and accelerating). Our ability to leverage and scale the accountability that such reporting provides turns on the universal adoption of stricter and more consistent metrics. That will help prevent the likely greenwashing of many funds, rebranded by opportunistic marketeers with an ESG halo (and often charging much higher fees than regular index funds, according to Morningstar[180]). All stakeholders must remain vigilant about mere virtue signaling from some ESG talk, as our collective future is at stake.

LEAD WITH WE investing should never promote or support hollow claims of environmental concern. Thoroughly research and vet all potential investments in the ESG space as you would any other—don't simply rely on someone's having put them on a list of "responsible investments."

But does some economic misreporting and the likely presence of some greenwashed ESG funds somehow diminish business's need—its responsibility—to act and act now? Do those likelihoods mean we're not moving in the right direction overall? *Lead With We* pressure from activist investors is working: On May 26, 2021, small activist fund Engine No.1, after recruiting larger investors, won its proxy war against ExxonMobil's board for its recalcitrance on transitioning to lower-carbon energy.[181] Such activist investors, along with the 2021 advent of Gary Gensler as chair of the US Securities and Exchange Commission, JUST Capital reports, "will be critical in driving (and enforcing) disclosure standards on climate risk and emissions, as well as holding companies to account on ESG more broadly."[182]

So, *Lead With We* investors should continue to seek out impact-targeting vehicles that solve major challenges while making money. Like FullCycle, which invests in growth-stage companies with developed climate-critical infrastructure technology. Or the holding company structure of ix Investments, which offers its investors the opportunity to create long-term economic growth and sustained social and environmental impact in areas such as housing, green real estate, and gender equality. Impact-focused funds are indeed becoming increasingly ubiquitous. Founded in 2004, London-based Generation Investment Management (GIM) has $26 billion[183] in sustainable assets under management (AUM). Launched in 2016 with partners such as The Rise Fund, the $5 billion[184] standard-bearer impact fund from U2's Bono and disruptive investment firm TPG ($85 billion),[185] GIM develops growth-stage, purpose-driven *Lead With We* companies. Bain Capital's Double Impact fund partners with companies that offer products, services, or business models that can create positive social impact at scale.[186] The fund recently raised $800 million in fresh capital to back impact-oriented businesses, even as the pandemic dramatically slowed fundraising across the board.[187]

For an up-to-date list where new and experienced investors can access *Lead With We*–type entrepreneurs, fund managers, and nonprofits best positioned to deliver on a range of financial opportunities that also serve ESGs, try ImpactAssets. org. If we want to review our personal or business bank's ethical track record—including the activities it finances worldwide—we can visit the lobbying organization BankTrack. For example, ethical bank Triodos, which enjoys the support of Friends of the Earth, funds projects only when they "create positive cultural, social and environmental outcomes."[188]

If we're not already sold on the *Lead With We* investment imperative, we can consider recent research by the San Diego–based Torrey Project, a global catalyst for multi-stakeholder balanced businesses. Its twenty-year study reveals that so-called ethical companies enjoy a 50 percent higher level of stock price growth over the S&P 500—but that stakeholder-focused (read: *LEAD WITH WE*) companies see *100 percent higher growth* over the same period.[189]

Transform Standard Practices with Increased ESG Credibility

Between 2018 and 2020, the US AUM employing ESG strategies increased by nearly 50 percent.[190] Here are five practical steps[191] we can follow to leverage our *LEAD WITH WE* purpose into becoming part of that trend, incentivizing smart, progressive investors to work *WITH* us on activating our shared purpose, ultimately advancing financial performance for all parties:

➠ ***Understand ESG ratings.*** Because ESGs are so tied to corporate purpose, and purpose is at the core of the *LEAD WITH WE* journey, some facet of the ESG spectrum will likely be a foundational aspect of a company's core being, criticisms of them notwithstanding. The WEF informs us that nearly nine of ten business executives in 2021 believe that detailed ESG reporting benefits individual companies and industries.[192] Yet there remains a dizzying variance in interpretations of ESG metrics; they are by nature vaguer than, say, the UN's SDGs, albeit implementation of those standards can be just as bureaucratic and complex.[193] So, yes, we need universally understood and adopted standards. We need consolidation and alignment across the various ESG frameworks to make validation and verification easier and clearer. Multiple organizations have crafted viable, sensible, trackable metrics, indices, and inventories of the highest-rated companies that *LEAD WITH WE*. We can study them for ideas about how to interpret and apply them practically at home. Generally, these rating systems assess key performance indicators ranging from employee diversity to corporate scandals and transparency, from energy footprint to healthful interactions in communities.

Let's pick a system that works for us and our industry, business, purpose, goals, and resources. We can employ Sustainalytics; Bloomberg ESG Data; the Global Reporting Initiative (GRI); or CDP Worldwide, the charity that runs a global disclosure system for investors, companies, cities, states, and regions to manage their environmental impacts. The merger, underway now, of the Sustainability Accounting Standards Board (SASB) and the International Integrated Reporting Council (IIRC), will provide a comprehensive corporate reporting framework to drive global sustainability performance.[194] CSRHub offers consensus ESG ratings to benchmark performance, analyze supply chains, improve reporting, and build portfolios.[195] On the investing side, the Morningstar Sustainability Rating for funds allows investors to understand how the companies in their portfolios manage ESG risks *relative to their peers.*[196] Directly from the source, the WEF itself unveiled a set of universal ESG measures and disclosures in 2020. Its "Stakeholder Capitalism Metrics," including ESG indicators and disclosures for financial markets, investors, and society are designed to make benchmarking sustainable business performance easier.[197] San Francisco–based Truvalue Labs provides a suite of AI-driven ESG data analytics that capture both positive and negative company ESG performance, uncovering both risks and opportunities.[198] GINN's IRIS+ is another generally accepted system for measuring, managing, optimizing, and comparing/contrasting impact across various interpretations of sustainability.[199] It uses a super-extensive set of metrics in many ESG categories, from the extent to which a company's operations stunt child growth, to the number of microenterprises that serve as distributors; from how many female employees get promoted, to its various GGEs.

Finally, a quiet but critical revolution is unfolding that might finally unify ESG standards for companies, investors, and governments. The foundation serving the group that oversees the work of the International Accounting Standards Board in establishing financial reporting requirements for many of the world's jurisdictions (and thus most companies) proposed in 2020 the creation of a Sustainability Standards Board. In the US, it would operate parallel to the Financial Accounting Standards Board it already oversees.[200] Such a new board has the support of the likes of Paul Polman and Oxford University's Saïd Business School. In September 2020, five of the leading standard-setters for voluntary ESG reporting (GRI, the Climate Disclosure Standards Board, SASB, IIRC, and CDP) struck a deal to create a comprehensive corporate reporting system.[201]

➠ ***Improve our ESG ratings.*** Once accustomed to our preferred ESG rating system(s), we triage and thread best practices through our operations—supply chain, product sourcing, employee contentment, energy consumption, diversity, and so forth. The GRI's Sustainability Reporting Guidelines are an excellent place to start, though there remains as of this writing no easy way to measure the "networking effect" in supply chains: If we better our materiality, our trucking, our manufacturing, and more, how do we calculate the compounding effect of addressing all those areas at once?

➠ ***Get ourselves rated.*** First, we focus on the advantages we're providing to the Higher *WE* in and of themselves—not on any good PR that might come our way as an ancillary benefit to us. This is not a marketing trick. Nor is ESG investing, as Sony Kapoor, managing director of the think tank Nordic Institute for Finance, Technology and Sustainability, a mere "ruse to launder reputations, maximise fees and assuage guilt."[202] We do this because it's the right thing to do, and thousands of companies—as well as the world at large—benefit. So, when we're well along the process of applying and assessing our *LEAD WITH WE* purpose activations, it's okay to seek credibility and distinguish ourselves from the competition mired in the status quo—as long as that's not the only reason why we're on this journey. We can contact one of the rating agencies to evaluate our business. Then we can transparently release our ESG data, along with financial statements to back it up, to our potential partners and the public—even when there's marked room for improvement.

➠ ***Expand our compass of impact.*** Once we've optimized our ESG ratings, we can partner with financial professionals whose specialty is studying risk/reward ratios, then matching capital investment opportunities with socially/environmentally conscious investors. Calvert Research Management of Bethesda, Maryland, and the strategic alliance between the American Sustainable Business Council and the Social Venture Circle are good examples. Such "shareholder activists" are a key component in the virtue-value spiral, both by supporting the company and demanding that boards commit to longer-term outlooks, thus expanding impact.

And while we're at it, let's innovate! Set sail for those blue oceans of unmet need. What new letter can we add to ESG? D for Data Stewardship? Perhaps our business is ready, willing, and able at this point to tackle one of the SDGs. Among the premier SDG interpretation and selection tools are SDG Compass, SDG Industry Matrix, SDG Selector, Business for 2030, and Future-Fit Goals. SDG goals most frequently addressed by the private sector are Climate Action, Clean Water and Sanitation, and Decent Work and Economic Growth. A huge opportunity for progressive *LEAD WITH WE* companies, the goals *least* frequently tackled are No Poverty; Peace, Justice, and Strong Institutions; and Reduced Inequality.

➡ ***Share our success.*** Tell this story widely and consistently—even the "chapters" where we currently stumble. Process improvements and complementary storytelling of our acting on purpose—and its real-world impact—are staples of today's corporate websites, big and small. Also, we should aim to expand our network—the Breadth of Our *WITH*—and to trigger investors' interest in our brand by spending resources on collaborating with like-minded *LEAD WITH WE* advocates. The SRI Conference, the *Economist*'s Impact Investing Conference, Sustainable Brands (SB), Greenbiz, and the USSIF Annual Conference are just a few of the ever-expanding opportunities to interact with socially responsible investors and assemble coalitions.

In addition to broad ESG metrics, the specific SDGs, standard CSR, and B Corp guiding principles, a number of emerging entities[203] also provide guidelines for the evolving social, financial, environmental, and geopolitical imperatives affecting the business world. These can aid us in transforming attitudes, identifying impact areas, acting on initiatives, tracking metrics, and reporting progress for *LEAD WITH WE* companies, large and small. We can follow any or some combination of these metric sets and benchmarks:

- The International Business Council[204]
- The Toxicity Characteristic Leaching Procedure process for waste management and reporting[205]
- The Human Rights Reporting and Assurance Framework Initiative[206]
- The Corporate Reporting Dialog[207]
- The Impact Management Project[208]
- The Task Force on Climate-Related Financial Disclosure[209]

But it's not just about the clear communication of purpose to manage one's reputation—most of all, it's about sharing *impact*. Over the past thirty-five years or so, investors have increasingly demanded such impact data points, such as compliance with the SDGs.[210] The great news here is that once we've set ambitious but attainable goals, in line with the appropriate emerging "regulatory" or benchmarking body like one of those above, it's progress that matters most. We also get the benefit of the support, best practices, and other expertise of those in-built communities. Innumerable companies annually report on their headway even before they hit their goals. A transparent process of confronting, analyzing, and communicating meaningful improvements works to fortify the 75 percent of our business's value that, according to *Fortune's* famous survey,[211] hovers in the realm of the immaterial. That includes goodwill, reputation, innovation, and potential. It's a number that by 2019 was estimated at an incredible 84 percent of the value of the S&P 500.[212] This would mean that our goal-setting and metrics calculation, revenue, and other tangible effects (real estate, inventory, cash, etc.) must be viewed alongside adequately incorporated intangibles. What's the real value of our brand in consumers' hearts and minds? Not to mention our value based on real impact on the world, which can be difficult to quantify in the same way you could measure sales.

"As more companies and state actors disclose their GGEs, for example, global policy-makers and regulators act in the form of climate treaties and carbon taxation or markets," according to Nixon at Thomson Reuters. "Contrary to a more cynical view, there are real and biting regulatory actions that can and do affect the behavior of the great powers in global commerce."[213]

Increasingly, organizations such as Transparency International[214] have emerged that collect, analyze, and curate ESG data—and republish it with benchmarking for consumers and investors. GRI is the international independent standards organization that more than three-quarters of all businesses that report on ESGs use to understand and communicate their impacts on *LEAD WITH WE* metrics such as human rights, corruption, and environmental impact. The NPF known as the Sustainability Consortium, with more than one hundred members such as Amazon, Mars, and Wrangler, extends through supply chains to thousands of other companies; provides various tools, trainings, trackers; and reports to subscribers. A key component, its Sustainability Index, works with partner organizations on THESIS (The Sustainability Insight System), which focuses on product-related interactions between suppliers and retailers.[215] The era of radical transparency is upon us. Let's get some help with it and get in gear. Then get ready to use it as a growth driver, intertwined with our purpose, culture, and community architecture.

The fashion industry, traditionally opaque, elitist, and secretive,[216] is now staying considerably ahead of the transparency curve, partly because of its excellent ESG improvements. One example is the NPF known as Fashion Revolution, which in 2017 launched its Fashion Transparency Index, a benchmark tracking the extent to which brands like Target and G-Star Raw divulge their "social and environmental policies, practices and impacts." It looks at metrics such as adherence to the Bangladesh Safety Accord, "a breakthrough in holding garment companies to account for the working conditions in their supply chains, and covers around sixty major international brands using 1,200 Bangladeshi factories."[217] Along similar lines, starting in 2015, the entire fashion industry began addressing its use of forced labor, which nonprofits and journalistic reporting had revealed at brands previously considered leaders in environmental and worker best practices. This despite the best efforts to avoid such abuses through a combination of in-house audits by brands like Patagonia; third-party oversight (like Fair Trade USA); and industry-wide fair labor tracking by the SAC, including all tiers and far-flung stations in everyone's supply chains.[218] Since that scandal broke, Patagonia's remediation efforts, in particular, provide a model *LEAD WITH WE* response.[219] Issues arise in the very best of companies and it's important to remember that in an increasingly global economy, *WE* might mean people far away, pursuing lives we might find unrecognizable from our siloed perspective.

Transform our Goals

An estimated 54 million Americans struggled with hunger in the winter of 2020, according to the US Department of Agriculture. Shoplifting of baby formula, bread, and pasta was up sharply during the height of the pandemic.[220] Does it make sense for us to carry on with business as usual while parents next door can't feed their children? In 2020's *Moral Capitalism: Why Fairness Won't Make Us Poor,*

Washington Post business writer Steven Pearlstein argues that we can create a more equitable and sustainable financial framework: "An economic system that regularly ignores" people's "moral sentiments such as compassion, generosity, and sense of fair play . . . forfeits its moral legitimacy. And, in time, it will forfeit its prosperity as well."[221] Like LEAD WITH WE, moral capitalism is interested in restoring income equality, reversing erosion of institutional trust, and reestablishing true competition in the face of monopolies and duopolies, among other ambitions that might appear lofty, but are entirely realistic to expect as outcomes of this revolution.

Yes, we'll each LEAD WITH WE through our own, unique expressions. But a few major and interrelated shifts are critical to move us all rapidly forward in a healthy and prosperous way. Businesses that address one or more of these problems most effectively in the near term will be well positioned for the future. This list is highly compressed, of course, and subjective, but it points at pressing, fundamental shifts WE must continue to LEAD:

1. ***Clean and Renewable Energy.*** A comprehensive clean energy transition is necessary as the cornerstone of climate action, the number one priority for any business intending to maintain relevance and prosper over the long run. Not only because the concurrent transitions into AI and electric vehicles will require so much energy (not to mention the environmental liability of lithium[222]), but because insurance, home, and product prices have already been rising; the wealth gap is widening; food has become more scarce, more expensive, and less nutritious; and climate refugees are on the move in droves.[223] In short, the climate emergency is affecting both business and consumers in a negative feedback loop. Carbon sequestration, a pervasive headline in the world press, is the first order of business, and non-negotiable if we are to address the coming environmental apocalypse. We've touched on companies working on this, but whole regions are doing it, too: Barcelona, for example, is introducing "green zones."[224]

   Of course, NPFs are also propelling such shifts. Of note, Paul Hawken's Project Drawdown, founded in 2014, collaborates on a program to help the world reach "Drawdown"—the future point (it proposes within a generation) when levels of greenhouse gases in Earth's atmosphere peak, then start to steadily drop. But we will need more effective policies, incentives, and collaborations to achieve this, rather than relying on voluntary altruism. The US rejoining the Paris Accord is an important step in the right direction. And when Jeff Bezos, the richest man in the world as of this writing, begins spending the better part of a billion dollars[225] on climate action, that's also a sign of good things to come.

Consumers can speed these changes simply via their purchases and advocacy. For instance, there's the global generosity movement of #GivingTuesday.[226] Climate Neutral, an independent NFP, certifies *LEAD WITH WE*–like companies. Qantas, and Etihad airlines, and British Airways owner IAG, are all aiming to reach net-zero emissions by 2050—and Delta pledged $1 billion to become the world's first carbon-neutral airline by 2030.[227] United Airlines's Eco-Skies Alliance is a first-of-its-kind program involving leading global corporations such as Switzerland's CEVA Logistics and Denmark's BSG. Employees of the latter who fly with the airline can optionally reduce their environmental impact by paying a premium for more sustainable aviation fuel.[228]

Of late, we're even witnessing old-school oil and gas companies shifting to renewables. Struggling oil refineries in particular are increasingly turning away from fossil fuels and toward renewable-diesel production, according to the *New York Times*; biodiesel is known to reduce GGEs.[229]

This follows many large companies' shift to green energy for their fleets, such as FedEx, Frito-Lay, A. Duie Pyle, UPS, and Waste Management.[230] Safeway, the US's third-largest grocery chain, converted to biodiesel as early as 2008.[231] In the past few years, we've seen impactful (billion-plus dollar) commitments from Amazon ($2 billion climate pledge fund that unites signatories such as Norway, Britain, Colombia's Daabon, the Netherlands's Vanderlande, and Spain's Acciona to be Net Zero Carbon by 2040, ten years ahead of the Paris Climate Agreement);[232] Kellogg, GM, and PepsiCo (curbing the devastating effects of climate emergency on food supply,[233] the latter massively scaling regenerative farming by 2030[234]); Mars (Sustainable in a Generation and Palm Positive plans);[235] Johnson & Johnson (Healthy Lives Mission);[236] Microsoft and Apple (net zero by 2030);[237] BlackRock, Etsy, Ford Motor Company, PayPal, Visa, and Vanguard (net zero; Ford alone is investing more than $29 billion in electric and autonomous vehicles through 2025[238] in service of its goal of net zero by 2050[239]); Starbucks (resource-positive future);[240] Mastercard (Priceless Planet Coalition);[241] Unilever ($1 billion for nature and environment fund);[242] M&S (science-based

Plan A commitments);[243] JPMorgan Chase (Paris-aligned finance commitment);[244] Google (massive carbon offset program);[245] AT&T (carbonneutral future);[246] The Goodyear Tire & Rubber Company (replacing all petroleum-based products with soybean oil by 2040[247]); and many more. And because "investors, companies, and governments need to be able to predict the way climate-related changes will interact and affect economies, industries, companies, and assets," the Open Source Climate initiative has brought together companies like France's BNP Paribas and Germany's Allianz Investment Management around a new predictive AI platform.[248] Of note, several companies now committed to LEAD WITH WE on the climate emergency have faced challenges and past accusations about pollution and various other hypocrisies.[249] They have responded by turning those potential business-killers into marketplace and innovation opportunities that deliver relevance, resonance, and reach.

Simultaneously, we see two frameworks aligning for institutional investors to move their portfolios to net zero by 2050 in pursuit of meeting Paris Agreement goals. Launched in early 2019, Natixis's Net Zero Asset Owners Alliance gathers a set of climate-conscious international institutional investors. The Institutional Investors Group on Climate Change is another European-membership body for investor collaboration on ameliorating the climate emergency. With more than 270 members (mainly pension funds and asset managers), it has more than €35 trillion[250] in AUM. Each of these frameworks for large pensions and huge investors allows managers and clients to direct their money into portfolios including mutual funds, bonds, and public equities that aim for lower carbon emissions. The UN's Intergovernmental Panel on Climate Change continues to assess the science related to the climate crisis and inform policymakers and business leaders on current and upcoming risk—as well as science-backed solutions for mitigation. And now, in addition to green bonds and sustainable bonds, there is the Transition Bond, which is the latest financial vehicle for the banking world to incentivize carbon reduction.[251] John Kerry, President Biden's climate envoy, spoke of the proliferation of corporate climate emergency pledges: "US banks have committed $4.15 trillion to finance low carbon projects by 2030, while US asset managers have made more than $19 trillion in commitments."[252]

2. ***Circular, Regenerative, Net-Positive Systems.*** Large companies, such as Nestlé and its "Net Zero Roadmap" for a carbon-free future,[253] are making regenerative agriculture commitments and major efforts to shift consumer buying habits. Walmart, the world's largest retailer, launched its Project Gigaton, which aims to reduce a billion metric tons of GGEs from the global value chain by 2030.[254] Walmart is partnering with suppliers like Procter & Gamble (which has pledged to cut 50 million metric tons of GGEs from its operations and value chain by 2030).[255] Meanwhile, Madewell wants to buy your old clothes to prolong the lives of garments.[256] Levi's, too, will pay you as much as $25 for your old jeans, because they can clean them, then resell them in a new online store called Levi's SecondHand.[257]

Let's remember that investing in initiatives such as regenerative agriculture (soil management, crop rotation, cover crops, etc.) provides its own rewards, both for the Earth and its inhabitants, as well as our balance sheets. Shell's investment of $300 million in natural ecosystems[258] and GM's plan to regenerate one million acres of farmland[259] are just two examples of a worldwide shift led by business. If enacted globally, they "could theoretically suck a trillion tons of CO_2 from the atmosphere, or as much as humans have emitted since the Industrial Revolution," says *Fast Company*.[260]

But this is not only the province of megacorps. Small but growing companies can participate, too. There's indoor urban farming company Square Roots, one of several scalable "farm tech" startups that connect people in big cities to local, fresh produce, so that retail grocers can act as their own supply chain in the regenerative agriculture space. Iron Ox—"Grown By Robots With Love"—of San Carlos, California, is also reinventing the growing process, by using a human-led, robotics-first process from seed to harvest. It requires less energy and water, increases crop yield, and expands access to high-quality, consistent produce for everyone.[261] Plenty, another "ag tech" startup based in the US Pacific Northwest, proves that AI and robots on an indoor vertical farm can achieve four hundred times more yield than standard ground farming using 95 percent less water and 99 percent less space. After all, "they're not making any more land," says Nate Storey, Plenty's co-founder and chief science officer.[262]

Or consider fifty-year-old Earth-friendly winegrower, Fetzer Vineyards of California, which calls its purpose activation journey a "Road to Regeneration . . . We are committed to putting more back into the world than we are taking out," with the goal of net zero by 2030. The long goal, almost since the company's founding in 1968, is "net-positive wine." And each year it reports on the key milestones it's made along that road, every step forward closer to zeroing out its footprint. Fetzer continues to improve its B Corp certification score since 2016, by reducing its "water intensity per gallon" of wine produced and "continuing a trajectory of improvement" in waste diversion.[263] It has become the first US winery certified "CarbonNeutral" by Natural Capital Partners, a third-party framework that has offered the protocol and endorsement since 2002.[264]

Circular Leap Asia (CLA) assists major upstream fashion brands in making and delivering on commitments to advance circular solutions in their industry. Supported by Laudes Foundation as part of the Bridging the Gap initiative of the Forum for the Future, CLA guides brands in its small but growing coalition to identify circular fashion challenges that each is best resourced to lead.[265]

Instead of waiting for some miraculous, high-tech solution to bail us out of our climate-change disaster," says Patagonia's Yvon Chouinard, "the real miracle turns out to be simply working with nature instead of against it."[266] Multiple global movements are underway to reengineer business this way, from Conscious Capitalism to SB's "Brands for Good," a roadmap for how brands make sustainable living the good life of tomorrow. Imperative 21 is a dynamic business-led coalition driving a reset from shareholder primacy to stakeholder capitalism, fostering cross-sector collaboration to shift the cultural narrative about the role of business in society. The outcomes-based Carbon Underground, launched in 2013, operates with two core goals: "to coalesce the emerging science on soil's relationship to climate change and tell the world about a possibility to not simply slow down this threat, but reverse it." It creates tools, alliances, and opportunities to achieve scale at efforts proven to draw down carbon and mitigate the climate emergency.[267] On a larger scale, in Oxford economist Kate Raworth's 2017 book, *Doughnut Economics: Seven Ways to Think Like a 21st-Century Economist*,[268] the author promotes Doughnut Economic Theory, which argues that twentieth-century economic thinking is not equipped to deal with the twenty-first-century reality of a planet teetering on the edge of climate breakdown. Rather than paralleling a growing GDP with a healthy society, our goal should be to fit all of human life into what Raworth calls the "sweet spot" between the "social foundation," where everyone has what they need to live a good life, and the "environmental ceiling."[269]

Imagine if all our cities did that—not to mention the business world! But for this kind of circular system to work at scale, for entire supply chains to become at least sustainable, and ideally, regenerative, we'll need much policy help, external incentive, and inventive trial and error. Policymakers and their regulations are slowly beginning to catch up. The "EU Taxonomy," for example, is a classification system that establishes a list of environmentally sustainable economic activities related to the European Green Deal (EGD). It creates more security, protecting private investors from greenwashing efforts on the part of disingenuous players.[270] Critically, "Voluntary reporting wasn't cutting it,"[271] and the US Securities and Exchange Commission will be requiring more ESG reporting soon to better serve investors, the planet, and our collective future. In the US, President Biden and his environmental czar, John Kerry, are embracing the latest version of a "Green New Deal," intending to ensure the country achieves a 100 percent clean energy economy and reaches net-zero emissions no later than 2050—with much of that result coming from shifting business practices.[272]

From a capital market and financing perspective, more "circular economy principles are crucial in moving the world we share beyond a problematic 'take-make-waste' approach to scarce natural resources," according to Saker Nusseibeh, international CEO at investment management firm Federated Hermes, "to recognise the financial opportunity in resilient, circular models of resource use, and shift financing to enterprises focusing capital allocation on circular products, processes and value chains."[273] All the climate emergency commitments we've seen of late are a great start. But next we need to see legitimate, effective "nature restoration" commitments at scale.[274]

3. *Fair & Just Human Relations.* This is a catch-all category that spans such necessities as a universal living wage; clean water, healthful food,

sanitation, and energy available to all citizens; affordable housing; medicine and healthcare provided to all at economical rates; safe and respectful working conditions; democratic and equitable civil and criminal laws; voting rights; the protection of children, the elderly, the disabled, the poor, and other disadvantaged citizens from abuse and neglect; the freedom to express the panoply of sexuality, political leanings, gender, and religious beliefs—and the complete equity arising from them; free and equal primary and secondary education; an equitable distribution of public resources; and the right to organize and redress grievances without fear of reprisal, among other things.

Our businesses can start by working to ensure that our own associates gain and maintain access to all these necessities. Then all persons in our supply chain and the communities we serve. Then all our consumers. Then *WE* continue to expand our compass of impact to our brand communities and beyond, by leading cultural conversations in these areas. None of this is utopian; rather, it's critical if business and the communities it enables are to survive. It's the reason why Adepeju Jaiyeoba founded Colourful Giggles Nutrition to provide affordable nutrition to African children, using local ingredients to support other small enterprises.[275] It's why Israel's Inna Braverman, at twenty-four, founded the clean electricity company Eco Wave Power. Born just two weeks after the Chernobyl nuclear disaster, she suffered respiratory arrest in her crib, requiring her mother to perform mouth-to-mouth resuscitation. Getting this "second chance in life," she "decided to devote it to the development of a clean and safe method of electricity production."[276] It's why social entrepreneur Latifa Al-Khalifa co-founded Clever Play, a Bahrain-based social-purpose-driven startup aiming to inspire, educate, and empower one million children in STEAM skills by 2030.[277] It's why Old Navy, Tory Burch, and Target paid their employees not only to go vote in 2020—but to be poll workers at local precincts.[278]

To continue this trajectory toward a more *LEAD WITH WE* world, we need major shifts/continuations of these processes variously underway. If we're wondering where and how exactly we can and should *LEAD*, here are a few imperatives, all of which must work together for us to achieve the kinds of large-scale solutions we need:

1. ***Pragmatism.*** We need less idealistic "altruism" and fewer unrealistic standards that stall adoption of new, more collective ways to do business in the world. Anyone who still requires a business case for a stakeholder model, for dealing with the climate, or for preventing future crises is simply not paying attention.

2. ***New consumerism.*** We need shoppers to continue to vote with their wallets and otherwise understand, value, and leverage their massive influence. This could be the single strongest driver of a business shift to *LEAD WITH WE* priorities.

3. ***Policy change.*** We need more regulatory support/pressure to drive change. We need stricter and clearer government standards, frameworks, consequences, and rewards to foster ecosystemic solutions. We must explore what more governments can do to create an enabling environment for business to be both good actors and also create market-based solutions to social, environmental, and public problems. Where policy and incentives meet, that's when change really accelerates.

4. ***Philanthropy.*** We need all the fine organizations that raise and distribute moneys to causes to continue to do so, but in more participatory, silo-busting, pooled, efficient, and effective ways. For example, they must not only direct billions of well-intended donor dollars to sudden disasters, but also gradually alter their focus on injecting urgent (reactive) disaster relief, and start nourishing with more proactive, "risk-tolerant, 'patient' capital."[279] More consumer and wealthy donor engagement must be guided by experts, especially utilizing technology not traditionally used for such giving, such as payment apps. Examples of such a frictionless mobile donation app include Pledge, which works seamlessly across live or virtual events, and GiveDirectly, boosted by the Gates's foundations and Twitter CEO, Jack Dorsey.

5. ***Innovation.*** We also need to speed up innovation of technology that promotes collective good, that helps all sectors connect with one another and communicate transparently about problems and potential solutions— then embed it where most impactful ASAP. And we need to leverage extant technology. For just one narrow example, consider video games, played by 55 percent of people in the US during the first phase of lockdowns in 2020, according to Nielsen.[280] Pew Research finds that 90 percent of people between the ages of thirteen and seventeen play video games, which

represent a major new vehicle for social-good integrations.[281] Note that in 2019, Riot Games—in celebration of the tenth anniversary of its online multiplayer battle arena game, *League of Legends*—launched the Riot Games Social Impact Fund, in partnership with ImpactAssets. In its first six months, the fund raised more than $10 million.[282] But because every new technology comes with potential unintended consequences—such as toxic sexual behaviors[283]—we need more *ethical* tech and better training for using it properly. New research reveals that trust in the tech sector is the lowest since Edelman began tracking it in 2000. "The tech industry is now being held to account for all manner of societal ills, from information bankruptcy, to job loss, to human rights, to the mass-class divide," CEO Richard Edelman writes.[284]

There's certainly a plethora of mistrust about the future of AI, which, as the *New York Times* notes, is already transforming industries like transportation[285] and healthcare,[286] but is also linked to mass surveillance,[287] identity theft,[288] and the (ubiquitous, dangerous) proliferation of false news.[289] Of course, some applications of AI are also fighting the climate emergency, countering the fake news problem, and working to reduce inequality and poverty.[290]

6. *Synergy.* All of us—the WE—need to work WITH each other on this program. We need government, companies, schools, churches, NGOs, and private citizens to inspire and drive everyone toward this critical shift. Pope Francis audaciously taking on the climate crisis, poverty, and homophobia has been huge. The political class slowly waking up to societal crises (if not always keeping up with them) and providing various pandemic stimuli has also been a watershed moment. The 2021 UN Climate Change Conference (COP26) will be influenced by the first Global Assembly that anyone on Earth can join, including governments, businesses, artists, scientists, and social movements,[291] because everyone is a shareholder in our collective future. We need all participants in We First Capitalism to play their part boldly, effectively, and publicly so we can present a united front of complementary powers to combat those unified forces, such as monopolies, that are maliciously seeking to hold us back. We need to work together within companies and industries, across sectors and geography, as well as on the ground, neighbor to neighbor, to take on the forces compromising our future.

Transform the World Through Cross-Sector Alliances

In some cases, cross-sector collaboration is desirable or even necessary, such as in public–private partnerships between government and business, but also well beyond. The Deep South Economic Mobility Collaborative, which includes Hope Enterprise Corporation; Goldman Sachs's 10,000 Small Businesses initiative; seven cities; nine Historically Black Colleges and Universities; the Ford Foundation; and novelist, philanthropist, and Giving Pledge signatory MacKenzie Scott, seeks to invest in small businesses in the economically hard-hit region.[292] But we want to widen the Spiral one level further still. In fact, the highest order of LEAD WITH WE practice—and the penultimate level of the Spiral—is cross-sector collaboration. We must ask the following questions of these sectors:

1. **Business.** How can business (ours and the business world in general) advocate for policy changes that will prioritize DI&E, social justice, climate and biodiversity solutions, and gender and pay equity, among other things? Are we setting a positive example in our industry?

2. **Investors.** What standardized ESG metrics, innovative instruments, and industry practices can we use to reward entrepreneurs and corporate leaders for reengineering their companies and industries to provide social and environmental solutions that enable a regenerative future? Is our money supporting improvements in capital markets and the world?

3. **Government.** What policy or regulatory changes can we enact to accelerate and reward business for prioritizing long-term and regenerative solutions that benefit all stakeholders? Are we partnering with business to scale positive change—or regulating in ways that make that harder?

4. **Civil Society.** How can our organizations and citizen movements collaborate more effectively in the context of a participatory, We First form of capitalism that better meets the needs of the underserved? Are we engaging, contributing, and collaborating—or just complaining?

5. **Philanthropy.** How can our capital and knowledge get invested, combined, compounded, and shared to provide long-term systemic solutions in partnership with other sectors? How much of our charity efforts are wasted by our not partnering with the most effective business leadership?

In my client experience at We First, effective coalitions operate best at a local level, because only in their neighborhoods of expertise and easy access can each partner create programs and impact specific to their unique circumstances and conditions. This is how large-scale change occurs: person by person, small group to small group, across digital, racial, and regional divides, with each node in the network localizing their impact through their novel skills, connections, and community resources. Expanding upward to ever wider movements of change, and combining to compound resources, reach, and resonance, because the larger they get, the more leverage these movements have to shift behavior, create markets, and drive change. This framing avoids the exercise of cross-sector collaboration becoming just some lofty, unattainably challenging notion. It's not. You can have a tangible impact on the ground, local to home. And when several local communities act in concert, you have the beginning of global scale. This is where Starbucks excels, in uniting and mobilizing local communities around pressing social issues.

The natural benefit of effective cross-sector collaboration is, of course, the automatic "plussing" we get by expanding our base of expertise and other resources. The potential negative is tension between sectors. We can lessen the latter by focusing on our shared impact goals and using the collective purpose as the touchstone. Then we can have all parties ask of themselves and each other the following questions to help resolve any lingering friction, mistrust, or conflict:

1. **How** does the short-term cost of embracing the *LEAD WITH WE* approaches described here contrast to the long-term cost of continuing with a Me First mindset and action plan?

2. **What** limiting beliefs or behaviors serve as obstacles to enabling a collaborative and regenerative practice of business? How do we overcome them?

3. **What** risk will we assume and even increase by stalling the wholesale shift toward regenerative mindsets and behaviors?

4. **How much** more quickly and effectively could the desired impact be achieved through this or some other cross-sector collaboration? How can we best help each other solve the bigger problems, rather than merely troubleshoot smaller issues?

5. **How** can we work *WITH* each other in ways that spark measurable local impact while creating long-term value across all sectors?

6. **What** policy or regulatory changes would make this more possible, more quickly?

7. **How** better served will all stakeholders be by a long-term, participatory, and regenerative approach to the problem(s)?

8. *How much* more effective will our impact efforts be with cross-sector support?

9. *What* unexpected partnerships, collaborations, or opportunities will be unlocked by working cross-sector?

10. *What* future do we seek to create in our lifetimes for this and following generations?

When *WE* together achieve this, we're ready to move from transformation into the realm of transcendence. Are we ready for that? Read on!

Key Takeaways

⇒ Brands must define and *LEAD* the cultural conversations they are best qualified to address, with the goal of positively shaping culture and society.

⇒ Pre-competitive collaboration unlocks and scales profitable innovations, elevates industry reputation, and scales solutions for a regenerative and sustainable future, while fortifying trust that insulates against future controversy.

⇒ A requisite coalition of stakeholders, including the critical participation of the investor class, is enabling new market forces with the potential to regenerate our collective future.

Action Items

1. *LEAD*—Drive cultural conversations with clearly defined pillars and proof points to achieve lasting business growth and societal impact.

2. *WITH*—Be proactive, responsive, and/or reactive in service of these cultural conversations and changes you seek to co-create *WITH* other stakeholders.

3. *WE*—Participate in pre-competitive collaborations, industry coalitions, and cross-sector alliances to accelerate and scale industry-wide shifts, net positive solutions, and regenerative practices.

PART THREE

WE

Ultimately, all our efforts lead to *WE*. This Higher *WE* encompasses us all working together with empathy, respect, and diligence for the benefit of each other, ourselves, other species, and the planet itself. Recasting *WE* the way it was always meant to be, and for tens of thousands of years was well understood: as a true collective, where the results of our efforts at last compound faster than our problems do. One that we all operate in a way that benefits all life, actually living and doing business that synergizes, enhances, nurtures, and bolsters—rather than steadily ruins—nature. Humanity in this imperative conception becomes a symbiotic, no longer opportunistic, life form. This requires a fundamental shift in the way we perceive the world so that we can change the way we behave upon it.

HUMANITY & PLANET

TRANSCENDENCE
FOSTER REGENERATIVE
& ABUNDANT FUTURE
Evolve principles & practices to
scale human & planetary health

SOCIETY
COLLABORATE CROSS-
SECTOR & SHAPE CULTURE
Drive cultural conversations &
coalitions that improve society
Citizens, Collaborators & Sectors

COMMUNITY
MOBILIZE BRAND
COMMUNITIES &
BUILD MOVEMENTS
Engage external stakeholders
around purpose-led movements
Customers, Consumers & Partners

COMPANY
ACTIVATE PURPOSE
& ALIGN INTERNAL
STAKEHOLDERS
Integrate & apply purpose
throughout company
Execs, Employees & Supply Chain

LEADERS
DEFINE COMPANY
PURPOSE & GOALS
Conduct honest audit &
determine reason for being
Corporations, Businesses & Startups

ME
ADOPT *LEAD WITH WE*
MINDSET & BEHAVIOR
Recognize new reality, grasp
urgency & shift thinking
Every Individual

8

Transcendence

Committing to Each Other & the Planet

Never before has humanity all at once faced a combination of crises so exacting, so treacherous, so punishing. If a silver lining is possible in this grave situation, though, it's that we are now awake—or at least more of us are, more than ever before—about the most critical of our challenges. But, given our track record in the face of relentless warnings, it's fair to ask why this attempt at cultural recalibration will be any different, will really last. I believe it absolutely will.

The reason turns on a conspiracy of circumstances that has not occurred before. First, the shared values and commitment of a requisite coalition of stakeholders. Second, our escalating awareness of the challenges we face, amplified by a tidal wave of young leaders, employees, entrepreneurs, investors, and citizens refusing to forgo a healthful and abundant future. Third, our visceral experience of COVID-19. We all lived the waking nightmare together at the same time, an existential crisis unleashed on the human family—and yet it also revealed and exacerbated longstanding divisions and disparities. The pandemic is still driving in-depth dialogue around what we value, who we are, and what future(s) we face.

It's this *combination of stakes, stakeholders, and story* that makes it all different this time.

This uniting of new forces is already inspiring early drafts of a new role for business based on our imminent future, undeniable science, and unconscionable suffering. The story is grounded in optimism because pessimism seals our fate. This fundamental change in the way we do business is rooted in an enduring belief in our innate goodness, imaginative capacity, and boundless ingenuity. We don't simply believe that a regenerative future is achievable; rather, we engage our individual and collective agency in order to realize that optimal outcome: a plentiful and regenerative economy embodying the dynamics of living systems. Evidence of successes abound. Examples are manifold. This revolution is proceeding, accelerating, working. But we have far to go.

The individual people on whom the revolution depends—*WE*—are not coin-operated automatons. We're also well entrenched in our old ways. For this story to have effect, it must be shared with empathy and urgency, because each person must overcome their habits, inertia, and obstacles to change so much so quickly. Every one of us must each (and all) consciously choose to change for ourselves, for each other, and for the betterment of our shared planetary home.

This new story must be an emotionally resonant one. This revolution won't work unless *WE* all join together. It is inspired by the emotional power to drive behavioral shifts by tapping into instincts hardwired within all of us; our connection as a human family; our deep bonds to nature; our intuitive understanding of the value of coherence and unity versus separation and division. This narrative and its recalibration leverage centuries of experience, from traditional storytelling to modern mass media, that all employ real-time, trust-building, and ethically directed tools in everyone's hands; that apply inclusive messaging to bridge deeply polarized people, issues, and politics and build social movements that shift thinking and behavior, ultimately reshaping society and reforming our future. Nobody loses.

The story and the unfolding real benefits of putting this prescription into action continue to restore a sense of meaning to all of us, the *WE*. It's subsuming not our individualism, self-reliance, and independence—but our self-centeredness. Together we can all realize a shared vision, a collective future, a profusion of mutual benefits.

This course correction does not derive from fear, which can cause apathy, passivity, and denial, as we learned from economist and psychologist Per Espen

Stoknes's research into "global warming fatigue."[1] Instead, given a plethora of evidence, it presupposes a positive experience for us, the characters engaged in reimagining and reengineering capitalism. The future is a story we write each day, in the vast and thrilling potentiality extant within the uppermost reaches of our Virtuous Spiral. What is possible at the top? What can we achieve? How will we make the world a better place?

The more of us who participate, the less likely that egregious polarization will derail our collective efforts. WE all must fortify meaning through our exertions in the right direction. Every action we take one way or the other is a chip we wager on our future. An aggregate of endless everyday decisions and actions will get us all there. A product of what we inside companies, within industries, across communities, throughout supply chains, and between sectors can achieve with a LEAD WITH WE mindset and a practice of We First Capitalism. Of how we earn, spend, and donate our dollars. How we treat our finite resources, wherever we are in the world or on our purpose journey. Each recalibration is an installment in this transformative story. The momentum of our decisions will build critical resilience for withstanding the temptation to default to self-serving habits.

The aim is a world in which we've learned at last to work WITH—not against—each other and the true, natural order of things: mutual, reciprocal, and interdependent. Resensitizing ourselves to what our species used to know before the unintended consequences of all our scientific advances changed our daily lives. Until we do, we're not only at war with nature, but also with our own better natures. And if we don't, the foundations of life will buckle, break, and collapse, taking humanity with it. Self-termination will ensue because the natural world will reject us like a pathogen—a virus. The interdependence between humanity and the planet will either save or destroy us.

We are headed in the right direction, but we must evolve faster. Each day we are restoring more land, drawing down more carbon, and reengineering more companies. We are moving beyond binary mindsets, false dichotomies, and limiting beliefs that pit one against another and all of us against the planet. We are integrating the historic humbling brought by COVID-19, conscious of the liminal phase we are in, where we realize that breakdown is in fact breakthrough to a more pluralistic, transpersonal, and collectivist paradigm of democracy and capitalism. Through an equitable, sustainable, and regenerative practice of We First Capitalism, we are future-proofing business and humanity by future-proofing the planet, and vice versa.

Yes, a LEAD WITH WE attitude and approach allows us to tackle current conditions on the ground, and go a long way together in reversing the damage our species has already done. But gaining LEAD WITH WE traction and momentum will also help preempt and remedy inevitable future global challenges . . . the as-yet-unforeseen predicaments a failure of our imagination must not cause us to ignore. The rising specter of an AI that outstrips humanity in terms of intelligence, productivity, and self-sufficiency. The ethical, social, and practical fallout of life-extension hacks and other human upgrades through advancing biotechnology. The predictable interplanetary tension between off-world homes as they compete over rights, resources, and prosperity. The ownership, regulation, and distribution of countless extinct animal and plant species as science unlocks the secrets to their restoration.

LEAD WITH WE mindsets and methods already in progress are paving the way toward envisioning, articulating, and executing a new and long-term human-ecological equilibrium. A new beginning, really. A brighter future for our species, and the world. The Higher WE. This is our best and only hope. We must leverage this guiding narrative, to LEAD WITH WE in all things, embracing our interdependence as a fulcrum of strength, and let its essence serve as an enabling, inclusive, and calibrating compass, a new North Star to direct us sensibly to resolve the accelerating, dizzying, stupefying challenges we will all face. A target to aim for in the center of kaleidoscopic options.

Naïve? Oversimplified? I'm arguing only that we must avoid inertia, or worse, backsliding. We must resist the division and damage often wrought by overcomplexity, especially in the context of an already compromised future. The moment demands an organizing principle for the next chapter in humanity's evolution. We have either everything to lose, or everything to gain. And WE are in this together.

This is the calling of our lifetimes. A *cri de coeur* to echo through generations. Our "Earthshot." A Copernican moment, where we reorient, restore, and renew our systems around the WE. There is no Me. Me is a mirage. As the architects, engineers, and artists of renewal and reintegration, WE get to give the gift of life, of healing and justice, to each other. To live WITH, not *on*, this Earth, as co-creators of humanity and planetary well-being. WE reveal, together, the true measure of humanity.

The future we need is within us. It is us. We are our own transcendent heroes. Our job is to share this story. And to live it. It is the story of WE, working WITH each other. It is the time for us all to LEAD.

Acknowledgments

This book is a pure expression of *Lead With We*.

First, my deepest admiration and gratitude belongs with those iconic leaders that inspired in me a love and belief in the power of words to change lives, most notably the Rev. Dr. Martin Luther King Jr., John F. Kennedy, and Barack Obama, from all of whom I draw sustaining insight and inspiration.

Lead With We is a new installment in a longstanding movement that extends back to inventor and visionary Richard Buckminster Fuller in the 1950s, but whose roots go far deeper still, into the enduring genius—returning at last to broad consciousness—of indigenous cultures.

I am neither economist nor academician, but rather a practitioner of purposeful business who's been applying the "how" of responsible business across many of the world's most exciting startups and well-known brands. That practice builds on the research and insights of firms such as GlobeScan, Edelman, JUST Capital, Kantar Consulting, InSite Consulting, Forrester, Stockholm Resilience Center, and more; as well as from EY, PwC, Accenture, and Deloitte, to all of whom I extend my respect and gratitude.

This book has been intensely informed by the wisdom and real-world efforts of thought leaders, scholars, and masters of responsible, regenerative business, many of whom I reference in the foregoing pages. Peers and friends that include Janine Beynus, John Elkington, John Fullerton, Jay Cohen Gilbert, Jeffrey Hollander, Mark Kramer, Mark Lee, Hunter Lovins, John Mackey, John Porritt, Michael Porter, Rick Ridgeway, Raj Sisodia, KoAnn Skrzyniarz, Josh Ticknell, Sally Uren, Andrew Winston, and others.

As the second installment to a thesis that began with the first edition of my first book, *We First*, this volume was enabled and supported by the dialogues driven by, and communities fostered by, organizations I consider part of the We First family, most notably Sustainable Brands, Conscious Capitalism, B Corp, the UN Foundation, WORLDZ, the Forbes Business Council, the Royal Society of Arts, Real Leaders Impact Collaborative, and METal. You are all at the vanguard of this revolution.

I have detailed in these pages the cases of many We First clients, partners whose passion, courage, and impact motivate me daily. Our collaboration with companies such as the VF Corporation, Timberland, VSP Global, Mammut, Traditional Medicinals, TOMS, Clif Bar & Company, Coca-Cola, Fishpeople Seafood, Eagle Creek, Wrangler, Toyota, Thrive Farmers, Virgin Unite, Veggie Grill, SAP, Avery Dennison, JanSport, Maybelline, B Lab, X Prize Foundation, and more has informed my professional development, the *Lead With We* thesis, and all you've just read. In the narrative, however, I eschewed naming them as clients, to avoid self-promotion or bias. And my deep appreciation extends to their other partners—consultants, advertising agencies, PR firms, too many to name—helping to make purposeful business possible. *We* are in this together—and I am in all your debt.

My thanks also extend to the hundreds of guests who were interviewed for the book, my *Forbes* "Purpose at Work" column, and my *Lead With We* podcast. Equally important are the readers and listeners who respond daily, invest their time and interest, then apply the learnings to their own companies and lives. Thank you for the constant encouragement and support. I draw great optimism from your efforts.

The thinking in this book—from the philosophy to the paradigm—was co-created *With* the whole We First team over the last ten years. Our business family has evolved, but includes Karina Alvarez, Stacy Anderson, Anne Brashier, Dana Byerlee, Melissa Cunningham, Logan Eastman, Alexis Hay, Chad Kaszer, Serena Leung, Jill Lindeman, Shannon Pfeffer, Scott Sparks, Morgan Wells, and Jed Wolf. Not to mention Greg Mollner and Caroline Halter at Goal 17 Media, our partners in the *Lead With We* podcast.

The We First family will always include those who helped me start my purpose journey. They include a cast of colleagues, mentors, and friends, among them Mark Ankner, Sekou Andrews, Rick Benzel, Chuck Carey, Stephen and Patty Dewey, Michael Frick, Liz Heller, Chris Leahy, Ken Rutkowski, and Aaron Sherinian.

What makes this book publication even more exciting is the magnificent consortium of teams that has supported it. Chuck Joe and Target Marketing teams doing social media; Mark Fortier and Elena Christie at Fortier PR; and Compadre and Sisu, creators of our company and book websites. All of you share a passion for the LEAD WITH WE mindset and methodology. I learn from you always, and I'm privileged to work with you.

In terms of the production of LEAD WITH WE itself, it serves as its own testament to the prescription set within it: that the most meaningful and impactful endeavors are those conducted collaboratively. Much gratitude to Letitia Webster for her insightful feedback on early drafts. And my deep appreciation goes to Jill Lindeman, who kept the We First machine running while tirelessly helping me balance the demands of the business and a book. My utmost respect and gratitude go to Ian Blake Newhem, without whom the writing, editing, and final manuscript would simply not be what it is today. To Logan Eastman for his indispensable and dogged research and citation support. To Anne Brashier, Lara Lile, and Michelle Elyse Ambrosio, the production managers who kept all the moving parts well-oiled and working together. And to my wonderful agent, Lisa Gallagher, who not only found me the best publisher for this book, but tirelessly helped me navigate the nuanced process. This book team worked diligently through what was perhaps the hardest professional period in all their lives—our collective life—and never missed a beat.

Speaking of which, this book you hold in your hands would not have been possible without editor-in-chief of Matt Holt Books at BenBella, Matt Holt (a true gent and titan of his industry); senior editor Katie Dickman, who believed in, understood, then elevated the manuscript; Camille Cline, my developmental editor, who helped guide us to the final draft; James Fraleigh, my copy editor, who had the thankless task of ensuring all the i's were dotted and t's crossed (which hardly describes the copyediting burden when the author is me); Jessika Rieck, who shepherded this book through the final stages; Sarah Avinger and Heather Butterfield, who both rocked this cover design. I'm privileged to be part of the BenBella family and thanks to the whole team.

Coming closer to home, I cannot express my love and gratitude enough to my family and friends, who endured my persistent distraction and absence as busy work weeks melded into even busier writing weekends, over the course of nearly three years. To my wife, Monna, your tireless patience, support, and love made all this possible (and now I get to make up for it!); and to my two sweet daughters,

Aisha and Talia, your love, joy, and humor kept me smiling, even as your futures were constantly on my mind.

To my brother, Paul, and sister, Justine, deep thanks for your constant encouragement and belief in me. To my devoted mum, Fruzsina, for always being there for me, for loving me unconditionally, and instilling in me a strong desire to be of service. And to my dad, Nigel, whose sudden passing long ago and far too soon started me on the We First journey: You are never far from my thoughts.

Finally, *LEAD WITH WE* is nothing without you, the reader. For your attention to the book, love for each other, care for the planet, and stewardship of our future, I extend my respect, friendship, and boundless appreciation. The future we want for ourselves and our children is possible because *WE* are in reach of each other, and there is nothing we cannot achieve together.

Notes

Notes on Case Studies, Language & Resources

1. Neil Parker, "Five reasons to kill the word 'consumer' right now," *Forbes*, December 8, 2016, https://www.forbes.com/sites/onmarketing/2015/12/08/five-reasons-to-kill-the-word-consumer-right-now/?sh=295fcf341f51.

Introduction

1. Heba Aly, "The humanitarian system: 'A mammoth machinery losing track of what it is for,'" *Guardian*, May 22, 2016, https://www.theguardian.com/global-development-professionals-network/2016/may/22/humanitarian-aid-system-power-concentrated-hands-of-few-losing-track.
2. Anneken Tappe, "Record 20.5 million American jobs lost in April. Unemployment rate soars to 14.7%," *CNN Business*, May 8, 2020, https://www.cnn.com/2020/05/08/economy/april-jobs-report-2020-coronavirus/index.html.
3. Sam Cartmell, "Lack of disaggregated data a glaring gap in Southeast Asia's COVID-19 response," *Minority Rights Group*, May 20, 2020, https://minorityrights.org/2020/05/20/data-southeast-asia-covid/.
4. Mike Davis, "Mike Davis: The coronavirus crisis is a monster created by capitalism," *In These Times*, March 20, 2020, https://inthesetimes.com/article/22394/coronavirus-crisis-capitalism-covid-19-monster-mike-davis.
5. Heather Long and Andrew Van Dam, "The black-white economic divide is as wide as it was in 1968," *Washington Post*, June 4, 2020, https://www.washingtonpost.com/business/2020/06/04/economic-divide-black-households/.
6. Larry Buchanan, Quoctrung Bui, and Jugal K. Patel, "Black Lives Matter may be the largest movement in US history," *New York Times*, July 3, 2020, https://www.nytimes.com/interactive/2020/07/03/us/george-floyd-protests-crowd-size.html.
7. Insurance Information Institute, "Fact + Statistics: Civil disorders," accessed October 26, 2020, https://www.iii.org/fact-statistic/facts-statistics-civil-disorders.
8. Cybersecurity & Infrastructure Security Agency, "Joint statement from Elections Infrastructure Government Coordinating Council & the Election Infrastructure Sector Coordinating Executive Committees," November 12, 2020, https://www.cisa.gov/news/2020/11/12/joint-statement-elections-infrastructure-government-coordinating-council-election.
9. John A. Tures, "Even Republicans are aware that climate change is happening," *Observer*, July 10, 2019, https://observer.com/2019/07/climate-change-republicans-conservative-solution/.

10. United Nations, "Take action for the sustainable development goals," accessed October 26, 2020, https://www.un.org/sustainabledevelopment/sustainable-development-goals/.

11. Center for Effective Policy Change, *The Future of Foundation Philanthropy: The CEO Perspective*, 2016, http://cep.org/wp-content/uploads/2016/12/CEPs-The-Future-of-Foundation-Philanthropy-December-2016.pdf.

12. Karn Vohr, Alina Vodonos, Joel Schwartz, Eloise A. Marais, Melissa P. Sulprizio, and Loretta J. Mickley, "Global mortality from outdoor fine particle pollution generated by fossil fuel combustion: Results from GEOS-Chem," *Environmental Research* 195 (2021), https://doi.org/10.1016/j.envres.2021.110754.

13. Damian Carrington, "Depression and suicide linked to air pollution in new global study," *Guardian*, December 18, 2020, https://www.theguardian.com/environment/2019/dec/18/depression-and-suicide-linked-to-air-pollution-in-new-global-study?fbclid=IwAR2vXZ5yxWDhfO_oTQYONDf-T5xACWlHZ89e3s7t0hBdKUrzGy4gsKRerTE.

14. Centers for Disease Control & Prevention, "History of smallpox," August 30, 2016, https://www.cdc.gov/smallpox/history/history.html.

15. Christopher Rowland and Laurie McGinley, "Merck will help make Johnson & Johnson coronavirus vaccine as rivals team up to help Biden accelerate shots," *Washington Post*, March 3, 2021, https://www.washingtonpost.com/health/2021/03/02/merck-johnson-and-johnson-covid-vaccine-partnership/.

16. Patagonia, "Patagonia's mission statement," accessed February 2, 2021, https://www.patagonia.com.au/pages/our-mission.

17. Hans Rosling, Ola Rosling, and Anna Rosling Rönnlund, *Factfulness: Ten Reasons We're Wrong About the World—And Why Things Are Better Than You Think* (New York: Flatiron Books, 2018).

18. The Asset, "Multi-billionaire Kakao boss to give away half his fortune," March 16, 2021, https://www.theasset.com/article/43182/multi-billionaire-kakao-boss-to-give-away-half-his-fortune.

19. World Economic Forum, *The Global Risks Report 2019*, 14th Edition, accessed October 26, 2020, http://www3.weforum.org/docs/WEF_Global_Risks_Report_2019.pdf.

20. Sebastian Herrera, "Amazon's profit run continues, bolstered by sustained demand," *Wall Street Journal*, April 29, 2021, https://www.wsj.com/articles/amazon-amzn-1q-earnings-report-2021-11619649081.

21. United Nations Development Programme, "World's largest survey of public opinion on climate change: A majority of people call for wide-ranging action," January 27, 2021, https://www.undp.org/content/undp/en/home/news-centre/news/2021/Worlds_largest_survey_of_public_opinion_on_climate_change_a_majority_of_people_call_for_wide_ranging_action.html; *The Peoples' Climate Vote*, January 26, 2021, https://www.undp.org/content/undp/en/home/librarypage/climate-and-disaster-resilience-/The-Peoples-Climate-Vote-Results.html.

22. Yola Robert, "Here's how brands have pivoted since the COVID-19 outbreak," *Forbes*, April 20, 2020, https://www.forbes.com/sites/yolarobert1/2020/04/20/heres-how-brands-have-pivoted-since-the-covid-19-outbreak/#71f360fa3beb.

23. Greta Thunberg, "Transcript: Greta Thunberg's speech at the U.N. Climate Action Summit," *NPR*, September 23, 2019, https://www.npr.org/2019/09/23/763452863/transcript-greta-thunbergs-speech-at-the-u-n-climate-action-summit.

24. Worldometer, "World population," accessed October 26, 2020, https://www.worldometers.info/world-population/.

25. Matt Rosenberg, "Current world population and future projections," ThoughtCo., February 18, 2020, https://www.thoughtco.com/current-world-population-1435270.

26. International Institute for Environment and Development, "About us," accessed October 26, 2020, https://www.iied.org/about.

27. Adam Vaughan, "Humanity driving 'unprecedented' marine extinction," *Guardian*, September 14, 2016, https://www.theguardian.com/environment/2016/sep/14/humanity-driving-unprecedented-marine-extinction

28. Center for Biological Diversity, "Human population growth and extinction," accessed April 22, 2021, https://www.biologicaldiversity.org/programs/population_and_sustainability/extinction/index.html.

29. Intergovernmental Panel on Climate Change, "Summary for policymakers of IPCC Special Report on Global Warming of 1.5°C approved by governments," October 8, 2018, https://www.ipcc.ch/20 18/10/08/summary-for-policymakers-of-ipcc-special-report-on-global-warming-of-1-5c-approved -by-governments/.

30. Intergovernmental Science-Policy Platform on Biodiversity and Ecosystem Services, "Nature's dangerous decline 'unprecedented'; species extinction rates 'accelerating'" (media release), accessed October 26, 2020, https://ipbes.net/news/Media-Release-Global-Assessment.

31. Jessie Yeung, "We have 10 years to save Earth's biodiversity as mass extinction caused by humans takes hold, UN warns," *CNN World*, January 14, 2020, https://www.cnn.com/2020/01/14/world /un-biodiversity-draft-plan-intl-hnk-scli-scn/index.html.

32. Sustainable Brands, "WWF reveals biggest losers in unchecked nature and climate crisis," February 12, 2020, https://sustainablebrands.com/read/defining-the-next-economy/wwf-reveals-biggest -losers-in-unchecked-nature-and-climate-crisis."

33. Rebecca Harrington, "By 2050, the oceans could have more plastic than fish," *Business Insider*, January 26, 2017, https://www.businessinsider.com/plastic-inl-ocean-outweighs-fish-evidence-report -2017-1.

34. Jen Fela, "Every minute of every day, the equivalent of one truckload of plastics enter the sea," Greenpeace, April 13, 2018, https://www.greenpeace.org/international/story/15882/every-minute -of-every-day-the-equivalent-of-one-truckload-of-plastic-enters-the-sea/.

35. Fela, "Every minute."

36. Damian Carrington, "Plastic fibres found in tap water around the world, study reveals," *Guardian*, September 5, 2017, https://www.theguardian.com/environment/2017/sep/06/plastic-fibres-found -tap-water-around-world-study-reveals.

37. The World Counts, "Earth's forests are being cut down. And they are being cut down fast," accessed October 26, 2020, https://www.theworldcounts.com/challenges/planet-earth/forests-and-deserts /rate-of-deforestation.

38. Christina Nunez, "Deforestation explained," *National Geographic*, February 7, 2019, https://www .nationalgeographic.com/environment/global-warming/deforestation/.

39. Lisa Warden, "A palate for pestilence: Ominous links between COVID-19 and industrial animal farming," *Sentient Media*, March 19, 2020, https://sentientmedia.org/ominous-links-between-covid -19-and-industrial-animal-farming/?fbclid=IwAR3qRKvAZSsKHezwK5-vn8gtdBCFPuB99Jf Et9BSjXaAZsBEbCD_4JLZ73E.

40. Bibi van der Zee, "Why factory farming is not just cruel—but also a threat to all life on the planet," *Guardian*, October 4, 2017, https://www.theguardian.com/environment/2017/oct/04/factory -farming-destructive-wasteful-cruel-says-philip-lymbery-farmageddon-author.

41. Scott Weathers, Sophie Hermanns, and Mark Bittman, "Health leaders must focus on the threats from factory farms," *New York Times*, May 21, 2017, https://www.nytimes.com/2017/05/21 /opinion/who-factory-farming-meat-industry-.html.

42. David Armano, "How the pandemic is pressure-testing a brand's purpose," Edelman, March 30, 2020, https://www.edelman.com/covid-19/perspectives/testing-brands-purpose.

43. Deloitte, "2030 Purpose: Good business and a better future," accessed October 26, 2020, https:// www2.deloitte.com/global/en/pages/about-deloitte/articles/purpose-2030-good-business-better -future.html.

44. Simon Mainwaring, "Purpose at work: SanMar, sustainability and pivoting during Covid-19," *Forbes*, July 28, 2020, https://www.forbes.com/sites/simonmainwaring/2020/07/28/purpose-at-work -sanmar-sustainability-and-pivoting-during-covid-19/.

45. IKEA, "People & Planet Positive: IKEA Group Sustainability Strategy for 2020," accessed October 26, 2020, https://preview.thenewsmarket.com/Previews/IKEA/DocumentAssets/511938_v3.PDF.

46. Virgin Unite, "10 global companies that are environmentally friendly," June 1, 2016, https://www .virgin.com/virgin-unite/10-global-companies-are-environmentally-friendly.

47. IKEA, "IKEA sustainability strategy—people & planet positive," June 7, 2018, https://newsroom .inter.ikea.com/publications/ikea-sustainability-strategy---people---planet-positive/s/5b72986f-d8 c5-42fe-b123-f5f9d00a17bb.

48. Starbucks, "Navigating through COVID-19," July 17, 2020, https://stories.starbucks.com/stories /2020/navigating-through-covid-19.

49. "Vaccinations: Employers consider incentives, mandates," *The Week*, January 29, 2021.

50. Harriet Grant and Joshua Carroll, "COVID led to 'brutal crackdown' on garment workers' rights, says report," *Guardian*, August 7, 2020, https://www.theguardian.com/global-development/2020 /aug/07/covid-led-to-brutal-crackdown-on-garment-workers-rights-says-report.

51. Jay Lombard, *The Mind of God: Neuroscience, Faith, and a Search for the Soul* (New York: Harmony Books, 2017).

52. Michael K. Honey, "Martin Luther King's forgotten legacy? His fight for economic justice," *Guardian*, April 3, 2018, https://www.theguardian.com/commentisfree/2018/apr/03/martin-luther-king -50th-anniversary-.

53. Donald Davis, "How the story transforms the teller," TEDxCharlotteville," YouTube video, December 23, 2014, 17:33, https://www.youtube.com/watch?v=wgeh4xhSA2Q.

54. William S. Burroughs, *The Ticket That Exploded* (Paris: Olympia Press, 1962).

55. David Gelles, "Marc Benioff of Salesforce: 'Are we not all connected?'" *New York Times*, June 15, 2018, https://www.nytimes.com/2018/06/15/business/marc-benioff-salesforce-corner-office.html.

56. Blake Morgan, "101 companies committed to reducing their carbon footprint," *Forbes*, August 26, 2019, https://www.forbes.com/sites/blakemorgan/2019/08/26/101-companies-committed-to -reducing-their-carbon-footprint/.

Chapter One: The Rise of We First Capitalism

1. Matt Phillips, "Repeat after me: The markets are not the economy," *New York Times*, May 10, 2020, https://www.nytimes.com/2020/05/10/business/stock-market-economy-coronavirus.html.

2. Joseph Stiglitz, "Beyond GDP," *Social Europe*, January 7, 2019, https://www.socialeurope.eu /beyond-gdp.

3. Arianne Cohen, "A Nobel-winning economist says it's time to kill the GDP," *Fast Company*, November 25, 2019, https://www.fastcompany.com/90435788/a-nobel-winning-economist-says -its-time-to-kill-the-gdp.

4. *BBC News*, "Iceland puts well-being ahead of GDP in budget," December 3, 2019, https://www.bbc .com/news/world-europe-50650155.

5. James Ellsmoor, "New Zealand ditches GDP for happiness and well-being," *Forbes*, July 11, 2019, https://www.forbes.com/sites/jamesellsmoor/2019/07/11/new-zealand-ditches-gdp-for-happiness -and-well-being/.

6. John Helliwell, Richard Layard, Jeffrey Sachs, and Jan-Emmanuel De Neve, eds., *World Happiness Report 2020*, Sustainable Development Solutions Network, https://worldhappiness.report /ed/2020/.

7. David Marchese, "Ben & Jerry's radical ice cream dreams," *New York Times*, July 27, 2020, https:// www.nytimes.com/interactive/2020/07/27/magazine/ben-jerry-interview.html.

8. John Elkington, *Green Swans: The Coming Boom in Regenerative Capitalism* (New York: Fast Company Press, 2020).

9. "Economists are rethinking the numbers on inequality," *Economist*, November 28, 2019, https://www.economist.com/briefing/2019/11/28/economists-are-rethinking-the-numbers-on -inequality?fsrc=scn/fb/te/bl/ed/economistsarerethinkingthenumbersoninequalitymeasuringthe1.

10. Institute for Policy Studies, "Global inequality," Inequality.org, accessed October 26, 2020, https:// inequality.org/facts/global-inequality/.

11. Michael Grothaus, "82% of all the wealth in the world went to just 1% of its people last year," *Fast Company*, January 22, 2018, https://www.fastcompany.com/40519523/82-of-all-the-earth-in-the -world-went-to-just-1-of-its-people-last-year.

12. Alison Beard, interview with Rebecca Henderson, "Why capitalists need to save democracy," *HBR IdeaCast*, podcast audio, March 10, 2020, https://hbr.org/podcast/2020/03/why-capitalists-need-to -save-democracy.

13. Centre for the Future of Democracy, *Youth and Satisfaction with Democracy*, Bennett Institute for Public Policy, accessed February 4, 2021, https://www.cam.ac.uk/system/files/youth_and _satisfaction_with_democracy.pdf.

14. Martin Wolf, "Why rigged capitalism is damaging liberal democracy," *Financial Times*, September 17, 2019, https://www.ft.com/content/5a8ab27e-d470-11e9-8367-807ebd53ab77.

15. Millionaires for Humanity, "Over 80 millionaires around the world call for higher taxes on the richest to help COVID-19 global recovery," Oxfam International, July 13, 2020, https://www .oxfam.org/en/press-releases/over-80-millionaires-around-world-call-higher-taxes-richest-help -covid-19-global.

16. Donna Lu, "2020 in review: Calls for universal basic income on the rise," *New Scientist*, December 16, 2020, https://www.newscientist.com/article/mg24833135-600-2020-in-review-calls-for-universal -basic-income-on-the-rise/.

17. Sam Meredith, "The coronavirus crisis could pave the way to universal basic income," *CNBC*, April 16, 2020, https://www.cnbc.com/2020/04/16/coronavirus-crisis-could-pave-the-way-to-a -universal-basic-income.html.

18. Union Bank of India, "UBI: A brave experiment or just welfare renamed?" *The Week*, April 9, 2021, https://www.pressreader.com/usa/the-week-us/20210409/282359747506493.

19. Oscar Williams-Grut, "Billionaire Salesforce founder: 'Capitalism as we know it is dead,'" *Yahoo! Finance*, January 21, 2020, https://finance.yahoo.com/news/davos-2020-salesforce-founder-capitalism -is-dead-181643945.html.

20. Forbes, "#69 Marc Benioff," accessed October 26, 2020, https://www.forbes.com/profile/marc -benioff.

21. Robert Safian, "Salesforce's Marc Benioff on the power of values," *Fast Company*, April 17, 2017, https://www.fastcompany.com/40397514/salesforces-marc-benioff-on-the-power-of-values.

22. Will Feuer, "Salesforce CEO Marc Benioff says over 300 companies have agreed to help plant one trillion trees," *CNBC*, January 23, 2020, https://www.cnbc.com/2020/01/23/salesforce-ceo-marc -benioff-300-companies-to-help-plant-1-trillion-trees.html.

23. Feuer, "Salesforce CEO Marc Benioff."

24. Trillion Trees, "Home," accessed October 27, 2020, https://www.trilliontrees.org/.

25. Aaron K. Chaterji and Michael W. Toffel, "Divided we lead," *Harvard Business Review*, March 22, 2018, https://hbr.org/2018/03/divided-we-lead.

26. Pippa Stevens, "Stakeholder capitalism has reached a 'tipping point,' says Salesforce CEO Benioff," *CNBC*, January 21, 2020, https://www.cnbc.com/2020/01/21/stakeholder-capitalism-has-reached -a-tipping-point-says-salesforce-ceo-benioff.html.

27. Addisu Lashitew, "Stakeholder capitalism arrives at Davos," *Future Development* (blog), World Bank and Brookings Institution, January 21, 2020, https://www.brookings.edu/blog/future -development/2020/01/21/stakeholder-capitalism-arrives-at-davos/.

28. Peter Vanham, "Klaus Schwab releases 'stakeholder capitalism'; making the case for a global econ-omy that works for progress, people and planet," World Economic Forum (news release), January 29, 2021, https://www.weforum.org/press/2021/01/klaus-schwab-releases-stakeholder-capitalism -making-the-case-for-a-global-economy-that-works-for-progress-people-and-planet/.

29. Klaus Schwab, "Now is the time for a 'great reset,'" World Economic Forum, June 3, 2020, https:// www.weforum.org/agenda/2020/06/now-is-the-time-for-a-great-reset/.

30. Salesforce, "'CEOs must mandate for all stakeholders, not just shareholders': Marc Benioff joins Davos panel on stakeholder capitalism," January 26, 2021, https://www.salesforce.com/news /stories/marc-benioff-on-stakeholder-capitalism-davos-2021/.

31. Andrew Ross Sorkin, "BlackRock's message: Contribute to society, or risk losing our support," *New York Times*, January 15, 2018, https://www.nytimes.com/2018/01/15/business/dealbook/blackrock -laurence-fink-letter.html.

32. Kallen Diggs, "Why corporate philanthropy is the 21st century standard," *HuffPost*, December 6, 2017, https://www.huffpost.com/entry/why-corporate-social-resp_1_b_9671642.

33. Diggs, "Why corporate philanthropy is the 21st century standard."

34. Edelman, "Edelman Trust Barometer 2020," January 19, 2020, https://www.edelman.com/trust /2020-trust-barometer.

35. Tristan Harris, interview with Lawrence O'Donnell, *Last Word*, January 14, 2021, https://www .msnbc.com/the-last-word/watch/former-google-ethicist-we-have-been-watching-different-movies -of-reality-99504709530.

36. Adam Grant, *Think Again: The Power of Knowing What You Don't Know* (New York: Viking, 2021).

37. Edelman, "Edelman Trust Barometer 2020."

38. David Brooks, "America is having a moral convulsion," *Atlantic*, October 5, 2020, https://www.the atlantic.com/ideas/archive/2020/10/collapsing-levels-trust-are-devastating-america/616581/.

39. Edelman, "Trust Barometer special report: Brand trust in 2020," June 25, 2020, https://www .edelman.com/research/brand-trust-2020.

40. Edelman, "Brands take a stand," accessed October 29, 2020, https://www.edelman.com/sites/g /files/aatuss191/files/2018-10/2018_Edelman_Earned_Brand_Global_Report.pdf.

41. Edelman, "2020 Edelman Trust Barometer spring update," May 5, 2020, https://www.edelman .com/research/trust-2020-spring-update.

42. Andrew C. Wicks and Brian T. Moriarty, "Public trust in business: What's the problem and why does it matter?" in *Public Trust in Business*, ed. Jared D. Harris, Brian Moriarty, and Andrew C. Wicks (Cambridge, UK: Cambridge University Press, 2014), doi.org/10.1017/CBO9781139152389.002.

43. André Gonçalves, "Globally, business and government lack trust, a new survey shows," Youmatter, February 27, 2020, https://youmatter.world/en/business-government-trust/.

44. Laura Poppo and Donald J. Schepker, "The repair of public trust following controllable or uncon- trollable organization failures: A conceptual framework," in *Public Trust in Business*, ed. Jared D. Harris, Brian Moriarty and Andrew C. Wicks (Cambridge, UK: Cambridge University Press, 2014), doi.org/10.1017/CBO9781139152389.002.

45. Page Knowledge Base, *The Dynamics of Public Trust in Business—Emerging Opportunities for Lead- ers*, accessed January 22, 2021, https://knowledge.page.org/report/the-dynamics-of-public-trust-in -business-emerging-opportunities-for-leaders/.

46. Page Knowledge Base, *The Dynamics of Public Trust in Business*.

47. Page Knowledge Base, *The Dynamics of Public Trust in Business*.

48. Michael Pirson and Kristen Martin, "Public trust in business and its determinants," in *Public Trust in Business*, ed. Jared D. Harris, Brian Moriarty, and Andrew C. Wicks (Cambridge, UK: Cam- bridge University Press, 2014), doi.org/10.1017/CBO9781139152389.002.

49. Ethisphere, "The world's most ethical companies," accessed April 7, 2021, https://www.worldsmost ethicalcompanies.com/.

50. Alex Edmans, *Grow the Pie: How Great Companies Deliver Both Purpose and Profit* (Cambridge, UK: Cambridge University Press, 2020).

51. Medard Gabel, "Buckminster Fuller and the game of the world," in *Buckminster Fuller: An Anthol- ogy for the New Millennium* (New York: St. Martin's Press, 1999).

52. Daniel Christian Wahl, "Visionaries of regenerative design III: R. Buckminster Fuller (1895– 1983)," *Age of Awareness*, March 18, 2017, https://medium.com/age-of-awareness/visionaries-of -regenerative-design-iii-r-buckminster-fuller-1895-1983-51ada798f11.

53. James F. Moore, "Predators and prey: A new ecology of competition," *Harvard Business Review*, May–June 1993, https://hbr.org/1993/05/predators-and-prey-a-new-ecology-of-competition.

54. Lynne Twist, *The Soul of Money: Transforming Your Relationship with Money and Life* (New York: W.W. Norton, 2017); *Buckminster Fuller*.

55. Twist, *The Soul of Money*; *Buckminster Fuller*.

56. Albert Schweitzer, "The meaning of ideals in life" (speech, Silcoates School, Wakefield, England, December, 3, 1935).

57. Cara Buckley, "Apocalypse got you down? Maybe this will help?," *New York Times*, November 15, 2019, https://www.nytimes.com/2019/11/15/sunday-review/depression-climate-change.html.

58. David J. Schwartz, *The Magic of Thinking Big* (New York: Simon and Schuster, 1987).

59. Ben Soltoff, "Leaders from Unilever, WWF, others reflect on what's changed since the first Earth Day," GreenBiz, April 22, 2020, https://www.greenbiz.com/article/leaders-unilever-wwf-others -reflect-whats-changed-first-earth-day.

60. Yale School of Management, Yale Business Sustainability Summit April 2020, accessed October 26, 2020, https://som.yale.edu/sites/default/files/files/Yale%202020%20Yale%20Business%20 Sustainability_Key%20Themes_v8.pdf.

61. Judith Humphrey, "Using collaborative language is essential in time of crisis," *Fast Company*, March 3, 2020, https://www.fastcompany.com/90481201/using-collaborative-language-is-essential -in-times-of-crisis.

62. Gillian Teff et al., "Coronavirus poses 'acid test' for conscious capitalism; climate pressure continues," *Financial Times*, March 18, 2020, https://www.ft.com/content/b0620412-846b-4dcb-9451 -d0887c3d8aba?fbclid=IwAR0T-uCLS6q1wQqw5bhMbAb9LHGWiNbGPZ8BpTmHA-lwTww TGfVQgGmfZs8.

63. Kevin Stankiewicz, "Mark Cuban says how companies treat workers during pandemic could define their brand 'for decades,'" *CNBC*, March 25, 2020, https://www.cnbc.com/2020/03/25/coronavirus -mark-cuban-warns-against-rushing-employees-back-to-work.html.

64. Byron Loflin, "The coronavirus crisis will speed up the end of shareholder primacy," *Fast Company*, April 14, 2020, https://www.fastcompany.com/90489502/the-coronavirus-crisis-will-speed-the -end-of-shareholder-primacy.

65. Business Roundtable, "Business Roundtable redefines the purpose of a corporation to promote 'an economy that serves all Americans,'" August 19, 2019, https://www.businessroundtable.org /business-roundtable-redefines-the-purpose-of-a-corporation-to-promote-an-economy-that-serves -all-americans.

66. Solgaard, "Our Mission," accessed February 2, 2021, https://solgaard.co/pages/our-mission.

67. "H&M, Nike face boycotts in China as Xinjiang dilemma deepens," *Bloomberg News,* March 24, 2021, https://www.bloomberg.com/news/articles/2021-03-25/h-m-nike-face-boycotts-in-china-as -xinjiang-becomes-wedge-issue.

68. Sam Levin and Laura Snapes, "Rihanna wipes $1bn off Snapchat after criticizing app for making a 'joke' of domestic violence," *Guardian*, March 15, 2018, https://www.theguardian.com/music/2018 /mar/15/rihanna-snapchat-ad-domestic-violence-chris-brown.

69. Emma Stefansky, "Snapchat lost $800 million after Rihanna criticized its offensive ad," *Vanity Fair*, March 17, 2018, https://www.vanityfair.com/style/2018/03/rihanna-chris-brown-snapchat-ad.

70. John Mackey and Raj Sisodia, *Conscious Capitalism: Liberating the Heroic Spirit of Business* (Cambridge, MA: Harvard Business Review Press, 2013).

71. Rajendra Sisodia, David B. Wolfe, and Jagdish N. Sheth, *Firms of Endearment: How World-Class Companies Profit from Passion and Purpose* (Upper Saddle River, NJ: Pearson Prentice Hall, 2007).

72. Marissa Beechuk and Brittany VanderBeek, "'Firms of endearment' find enlightenment by engaging stakeholders," GreenBiz, March 3, 2014, https://www.greenbiz.com/article/firms-endearment -find-enlightenment-engaging-stakeholders.

73. Stephen P. Ashkin, "Sustainability: history of the word and its meaning today," *Restoration Remediation*, July 16, 2018, https://www.randrmagonline.com/articles/88041-sustainability-history-of -the-word-its-meaning-today.

74. Corporate Citizenship, "Sustainability Timeline," accessed October 26, 2020, https://corporate -citizenship.com/sustainability-timeline/.

75. Bethany Hubbard, "The Ecologist January 1972: A blueprint for survival," *Ecologist*, January 27, 2012, https://theecologist.org/2012/jan/27/ecologist-january-1972-blueprint-survival.

76. United Nations, *Report of the World Commission on Environment and Development: Our Common Future*, accessed October 26, 2020, https://sustainabledevelopment.un.org/content/documents/598 7our-common-future.pdf.

77. Corporate Citizenship, "Sustainability timeline," accessed October 26, 2020, https://corporate -citizenship.com/sustainability-timeline/.

78. D. L. Cooperrider and R. Fry, "Mirror flourishing and the positive psychology of sustainability," *Journal of Corporate Citizenship* 46 (2013): 3–12.

79. David Cooperrider, "Mirror flourishing: The new business north star," *Kosmos Journal*, Spring/Summer 2016, https://www.kosmosjournal.org/article/mirror-flourishing-the-new-business-north-star/.

80. J. R. Ehrenfeld and A. J. Hoffman, *Flourishing: A Frank Conversation About Sustainability* (Stanford, CA: Stanford University Press, 2013).

81. Planetiers World Gathering, "Planetiers Home Gathering #33—John Elkington & Paul Hawken," YouTube video, September 5, 2020, 27:33, https://www.youtube.com/watch?v=V4RvNgGaqvM.

82. Tom Moore, "A moment of truth for purpose-driven businesses," *B the Change, Medium*, May 7, 2020, https://bthechange.com/a-moment-of-truth-for-purpose-driven-businesses-caa898e000c8.

83. Simon Mainwaring, "Purpose at work: How CleanWell's sustainability commitment wins market share," *Forbes*, August 25, 2020, https://www.forbes.com/sites/simonmainwaring/2020/08/25/purpose-at-work-how-cleanwells-sustainability-commitment-wins-market-share/?sh=6707c9b7efd5.

84. Aaron Hall, "Renaming climate change: Can a new name finally make us take action?" Ad Age, November 27, 2019, https://adage.com/article/industry-insights/renaming-climate-change-can-new-name-finally-make-us-take-action/2218821.

85. Elijah Wolfson, "'Global warming' and 'climate change' are disasters at conveying our environmental predicament," *Quartz*, January 31, 2019, https://qz.com/1539285/global-warming-and-climate-change-are-disasters-at-conveying-our-environmental-predicament/.

86. Michael J. Coren, "Global warming will hit states that support Donald Trump the hardest," *Quartz*, January 29, 2019, https://qz.com/1535932/global-warming-will-hit-states-supporting-donald-trump-hardest/.

87. Bryan Bender, "The new language of climate change," *Politico*, January 27, 2019, https://www.politico.com/magazine/story/2019/01/27/climate-change-politics-224295.

88. Per Epsen Stoknes, "How to transform apocalyptic fatigue into action on global warming," filmed at TEDGlobal, September 2017, New York City, 4:52, https://www.ted.com/talks/per_espen_stoknes_how_to_transform_apocalypse_fatigue_into_action_on_global_warming?language=en.

89. Caroline Hickman, "Our environmental problem is also a mental problem," *Fast Company*, June 8, 2019, https://www.fastcompany.com/90358827/our-environmental-problem-is-also-a-mental-problem.

90. Elizabeth Boulton, "Climate change as a 'hyperobject': A critical review of Timothy Morton's reframing narrative," ed. Mike Hulme, *Wiley Interdisciplinary Review* 7, no. 5 (2016), https://www.researchgate.net/publication/303801414_Climate_change_as_a_'hyperobject'_a_critical_review_of_Timothy_Morton's_reframing_narrative_Climate_change_as_a_hyperobject.

91. Joel Makower, "Capitalism's change of climate," GreenBiz, August 6, 2019, https://www.greenbiz.com/article/capitalisms-change-climate.

92. Makower, "Capitalism's change of climate."

93. Mark R. Kramer, "Larry Fink isn't going to read your sustainability report," *Harvard Business Review*, January 20, 2020, https://hbr.org/2020/01/larry-fink-isnt-going-to-read-your-sustainability-report.

94. Bryan Bender, "The new language of climate change," *Politico*, January 27, 2019, https://www.politico.com/magazine/story/2019/01/27/climate-change-politics-224295.

95. Hall, "Renaming climate change."

96. Mark Fischetti, "We are living in a climate emergency, and we're going to say so," *Scientific American*, April 12, 2021, https://www.scientificamerican.com/article/we-are-living-in-a-climate-emergency-and-were-going-to-say-so/.

97. Damian Carrington, "Why the *Guardian* is changing the language it uses about the environment," *Guardian*, May 17, 2019, https://www.theguardian.com/environment/2019/may/17/why-the-guardian-is-changing-the-language-it-uses-about-the-environment.

98. Max Roser, "Economic growth," Our World in Data, accessed October 26, 2020, "https://ourworldindata.org/economic-growth.

99. Jonathan Tapper with Denise Hearn, *The Myth of Capitalism* (Hoboken, NJ: Wiley, 2018).

100. Rebecca Henderson, *Reimagining Capitalism in a World on Fire* (New York: Public Affairs, 2020).

101. Peter Diamandis and Steven Kotler, *Abundance: The Future Is Better Than You Think* (New York: Free Press, 2012).

102. Derin Cag, "Michael Porter's approach: How to create shared value in business (top 3 tips)," Richtopia, accessed October 26, 2020, https://richtopia.com/effective-leadership/michael-porter-shared-value.

103. Mary Mazzoni, "5 Steps to reimagine capitalism in a changing world," TriplePundit, March 31, 2020, https://www.triplepundit.com/story/2020/reimagine-capitalism-COVID-19/87056.
104. Cag, "Michael Porter's approach."
105. B the Change, "Dear Business Roundtable CEOs: Let's get to work," *Medium*, August 25, 2019, https://bthechange.com/dear-business-roundtable-ceos-lets-get-to-work-25f06457738c.
106. Hubert Joy, "A time to lead with purpose and humanity," *Harvard Business Review*, March 24, 2020, https://hbr.org/2020/03/a-time-to-lead-with-purpose-and-humanity.
107. Martin Luther King Jr., "Remaining awake through a great revolution" (speech, Washington, DC, March 31, 1968), Martin Luther King Jr. Research and Education Institute.
108. Simon Mainwaring, "Purpose at work: How Traditional Medicinals powerfully combines purpose and profit," *Forbes*, April 23, 2019, https://www.forbes.com/sites/simonmainwaring/2019/04/23/purpose-at-work-how-traditional-medicinals-powerfully-combines-purpose-and-profit/.
109. Triple Pundit, "How brands communicated purpose in 2019," January 1, 2020, https://www.triplepundit.com/story/2020/how-brands-communicated-purpose-2019/86071.
110. Nathan Bomey, "Under Armour CEO Kevin Plank steps down as turnaround effort continues," *USA Today*, October 22, 2019, https://www.usatoday.com/story/money/2019/10/22/under-armour-ceo-kevin-plank-patrik-frisk/4060838002/.
111. Bomey, "Under Armour CEO Kevin Plank."
112. US Department of Justice, "Ohio man sentenced to life in prison for federal hate crimes related to August 2017 car attack at rally in Charlottesville, Virginia," June 28, 2019, https://www.justice.gov/opa/pr/ohio-man-sentenced-life-prison-federal-hate-crimes-related-august-2017-car-attack-rally.
113. Angie Drobnic-Holan, "In Context: Donald Trump's 'very fine people on both sides' remarks (transcript)," *Politifact*, April 26, 2019, https://www.politifact.com/article/2019/apr/26/context-trumps-very-fine-people-both-sides-remarks/.
114. David Gelles, "The moral voice of corporate America," *New York Times*, August 19, 2017, https://www.nytimes.com/2017/08/19/business/moral-voice-ceos.html.
115. Simon Mainwaring, "Top 17 in purposeful branding for 2017: The We First year in review," *We First Branding* (blog), December 29, 2017, https://www.wefirstbranding.com/we-first/top-17-purposeful-branding-2017-first-year-review/.
116. Simon Mainwaring, "Purpose at work: How Ben & Jerry's combines growth and brand activism," *Forbes*, February 26, 2020, https://www.forbes.com/sites/simonmainwaring/2020/02/26/purpose-at-work-how-ben--jerrys-combines-growth-and-brand-activism/.
117. Interface, "Carbon Negative," accessed October 30, 2020, https://www.interface.com/US/en-US/sustainability/carbon-negative-en_US.
118. Simon Mainwaring, "Purpose at work: How Interface is building a climate movement with business solutions," *Forbes*, October 21, 2019, https://www.forbes.com/sites/simonmainwaring/2019/10/21/purpose-at-work-how-interface-is-building-a-climate-movement-with-business-solutions/; Interface, "Interface announces mission zero success, commits to climate take back," *PR Newswire*, November 4, 2020, https://www.prnewswire.com/news-releases/interface-announces-mission-zero-success-commits-to-climate-take-back-300949740.html.
119. Mainwaring, "Purpose at work: How Interface is building."
120. Interface, "Climate take back," accessed October 27, 2020, https://www.interface.com/US/en-US/sustainability/climate-take-back-en_US.
121. Mainwaring, "Purpose at work: How Interface is building."
122. Laura Feiner, "Salesforce bans companies that sell certain types of guns from using its software," *CNBC*, May 30, 2019, https://www.cnbc.com/2019/05/30/salesforce-bans-some-gun-sellers-from-using-its-software.html.
123. Chris Isidore, "Dick's Sporting Goods will stop selling assault-style rifles," *CNN Money*, February 28, 2018, https://money.cnn.com/2018/02/28/news/companies/dicks-weapon-ban/index.html.
124. Isidore, "Dick's Sporting Goods."
125. Adam Peck, "Dick's Sporting Goods removed guns from their stores and sales are climbing," *ThinkProgress*, August 25, 2019, https://archive.thinkprogress.org/dicks-sporting-goods-sales-rise-gun-ban-78e1cbb7b23c/.

126. Zlati Meyer, "Dick's Sporting Goods is doing just fine without guns," *Fast Company*, November 26, 2019, https://www.fastcompany.com/90436511/dicks-sporting-goods-is-doing-just-fine-without -guns.

127. Peck, "Dick's Sporting Goods."

128. Terry Nguyen, "Dick's Sporting Goods destroyed $5 million worth of guns it pulled from its stores," *Vox*, October 8, 2019, https://www.vox.com/the-goods/2019/10/8/20904713/dicks-destroyed-guns -5-million-dollars.

129. Sarah Nassauer, "Walmart to stop selling ammunition for assault-style weapons," *Wall Street Journal*, September 3, 2019, https://www.wsj.com/articles/walmart-to-stop-selling-ammunition-for -assault-style-weapons-11567530289.

130. Kate Taylor, "Here are all the retailers that have stopped selling assault-style rifles and changed firearm policies following gun-control activists' protests," *Business Insider*, March 2, 2018, https:// www.businessinsider.com/retailers-change-gun-policies-after-gun-control-protests-2018-3.

131. Daniel Korschun, "Companies that stay silent on political issues can pay a hefty price," *Fast Company*, February, 7, 2017, https://www.fastcompany.com/3067944/political-neutrality-can-be -costly.

132. Adam Rosenberg, "Lyft pledges $1 million ACLU donation in response to Trump's #MuslimBan," *Mashable*, January 29, 2017, https://mashable.com/2017/01/29/lyft-aclu-donation-trump-muslim -ban/.

133. Kate Rooney, "Coinbase CEO discourages politics at work, offers generous severance to employees who want to quit," *CNBC*, September 30, 2020, https://www.cnbc.com/2020/09/30/coinbase-ceo -offers-severance-to-employees-leaving-over-politics.html.

134. Taylor Hatmaker, "Basecamp sees mass employee exodus after CEO bans political discussions," *TechCrunch*, April 30, 2021, https://techcrunch.com/2021/04/30/basecamp-employees-quit-ceo -letter/.

135. Richard Feloni and Amanda Keating, "The attack on the Capitol prompted an unprecedented wave of responses from corporate America—we've collected them," JUST Capital, January 14, 2021, https://justcapital.com/news/corporate-responses-to-us-capitol-attack-01-2021/.

136. Mike Isaac, "Facebook oversight board upholds social network's ban of Trump," *New York Times*, May 5, 2021, https://www.nytimes.com/2021/05/05/technology/facebook-trump-ban-upheld .html.

137. Jane C. Timm, "Hundreds of CEOs, celebrities, corporations join forces to oppose 'discriminatory' voting legislation," *NBC News*, April 14, 2021, https://www.nbcnews.com/politics /elections/hundreds-ceos-celebrities-corporations-join-forces-oppose-discriminatory-voting -legislation-n1264034.

138. Jeff Beer, "Patagonia CEO calls on U.S. business leaders to act on restrictive voting laws," *Fast Company*, April 6, 2021, https://www.fastcompany.com/90622444/patagonia-ceo-calls-on-u-s -business-leaders-to-act-on-restrictive-voting-laws.

139. Deloitte, "Culture of purpose: Building business confidence; driving growth," accessed February 3, 2021, https://www2.deloitte.com/content/dam/Deloitte/us/Documents/about-deloitte/us -leadership-2014-core-beliefs-culture-survey-040414.pdf.

140. Business & Sustainable Development Commission, "Better business, better world," accessed October 26, 2020, https://d306pr3pise04h.cloudfront.net/docs/news_events%2F9.3%2Fbetter -business-better-world.pdf.

141. Business & Sustainable Development Commission, "Better business, better world."

142. Larry Fink, "A fundamental reshaping of finance," BlackRock, January 14, 2020, https://www .blackrock.com/us/individual/larry-fink-ceo-letter.

143. Larry Fink, "Larry Fink's 2021 letter to CEOs," accessed February 12, 2021, https://www .blackrock.com/corporate/investor-relations/larry-fink-ceo-letter.

144. Rachel Zurer, "On Transit," *Conscious Company*, Spring 2018, 5.

145. Peter Whoriskey, Douglas MacMillan, and Jonathan O'Connell, "'Doomed to fail': Why a $4 trillion bailout couldn't revive the American economy," *Washington Post*, October 5, 2020, https:// www.washingtonpost.com/graphics/2020/business/coronavirus-bailout-spending/.

146. United Nations, "UN Report: Nature's dangerous decline 'unprecedented'; species extinction rate 'accelerating'," Sustainable Development Goals (blog), May 6, 2019, https://www.un.org/sustainabledevelopment/blog/2019/05/nature-decline-unprecedented-report/.

Chapter 2: Urgency

1. Simon Mainwaring, "Podcast," accessed October 27, 2020, https://simonmainwaring.com/podcast/.
2. Gus Lubin, "The US is making a big shift away from factory farming," *Business Insider*, February 8, 2017, https://www.businessinsider.com/factory-farming-on-the-decline-2017-2.
3. Jonathan Lowe, "Worldwide shutdown leads to visible, positive environmental impacts," *Spectrum News 1*, April 6, 2020, https://spectrumlocalnews.com/nc/charlotte/news/2020/04/06/worldwide-shutdown-leads-to-visible--positive-environmental-impacts.
4. Alisha Ebrahimji, "Sea turtles are thriving as coronavirus lockdown empties Florida beaches," *CBS 58*, April 18, 2020, https://www.cbs58.com/news/sea-turtles-are-thriving-as-coronavirus-lockdown-empties-florida-beaches.
5. Lucas Shaw, "Netflix to shift $100 million in cash into Black-owned banks," *Bloomberg*, June 30, 2020, https://www.bloomberg.com/news/articles/2020-06-30/netflix-will-shift-100-million-of-cash-into-black-owned-banks.
6. Jonathan Stempel, "McKinsey settles with holdout Nevada for $45 million over role in opioid crisis," *Reuters*, March 22, 2021, https://www.reuters.com/article/us-usa-mckinsey-nevada/mckinsey-settles-with-holdout-nevada-for-45-million-over-role-in-opioid-crisis-idUSKBN2BE2XH.
7. McKinsey & Company, "Igniting individual purpose in times of crisis," August 18, 2020, https://www.mckinsey.com/business-functions/organization/our-insights/igniting-individual-purpose-in-times-of-crisis.
8. Simon Mainwaring, "Purpose at work: How brands must respond in times of social crisis," *Forbes*, July 13, 2020, https://www.forbes.com/sites/simonmainwaring/2020/07/13/purpose-at-work-how-brands-must-respond-in-times-of-social-crisis.
9. John Elkington, *Green Swans: The Coming Boom in Regenerative Capitalism* (New York: Fast Company Press, 2020).
10. Rebecca Henderson, *Reimagining Capitalism in a World on Fire* (New York: Public Affairs, 2020), 8.
11. Henderson, *Reimagining Capitalism in a World on Fire*.
12. Simon Mainwaring, "Purpose at work: How Vita Coco is starting a COVID-19 impact movement," *Forbes*, April 22, 2020, https://www.forbes.com/sites/simonmainwaring/2020/04/22/purpose-at-work-how-vita-coco-is-starting-a-covid-19-impact-movement/.
13. Mainwaring, "Purpose at Work: How Vita Coco is starting a COVID-19 impact movement."
14. Bombas, "About Us," accessed October 27, 2020, https://bombas.com/pages/about-us.
15. Simon Mainwaring, "Purpose at work: SanMar, sustainability and pivoting during COVID-19," *Forbes*, July 28, 2020, https://www.forbes.com/sites/simonmainwaring/2020/07/28/purpose-at-work-sanmar-sustainability-and-pivoting-during-covid-19/.
16. Hubert Joly, "A time to lead with purpose and humanity," *Harvard Business Review*, March 24, 2020, https://hbr.org/2020/03/a-time-to-lead-with-purpose-and-humanity.
17. Simon Mainwaring, "Purpose at work: How brands lead with their purpose to combat the coronavirus," *Forbes*, March 18, 2020, https://www.forbes.com/sites/simonmainwaring/2020/03/18/purpose-at-work-how-brands-lead-with-their-purpose-to-combat-the-coronavirus/.
18. Carol Cone and Kristin Kenny, "The COVID-19 pandemic is sparking an era of 'smart generosity,'" *Fast Company*, April 27, 2020, https://www.fastcompany.com/90496736/the-covid-19-pandemic-is-sparking-an-era-of-smart-generosity.
19. Mainwaring, "Purpose at work: SanMar."
20. Tazo, "Our tree corps ambassador," accessed March 26, 2021, https://www.tazo.com/us/en/treecorps.html.
21. Elizabeth D. Samet, *Leadership Essentials by Our Greatest Thinkers* (New York: W. W. Norton & Company, 2015).

22. Joshua Rothman, "Shut up and sit down," *New Yorker*, February 22, 2016, https://www.newyorker.com/magazine/2016/02/29/our-dangerous-leadership-obsession.

23. Adele Peters, "Coke's newest bottle is made from paper," *Fast Company,* February 21, 2021, https://www.fastcompany.com/90604514/cokes-newest-bottle-is-made-from-paper.

24. "What is Nestlé doing to tackle plastic packaging waste?," Nestlé, accessed March 26, 2021, https://www.nestle.com/ask-nestle/environment/answers/tackling-packaging-waste-plastic-bottles.

25. "Nestlé aiming at 100% recyclable or reusable packaging by 2025," Nestlé, April 10, 2018, https://www.nestle.com/media/pressreleases/allpressreleases/nestle-recyclable-reusable-packaging-by-2025.

26. Thomas L. Friedman, "We Need Great Leadership Now, and Here's What It Looks Like," *New York Times*, April 21, 2020, https://www.nytimes.com/2020/04/21/opinion/covid-dov-seidman.html.

27. Diana Pearl, "Adidas and Allbirds are teaming up to create a shoe with a low carbon footprint," *Adweek*, May 28, 2020, https://www.adweek.com/brand-marketing/allbirds-and-adidas-team-up-to-reduce-the-footwear-industrys-carbon-footprint.

28. "Parley Ocean Plastic," Adidas, accessed May 18, 2021, https://www.adidas.com/us/sustainability-parley-ocean-plastic.

29. John G. Neihardt, *Black Elk Speaks: Being the Life Story of a Holy Man of the Oglala Sioux* (Lincoln, NE: Bison Books, 2014).

30. Pablo Strong, "Man predicts future of the world," YouTube video, February 28, 2019, 13:53, https://www.youtube.com/watch?v=Gh-NdehdZfc.

31. Maria Chiorando, "We have 'urgent responsibility' to protect wildlife and the planet, says Dalai Lama," *Plant Based News*, February 17, 2020, https://www.plantbasednews.org/news/urgent-responsibility-protect-wildlife-and-planet-dalai-lama.

32. "What is biomimicry?," Biomimicry Institute, accessed October 28, 2020, https://biomimicry.org/what-is-biomimicry/.

33. "The Biomimicry Institute," Biomimicry Institute, accessed October 28, 2020, https://biomimicry.org/.

34. Gregory Unruh, "Mimicking nature, but not as nature intended: An introduction to geomimicry," November 5, 2018, https://sustainablebrands.com/read/product-service-design-innovation/mimicking-nature-but-not-as-nature-intended-an-introduction-to-geomimicry.

35. Unruh, "Mimicking Nature.

36. David H. Saiia, "Corporate ecology," in *Encyclopedia of Business Ethics and Society*, ed. Robert W. Kolb (2008), 467–68, doi: 10.4135/9781412956260.n196.

37. Twist, *The Soul of Money*.

38. "How trees secretly talk to each other," *BBC News*, YouTube video, June 29, 2018, 1:15, https://www.youtube.com/watch?v=yWOqeyPIVRo&feature=emb_title.

39. Robert Macfarlane, "The secrets of the Wood Wide Web," *New Yorker*, August 7, 2016, https://www.newyorker.com/tech/annals-of-technology/the-secrets-of-the-wood-wide-web.

40. David K. Hurst, "Forces of nature," *strategy+business*, April 30, 2020, https://www.strategy-business.com/article/Forces-of-nature.

41. C. S. Holling, "Understanding the complexity of economic, ecological, and social systems," *Ecosystems* 4 (2001): 390–405, https://doi.org/10.1007/s10021-001-0101-5.

42. Janine Benyus, 2009, "Biomimicry in action," TedGlobal video, Oxford, UK, 17:24, https://www.ted.com/talks/janine_benyus_biomimicry_in_action.

43. Biomimicry Institute, "What is biomimicry?"

44. Janine Benyus, "Designing society through the natural world," *The Environment* (blog), Aspen Institute, June 26, 2018, https://www.aspeninstitute.org/blog-posts/designing-society-through-the-natural-world/.

45. Brandon Keim, "Nature, heal thyself: The lessons of restoration ecology," *Anthropocene*, April 11, 2018, https://www.anthropocenemagazine.org/2018/04/nature-heal-thyself-the-lessons-of-restoration-ecology/.

46. Tim Idle, "Benyus: COVID-19 offers 'utopian glimmer' of new world, but we must give back to nature,'" Sustainable Brands, May 25, 2020, https://sustainablebrands.com/read/defining-the-next -economy/benyus-covid-19-offers-utopian-glimmer-of-new-world-but-we-must-give-back-to-nature.

47. Jianxi Gao, Baruch Barzel, and Albert-László Barabási, "Universal resilience in complex networks," *Nature* 530 (2016): 307–12, https://doi.org/10.1038/nature16948.

Chapter 3: Paradigm

1. Anand Giridharadas, *Winners Take All: The Elite Charade of Changing the World* (New York: Vintage, 2018).

2. Giridharadas, *Winners Take All*.

3. Giridharadas, *Winners Take All*.

4. Anand Giridharadas, "The new elite's phony crusade to save the world—without changing anything," *Guardian*, January 22, 2019, https://www.theguardian.com/news/2019/jan/22/the-new -elites-phoney-crusade-to-save-the-world-without-changing-anything.

5. Diana O'Brien, Andy Main, Suzanne Kounkel, and Anthony R. Stephan, "Purpose is everything: How brands that authentically lead with purpose are changing the nature of business today," Deloitte, October 16, 2019, https://www2.deloitte.com/us/en/insights/topics/marketing-and-sales -operations/global-marketing-trends/2020/purpose-driven-companies.html.

6. O'Brien et al., "Purpose is everything."

7. O'Brien et al., "Purpose is everything."

8. VFC, "Financial results: Fourth quarter fiscal 2020," accessed October 28, 2020, https:// d1io3yog0oux5.cloudfront.net/_b62fdec333c75ff6ed5e3aa64796c78b/vfc/db/409/70380 /infographic/VF_IR-Q4-2020_Final.pdf.

9. "Five case studies proving the ROI of sustainability," Sustainable Brands, accessed December 3, 2020, https://events.sustainablebrands.com/newmetrics19/5-case-studies-proving-the-roi-of -sustainability/.

10. Claudine Madras Gartenberg, Andrea Prat, and George Serafeim, "Corporate Purpose and Financial Performance," *Organization Science* 30 (2016): 1–18, https://papers.ssrn.com/sol3/papers.cfm ?abstract_id=2840005.

11. Scott Broomfield and Dimitar Vlahov, "Redesigning the purpose of business for humanity: Let's talk know-how," Sustainable Brands, September 23, 2019, https://sustainablebrands.com/read /leadership/redesigning-the-purpose-of-business-for-humanity-let-s-talk-know-how.

12. Charlie Mahoney and Steffen Bixby, "Chart of the week: JUST businesses have a higher return on equity," JUST Capital, October 28, 2020, https://justcapital.com/news/chart-of-the-week-just -businesses-have-a-higher-return-on-equity/.

13. Martin Whittaker and Simon Mainwaring, "3BL Forum: Ep 3: Session 5 ft. JUST Capital & We First," 2020 3BL Virtual Forum, October 22, 2020.

14. Whittaker and Mainwaring, "3BL Forum."

15. "Consumer spending," Bureau of Economic Analysis, October 1, 2020, https://www.bea.gov/data /consumer-spending/main.

16. David Cooperrider and Audrey Seilan, "Business as an agent of world benefit," Scoop post, January 2, 2020, https://www.scoop.it/topic/business-as-an-agent-of-world-benefit.

17. Giovanni Rodriguez, "This is your brain on storytelling: The chemistry of modern communication," *Forbes*, July 21, 2017, https://www.forbes.com/sites/giovannirodriguez/2017/07/21/this-is -your-brain-on-storytelling-the-chemistry-of-modern-communication/.

18. "Armory of Harmony," accessed February 3, 2021, https://www.armoryofharmony.com/.

19. "Armory of Harmony."

20. Afdhel Aziz, "The power of purpose: How Armory of Harmony is turning guns into musical instruments for children," *Forbes*, December 2, 2019, https://www.forbes.com/sites/afdhelaziz/2019/12 /02/the-power-of-purpose-how-armory-of-harmony-is-turning-guns-into-musical-instruments-for -children/?sh=2eeebd0f5a71.

21. Ye Yuan, Judy Major-Girardin, and Steven Brown, "Storytelling is intrinsically mentalistic: A functional magnetic resonance imaging study of narrative production across modalities," *Journal of Cognitive Neuroscience* 30, no. 9 (2018): 1298–1314, doi: 10.1162/jocn_a_01294.

22. McMaster University, "The art of storytelling: Researchers explore why we relate to characters," *Science Daily*, September 13, 2018, https://www.sciencedaily.com/releases/2018/09/180913113822.htm.

23. "Ari Wallach," Longpath Labs, accessed October 29, 2020, https://www.longpath.org/ari-wallach.

24. Kim Polman, "It's time to reboot your future," *Real Leaders*, April 8, 2020, https://real-leaders.com/its-time-to-reboot-your-future/.

25. Paul Valéry, *Reflections on the World Today* (New York: Pantheon Books, 1948).

26. Oliver Milman, "Greta Thunberg condemns world leaders in emotional speech at UN," *Guardian*, September 23, 2019, https://www.theguardian.com/environment/2019/sep/23/greta-thunberg-speech-un-2019-address.

27. David H. Pink, *Drive: The Surprising Truth About What Motivates Us* (New York: Riverhead Books, 2009).

28. Pink, *Drive*.

29. Michelle Greene, "A principles-based approach," Long Term Stock Exchange, accessed October 29, 2020, https://longtermstockexchange.com/listings/principles/.

30. "Extinction Rebellion: Jury acquits protesters despite judge's direction," *BBC News*, April 23, 2021, https://www.bbc.com/news/uk-england-london-56853979.

31. "Become an earth protector," Stop Ecocide, accessed May 18, 2021, https://www.stopecocide.earth/become-an-earth-protector-.

32. "Top 10 tips for telling your sustainability story," Edie, May 14, 2018, https://www.edie.net/library/Top-10-tips-for-telling-your-sustainability-story/6815.

33. "From me to we: The rise of the purpose-led brand," Accenture, December 5, 2018, https://www.accenture.com/us-en/insights/strategy/brand-purpose.

34. Mallika Shankarnarayan, "Havas Horizon: Meaningful trends for 2020," Havas Group, December 19, 2019, https://dare.havas.com/posts/havas-horizon-meaningful-trends-for-2020/.

35. "Building meaningful is good for business: 77% of consumers buy brands who share their values," Havas Media Group, February 21, 2019, https://havasmedia.com/building-meaningful-is-good-for-business-77-of-consumers-buy-brands-who-share-their-values/.

36. Brittany Wong, "10 life changes that will actually make a difference for the environment," *HuffPost*, January 17, 2020, https://www.huffpost.com/entry/how-to-help-the-environment_l_5e1f9811c5b674e44b92119a.

37. Anna Berrill et al., "50 simple ways to make your life greener," *Guardian*, February 29, 2020 https://www.theguardian.com/environment/2020/feb/29/50-ways-to-green-up-your-life-save-the-planet.

38. "Choose the greenest option," World Wide Fund for Nature, accessed February 9, 2021, https://wwf.panda.org/act/live_green/out_shopping/.

39. Zeynep Ahmet Vidal, "5 ideas on how to promote a sustainable lifestyle," *Ericsson Blog*, June 5, 2020, https://www.ericsson.com/en/blog/2020/6/how-to-promote-a-sustainable-lifestyle.

40. Katherine White, David J. Hardisy, and Rishad Habib, "The elusive green consumer," *Harvard Business Review*, July–August 2019, https://hbr.org/2019/07/the-elusive-green-consumer.

41. HBR Editors, "The best-performing CEOs in the world 2017," *Harvard Business Review*, November–December 2017, https://hbr.org/2017/11/the-best-performing-ceos-in-the-world-2017

42. HBR Editors, "The best-performing CEOs in the world, 2019," *Harvard Business Review*, November–December 2019, https://hbr.org/2019/11/the-best-performing-ceos-in-the-world-2019.

43. "The Just 100: Companies leading the new era of responsible capitalism," *Forbes*, October 14, 2020, https://www.forbes.com/just-companies.

44. Whittaker and Mainwaring, "3BL Forum: Ep 3."

45. Whittaker and Mainwaring, "3BL Forum: Ep 3."

46. Evie Liu, "The 100 most sustainable companies, reranked by social factors," *Barron's*, June 28, 2020, https://www.barrons.com/articles/these-companies-rank-best-on-social-criteriaand-could-reward-investors-51593215993.

47. Hamdi Ulukaya, "The anti-CEO playbook," filmed April 2019, TED video, 17:10, Vancouver, CA, https://www.ted.com/talks/hamdi_ulukaya_the_anti_ceo_playbook.

48. Ulukaya, "The anti-CEO playbook."

49. Sheridan Prasso, "Chobani: The unlikely king of yogurt," *CNN Money*, November 30, 2011, https://money.cnn.com/2011/11/29/smallbusiness/chobani_yogurt_hamdi_ulukaya.fortune/index.htm.

50. John Kell, "General Mills loses the culture wars," *Fortune*, May 22, 2017, https://fortune.com/2017/05/22/general-mills-yoplait-greek-yogurt/.

51. Mamta Badkar, "Trendy Greek yogurt Chobani is officially the top selling brand in America," *Business Insider*, October 8, 2011, https://www.businessinsider.com/americas-favorite-yogurt-2011-10.

52. Badkar, "Trendy Greek yogurt Chobani."

53. Larry Rulison, "Chobani, yogurt maker founded by UAlbany grad, eyes IPO," *Times Union*, February 5, 2021, https://www.timesunion.com/business/article/Chobani-yogurt-maker-founded-by-UAlbany-grad-15928195.php.

54. Stephanie Strom, "At Chobani, now it's not just the yogurt that's rich," *New York Times*, April 26, 2016, https://www.nytimes.com/2016/04/27/business/a-windfall-for-chobani-employees-stakes-in-the-company.html.

55. Hannah Furlong, "'Better food for more people:' Chobani incubator seeking purpose-driven food startups," Sustainable Brands, August 1, 2016, https://sustainablebrands.com/read/product-service-design-innovation/better-food-for-more-people-chobani-incubator-seeking-purpose-driven-food-startups.

56. Elaine Watson, "Chobani Simply 100 ad campaign sparks legal spat with Dannon," FoodNavigator-USA, January 11, 2016, https://www.foodnavigator-usa.com/Article/2016/01/11/Chobani-Simply-100-ad-campign-lands-it-in-legal-hotwater.

57. "Chobani: Most innovative company," *Fast Company*, accessed December 3, 2020, https://www.fastcompany.com/company/chobani.

58. "Chobani: Most innovative company," *Fast Company*.

59. Klaus Schwab, "Davos manifesto 2020: The universal purpose of a company in the fourth industrial revolution," World Economic Forum, December 2, 2019, https://www.weforum.org/agenda/2019/12/davos-manifesto-2020-the-universal-purpose-of-a-company-in-the-fourth-industrial-revolution/.

60. Lisa Earle McLeod, "From bottom lines to higher callings: The new era of purpose-driven boards," *Forbes*, August 20, 2020, https://www.forbes.com/sites/lisaearlemcleod/2020/08/20/from-bottom-lines-to-higher-callings-the-new-era-of-purpose-driven-boards/#50cf8f0f7502.

61. Seymour Burchman, "A new framework for executive compensation," *Harvard Business Review*, February 26, 2020, https://hbr.org/2020/02/a-new-framework-for-executive-compensation.

62. Jeff Fromm, "From palm oil to purpose: Mars VP weighs in on why private companies must focus on sustainability," *Forbes*, February 25, 2021, https://www.forbes.com/sites/jefffromm/2021/02/25/from-palm-oil-to-purpose-mars-vp-weighs-in-on-why-private-companies-must-focus-on-sustainability/?sh=33e271d94691.

63. Morgan Fecto, "Uber sets diversity goals, ties executive compensation to D&I success," *Industry Drive*, July 17, 2019, https://www.hrdive.com/news/uber-sets-diversity-goalsexecutive-ties--compensation-to-di-success/558935/.

64. Jincong Zhao, "These companies are tying executive bonuses to diversity goals," PayScale, March 7, 2019, https://www.payscale.com/compensation-today/2019/03/tie-bonuses-to-diversity-goals.

65. Johnson & Johnson, Form 10-K, February 18, 2020.

66. Bayer, "Our sustainability story," accessed February 12, 2021, https://www.bayer.com/en/sustainability/sustainability-strategy.

67. "Sustainability matters: The rise of ESG metrics in executive compensation," Sullivan & Cromwell, March 10, 2020, https://www.sullcrom.com/files/upload/SC-Publication-Sustainability-Matters-The-Rise-of-ESG-Metrics-in-Executive-Compensation.pdf.

68. "2019 proxy season review: Part 1," Sullivan & Cromwell, July 12, 2019, https://www.sullcrom .com/files/upload/SC-Publication-2019-Proxy-Season-Review-Part-1-Rule-14a-8-Shareholder -Proposals.pdf.

69. Hope Reese, "Living machines: MIT's former president on the next technology revolution," *Fast Company*, May 28, 2019, https://www.fastcompany.com/90353523/living-machines-susan -hockfield-next-technology-revolution.

70. Susan Hockfield, *Age of Living Machines: How Biology Will Build the Next Technology Revolution* (New York: W.W. Norton & Company, 2019).

71. Simon Mainwaring, "Purpose at work: How Omaze reinvented philanthropy to unlock exponential growth and impact," *Forbes*, September 9, 2020, https://www.forbes.com/sites/simonmainwaring /2020/09/09/purpose-at-work-how-omaze-reinvented-philanthropy-to-unlock-exponential -growth-and-impact/?sh=1ab0b7b0ce80.

72. "It all starts with clean water," WaterAid, accessed October 30, 2020, https://www.wateraid.org/us /why-wateraid.

73. Ben Paynter, "How Charity: Water uses data to connect donors and the people they're helping," *Fast Company*, March 20, 2017, https://www.fastcompany.com/3068686/how-charity-water-uses-data -to-connect-donors-and-the-people-theyre-hel.

74. "It all starts with clean water," WaterAid.

75. "Unlocking technology for the global goals," World Economic Forum, accessed October 30, 2020, http://www3.weforum.org/docs/Unlocking_Technology_for_the_Global_Goals.pdf.

76. "Unlocking technology for the global goals," World Economic Forum.

77. Douglas Rushkoff, "How tech's richest plan to save themselves after the apocalypse," *Guardian*, July 24, 2018, https://www.theguardian.com/technology/2018/jul/23/tech-industry-wealth-futurism -transhumanism-singularity.

78. Simon Mainwaring, "Purpose at work: How MOD Pizza's culture drives growth and impact," October 31, 2018, https://www.forbes.com/sites/simonmainwaring/2018/10/31/how-mod-pizzas -culture-drives-growth-and-impact/.

79. Business & Sustainable Development Commission, "Better business, better world."

80. United Nations Development Programme, "Our Perspectives," August 25, 2017, https://www.undp .org/content/undp/en/home/blog/2017/8/25/More-than-philanthropy-SDGs-present-an-estimated -US-12-trillion-in-market-opportunities-for-private-sector-through-inclusive-business.html.

81. Tom Metcalf and Pei Yi Mak, "These billionaires made their fortunes by trying to stop cli- mate change," *Bloomberg*, January 21, 2020, https://www.bloomberg.com/features/2020-green -billionaires/.

Part Two: With

1. Steven Sieden, *A Fuller View: Buckminster Fuller's Vision of Hope and Abundance for All* (Studio City, CA: Divine Arts, 2012).

Chapter 4: Purpose

1. Paul J. Zak, "Why your brain loves good storytelling," *Harvard Business Review*, October 28, 2014, https://hbr.org/2014/10/why-your-brain-loves-good-storytelling.

2. Bruce Eckfeldt, "How the Japanese word 'ikigai' can help your business be more successful," *Inc.*, October 16, 2020, https://www.inc.com/bruce-eckfeldt/how-japanese-word-ikigai-can-help-your -business-be-more-successful.html.

3. Brian Chesky, "Belong Anywhere," *Medium*, July, 16, 2014, https://medium.com/@bchesky/belong -anywhere-ccf42702d010.

4. "Open letter to the Airbnb community about building a 21st century company," Airbnb, Janu- ary 25, 2018, https://news.airbnb.com/brian-cheskys-open-letter-to-the-airbnb-community-about -building-a-21st-century-company/.

5. Simon Mainwaring, *We First: How Brands Use Social Media to Build a Better World* (New York: St. Martin's Press, 2011).

6. Daniel Victor, "Pepsi pulls ad accused of trivializing Black Lives Matter," *New York Times*, April 5, 2017, https://www.nytimes.com/2017/04/05/business/kendall-jenner-pepsi-ad.html.

7. Joe Berkowitz, "How that Pepsi Kendall Jenner ad taught brands to respond in this moment," *Fast Company*, June 2, 2020, https://www.fastcompany.com/90511890/how-that-pepsi-kendall-jenner -ad-taught-brands-to-respond-in-this-moment.

8. Fabiola Cineas, "'The march is not over': Read Barack Obama's eulogy for John Lewis," *Vox*, July 30, 2020, https://www.vox.com/2020/7/30/21348062/john-lewis-funeral-barack-obama-eulogy.

9. Glenn Llopis, "The cultural demographics," accessed November 12, 2020, https://www.glennllopis .com/research/the-cultural-demographic-shift/.

10. William H. Frey, "The US will become 'minority white' in 2045, Census projects," *The Avenue* (blog), Brookings Institution, March 14, 2018, https://www.brookings.edu/blog/the-avenue/2018 /03/14/the-us-will-become-minority-white-in-2045-census-projects/.

11. Llopis, "The cultural demographics."

12. Llopis, "The cultural demographics."

13. Jeff Desjardins, "Millennials are investing with purpose, and it's changing wealth management," Visual Capitalist, August 11, 2017, https://www.visualcapitalist.com/millennials-sustainable -investing-mainstream/.

14. Ben Schiller, "As wealthy millennials take control of family fortune, impact investing is set for a big boost," *Fast Company*, September, 15, 2017, https://www.fastcompany.com/40466206/as-wealthy -millennials-take-control-of-family-fortunes-impact-investing-is-set-for-a-big-boost.

15. "Generation Z is willing to pay more for eco-friendly products," Ad Age, January 14, 2020, https:// adage.com/article/cmo-strategy/generation-z-willing-pay-more-eco-friendly-products/2227101.

16. Desjardins, "Millennials are investing with purpose."

17. International Finance Corporation, "Creating Impact: The Promise of Impact Investing," April 2019, https://www.ifc.org/wps/wcm/connect/66e30dce-0cdd-4490-93e4-d5f895c5e3fc/The-Promise -of-Impact-Investing.pdf.

18. International Finance Corporation, *Creating Impact*.

19. Vivek Pandit and Toshan Tamhane, "A closer look at impact investing," *McKinsey Quarterly*, February 29, 2018, https://www.mckinsey.com/industries/private-equity-and-principal-investors/our -insights/a-closer-look-at-impact-investing.

20. Cary Funk and Alec Tyson, "Millennial and Gen Z Republicans stand out from their elders on climate and energy issues," Pew Research Center, June 24, 2020, https://www.pewresearch.org/fact -tank/2020/06/24/millennial-and-gen-z-republicans-stand-out-from-their-elders-on-climate-and -energy-issues/.

21. "2019 Deloitte Millennial Survey," Deloitte, accessed February 9, 2021, https://www2.deloitte .com/content/dam/Deloitte/global/Documents/About-Deloitte/gx-2018-millennial-survey-report .pdf.

22. "2015 Cone Communications millennial CSR study," Cone Communications, September 23, 2015, https://www.conecomm.com/2015-cone-communications-millennial-csr-study-pdf.

23. "Retail trends 2020," Deloitte, accessed February 9, 2021, https://www2.deloitte.com/content/dam /Deloitte/dk/Documents/Imagine/Retail%20trends%202020_Full%20presentation.pdf.

24. "Retail trends 2021," Deloitte, accessed February 9, 2021, https://www2.deloitte.com/ch/en/pages /consumer-business/articles/retail-trends.html

25. "Millennials coming of age," Goldman Sachs, accessed February 9, 2021, https://www.goldmansachs .com/insights/archive/millennials/.

26. "From fringe to mainstream: Companies integrate CSR initiatives into everyday business," Wharton School of the University of Pennsylvania, May 23, 2012, https://knowledge.wharton.upenn.edu /article/from-fringe-to-mainstream-companies-integrate-csr-initiatives-into-everyday-business/.

27. Achieve Consulting, "Millennial impact report," accessed February 9, 2019, http://www .themillennialimpact.com/sites/default/files/reports/MIR_2014.pdf.

28. "About us," As You Sow, accessed February 9, 2021, http://www.asyousow.org/about-us.

29. "How millennials are leading change in the 21st century," TriplePundit, January 11, 2016, https:// www.triplepundit.com/story/2016/how-millennials-are-leading-change-21st-century/29231.

30. Nick Ranger, "How the modern CEO creates value," accessed November 12, 2020, http://www .brandquarterly.com/millennials-new-push-purpose-b2b-branding.

31. "People, planet and profit: Highlights from Bentley on Bloomberg," Bentley University, February 16, 2016, https://www.bentley.edu/news/people-planet-and-profit-highlights-bentley-bloomberg.

32. "People, planet and profit," Bentley University.

33. Sparks & Honey, "Meet Generation Z: Forget everything you learned about millennials," June 17, 2014, https://www.slideshare.net/sparksandhoney/generation-z-final-june-17.

34. "Your future consumers' views on social activism and cause marketing and how it differs from what millennials think," Fuse Marketing, accessed November 12, 2020, https://www.fusemarketing .com/thought-leadership/future-consumers-views-cause-marketing-social-activism/.

35. Greg Petro, "Sustainable retail: How Gen Z is leading the pack," Forbes, January 31, 2020, https:// www.forbes.com/sites/gregpetro/2020/01/31/sustainable-retail-how-gen-z-is-leading-the-pack/.

36. Taylor Lorenz, Kellen Browning, and Sheera Frenkel, "TikTok teens and K-pop stans say they sank Trump rally," New York Times, June 21, 2020, https://www.nytimes.com/2020/06/21/style/tiktok -trump-rally-tulsa.html.

37. Stephanie Akin and Bridget Bowman, "3 takeaways from the Georgia runoffs," Roll Call, January 7, 2021, https://www.rollcall.com/2021/01/07/3-takeaways-from-the-georgia-runoffs-warnock-ossoff -perdue-loeffler/.

38. Matthew Ballew et al., "Do younger generations care more about global warming?" Yale Program on Climate Change Communication, June 11, 2019, https://climatecommunication.yale.edu /publications/do-younger-generations-care-more-about-global-warming/.

39. Kevin Roose, "Why napalm is a cautionary tale for tech giants pursuing military contracts," New York Times, March 4, 2019, https://www.nytimes.com/2019/03/04/technology/technology-military -contracts.html.

40. Sujan Patel, "The 5 biggest PR failures of the last decade," Inc., August 19, 2017, https://www.inc .com/sujan-patel/the-5-biggest-pr-failures-of-the-last-decade.html.

41. Natalie Sherman, "Purdue Pharma to plead guilty in $8bn opioid settlement," BBC News, October 21, 2020, https://www.bbc.com/news/business-54636002.

42. Katherine Rosman and Lauren Hard, "Will CrossFit survive?" New York Times, June 24, 2020, https://www.nytimes.com/2020/06/08/style/crossfit-black-lives-matter-apology.html.

43. Andrew Edgecliffe-Johnson and Billy Nauman, "CEOs' plans to reset capitalism bump into reality of pandemic," Financial Times, August 21, 2020, https://www.bizjournals.com/charlotte/news /2020/08/21/ceos-plans-to-reset-capitalism-bump-into-reality.html.

44. "Capitalism: A pledge of reform, one year on," The Week, September 4, 2020, https://theweek.com /print/484229/123575/capitalism-pledge-reform-year.

45. Kristin Toussaint, "Another study finds the Business Roundtable's revolutionary pledge didn't translate to action," Fast Company, September 22, 2020, https://www.fastcompany.com/90553830 /another-study-finds-the-business-roundtables-revolutionary-pledge-didnt-translate-to-action.

46. Simon Mainwaring, "Purpose at work: How Grove Collaborative is disrupting the consumer goods industry," Forbes, June 12, 2020, https://www.forbes.com/sites/simonmainwaring/2020/06/12 /purpose-at-work-how-grove-collaborative-is-disrupting-the-consumer-goods-industry/.

47. Rosabeth Moss Kanter, "From spare change to real change: The social sector as beta site for business innovation," Harvard Business Review, May 1999, https://hbr.org/1999/05/from-spare-change-to -real-change-the-social-sector-as-beta-site-for-business-innovation.

48. "M&S basis of reporting plan A," Marks and Spencer, accessed November 16, 2020, https:// corporate.marksandspencer.com/documents/reports-results-and-publications/plan-a-reports/2020 /2020-plan-a-basis-of-reporting-26.5.2020.pdf.

49. Andrew Busby, "Why COVID-19 might just be the making of Marks and Spencer," Forbes, May, 5, 2020, https://www.forbes.com/sites/andrewbusby/2020/05/20/why-covid-19-might-just-be-the -making-of-marks--spencer/.

50. Marianne Calnan, "M&S to relaunch its 'Plan A' sustainability programe," The Grocer, December 15, 2020, https://www.thegrocer.co.uk/marks-and-spencer/mands-to-relaunch-its-plan-a -sustainability-programme/651342.article.

51. "Walmart sets goal to become a regenerative company" (press release), Walmart, September 21, 2020, https://corporate.walmart.com/newsroom/2020/09/21/walmart-sets-goal-to-become-a-regenerative-company.

52. "President Clinton and leading CEOs call on private sector to develop corporate solutions to global challenges" (press release), Clinton Foundation, May 13, 2009, https://www.clintonfoundation.org/main/news-and-media/press-releases-and-statements/press-release-president-clinton-and-leading-ceos-call-on-private-sector-to-devel.html.

53. Roose, "Why napalm is a cautionary tale."

54. Roose, "Why napalm is a cautionary tale."

55. A. Schneider, M. A. Friedl, and D. Potere, "A new map of global urban extent from MODIS satellite data," *Environmental Research Letters* 4, no. 4 (2009), https://doi.org/10.1088/1748-9326/4/4/044003.

56. Pat Brown, "The mission that motivates us," *Medium*, January 23, 2018, https://medium.com/impossible-foods/the-mission-that-motivates-us-d4d7de61665.

57. Douglas John Atkin, "How Airbnb found its purpose and why it's a good one," *Medium*, March 10, 2019, https://medium.com/@douglas.atkin/how-airbnb-found-its-purpose-and-why-its-a-good-one-b5c987c0c216.

58. Simon Mainwaring, "Purpose at work: How Amgen builds scientific literacy to grow its business and positive impact," *Forbes*, August 27, 2019, https://www.forbes.com/sites/simonmainwaring/2019/08/27/purpose-at-work-how-amgen-builds-scientific-literacy-to-grow-its-business-and-positive-impact/#7c47fec66ac1.

59. Amgen, "Amgen Foundation launches Amgen biotech experience in Pittsburgh," *PRNewswire*, October 9, 2019, https://www.prnewswire.com/news-releases/amgen-foundation-launches-amgen-biotech-experience-in-pittsburgh-300934701.html.

60. Mainwaring, "Purpose at work: How Amgen builds scientific literacy."

61. Simon Mainwaring, "Purpose at work: How Hershey stands behind youth to create the future," *Forbes*, December 12, 2019, https://www.forbes.com/sites/simonmainwaring/2019/12/03/purpose-at-work-how-hershey-stands-behind-youth-to-create-the-future/.

62. Simon Mainwaring, "Purpose at work: 10 brands leading with purpose in 2019," *Forbes*, December 31, 2019, https://www.forbes.com/sites/simonmainwaring/2020/12/31/purpose-at-work-10-brands-leading-with-purpose-in-2019/.

63. "Built on connections between people and the world," Hershey, accessed November 13, 2020, https://www.thehersheycompany.com/en_us/our-story.html.

64. "Purpose moves us," Nike, accessed February 12, 2021, https://purpose.nike.com/.

65. "Product Sustainability," Mammut, accessed May 18, 2021, https://www.mammut.com/us/en/support/sustainability.

66. "Clif Bar," Clif Bar & Company, accessed November 13, 2020, https://www.clifbar.com/.

67. Afdhel Aziz, "The power of purpose: Gary Erickson, founder of Clif Bar, reflects on a life of purpose" (part one), *Forbes*, May, 7, 2020, https://www.forbes.com/sites/afdhelaziz/2020/05/07/the-power-of-purpose-gary-erickson-founder-of-clif-bar-reflects-on-a-life-of-purpose-part-one/.

68. Aziz, "The power of purpose: Gary Erickson."

69. "Who we are," Clif Bar & Company, accessed November 13, 2020, https://www.clifbar.com/who-we-are.

70. "Recruiting is easier," *Conscious Company*, September/October 2017, 15.

71. "Daniel Lamare: 'I don't have a job; I have a lifestyle,'" *Globe and Mail*, May 1, 2016, https://www.theglobeandmail.com/report-on-business/careers/career-advice/life-at-work/daniel-lamarre-i-dont-have-a-job-i-have-a-lifestyle/article29805629/.

72. Carmine Gallo, "What Starbucks CEO Howard Schultz taught me about communication and success," *Forbes*, December 13, 2019, https://www.forbes.com/sites/carminegallo/2013/12/19/what-starbucks-ceo-howard-schultz-taught-me-about-communication-and-success/.

73. "The business case for purpose," *Harvard Business Review*, accessed November 16, 2020, https://hbr.org/resources/pdfs/comm/ey/19392HBRReportEY.pdf

74. Mainwaring, "Purpose at work: How Traditional Medicinals powerfully combines purpose and profit."

75. "Purpose 2020: Igniting purpose-led growth," Kantar, accessed November 16, 2020, https://consulting.kantar.com/wp-content/uploads/2019/06/Purpose-2020-PDF-Presentation.pdf.

76. "Unveiling the 2020 Zeno Strength of Purpose Study," Zeno Group, June 17, 2020, https://www.zenogroup.com/insights/2020-zeno-strength-purpose.

77. "Brands with purpose grow—and here's the proof," Unilever, June 11, 2019, https://www.unilever.com/news/news-and-features/Feature-article/2019/brands-with-purpose-grow-and-here-is-the-proof.html.

78. "Release: Sustainable business can unlock at least US$12 trillion in new market value, and repair economic system," Business and Sustainable Development Commission, January 16, 2017, http://businesscommission.org/news/release-sustainable-business-can-unlock-at-least-us-12-trillion-in-new-market-value-and-repair-economic-system.

79. "Our strategy for sustainable growth," Unilever, accessed November 13, 2020, https://www.unilever.com/sustainable-living/our-strategy/.

80. "Unilever will divest brands that aren't purpose driven," SmartBrief, June 20, 2019, https://www.smartbrief.com/s/2019/06/ceo-unilever-will-divest-brands-arent-purpose-driven/.

81. "Culture of purpose—Building business confidence, driving growth," Deloitte, accessed November 16, 2020, https://www2.deloitte.com/content/dam/Deloitte/us/Documents/about-deloitte/us-leadership-2014-core-beliefs-culture-survey-040414.pdf.

82. "B Corp analysis reveals purpose-led businesses grow 28 times faster than national average," Sustainable Brands, March 1, 2018, https://sustainablebrands.com/read/business-case/b-corp-analysis-reveals-purpose-led-businesses-grow-28-times-faster-than-national-average.

83. Alan Murray, "The 2019 Fortune 500 CEO survey results are in," *Fortune*, May 16, 2019, https://fortune.com/2019/05/16/fortune-500-2019-ceo-survey/.

84. "Meaningful brands powered by Havas," Meaningful Brands, accessed November 13, 2020, https://www.meaningful-brands.com/en.

85. "Earned brand 2017," Edelman, June 12, 2017, https://www.edelman.com/research/earned-brand-2017.

86. Oliver McAteer, "No one would care if 77% of brands died overnight, study claims," *Campaign*, February, 22, 2019, https://www.campaignlive.com/article/no-one-care-77-brands-died-overnight-study-claims/1526400.

87. "From me to we: The rise of the purpose-led brand," Accenture, December 5, 2018, https://www.accenture.com/us-en/insights/strategy/brand-purpose.

88. "B Corp analysis," Sustainable Brands.

89. "Giving back," Bombas, accessed February 9, 2021, https://bombas.com/pages/giving-back.

90. Abigail Jones, "The silence that still surrounds periods," *Independent*, April 25, 2016, https://www.independent.co.uk/life-style/health-and-families/silence-around-menstruation-a7000051.html.

91. Ella Chochrek, "As Toms' challenges continue, brand reveals it has donated almost 100M pairs of shoes," *Footwear News*, November 20, 2019, https://footwearnews.com/2019/business/financial-news/toms-shoe-donations-impact-report-1202876080/.

92. "Steve Jobs: 'There's sanity returning,'" *Bloomberg BusinessWeek*, May 25, 1998, https://www.bloomberg.com/news/articles/1998-05-25/steve-jobs-theres-sanity-returning.

93. "Impact," TOMS, accessed November 16, 2020, https://www.toms.com/us/impact.html.

94. Simon Mainwaring, "Purpose at work: How TOMS is evolving its brand to scale its impact," *Forbes*, January 12, 2019, https://www.forbes.com/sites/simonmainwaring/2019/06/12/purpose-at-work-how-toms-is-evolving-its-brand-to-scale-its-impact/.

95. Mainwaring, "Purpose at work: How TOMS is evolving."

96. Greg Roumeliotis, "Exclusive: TOMS Shoes creditors to take over the company," *Reuters*, December 27, 2019, https://www.reuters.com/article/us-tomsshoes-m-a-creditors-exclusive/exclusive-toms-shoes-creditors-to-take-over-the-company-idUSKBN1YV1PT.

97. Amanda Taub, "Buying TOMS shoes is a terrible way to help poor people," *VOX*, July, 23, 2015, https://www.vox.com/2015/7/23/9025975/toms-shoes-poverty-giving.

98. Mainwaring, "Purpose at work: How TOMS is evolving."

99. Simon Mainwaring, "Purpose at work: How Timberland is planting a climate change movement," *Forbes*, October 10, 2019, https://www.forbes.com/sites/simonmainwaring/2019/10/08/purpose-at -work-how-timberland-is-planting-a-climate-change-movement/.

100. "United States," Organisation for Economic Co-operation and Development, accessed November 16, 2020, http://www.oecd.org/unitedstates/.

101. Responsible Minerals Initiative, accessed November 16, 2020, http://www.responsibleminerals initiative.org/.

102. "Responsible Minerals Sourcing policy for Intel' products," Intel, accessed November 16, 2020, https://www.intel.com/content/www/us/en/policy/policy-responsible-minerals.html.

103. Jim Edwards, "Intel says it will never use minerals from African war zones ever again," *Business Insider*, January 7, 2014, https://www.businessinsider.com/intel-conflict-free-minerals-2014-1.

104. Richard Wilson, "CES: Intel CEO makes conflict-free minerals challenge to the industry," *Electronics Weekly*, January 7, 2014, https://www.electronicsweekly.com/news/business/finance/ces-intel -ceo-makes-conflict-free-minerals-challange-to-the-industry-2014-01/.

105. "I Drink Your Milkshake!—There Will Be Blood (7/8) Movie Clip (2007)," Movieclips, YouTube video, 2:39, October 6, 2011, https://www.youtube.com/watch?v=s_hFTR6qyEo.

106. Ariella Gintzler, "Clif Bar and KIND are fighting. Here's why," *Outside,* June 12, 2019, https:// www.outsideonline.com/2398140/clif-bar-kind-fight.

107. Amelia Lucas, "Bud Light brewer Anheuser-Busch-Bush accuses MillerCoors of stealing beer recipes," *CNBC*, October 18, 2019, https://www.cnbc.com/2019/10/18/bud-lights-parent-accuses -millercoors-of-stealing-its-beer-recipes.html.

108. B Lab, "Dear Business Roundtable CEOs: Let's get to work."

109. Thomas W. Malnight, Ivy Buche, and Charles Dhanarja, "Put purpose at the core of your strategy," *Harvard Business Review*, accessed February 9, 2021, https://hbr.org/2019/09/put-purpose-at-the -core-of-your-strategy.

110. Stephanie Strom, "Vision insurer asks justices to restore its tax exemption," *New York Times*, July 16, 2008, https://www.nytimes.com/2008/07/16/us/16exempt.html.

111. "Eyes of hope," VSP Global, accessed November 12, 2020, https://vspglobal.com/cms/vspglobal -outreach/home.html.

112. Simon Mainwaring, "Purpose at work: How VSP Global drives growth and impact through purpose*,"* *Forbes*, January 18, 2019, https://www.forbes.com/sites/simonmainwaring/2019/01/18/how -vsp-global-drives-growth-and-impact-through-purpose/.

113. Mainwaring, "Purpose at work: How VSP Global drives growth and impact through purpose."

114. Camila Domonoske, "'Not broken but simply unfinished': Poet Amanda Gorman calls for a better America," Wisconsin Public Radio, January 20, 2021, https://www.wpr.org/not-broken-simply -unfinished-poet-amanda-gorman-calls-better-america.

Chapter 5: Culture

1. "2019 Edelman Trust Barometer," Edelman, January 30, 2010.

2. Leaders on Purpose, "Purpose-driven leadership for the 21st century: How corporate purpose is fundamental to reimaging capitalism," accessed December 3, 2020, https://www.thegeniusworks .com/wp-content/uploads/2019/10/Leaders-on-Purpose.pdf.

3. Jeffrey A. Sonnenfeld, "PepsiCo's Indra Nooyi did it her way," *Chief Executive*, August 8, 2018, https://chiefexecutive.net/sonnenfeld-pepsicos-indra-nooyi-an-inspirational-figure/.

4. Sonnenfeld, "PepsiCo's Indra Nooyi did it her way."

5. Simon Mainwaring, "Mammut CEO Oliver Pabst on reinvigorating a legacy brand with purpose," *Lead With We* (podcast), October 9, 2020, https://podcasts.apple.com/us/podcast/mammut-ceo -oliver-pabst-on-reinvigorating-legacy-brand/id1518493080?i=1000497859484.

6. Charlie Osgood, "Barbie gets a makeover," *CBS News* video, 1:12, https://www.cbsnews.com/video /barbie-gets-a-makeover-2/.

7. Eliana Dockterman, "Barbie's got a new body," *Time*, January 28, 2016, https://time.com/barbie-new-body-cover-story/.

8. "An epidemic of body hatred," Dying to Be Barbie, accessed December 3, 2020, https://www.rehabs.com/explore/dying-to-be-barbie/.

9. Lateshia Beachum, "Barbie just got even more diverse, as Mattel adds dolls with vitiligo and no hair," *Washington Post*, January 29, 2020, https://www.washingtonpost.com/business/2020/01/29/new-diverse-vitiligo-barbies/.

10. "Gross sales of Mattel's Barbie brand worldwide from 2012 to 2019," Statista, accessed December 3, 2020, https://www.statista.com/statistics/370361/gross-sales-of-mattel-s-barbie-brand/.

11. "Denim jeans market 2020 global demand, growth, opportunities, top key players and forecast to 2026," MarketWatch, January 7, 2021, https://www.marketwatch.com/press-release/denim-jeans-market-2020-global-demand-growth-opportunities-top-key-players-and-forecast-to-2026-2021-01-07?tesla=y (site discontinued).

12. "Trending: Levi's, Dockers, Sheep Inc moving sustainable apparel ever forward," Sustainable Brands, July 21, 2020, https://sustainablebrands.com/read/waste-not/trending-levi-s-dockers-sheep-inc-moving-sustainable-apparel-ever-forward.

13. "Levi's presents Future Finish," Levi Strauss and Co., accessed December 3, 2020, https://www.levi.com/US/en_US/blog/article/levis-presents-future-finish/.

14. "Levi Strauss & Co. reports first-quarter 2020 earnings," Levi Strauss & Co., April 7, 2020, https://investors.levistrauss.com/news/financial-news/news-details/2020/Levi-Strauss-Co-Reports-First-quarter-2020-Earnings/default.aspx.

15. Leon Kaye, "Levi's 'Well-Being' programs to reach 300,000 workers by 2025," *TriplePundit*, October 18, 2016, https://www.triplepundit.com/story/2016/levis-well-being-programs-reach-300000-workers-2025/22076.

16. Ainsley Harris, "How PayPal CEO Dan Schulman is leading a more inclusive way forward," *Fast Company*, April 30, 2020, https://www.fastcompany.com/90490899/how-paypal-ceo-dan-schulman-is-leading-a-more-inclusive-way-forward.

17. Henry Cordes, "PayPal wants 'passionate employees.' So the company boosted pay, slashed health insurance costs," *Omaha World-Herald*, December 14, 2019, https://omaha.com/business/paypal-wants-passionate-employees-so-the-company-boosted-pay-slashed-health-insurance-costs/article_dcafe007-9c62-53b5-895e-87911e544ecc.htm.

18. "Open hiring: A human capital model that fuels the bottom line," Greyston, accessed December 3, 2020, https://www.greyston.org/open-hiring.

19. "About the SCBC," Second Chance Business Coalition, accessed May 18, 2021, https://secondchancebusinesscoalition.org/about.

20. Afdhel Aziz, "The power of purpose: How Greyston is championing radical inclusivity through open hiring," *Forbes*, May, 16, 2019, https://www.forbes.com/sites/afdhelaziz/2019/05/16/the-power-of-purpose-how-greyston-is-championing-radical-inclusivity-through-open-hiring.

21. Deborah Leipzinger, "Greyston Bakery: Combatting poverty by making a profit," Aspen Institute, December 18, 2013, https://www.aspeninstitute.org/wp-content/uploads/2019/01/Greyston_121813.pdf.

22. Michael J. de la Merced, "Shaving start-up Harry's will be sold to owner of Schick for $1.37 billion," *New York Times*, May 9, 2019, https://www.nytimes.com/2019/05/09/business/dealbook/harrys-edgewell-acquisition.html.

23. Richard Feloni, "The CEOs of shaving startup Harry's explain how they acquired a million customers in 2 years," *Business Insider*, December 17, 2015, https://www.businessinsider.com/harrys-ceos-explain-how-they-acquired-a-million-customers-in-2-years-2015-12.

24. Taylor Stanton, "Harry's growth is a cut above their manual shaving competitors," Rakuten Intelligence, February 23, 2019, https://www.rakutenintelligence.com/blog/2016/harrys-growth-cut-manual-shaving-competitors.

25. "Our plan," Harry's, Instagram highlight, accessed February 10, 2021, https://www.instagram.com/stories/highlights/17949893005337208/.

26. "Our story," Harry's, accessed February 10, 2021, https://www.harrys.com/en/us/our-story.

27. "Corporate Equality Index 2020," Human Rights Campaign, accessed December 3, 2020, https://www.hrc.org/resources/corporate-equality-index/.

28. "2020 Top 50 Companies for Diversity List," DiversityInc, accessed December 3, 2020, https://www.diversityinc.com/the-2020-top-50-diversityinc/.

29. "Closing the racial equality gap would generate $8 trillion in U.S. GDP growth," US Chamber of Commerce, June 25, 2020, https://www.uschamber.com/on-demand/economy/closing-the-racial-equality-gap-would-generate-8-trillion-in-u-s-gdp-growth.

30. "Kellogg's overview," Zippia, accessed February 10, 2021, https://www.zippia.com/kellogg-careers-6468/.

31. "The 2020 sustainability leaders," GlobeScan, December 8, 2020, https://globescan.com/wp-content/uploads/2020/08/GlobeScan-SustainAbility-Leaders-Survey-2020-Report.pdf.

32. Carol A. Massar, "Unilever CEO sees purpose-led businesses only gaining relevance," *Bloomberg Businessweek*, May 12, 2020, https://www.bloomberg.com/news/features/2020-05-12/unilever-ceo-on-coronavirus-pandemic-purpose-led-businesses.

33. Marguerite Ward, "JPMorgan's Jamie Dimon joins Ray Dalio, Mark Cuban, and other billionaires sounding the alarm on inequality in the US," *Business Insider*, May 19, 2020, https://www.businessinsider.com/jamie-dimon-mark-cuban-ray-dalio-billionaires-inequality-coronavirus-2020-5.

34. "COVID-19 and inequality: A test of corporate purpose (TCP)," GlobeScan, accessed February 10, 2021, https://globescan.com/wp-content/uploads/2020/09/Test-of-Corporate-Purpose-2020-GlobeScan-Stakeholder-Survey-Findings.pdf.

35. Marshall Ganz, "Leading Change: Leadership, Organization, and Social Movements," in *Handbook of Leadership Theory and Practice: A Harvard Business School Centennial Colloquium*, ed. Nitin Nohira and Rakesh Khurana (Boston: Harvard Business School, 2010).

36. Ganz, "Leading Change: Leadership, Organization, and Social Movements."

37. Jethro Pettit, "Unpacking the 'black box' of social movement leadership," Transformational Change Leadership, accessed December 3, 2020, http://tcleadership.org/introduction/.

38. Associated Press, "Apple's Tim Cook calls on Alabama to protect gay rights," *New York Times*, October 27, 2014, https://www.nytimes.com/2014/10/28/technology/apples-tim-cook-calls-on-alabama-to-protect-gay-rights.html.

39. Tim Cook, "Tim Cook: Pro-discrimination 'religious freedom' laws are dangerous," *Washington Post*, March 29, 2015, https://www.washingtonpost.com/opinions/pro-discrimination-religious-freedom-laws-are-dangerous-to-america/2015/03/29/bdb4ce9e-d66d-11e4-ba28-f2a685dc7f89_story.html.

40. "More than 100 major CEOs & business leaders urge North Carolina to repeal anti-LGBT Law," Human Rights Campaign, March 31, 2016, https://www.hrc.org/press-releases/more-than-100-major-ceos-business-leaders-demand-north-carolina-repeal-radi.

41. Oscar Williams-Grut, "Billonaire Salesforce founder: 'Capitalism as we know it is dead,'" *Yahoo! Finance*, January 21, 2020, https://finance.yahoo.com/news/davos-2020-salesforce-founder-capitalism-is-dead-181643945.html.

42. Aaron K. Chatterji and Michael W. Toffel, "Divided we lead," *Harvard Business Review*, March 22, 2018, https://hbr.org/cover-story/2018/03/divided-we-lead.

43. "The dawn of CEO activism," Weber Shandwick, accessed December 3, 2020, https://www.webershandwick.com/uploads/news/files/the-dawn-of-ceo-activism.pdf.

44. Frederick E. Allen, "Howard Schultz to anti-gay marriage Starbucks shareholder: 'You can sell your shares,'" *Forbes*, March 22, 2013, https://www.forbes.com/sites/frederickallen/2013/03/22/howard-schultz-to-anti-gay-marriage-starbucks-shareholder-you-can-sell-your-shares/.

45. Howard Schultz, "Remarks at 2013 annual meeting of shareholders" (speech, Seattle, WA, March, 13, 2013).

46. "8 employee engagement statistics you need to know in 2020 [INFOGRAPHIC]," Smarp, August 11, 2020, https://blog.smarp.com/employee-engagement-8-statistics-you-need-to-know.

47. Morgan Simon, "5 changes CEOs can make if they're serious about ending shareholder primacy," *Fast Company*, August 27, 2019, https://www.fastcompany.com/90395365/5-changes-ceos-can-make-if-theyre-serious-about-ending-shareholder-primacy.

48. Tensie Whelan and Carly Fink, "The comprehensive business case for sustainability," *Harvard Business Review*, October 21, 2016, https://hbr.org/2016/10/the-comprehensive-business-case-for-sustainability.

49. Richard Samans and Jane Nelson, *Integrated Corporate Governance: A Practical Guide to Stakeholder Capitalism for Board of Directors*, World Economic Forum, June 2020, http://www3.weforum.org/docs/WEF_Integrated_Corporate_Governance_2020.pdf.

50. Jeff Haynes, "The Black wealth gap," *The Week*, September 27, 2020, https://theweek.com/articles/939413/black-wealth-gap/.

51. Felix Salmon, "Wages hit record highs—for white Americans," *Axios*, April 29, 2021, https://www.axios.com/wages-gap-white-americans-6f38526d-8fc2-4e13-b447-6d1511d26cb6.html.

52. Haynes, "The Black wealth gap."

53. Haynes, "The Black wealth gap."

54. Martin Whittaker, "JUST Capital at 3BL Forum: Brands taking stands—Business elects to lead," 2020 3BL Virtual Forum, October 22, 2020.

55. Brendan Dunne, "Nike CEO addresses racial violence in heartfelt letter," Sole Collector, July 15, 2016, https://solecollector.com/news/2016/07/nike-ceo-mark-parker.

56. Bill Chappell, "Starbucks closes more than 8,000 stores today for racial bias training," *The Two-Way*, May 29, 2018, https://www.npr.org/sections/thetwo-way/2018/05/29/615119351/starbucks-closes-more-than-8-000-stores-today-for-racial-bias-training.

57. "Racism is another virus to eradicate," VF Corporation, May 30, 2020, https://www.vfc.com/news/feature-story/71112/racism-is-another-virus-to-eradicate.

58. "List: Women CEOs of the S&P 500," Catalyst, December 2, 2020, https://www.catalyst.org/research/women-ceos-of-the-sp-500/.

59. Vanessa Yukevich, "There are just four black CEOs of Fortune 500 companies. Here's how they are addressing the death of George Floyd," *CNN Business*, June 2, 2020, https://www.cnn.com/2020/06/01/business/black-ceos-george-floyd/index.html.

60. Jeanne Sahadi, "After years of talking about diversity, the number of Black leaders at U.S. companies is still dismal," *Philly Tribune*, June 2, 2020, https://www.phillytrib.com/news/business/after-years-of-talking-about-diversity-the-number-of-black-leaders-at-u-s-companies/article_a9bcd767-4e84-5c49-9fac-2f4131c3d6c2.html.

61. Will Heilpern, "Richard Branson told us his most surprising character trait," *Business Insider*, August 10, 2016, https://www.businessinsider.com/richard-branson-talks-about-public-speaking-2016-8.

62. Will Heilpern, "Billionaire Richard Branson told us his solution for inequality," *Business Insider*, August 11, 2016, https://www.businessinsider.com/richard-bransons-solution-to-inequality-2016-8.

63. Anjali Mullany, "Richard Branson is ready to take on Trump's 'worst ideas,'" *Fast Company*, November 11, 2016, https://www.fastcompany.com/3065614/richard-branson-is-ready-to-take-on-trumps-worst-ideas.

64. Loren Grush, "Richard Branson suspends Saudi Arabia's investment in space ventures over missing journalist," *Verge*, October 13, 2018, https://www.theverge.com/2018/10/13/17967954/virgin-galactic-richard-branson-saudi-arabia-jamal-khashoggi.

65. "Jamal Khashoggi: All you need to know about Saudi journalist's death," *BBC News*, July 2, 2019, https://www.bbc.com/news/world-europe-45812399.

66. Carmin Chappell, "Richard Branson suspends $1 billion Virgin investment talks with Saudi Arabia over missing journalist," *CNBC News*, October 11, 2018, https://www.cnbc.com/2018/10/11/richard-branson-halts-investment-over-jamal-khashoggis-disappearance.html.

67. Richard Branson, "Richard Branson: Why business leaders should advocate for the end of the death penalty," *Fast Company*, March 18, 2021, https://www.fastcompany.com/90615394/richard-branson-why-business-leaders-should-advocate-for-the-end-of-the-death-penalty.

68. Jeff Beer, "Exclusive: Patagonia founder Yvon Chouinard talks about the sustainability myth, the problem with Amazon—and why it's not too late to save the planet," *Fast Company,* October 16, 2019, https://www.fastcompany.com/90411397/exclusive-patagonia-founder-yvon-chouinard-talks -about-the-sustainability-myth-the-problem-with-amazon-and-why-its-not-too-late-to-save-the -planet.

69. "Patagonia's mission statement," Patagonia, accessed December 4, 2020, https://www.patagonia .com.au/pages/our-mission.

70. Beer, "Exclusive: Patagonia founder Yvon Chouinard."

71. Ryan Gellert, "Exclusive: Patagonia's new CEO talks about the future of the beloved brand," *Fast Company,* September 23, 2020, https://www.fastcompany.com/90553967/exclusive-patagonias -new-ceo-talks-about-the-future-of-the-beloved-brand.

72. Gellert, "Exclusive: Patagonia's new CEO."

73. "Glassdoor survey finds three in five U.S. employees have experienced or witnessed discrimina- tion based on age, race, gender or LGBTQ at work," Glassdoor, October 23, 2019, https://www .glassdoor.com/about-us/diversity-inclusion-2019/.

74. Chris Isidore, "Nasdaq to Corporate America: Make your boards more diverse or get out," *CNN Business,* December 2, 2020, https://www.cnn.com/2020/12/01/investing/nasdaq-rule-board-of -directors-diversity/index.html.

75. "Goldman Sachs' commitment to board diversity," Goldman Sachs, February 4, 2020, https://www .goldmansachs.com/what-we-do/investing-and-lending/launch-with-gs/pages/commitment-to -diversity.html.

76. "Stock exchanges: Nasdaq pushes for board diversity," *The Week,* December 18, 2020, 37.

77. "The bottom line," *The Week,* December 11, 2020, 40.

78. "Stock exchanges: Nasdaq pushes for board diversity," *The Week.*

79. Simon Mainwaring, "Purpose at work: Lessons from Lyft on how to transform lives through transportation," *Forbes,* May 17, 2021, https://www.forbes.com/sites/simonmainwaring/2021/05 /17/purpose-at-work-lessons-from-lyft-on-how-to-transform-lives-through-transportation/?sh =366e6ed66b8a.

80. Hanna Ziady, "Larry Fink says BlackRock 'isn't perfect.' These new incentives could help," *CNN Business,* April 7, 2021, https://www.cnn.com/2021/04/07/investing/blackrock-diversity-targets -loan/index.html.

81. Sundiatu Dixon-Fyle et al., "Diversity wins: How inclusion matters," McKinsey & Company, May 19, 2020, https://www.mckinsey.com/featured-insights/diversity-and-inclusion/diversity-wins-how -inclusion-matters.

82. John Csiszar, "10 companies that offer health insurance to part-time employees," *Yahoo! Finance,* February 23, 2021, https://finance.yahoo.com/news/10-companies-offer-health-insurance-1600 42290.html.

83. Ben Popken, Stephanie Ruhle, and Charlie Herman, "Over 150 top business executives urge Congress to back Biden's recovery bill," *NBC News,* February 24, 2021, https://www.nbcnews .com/business/economy/over-150-top-business-executives-urge-congress-back-biden-recovery -n1258752.

84. "Glassdoor unlocks employee sentiment & pay data by race/ethnicity, gender identity & more," Glassdoor, February 17, 2021, https://www.glassdoor.com/about-us/ratings-salaries -demographics/.

85. Nadine Saad, "Ratings firm Nielsen begins tracking diversity and inclusion in TV," *Los Angeles Times,* February 17, 2021, https://www.latimes.com/entertainment-arts/tv/story/2021-02-17/ratings -firm-nielsen-begins-tracking-diversity-and-inclusion-in-tv.

86. "McDonald's ties executive pay to diversity goals, releases data," Ad Age, February 18, 2021, https://adage.com/article/cmo-strategy/mcdonalds-ties-executive-pay-diversity-goals-releases-data /2315176.

87. "The corporate racial equity tracker," JUST Capital, accessed May 18, 2021, https://justcapital.com /reports/corporate-racial-equity-tracker/.

88. Afdhel Aziz, "The power of purpose: How Daniel Martínez-Valle, CEO of Orbia, led the company into a new era of purpose," *Forbes*, December 29, 2019, https://www.forbes.com/sites/afdhelaziz /2020/12/29/the-power-of-purpose-how-daniel-martinez-valle-led-orbia-into-a-new-era-of-purpose.

89. Aziz, "The power of purpose: How Daniel Martínez-Valle."

90. "Why you hate work," The Energy Project, accessed February 12, 2021, https://theenergyproject .com/why-you-hate-work-2/.

91. "Why you hate work," The Energy Project.

92. "2019 Workforce Purpose Index," Imperative, accessed February 12, 2021, https://www.2019wpi .com/.

93. "Putting purpose to work: A study of purpose in the workplace," PwC, accessed December 4, 2020, https://www.pwc.com/us/en/purpose-workplace-study.html.

94. "Statistics," Business of Purpose, accessed May 18, 2021, https://www.businessofpurpose.com /statistics.

95. "Our ImpactMark," Orbia, accessed December 4, 2020, https://www.orbia.com/this-is-orbia/our -impactmark/.

96. "Radically better future: The next gen reckoning for brands," BBMG and Globe Scan, accessed February 12, 2021, http://bbmg.com/radically-better-future/.

97. "Timberland marks 25 years of Path of Service employee volunteer program with a season of service celebrated around the world," Timberland, August 15, 2017, https://www.timberland.com /newsroom/press-releases/25-years-path-of-service.html.

98. "The top 3 brands in sportswear," Sports & Leisurewear, accessed December 4, 2020, https://www .sportsleisurewear.com/The-Top-3-Brands-in-Sportswear.html.

99. "PUMA launches financing programs to reward suppliers for sustainability performance," Sustainable Brands, September 8, 2016, https://sustainablebrands.com/read/organizational-change/puma -launches-financing-program-to-reward-suppliers-for-sustainability-performance.

100. "Taking the BS out of business—the disruptor's guide to transparency," Cannes Lions, accessed December 4, 2020, https://www.canneslions.com/about/news/taking-the-bs-out-of-business.

101. "The Business Case for Purpose": *Harvard Business Review*, accessed November 16, 2020, https:// hbr.org/resources/pdfs/comm/ey/19392HBRReportEY.pdf.

102. Steve Rochlin et al., *Project ROI: Defining the Competitive and Financial Advantages of Corporate Responsibility & Sustainability*, IO Sustainability, 2015, https://www.charities.org/sites/default/files /Project%20ROI%20Report.pdf.

103. "Latest research from NYU Stern Center for Sustainable Business and IRI shows that sustainability is surviving COVID-19," New York University Stern School of Business, July 16, 2020, https:// www.stern.nyu.edu/experience-stern/faculty-research/latest-research-nyu-stern-center-sustainable -business-and-iri-shows-sustainability-surviving-covid.

104. "Americans willing to buy or boycott companies based on corporate values, according to new research by Cone Communications," Cone Communications, May 17, 2017, https://www.conecomm.com /news-blog/2017/5/15/americans-willing-to-buy-or-boycott-companies-based-on-corporate-values -according-to-new-research-by-cone-communications.

105. Jeffrey Hollender and Bill Breen, *The Responsibility Revolution: How the Next Generation of Businesses Will Win* (Hoboken, NJ: Wiley, 2010).

106. Zameena Mejia, "Nearly 9 out of 10 millennials would consider taking a pay cut to get this," *CNBC Make It*, June 28, 2018, https://www.cnbc.com/2018/06/27/nearly-9-out-of-10-millennials-would -consider-a-pay-cut-to-get-this.html.

107. Shirin Panahi and Angelo Tremblay, "Sedentariness and health: Is sedentary behavior more than just physical inactivity," *Frontiers in Public Health* 6 (2018): 258, https://dx.doi.org/10.3389 %2Ffpubh.2018.00258.

108. Reggie Miller, personal interview with We First Inc., Los Angeles, August 24, 2020.

Chapter 6: Community

1. Simon Mainwaring, *We First: How Brands and Consumers Use Social Media to Build a Better World* (New York: St. Martin's Press, 2011).
2. Afdhel Aziz, "Global study reveals consumers are four to six times more likely to purchase, protect and champion purpose-driven companies," *Forbes*, June 17, 2020, https://www.forbes.com /sites/afdhelaziz/2020/06/17/global-study-reveals-consumers-are-four-to-six-times-more-likely-to -purchase-protect-and-champion-purpose-driven-companies/?sh=c382c9a435fe.
3. "'Badge' value: Finding and promoting products that inspire customer loyalty," Wharton School of the University of Pennsylvania, March 3, 2018, https://knowledge.wharton.upenn.edu/article /badge-value-finding-and-promoting-products-that-inspire-customer-loyalty/.
4. "Beer history," Craft Beer, accessed January 21, 2021, https://www.craftbeer.com/beer/beer-history.
5. "Beer history," Craft Beer.
6. Reuters, "Jessica Alba-backed Honest Company IPO raises $412.8 million," *CNBC*, May 5, 2021, https://www.cnbc.com/2021/05/05/jessica-alba-backed-honest-company-ipo-raises-412point 8-million.html.
7. "Our story," The Honest Company, accessed January 21, 2021, https://www.honest.com/about-us /our-story.html.
8. Jonathan Shieber, "With $23 million for its plant-based liquid meals, Kate Farms pushes into consumer and healthcare," *TechCrunch*, April 9, 2020, https://techcrunch.com/2020/04/09/with-23 -million-for-its-plant-based-liquid-meals-kate-farms-pushes-into-consumer-and-healthcare/.
9. "Kate Farms closes $51 million series b; investment led by Goldman Sachs and Kaiser Permanente Ventures," Kate Farms, November 12, 2020, https://www.katefarms.com/news/press-releases/kate -farms-closes-series-b-round-at-51-million/.
10. Mainwaring, "Purpose at work: Lessons from Lyft."
11. "2017 Edelman Earned Brand Study: Beyond no man's land," Edelman, June 18, 2017, https://www .slideshare.net/EdelmanInsights/2017-edelman-earned-brand.
12. "Radically better future," BBMG and GlobeScan.
13. Simon Mainwaring, "Purpose at work: How Fishpeople is changing its industry from the inside," *Forbes*, December 10, 2019, https://www.forbes.com/sites/simonmainwaring/2019/12/10/purpose -at-work-how-fishpeople-seafood-is-changing-its-industry-from-the-inside/?sh=31007d2934fa.
14. Mainwaring, "Purpose at work: How Fishpeople is changing its industry."
15. Arthur Power, *From the Old Waterford House* (London: Mellifont Press, 1940).
16. "Purpose: Shifting from why to how," McKinsey & Company, April 22, 2020, https://www .mckinsey.com/business-functions/organization/our-insights/purpose-shifting-from-why-to-how.
17. Sophia Bernazzani, "21 examples of successful co-branding partnerships (and why they're so effective)," HubSpot, accessed November 12, 2020, https://blog.hubspot.com/marketing/best -cobranding-partnerships.
18. Kyle O'Brien, "Burger King embraces McDonald's charity in 'Day Without Whopper' in Argentina," *Drum*, December 15, 2017, https://www.thedrum.com/news/2017/12/15/burger-king -embraces-mcdonald-s-charity-day-without-whopper-argentina.
19. Bob Schildgen, "Is any canned tuna truly dolphin safe," *Sierra*, April 28, 2019, https://www .sierraclub.org/sierra/2019-3-may-june/ask-mr-green/any-canned-tuna-truly-dolphin-safe.
20. "2020 Edelman Trust Barometer spring update," Edelman, May 5, 2020, https://www.edelman .com/research/trust-2020-spring-update.
21. Yuyo Chen, "84 percent of millennials don't trust traditional advertising," ClickZ, March 4, 2015, https://www.clickz.com/84-percent-of-millennials-dont-trust-traditional-advertising/27030/.
22. Tiffany Hsu, "The advertising industry has a problem: People hate ads," *New York Times*, October 28, 2019, https://www.nytimes.com/2019/10/28/business/media/advertising-industry-research.html.

23. "Aflac corporate social responsibility survey fact sheet," Aflac, accessed February 12, 2021, https://chronicle-assets.s3.amazonaws.com/7/items/biz/pdf/AflacCorporateSocialResponsibility.pdf.

24. David Marchese, "Ben & Jerry's radical ice cream dreams," *New York Times*, July 27, 2020, https://www.nytimes.com/interactive/2020/07/27/magazine/ben-jerry-interview.html.

25. Jay Curley, "The 6P's of Brand Activism," LinkedIn post, November 19, 2019, https://www.linkedin.com/pulse/6ps-brand-activism-jay-curley/.

26. Minda Zetlin, "This Elon Musk blog post from 2006 shows exactly why he's so successful," *Inc.*, July 28, 2017, https://www.inc.com/minda-zetlin/as-tesla-model-3-launches-11-year-old-blog-post-re.html.

27. Simon Mainwaring, "The Elon Musk leadership model: 3 key steps to building radical brand evangelism," *Forbes*, April 6, 2016, https://www.forbes.com/sites/simonmainwaring/2016/04/06/the-elon-musk-leadership-model-3-key-steps-to-building-radical-brand-evangelism/?sh=49f80066726e.

28. Brian Kateman, "Meatless meat is going mainstream. Now big food wants in," *Vox*, December 29, 2020, https://www.vox.com/future-perfect/22196077/impossible-foods-tesco-ikea-panera.

29. "Eco dog beds," Project Blu, accessed February 12, 2021, https://projectblu.co/collections/eco-dog-beds.

30. Martin Whittaker, "JUST Capital at 3BL Forum: Brands taking stands—Business elects to lead," 2020 3BL Virtual Forum, October 22, 2020.

31. "#OptOutSide—Will you go outside with us?" REI, accessed January 22, 2021, https://www.rei.com/blog/news/optoutside-will-you-go-out-with-us.

32. "REI again urging Americans to #OptOutside, studying link to human health," Sustainable Brands, October 24, 2018, https://sustainablebrands.com/read/behavior-change/rei-again-urging-americans-to-optoutside-studying-link-to-human-health.

33. Afdhel Aziz, "How Tieks Is Mobilizing Its Community To #SewTogether And Make Facemasks For Frontline Heroes," *Forbes*, April 28, 2020, https://www.forbes.com/sites/afdhelaziz/2020/04/28/how-tieks-is-mobilizing-its-community-to-sewtogether-and-make-facemasks-for-frontline-heroes/?sh=589f78157c40.

34. Afdhel Aziz, "How Tieks is mobilizing its community to #SewTogether and make facemasks for frontline heroes," *Forbes*, April 28, 2020, https://www.forbes.com/sites/afdhelaziz/2020/04/28/how-tieks-is-mobilizing-its-community-to-sewtogether-and-make-facemasks-for-frontline-heroes/?sh=3e238eb67c40.

35. "Sodexo campaigns aim to change behavior to save food, reduce water use and more," Sustainable Brands, October 31, 2016, https://sustainablebrands.com/read/behavior-change/sodexo-campaigns-aim-to-change-behavior-to-save-food-reduce-water-use-and-more.

36. Adele Peters, "This 'sustainable consumption' platform wants to help new parents buy fewer kids' clothes," *Fast Company*, August 6, 2019, https://www.fastcompany.com/90384951/this-sustainable-consumption-platform-wants-to-help-new-parents-buy-fewer-kids-clothes.

37. Jeremy Heimans and Henry Timms, *New Power: How Power Works in Our Hyperconnected World—and How to Make It Work for You* (New York: Doubleday, 2018).

38. "The hidden costs of hamburgers," *NewsHour*, August 2, 2012, https://www.pbs.org/newshour/science/the-hidden-costs-of-hamburgers.

39. "Impact Report 2020," Impossible Foods, accessed March 29, 2021, https://www.impossiblefoods.com/impact-report-2020.

40. "Impossible Foods: Creating plant-based alternatives to meat | Singapore, Hong Kong, USA, Macau," United Nations Climate Change, accessed January 22, 2021, https://unfccc.int/climate-action/momentum-for-change/planetary-health/impossible-foods.

41. "Impossible Foods," United Nations Climate Change.

42. "Impact Report 2020," Impossible Foods.

43. "Making a material difference," Avery Dennison, accessed January 22, 2021, https://sustainability.averydennison.com/en/home.html.

44. "Making a material difference: 2020 integrated sustainability report and annual report," Avery Dennison, accessed March 29, 2021, https://www.averydennison.com/content/dam/avery_dennison/corporate/global/english/documents/sustainability/AD-AnnualReport-2020-Web.pdf.

45. "2020 integrated sustainability report," Avery Dennison.

46. "History," Warby Parker, accessed March 29, 2021, https://www.warbyparker.com/history.

47. "Buy a pair, give a pair," Warby Parker, accessed March 29, 221, https://www.warbyparker.com/buy-a-pair-give-a-pair.

48. Simon Mainwaring, "Purpose at work: Warby Parker's keys to success," *Forbes*, December 1, 2020, https://www.forbes.com/sites/simonmainwaring/2020/12/01/purpose-at-work-warby-parkers-keys-to-success/?sh=91f868bdba79.

49. Simon Mainwaring, "Purpose at work: How Farmacy is disrupting the industry to scale clean beauty," *Forbes,* December 12, 2020, https://www.forbes.com/sites/simonmainwaring/2020/12/22/purpose-at-work-how-farmacy-is-disrupting-the-industry-to-scale-clean-beauty/?sh=5fca7c825675.

50. Marshall Ganz, *Leadership, Organizing, and Action: Organizing Workshop Participant Guide,* modified by Abel R. Cano, Harvard Graduate School of Education Doctor of Education Leadership (Ed.L.D.) program, accessed February 21, 2021, https://www.hrfn.org/wp-content/uploads/2018/02/Ganz-EdLD-Organizing-Participant-Guide-FINAL-2017-copy.pdf.

51. Simon Mainwaring, "Purpose at work: How Bombas gains competitive advantage with purpose and product," *Forbes*, September 30, 2020, https://www.forbes.com/sites/simonmainwaring/2020/09/30/purpose-at-work-how-bombas-gains-competitive-advantage-with-purpose-and-product/?sh=7c5772d73a8e.

52. Afdhel Aziz, "How this dad and his sons are creating good citizens: A 100% sustainable Australian sunglass range made from recycled plant bottles," *Forbes*, June 17, 2020, https://www.forbes.com/sites/afdhelaziz/2020/06/17/how-this-dad-and-his-sons-are-creating-good-citizens-a-100-sustainable-australian-sunglass-range-made-from-recycled-plastic-bottles/?sh=5fd9b2bb7571.

53. Ryan Skinner, "Consumer partners: Who they are and why you should care," Forrester, December 16, 2020, https://go.forrester.com/blogs/consumer-partners-who-they-are-and-why-you-should-care/.

54. Joeri Van den Bergh, "The conscious consumer," inSites Consulting, April 22, 2020, https://insites-consulting.com/blog/the-conscious-consumer/.

55. Ben Paynter, "Millennials are finding new models for driving change," *Fast Company*, March 28, 2018, https://www.fastcompany.com/40547260/millennials-are-finding-new-models-for-driving-change.

56. Mike Scott, "Companies look to supply chains for sustainability gains," *Forbes*, February 11, 2019, https://www.forbes.com/sites/mikescott/2019/02/11/companies-look-to-supply-chains-for-sustainability-gains/?sh=614d55881c55.

57. Suzy Welch, "To thrive at Under Armour, you have to answer Kevin Plank's three questions," LinkedIn post, June 20, 2016, https://www.linkedin.com/pulse/thrive-under-armour-you-have-answer-kevin-planks-three-suzy-welch.

58. Simon Mainwaring, "Purpose at work: Blume Honey Water's path to product and pollinator success," *Forbes*, February 20, 2019, https://www.forbes.com/sites/simonmainwaring/2019/02/20/purpose-at-work-blume-honey-waters-path-to-product-and-pollinator-success/?sh=39e967b251c1.

59. Aiman Bilal, "Lacoste changes crocodile logo with icons of endangered species," Research Snipers, accessed January 22, 2021, https://www.researchsnipers.com/lacoste-changes-crocodile-logo-with-icons-of-endangered-species/ (site discontinued).

60. "Gen Z vs Millenials: The Changing Landscape of Loyalty," CrowdTwist, accessed October 28, 2020, http://media.dmnews.com/documents/318/generation-z-vs-millennials-th_79333.pdf.

61. "Millennials, Gen Z and the coming 'youth boom' economy," Morgan Stanley, January 25, 2019, https://www.morganstanley.com/ideas/millennial-gen-z-economy.html.

62. "Radically better future," BBMG and GlobeScan.

63. Chris Coulter, interview with Simon Mainwaring, August 31, 2020.

64. Dante Disparte and Timothy H. Gentry, "Corporate activism is on the rise," *Real Leaders*, October 27, 2018, https://real-leaders.com/corporate-activism-rise/.

65. Alan Abitbol, "Razor burned: Why Gillette's campaign against toxic masculinity missed the mark," *The Conversation*, January 18, 2019, https://theconversation.com/razor-burned-why-gillettes-campaign-against-toxic-masculinity-missed-the-mark-109932.

66. Simon Mainwaring, "How your brand can better the best from Gillette," *Forbes*, January 17, 2019, https://www.forbes.com/sites/simonmainwaring/2019/01/17/how-your-brand-can-better-the-best-from-gillette/#3a4760616dcc.

67. Judann Pollack, "Hey, brands: Almost half of Americans don't find you honest," *Ad Age,* April 3, 2017, https://adage.com/article/special-report-4as-conference/mccann-survey-finds-half-america-trust-brand/308544.

68. "Radically better future," BBMG and GlobeScan.

69. "Always #LikeAGirl," YouTube video, Always, June 26, 2014, 3:18, https://www.youtube.com/watch?v=XjJQBjWYDTs.

70. "Help Always #EndPeriodPovery so no period holds her back," Always, accessed January 22, 2021, https://always.com/en-us/about-us/end-period-poverty.

71. Simon Mainwaring, "Purpose at work: How Greenbar Distillery crafts spirits with a sustainable twist," *Forbes*, May 7, 2020, https://www.forbes.com/sites/simonmainwaring/2020/05/07/purpose-at-work-how-greenbar-distillery-crafts-spirits-with-a-sustainable-twist/#38ac47596af2.

72. "Neighborhood of good," State Farm, accessed January 22, 2021, https://neighborhoodofgood.statefarm.com/.

73. "Neighborhood of good," State Farm.

74. Rachel Barnes, "Unilever's Paul Polman on why 'advertising' means nothing to him, plus his vision for magic, not metrics," *Campaign*, https://www.campaignlive.co.uk/article/unilevers-paul-polman-why-advertising-means-nothing-him-plus-vision-magic-not-metrics/1130728.

75. Simon Mainwaring, "Purpose at work: How Seventh Generation accelerates sustainable growth," *Forbes,* April 30, 2019, https://www.forbes.com/sites/simonmainwaring/2019/04/30/purpose-at-work-how-seventh-generation-accelerates-sustainable-growth/?sh=59e355071547.

76. "Home," Ben's Original, accessed May 18, 2021, https://www.bensoriginal.com/.

77. "Conagra Brands announces Mrs. Butterworths brand review," Conagra Brands, June 17, 2020, https://www.conagrabrands.com/news-room/news-conagra-brands-announces-mrs-butterworths-brand-review-prn-122733.

78. Atla Spells, "Eskimo Pie no more: Ice cream owners will drop 'derogatory' names," *CNN Business*, June 20, 2020, https://www.cnn.com/2020/06/20/business/eskimo-pie-ice-cream-name-change-trnd/index.html.

79. Samantha Leffler, "Food brands step up to change their racially insensitive names: Aunt Jemima, Uncle Ben's and more," *Us Weekly*, June 25, 2020, https://www.usmagazine.com/food/pictures/food-brands-changing-their-racially-insensitive-names-pics/eskimo-pie-ice-cream-bars/.

80. Jeremy Bergman, "Washington will go by 'Washington Football Team' until further notice," NFL, July 23, 2020, https://www.nfl.com/news/washington-football-team-nfl-name-change.

81. Paul Hoynes, "Paul Dolan will know by midyear if Cleveland Indians can change name for 2022 season," Cleveland.com, https://www.cleveland.com/tribe/2021/03/paul-dolan-will-know-by-midyear-if-cleveland-indians-can-change-name-for-2022-season.html.

82. Christopher Stjernholm, "The origin of the master bedroom," Trelora, July 2, 2018, https://www.trelora.com/blog/master-bedroom-origin/.

83. Marguerite Ward and Melissa Wiley, "15 racists, mascots, and logos that were considered just another part of American life," *Business Insider*, July 13, 2020, https://www.businessinsider.com/15-racist-brand-mascots-and-logos-2014-6#funny-face-drink-mix-1964-1965-13.

84. Hadley Meares, "The troubling history of Sambo's Pancake House," *KCET*, April 26, 2017, https://www.kcet.org/food-living/the-troubling-history-of-sambos-pancake-house.

85. Allan Smith and Frank Thorp V, "McConnell warns corporate America to 'stay out of politics'—but says donations are OK," *NBC News*, April 6, 2021, https://www.nbcnews.com/politics/congress/mcconnell-warns-corporate-america-stay-out-politics-says-donations-are-n1263173.

86. "Business & politics: Do they mix?" Global Consumer Group, accessed February 13, 2021, https://www.globalstrategygroup.com/thought-leadership/gsgs-third-annual-study-business-politics-do-they-mix/.

87. Tanya Dua, "People's BS detectors are high': Brands have given consumers cause fatigue," *Digiday*, April 14, 2016, https://digiday.com/marketing/brands-cause-marketing-fatigue/.

88. "Responsible care," American Chemistry Council, accessed May 18, 2021, https://responsiblecare .americanchemistry.com/.

89. Elizabeth Segran, "How a beauty brand raised an army of 30,000 political activists," *Fast Company*, March 3, 2018, https://www.fastcompany.com/40540039/how-a-beauty-brand-raised-an-army-of -30000-political-activists.

90. "Eileen Fisher," American Sustainable Business Council, accessed January 22, 2021, https://www .asbcouncil.org/platinum-business-member/eileen-fisher.

91. "Horizon 2030," Eileen Fisher, accessed January 22, 2021, https://www.eileenfisher.com /horizon2030.

92. "Horizon 2030," Eileen Fisher.

93. "Defend Bears Ears National Monument," Patagonia, accessed January 22, 2021, https://www .patagonia.com/actionworks/campaigns/defend-bears-ears-national-monument/.

94. Sam Murch, interview with Simon Mainwaring, recording, August 10, 2018, 50:00.

95. Whitney Bauck, "Patagonia's CEO on how saving the planet has been good for business," *Fashionista*, January 17, 2019, https://fashionista.com/2019/01/patagonia-politics-ceo-rose-marcario -interview.

96. Julie Creswell and Rachel Abrams, "Shopping becomes a political act in the Trump era," *New York Times*, February 10, 2017, https://www.nytimes.com/2017/02/10/business/nordstrom-trump.html.

Chapter 7: Society

1. Larry Fink, "A fundamental reshaping of finance," BlackRock, January 14, 2020, https://www .blackrock.com/corporate/investor-relations/larry-fink-ceo-letter.

2. Katherine Dunn, "BlackRock's Larry Fink to CEOs: Get serious on net-zero targets, or else," *Fortune*, January 26, 2021, https://fortune.com/2021/01/26/blackrock-larry-fink-serious-net-zero -target/.

3. "A regularly updated blog tracking brands' responses to racial injustice," Ad Age, January 13, 2021, https://adage.com/article/cmo-strategy/regularly-updated-blog-tracking-brands-responses-racial -injustice/2260291.

4. "Trust in global companies: A GlobeScan Public Opinion eBrief," GlobeScan, accessed February 21, 2021, https://globescan.com/wp-content/uploads/2017/07/Trust-in-Global-Companies -GlobeScan-Public-Opinion-eBrief-Feb2016.pdf.

5. Abraham J. Heschel, *Who Is Man* (Stanford, CA: Stanford University Press, 1965).

6. Abraham H. Maslow, *The Farther Reaches of Human Nature* (New York: Viking Press, 1971).

7. Kyle Krowder, "What is transcendence? The true top of Maslow's hierarchy of needs," Sloww, accessed January 22, 2021, https://www.sloww.co/transcendence-maslow/.

8. Maslow, *The Farther Reaches of Human Nature*.

9. Emanuela Barbiroglio, "Prince Charles wants companies to raise $10 billion for his Earth Charter," *Forbes*, January 15, 2021, https://www.forbes.com/sites/emanuelabarbiroglio/2021/01/15/prince -charles-wants-companies-to-raise-73bn-for-his-earth-charter/?sh=55e5766224f7.

10. "Executive Order on Climate-Related Financial Risk," White House, May 20, 2021, https:// www.whitehouse.gov/briefing-room/presidential-actions/2021/05/20/executive-order-on-climate -related-financial-risk/.

11. Amanda Keating, "Microsoft CEO Satya Nadella shares what he's learned about stakeholder capitalism as the head of America's most JUST company," JUST Capital, November 5, 2020, https://justcapital.com/news/microsoft-ceo-satya-nadella-shares-leadership-lessons-on-stakeholder -capitalism/.

12. "From System Shock to System Change—Time to Transform: The Future of Sustainability Report 2020," Futures Centre, October 2020, https://www.thefuturescentre.org/fos/.

13. "From System Shock to System Change," Futures Centre.

14. Andrei Cherny, interview with Simon Mainwaring, recording, January 5, 2021, 50:42.

15. "The Biden-Harris administration immediate priorities," White House, accessed January 22, 2021, https://www.whitehouse.gov/priorities/.

16. Matthew Daly, "Business leaders urge Biden to set ambitious climate goal," *AP News*, April 13, 2021, https://apnews.com/article/business-leaders-urge-biden-climate-goal-870b2d70a787693465 eedd20f85aaf3e.

17. "Businesses & investors call for ambitious U.S. NDC," We Mean Business Coalition, accessed May 18, 2021, https://www.wemeanbusinesscoalition.org/ambitious-u-s-2030-ndc/.

18. Laura Thornton and Emily Bonta, "These 10 companies are leading on environmental impact—here's why," JUST Capital, April 22, 2021, https://justcapital.com/news/these-10-companies-are -leading-on-environmental-impact-heres-why/.

19. "How to launch a purpose-led brand and go global," Unilever, September 16, 2020, https://www .unilever.com/news/news-and-features/Feature-article/2020/how-to-launch-a-purpose-led-brand -and-go-global.html?1=2345.

20. "Take Action This Election," Count on Us, accessed April 9, 2021, https://wecountonus.org/.

21. Fiona Harvey, "Campaign seeks 1bn people to save climate—one small step at a time," *Guardian*, October 10, 2020, https://www.theguardian.com/environment/2020/oct/10/campaign-seeks-1bn -people-to-save-climate-one-small-step-time.

22. "Plant a tree and change the world," Plant Your Change, accessed February 13, 2021, https://www .plantyourchange.com/.

23. "About us," OpenInvest, accessed February 13, 2021, https://www.openinvest.com/about.

24. "Adopt-a-Meter," The Carbon Underground, accessed February 13, 2021, https://thecarbon underground.org/adopt-meter/.

25. "WePledge," Twilio, accessed February 13, 2021, https://www.twilio.org/wepledge/.

26. "Empowering you to fight climate change," Pawprint, accessed February 13, 2021, https://www .pawprint.eco/.

27. "Climate action that matters," Joro, accessed February 13, 2021, https://www.joro.tech/.

28. "The app that lets you safely donate to your charity," Sustainably, accessed May 18, 2021, https:// www.sustainably.co/.

29. "The modern corporate social impact platform," Deed, accessed February 13, 2021, https://www .joindeed.com/.

30. Richard Edelman, "Systemic racism: The existential challenge for business," Edelman, September 8, 2020, https://www.edelman.com/research/systemic-racism.

31. Ani Turner, *The Business Case for Racial Equity: A Strategy for Growth* (Battle Creek, MI: W. K. Kellogg Foundation, 2018).

32. "Target reveals sweeping action plan to advance racial equity," Sustainable Brands, August 19, 2020, https://sustainablebrands.com/read/organizational-change/target-reveals-sweeping-action -plan-to-advance-racial-equity.

33. Matthew Boyle, "Target's hometown tragedy unearths its struggles with diversity," *Bloomberg Quint*, June 6, 2020, https://www.bloombergquint.com/onweb/target-s-hometown-tragedy-unearths-its -struggles-with-diversity.

34. Jan M. Olsen, "After 'monkey hoodie' scandal, H&M hires diversity leader," *USA Today*, January 17, 2018, https://www.usatoday.com/story/money/retail/2018/01/17/after-monkey-hoodie-scandal -h-m-hires-diversity-leader/1039748001/.

35. Associated Press, "From Gucci to Prada, luxury fashion brands challenged to confront racist attitudes," *USA Today*, June 22, 2020, https://www.usatoday.com/story/entertainment/celebrities /2020/06/22/luxury-fashion-brands-get-blowback-racism-gucci-prada-loreal/3234226001/.

36. Vivian Hunt, Dennis Layton, and Sara Prince, "Why diversity matters," McKinsey & Company, January 1, 2015, https://www.mckinsey.com/business-functions/organization/our-insights/why -diversity-matters.

37. Jemima McEvoy, "Sephora first to accept '15% Pledge,' dedicating shelf-space to Black-owned businesses," *Forbes*, June 10, 2020, https://www.forbes.com/sites/jemimamcevoy/2020/06/10/sephora -first-to-accept-15-pledge-dedicating-shelf-space-to-black-owned-businesses/?sh=70a0bdd24b02.

38. Richard Feloni, "Intel's Chief Diversity Officer explains why the company is spearheading tech alliance around racial equity, and shares what it's already learned," JUST Capital, April 29,

2021, https://justcapital.com/news/intel-chief-diversity-officer-dawn-jones-on-alliance-for-global -inclusion-with-dell-snap-nasdaq-ntt/.

39. "Alliance for Global Inclusion," Alliance for Global Inclusion, accessed May 18, 2021, https://www .allianceforglobalinclusion.com/.

40. "Rehumanizing marketing," *Forbes*, September 8, 2020, https://www.forbes.com/sites/insights -smartsheet/2020/09/08/re-humanizing-marketing-five-teams-of-executives-collaborate-on -a-purpose-driven-approach/?sh=4cfb8055611c.

41. Andrew J. Hoffman, "The next phase of business sustainability," *Stanford Social Innovation Review*, Spring 2018, https://ssir.org/articles/entry/the_next_phase_of_business_sustainability.

42. Monica Anderson, "For Earth Day, here's how Americans view environmental issues," *Fact Tank* (blog), Pew Research Center, April 20, 2017, https://www.pewresearch.org/fact-tank/2017/04/20 /for-earth-day-heres-how-americans-view-environmental-issues/.

43. "As economic concerns recede, environmental protection rises on the public's policy agenda," Pew Research Center, February 13, 2020, https://www.pewresearch.org/politics/2020/02/13/as -economic-concerns-recede-environmental-protection-rises-on-the-publics-policy-agenda/.

44. Andrew J. Hoffman, "The next phase of business sustainability," *Stanford Social Innovation Review*, Spring 2018, https://ssir.org/articles/entry/the_next_phase_of_business_sustainability.

45. Zoltán Szakály et al., "Attitudes of the lifestyle of health and sustainability segment in Hungary," *Sustainability* 9, no. 10 (2017): 1763, https://doi.org/10.3390/su9101763.

46. Timberland, "Timberland announces bold goal for products to be net positive by 2030, continues pursuit of a greener future," *Business Wire*, September 1, 2020, https://www.businesswire.com/news /home/20200901005414/en/Timberland-Announces-Bold-Goal-for-Products-to-be-Net-Positive -by-2030-Continues-Pursuit-of-a-Greener-Future.

47. "The restorative 20s: Why and how the 2020s can be the decade of regenerative business," Sustainable Brands, accessed January 25, 2020, https://sustainablebrands.com/conferences/sustainablebrands /the-restorative-20s-why-and-how-the-2020s-can-be-the-decade-of-regenerative-business/.

48. "Modern Meadow," Modern Meadow, accessed January 25, 2021, https://www.modernmeadow .com/.

49. "About us," Cariuma, accessed May 18, 2021, https://cariuma.com/pages/about-us.

50. Astrid Wendlandt, "Fashion's interest in alternative fabrics keeps growing," *New York Times*, November 12, 2017, https://www.nytimes.com/2017/11/12/style/alternative-fabrics-sustainability -recycling.html.

51. "Vivobarefoot x Bloom," Vivobarefoot, May 1, 2018, https://www.vivobarefoot.com/us/blog /vivobarefootxbloom.

52. Bridget Shirvell, "Regenerative agriculture startup Cooks Venture raises $4 million to expand national distribution," *Forbes*, January 28, 2020, https://www.forbes.com/sites/bridgetshirvell /2020/01/28/cooks-venture-raises-4-million-to-expand-national-distribution/?sh=59aabd5110ab.

53. "Cooks Venture raises $10m to breed chickens that are healthier inside and out," AlleyWatch, accessed January 25, 2021, https://www.alleywatch.com/2020/07/cooks-venture-chicken-farming -organic-regenerative-matthew-waldik/.

54. Ken Roseboro, "Cooks Venture offers regenerative alternative to industrial chicken production," *Organic & Non-GMO Report*, September 5, 2020, https://non-gmoreport.com/articles/cooks -venture-offers-regenerative-alternative-to-industrial-chicken-production/.

55. Simon Mainwaring, "Purpose at work: How Ripple Foods disrupts to drive growth and impact," *Forbes*, November 11, 2020, https://www.forbes.com/sites/simonmainwaring/2020/11/10/purpose -at-work-how-ripple-foods-disrupts-to-drive-growth-and-impact/?sh=251f80e54f98.

56. "The world's largest product sustainability database," HowGood, accessed March 29, 2021, https:// howgood.com/.

57. Mary Mazzoni, "5 steps to reimagine capitalism in a changing world," *TriplePundit*, March 31, 2020, https://www.triplepundit.com/story/2020/reimagine-capitalism-COVID-19/87056.

58. Henry Chesbrough, *Open Innovation: The New Imperative* (Brighton, MA: Harvard Business Review Press, 2003).

59. Chesbrough, *Open Innovation*.

60. Henry Chesbrough, "Open innovation," *Open Innovation Community*, accessed January 25, 2021, http://openinnovation.net/about-2/open-innovation-definition/.

61. Eric S. Raymond, "The cathedral and the bazaar," CATB.org, August 2, 2002, http://www.catb.org/esr/writings/homesteading/cathedral-bazaar/.

62. "Call for code," IBM, accessed October 30, 2020, https://developer.ibm.com/callforcode/.

63. "Call for code," IBM.

64. Adam Brandenburger and Barry Nalebuff, "The rules of co-opetition," *Harvard Business Review*, accessed January 25, 2021, https://hbr.org/2021/01/the-rules-of-co-opetition.

65. Johan Weigeit, "The case for open-access chemical biology. A strategy for pre-competitive medicinal chemistry to promote drug discovery," *EMBO Reports* 10, no. 9 (2009): 941–5, doi:10.1038/embor.2009.193.

66. Weigeit, "The case for open-access chemical biology."

67. John Fullerton, *Regenerative Capitalism: How Universal Principles and Patterns Will Shape Our New Economy*, Capital Institute, April 2015, http://fieldguide.capitalinstitute.org/uploads/1/3/9/6/13963161/_____whitepaper9-2-2015.pdf.

68. Lisa Schnirring, "China releases genetic data on new coronavirus, now deadly," CIDRAP, January 11, 2020, https://www.cidrap.umn.edu/news-perspective/2020/01/china-releases-genetic-data-new-coronavirus-now-deadly.

69. William Falk, "Editor's letter," *The Week*, December 25, 2020.

70. William Hoffman et al., "Collaborating for the common good: Navigating public-private data partnerships," McKinsey & Company, May 30, 2019, https://www.mckinsey.com/business-functions/mckinsey-analytics/our-insights/collaborating-for-the-common-good.

71. "Global homelessness statistics," Homeless World Cup Foundation, accessed February 13, 2021, https://homelessworldcup.org/homelessness-statistics/.

72. Lilah Beldner, "How Lava Mae brings showers to people experiencing homelessness," The Right to Shower, January 9, 2019, https://www.therighttoshower.com/make-difference/mobile-showers-for-homeless.

73. Elon Musk, "All our patent are belong to you," Tesla, June 12, 2014, https://www.tesla.com/blog/all-our-patent-are-belong-you.

74. Kyle Hyatt, "Toyota isn't stopping at opening its patents, will sell hybrid tech to rivals, report says," Roadshow by CNET, April 12, 2019, https://www.cnet.com/roadshow/news/toyota-patents-hybrid-component-sales-electrification/.

75. Rich Ceppos, "Toyota intends to move people in new ways with new kinds of vehicles," *Car and Driver*, December 7, 2019, https://www.caranddriver.com/news/a30153010/toyota-e-palette-mobility-olympics/.

76. Cromwell Schubarth, "Palo Alto unicorn Aurora Innovations is teaming up with Toyota on ride-hailing minivans," *Silicon Valley Business Journal*, February 9, 2021, https://www.bizjournals.com/sanjose/news/2021/02/09/aurora-teams-with-toyota-on-ride-hailing-minivans.html.

77. Simon Mainwaring, "Purpose at work: How Allbirds is redefining purposeful profit," *Forbes*, https://www.forbes.com/sites/simonmainwaring/2021/02/08/purpose-at-work-how-allbirds-is-redefining-progress/?sh=6e6d18cf6128.

78. Mainwaring, "Purpose at work: How Allbirds is redefining purposeful profit."

79. "Vaccinating the world," *The Week*, May 21, 2021, https://theweek.com/articles/982467/vaccinating-world.

80. Simon Mainwaring, "Purpose at work: How Interface transforms sustainability to rewrite our future," *Forbes*, December 8, 2020, https://www.forbes.com/sites/simonmainwaring/2020/12/08/purpose-at-work-how-interface-transforms-sustainability-to-rewrite-our-future/?sh=c23202b26734.

81. "Interface, Gensler, Skanska, Armstrong, CertainTeed and USG form Carbon Action Network," Interface, accessed January 25, 2021, https://www.interface.com/US/en-US/about/press-room/materialsCAN-Release-en_US.

82. Tom Metcalf and Pei Yi Mak, "These billionaires made their fortunes by trying to stop climate change," *Bloomberg*, January 22, 2020, https://www.bloomberg.com/features/2020-green -billionaires/.

83. "EC3 product brief," Carbon Leadership Forum, accessed January 25, 2021, https://static1 .squarespace.com/static/5c73f31eb10f25809eb82de2/t/5e88a668c77d204f57ad2d5c/1586 013802123/3+-+EC3-product+Brief.pdf.

84. "Transparent through and through," Logitech, accessed March 29, 2021, https://www.logitech .com/en-au/sustainability/carbon-transparency.html.

85. "Interface, Gensler, Skanska," Interface.

86. Bart King, "Can a carpet factory run like a forest?" GreenBiz, June 12, 2015, https://www.greenbiz .com/article/can-carpet-factory-run-forest.

87. Merlyn Mathews, "Factory as a forest: Reimagining facilities as ecosystems," Interface, August 24, 2018, https://blog.interface.com/factory-forest-reimagining-facilities-ecosystems/.

88. "Project Positive," Biomimicry, accessed January 25, 2021, https://biomimicry.net/project-positive/.

89. "Project Positive," Biomimicry.

90. "Salesforce Sustainability Cloud becomes generally available," Salesforce, accessed February 9, 2021, https://www.salesforce.com/news/stories/salesforce-sustainability-cloud-becomes-generally -available/.

91. Adele Peters, "Why this Scottish brewery just bought a forest," *Fast Company*, August 23, 2020, https://www.fastcompany.com/90542281/why-this-scottish-brewery-just-bought-a-forest.

92. "Make earth great again," BrewDog, accessed January 25, 2021, https://d1fnkk8n0t8a0e.cloudfront .net/docs/Make-Earth-Great-Again_4.pdf.

93. "BrewDog is now carbon-negative," BrewDog, accessed January 25, 2021, https://www.brewdog .com/uk/tomorrow.

94. "Make earth great again," BrewDog.

95. "Apple and Google partner on COVID-19 contact tracing technology," Apple, April 10, 2020, https://www.apple.com/newsroom/2020/04/apple-and-google-partner-on-covid-19-contact -tracing-technology/.

96. "Luxury shopping with purpose," Olivela, accessed November 16, 2020, http://www.olivela.com.

97. Thankyou, "Social enterprise Thankyou launches bold initiative to help end extreme poverty by seeking partnership from competitors P&G and Unilever, two of the world's largest companies," *PR Newswire*, September 29, 2020, https://www.prnewswire.com/news-releases/social-enterprise -thankyou-launches-bold-initiative-to-help-end-extreme-poverty-by-seeking-partnership-from -competitors-pg-and-unilever-two-of-the-worlds-largest-companies-301139404.html.

98. "About the Fashion Pact," Fashion Pact, accessed January 25, 2021, https://thefashionpact.org/.

99. "Cotton 2040," Forum for the Future, accessed January 25, 2021, https://www.forumforthefuture .org/cotton-2040.

100. "Supporting our member brands," Fair Wear Foundation, accessed January 25, 2021, https://www .fairwear.org/programmes/brands.

101. "About IDH," The Sustainable Trade Initiative, accessed February 13, 2021, https://www .idhsustainabletrade.com/about-idh/.

102. Sean O'Kane, "Tesla stops taking Bitcoin for vehicle purchases, citing environmental concerns," *Verge*, May 12, 2021, https://www.theverge.com/2021/5/12/22433153/tesla-suspend-bitcoin-vehicle -purchase-cryptocurrency-elon-musk.

103. "Commit to OneTen," OneTen, accessed January 25, 2021, https://www.oneten.org/.

104. "Fintech Equality Coalition," Fintech Equality Coalition, accessed January 25, 2021, https://www .fintechequality.com/.

105. "U.S. Plastics Pact," U.S. Plastics Pact, accessed April 9, 2021, https://usplasticspact.org/.

106. Shilpa Pai Mizar, "Successful corporate-NGO partnerships," *FM Magazine*, April 2019, 36–39, https://www.fm-magazine.com/content/dam/fmm/issues/2019/apr/fm-april-2019.pdf.

107. "For the oceans," Parley for the Oceans, accessed May 18, 2021, https://www.parley.tv/#for theoceans.

108. "Help solve climate change," Carbon Vault, accessed January 25, 2021, https://carbonvault.org/.

109. Alison Gould, "A framework for learning about cross-sector collaboration," Independent Sector, October 6, 2016, https://independentsector.org/resource/a-framework-for-learning-about-cross-sector-collaboration-2/.

110. Edmans, *Grow the Pie*.

111. "Farm like the world depends on it," Regenerative Organic, accessed January 25, 2021, https://regenorganic.org/#our-story.

112. "#BillionPersonMovement," ReGenFriends, accessed May 18, 2021, https://www.regenfriends.com/.

113. "Regenerative," ReGenFriends, accessed January 25, 2021, https://www.regenfriends.com/.

114. "The Emerging ReGen Customer," ReGenFriends, accessed January 25, 2021, https://www.regenfriends.com/regencustomerinsights.

115. "Regeneration International," Regeneration International, accessed January 25, 2021, https://regenerationinternational.org/.

116. "Our story," Sweetgreen, accessed January 25, 2021, https://www.sweetgreen.com/our-story/.

117. Nathaniel Ru, interview with Simon Mainwaring, recording, November 25, 2020, 56:51.

118. Caitlin Dewey, "Olympic athletes love McDonalds. But its role in PyeongChang will be the smallest in decades," *Washington Post,* February 9, 2018, https://www.washingtonpost.com/news/wonk/wp/2018/02/09/olympic-athletes-love-mcdonalds-but-its-role-in-pyeongchang-will-be-the-smallest-in-decades/.

119. Nathaniel Ru, interview with Simon Mainwaring.

120. Adele Peters, "How Sweetgreen plans to cut its carbon footprint in half in the next 6 years," *Fast Company,* February 24, 2021, https://www.fastcompany.com/90606733/how-sweetgreen-plans-to-cut-its-carbon-footprint-in-half-in-the-next-6-years.

121. Nathaniel Ru, interview with Simon Mainwaring.

122. Alex Nicoll, "This unicorn thrives on salad. Investors supply the other greens," *Fortune*, September 25, 2019, https://fortune.com/2019/09/25/unicorn-thrives-salad-investors-supply-other-greens/.

123. Daniel J. Murphy, "How Bombas built a $100 million brand by giving away socks," Privy, March, 18, 2020, https://www.privy.com/blog/bombas.

124. Charles Robinson, "Nike's value is up $26.2B since Colin Kaepernick endorsement. Now it's close to unveiling his shoe," *Yahoo! Sports*, November 21, 2019, https://sports.yahoo.com/nikes-value-is-up-262-b-since-colin-kaepernick-endorsement-now-its-close-to-unveiling-his-shoe-150012824.html.

125. "Cooks Venture," Craft, accessed January 25, 2021, https://craft.co/cooks-venture.

126. John Zimmer, "Every Lyft ride will now contribute to fighting climate change," Sustainable Brands, April 23, 2018, https://sustainablebrands.com/read/business-case/every-lyft-ride-will-now-contribute-to-fighting-climate-change.

127. Jessica Klein, "Lyft is helping nonprofits get low-income workers to their job interviews and first weeks of their new jobs," *Fast Company*, October 17, 2019, https://www.fastcompany.com/90418584/lyft-is-helping-nonprofits-get-low-income-workers-to-their-job-interviews-and-first-weeks-of-their-new-jobs.

128. "Braver together," Maybelline, accessed February 13, 2021, https://www.maybelline.com/bravetogether.

129. "UK advertising launches Ad Net Zero," Advertising Association, November 18, 2020, https://adassoc.org.uk/our-work/uk-advertising-launches-ad-net-zero/.

130. "Purpose holds the key to igniting brand growth," Kantar, April 19, 2020, https://consulting.kantar.com/news-events/purpose-holds-the-key-to-igniting-brand-growth/.

131. Tom Harries and Meredith Annex, "Orsted's profitable transformation from oil, gas and coal to renewables," Powering Past Coal Alliance, December, 12, 2018, https://poweringpastcoal.org/insights/economy/orsteds-profitable-transformation-from-oil-gas-and-coal-to-renewables.

132. David Cooperrider and Audrey Seilan, "Lead from the future: How to turn visionary thinking into breakthrough growth," Scoopit post, April 18, 2020, https://www.scoop.it/topic/business-as-an-agent-of-world-benefit.

133. "Hey, how's that lawsuit against the president going?" Patagonia, accessed February 13, 2021, https://www.patagonia.com/stories/hey-hows-that-lawsuit-against-the-president-going/story-72248.html.

134. "Polling the American people," JUST Capital, accessed January 25, 2021, https://justcapital.com/polling/.

135. "Global consumer & stakeholder insights," report, GlobeScan, September 22, 2020.

136. "Sustainable investing is more mainstream," JPMorgan, April 20, 2018, https://www.jpmorgan.com/insights/research/esg.

137. Simon Mainwaring, "Purpose at work: How Satori Capital's key embeds purpose to drive profits," *Forbes*, November 4, 2020, https://www.forbes.com/sites/simonmainwaring/2020/11/04/purpose-at-work-how-satori-capitals-key-embeds-purpose-to-drive-profits/?sh=2e920a2872b4.

138. Sunny Vanderbeck, interview with Simon Mainwaring, recording, October 6, 2020, 59:23.

139. Sarah Keohane Williamson, "US short termism on ESG investing will hurt growth," *Financial Times*, August 27, 2020, https://www.ft.com/content/c4f2cb56-b0cb-4fdd-9939-b30ef329a6bf.

140. Timothy Nixon, "Opinion: 7 promising signs we're moving toward a more sustainable world," Ensia, March 2, 2016, https://ensia.com/voices/7-reasons-the-world-will-be-sustainable/.

141. Fred Richards, "Sustainability: Separating the talk from the action," Sustainable Brands, April 29, 2016, https://sustainablebrands.com/read/product-service-design-innovation/sustainability-separating-the-talk-from-the-action.

142. Maitane Sardon, "Sustainability investors shift their focus to social issues," *Wall Street Journal*, October 10, 2020, https://www.wsj.com/articles/sustainability-investors-shift-their-focus-to-social-issues-11602342000?st=gze7ua7h2ct8jan.

143. Tina Casey, "ExxonMobil's climate change pivot speaks volumes about shareholder activism," TriplePundit, February 26, 2019, https://www.triplepundit.com/story/2019/exxonmobils-climate-change-pivot-speaks-volumes-about-shareholder-activism/82596/.

144. Alistair Gray and Patrick Temple-West, "Investor rebellion at Procter & Gamble over environmental concerns," *Financial Times*, October 13, 2020, https://www.ft.com/content/1dd92502-e95b-4c21-be1c-c18a598acf1a.

145. Emily Holbrook, "Record-setting 81% of DuPont shareholders approve plastics pollution proposal," *Environment + Energy Leader*, May 3, 2018, https://www.environmentalleader.com/2021/05/record-setting-81-of-dupont-shareholders-approve-plastics-pollution-proposal/.

146. Amanda Keating, "Microsoft CEO Satya Nadella shares what he's learned about stakeholder capitalism as the head of America's most JUST company," JUST Capital, November 5, 2020, https://justcapital.com/news/microsoft-ceo-satya-nadella-shares-leadership-lessons-on-stakeholder-capitalism/.

147. "2020 year in review," FCLTGlobal, December 22, 2020, https://www.fcltglobal.org/resource/2020-year-in-review/.

148. "Exxon's climate denial history: A timeline," Greenpeace, accessed May 18, 2021, https://www.greenpeace.org/usa/ending-the-climate-crisis/exxon-and-the-oil-industry-knew-about-climate-change/exxons-climate-denial-history-a-timeline/.

149. Jillian Ambrose, "ExxonMobil reports loss after $3bn wiped off value of oil reserve," *Guardian*, May 1, 2020, https://www.theguardian.com/business/2020/may/01/exxonmobile-hits-loss-as-us-oil-price-slide-delivers-3bn-writedown/.

150. Heather Long, "Dumping fossil fuels was great move for Rockefeller Brothers Fund," *CNN Business*, October 26, 2015, https://money.cnn.com/2015/10/26/investing/fossil-fuel-divestment-rockefeller-brothers-fund/.

151. Cathy Clark, Jed Emerson, and Ben Thornley, *The Impact Investor: Lessons in Leadership and Strategy for Collaborative Capitalism* (San Francisco: Jossey-Bass, 2014).

152. Gunnar Friede, Timo Busch, and Alexander Bassen, "ESG and financial performance: Aggregated evidence from more than 2000 empirical studies," *Journal of Sustainable Finance & Investment* 5, no. 4 (2015): 210–33.

153. Simon Mainwaring, "Purpose at work: How to use purpose to attract investors and drive profit," *Forbes*, January 26, 2017, https://www.forbes.com/sites/simonmainwaring/2017/01/26/how-to-use-purpose-to-attract-investors-and-drive-profit/#6a1c8ed33f7f.

154. "Project ROI: Defining the Competitive and Financial Advantage of Corporate Responsibility and Sustainability," IO Sustainability, 2015, https://www.charities.org/sites/default/files/Project%20ROI%20Report.pdf.

155. "2020 Global 100 ranking," Corporate Knights, January 21, 2020, https://www.corporateknights.com/reports/2020-global-100/2020-global-100-ranking-15795648/.

156. Matt Egan, "Pfizer and Moderna could score $32 billion in Covid-19 vaccine sales—in 2021 alone," *CNN Business*, December 11, 2020, https://www.cnn.com/2020/12/11/business/pfizer-vaccine-covid-moderna-revenue/index.html.

157. "Investors seeking profit—and pushing for change," *Forbes*, September 8, 2020, https://www.forbes.com/sites/forbeswealthteam/2020/09/08/impact-50-investors-seeking-profit-and-pushing-for-change-equality-and-healthcare/?sh=5ab105255dde.

158. Dean Hand et al., "2020 annual impact investor survey," Global Impact Investing Network, June 11, 2020, https://thegiin.org/research/publication/impinv-survey-2020.

159. "Report on US Sustainable, Responsible and Impact Investing Trends," US SIF Foundation, October 31, 2018, https://www.ussif.org/files/Trends/Trends%202018%20executive%20summary%20FINAL.pdf.

160. CoPeace, "The dramatic growth of impact investing," *SRI Conference*, April 13, 2020, https://www.sriconference.com/blog/the-dramatic-growth-of-impact-investing.

161. "Older and wiser: Is responsible investment coming of age? Private Equity Responsible Investment Survey 2019," PwC, accessed February 13, 2021, https://www.pwc.com/gx/en/services/sustainability/assets/pwc-private-equity-responsible-investment-survey-2019.pdf.

162. "Unlocking capital markets to finance the SDGs," World Economic Forum, accessed January 25, 2021, http://www3.weforum.org/docs/WEF_Unlocking_Capital_Markets_to_Finance_the_SDGs_2019.pdf.

163. Josh Friedman and Noah Buhayar, "BlackRock seeks $10 billion to buy stakes in companies," *Bloomberg*, February 7, 2018, https://www.bloomberg.com/news/articles/2018-02-08/blackrock-is-said-to-seek-10-billion-to-buy-stakes-in-companies.

164. Sam Meredith, "BlackRock CEO says the climate crisis is about to trigger 'a fundamental reshaping of finance,'" *CNBC*, January 14, 2020, https://www.cnbc.com/2020/01/14/blackrock-ceo-larry-fink-says-climate-change-will-soon-reshape-markets.html.

165. Larry Fink, "Larry Fink's 2021 letter to CEOs," accessed February 12, 2021, https://www.blackrock.com/corporate/investor-relations/larry-fink-ceo-letter.

166. Meredith, "BlackRock CEO says."

167. Harry Robertson, "BlackRock holds $85 billion in coal investments despite Larry Fink's focus on climate change, report shows," *Market Insider*, January 13, 2021, https://markets.businessinsider.com/news/stocks/blackrock-holds-85-billion-in-coal-despite-green-pledges-2021-1-1029964594.

168. Mindy Lubber, "What it means when the world's largest asset manager rings warning bell about the financial risks of climate change," *Forbes*, January 16, 2020, https://www.forbes.com/sites/mindylubber/2020/01/16/what-it-means-when-the-worlds-largest-asset-manager-rings-a-warning-bell-about-the-financial-risks-of-climate-change/#6763b34c3086.

169. "What is a benefit corporation?" Benefit Corporation, accessed February 13, 2021, https://benefitcorp.net/.

170. "B movement builders," B Lab, accessed January 25, 2021, https://bcorporation.net/b-movement-builders.

171. "Grow manifesto brands," Danone, accessed January 25, 2021, https://www.danone.com/integrated-annual-report-2019/performance/grow-manifesto-brands.html.

172. Christopher Marquis, "Danone sees long-term value of becoming a global benefit corporation," *B the Change* (blog), July 2, 2020, https://bthechange.com/danone-sees-long-term-value-of-becoming-a-global-benefit-corporation-81362ff9cde6?gi=c979dda9f0cc.

173. "Sustainable investor poll on TCFD implementation," Global Sustainable Investment Alliance, accessed January 25, 2021, http://www.gsi-alliance.org/members-resources/sustainable-investor-poll-on-tcfd-implementation/.

174. Emily Chasan, "Global sustainable investments rise 34 percent to $30.7 trillion," *Bloomberg*, April 1, 2019, https://www.bloomberg.com/news/articles/2019-04-01/global-sustainable-investments-rise-34-percent-to-30-7-trillion.

175. "GSIA report finds increase in sustainable investing," International Institute for Sustainable Development, April 16, 2019, https://sdg.iisd.org/news/gsia-report-finds-increase-in-sustainable-investing/.

176. Deborah Nason, "Sustainable investing is surging. How to decide if it's right for you," *CNBC*, November 5, 2020, https://www.cnbc.com/2020/11/05/sustainable-investing-is-surging-how-to-decide-if-its-right-for-you.html.

177. Gwladys Fouche, "Norway wealth fund to test business model of biggest CO_2 emitters," *Reuters*, September 3, 2020, https://www.reuters.com/article/us-norway-swf/norway-wealth-fund-to-test-business-model-of-biggest-co2-emitters-idUSKBN25U1MN.

178. Pippa Stevens, "Your complete guide to investing with a conscience, a $30 trillion market just getting started," *CNBC*, December 14, 2019, https://www.cnbc.com/2019/12/14/your-complete-guide-to-socially-responsible-investing.html.

179. Steve Johnson, "ESG outperformance narrative 'is flawed', new research shows," *Financial Times*, May 2, 2021, https://www.ft.com/content/be140b1b-2249-4dd9-859c-3f8f12ce6036.

180. Katherine Lynch, "Where to find low-cost ESG funds," *Morningstar*, June 6, 2020, https://www.morningstar.com/articles/987495/where-to-find-low-cost-esg-funds.

181. Kevin Crowley and Scott Deveau, "Exxon CEO is dealt a stinging setback at hands of new activist," *Bloomberg*, May 26, 2021, https://www.bloomberg.com/news/articles/2021-05-26/tiny-exxon-investor-notches-climate-win-with-two-board-seats.

182. Nick Masercola, "Corporate climate pledges proliferate," JUST Capital, April 17, 2021, https://justcapital.com/news/corporate-climate-pledges-proliferate/.

183. "Firm overview," Generation Investment Management, accessed January 25, 2021, https://www.generationim.com/firm-overview/.

184. "The Rise Fund," The Rise Fund, accessed January 25, 2021, https://therisefund.com/.

185. "TPG Capital," TPG Capital, accessed January 25, 2021, https://www.tpg.com/.

186. "Scaling mission-driven companies," Bain Capital, accessed January 25, 2021, https://www.baincapitaldoubleimpact.com/.

187. Laura Kreutzer, "Bain Capital raises $800 million for second impact investing fund," *Wall Street Journal*, November 22, 2020, https://www.wsj.com/articles/bain-capital-raises-800-million-for-second-impact-investing-fund-11606053601.

188. Anna Berrill et al., "50 simple ways to make your life greener," *Guardian*, February, 29, 2020, https://www.theguardian.com/environment/2020/feb/29/50-ways-to-green-up-your-life-save-the-planet.

189. David J. Ferran and Katy Sperry, "Ethics + stakeholder focus = greater long-run shareholder profits," Torrey Project, October 23, 2019, https://www.torreyproject.org/post/ethics-stakeholder-focus-greater-long-run-shareholder-profits.

190. Peter Gassmann and Colm Kelly, "How ESG will drive the next wave of transformation," PwC, January 26, 2021, https://www.pwc.com/gx/en/issues/reinventing-the-future/take-on-tomorrow/esg-transformation.html.

191. Mainwaring, "Purpose at work: How to use purpose to attract investors and drive profit."

192. "Measuring stakeholder capitalism: Top global companies take action on universal ESG reporting," World Economic Forum, September 22, 2020, https://www.weforum.org/press/2020/09/measuring-stakeholder-capitalism-top-global-companies-take-action-on-universal-esg-reporting/.

193. Charlotte Petri Gornitzka and Anthony F. Pipa, "A new type of leadership from national governments is essential for success of the SDGs," Brookings, April 24, 2018, https://www.brookings.edu/blog/up-front/2018/04/24/a-new-type-of-leadership-from-national-governments-is-essential-for-success-of-the-sdgs/.

194. Mainwaring, "Purpose at work: How to use purpose to attract investors and drive profit."

195. "Corporate social responsibility and sustainability reports," CSRHub, accessed January 25, 2021, https://www.csrhub.com/.

196. "Investing in a sustainable future," *Morningstar*, accessed January 26, 2021, https://www .morningstar.com/company/esg-investing.

197. Katherine J. Brennan et al., "World Economic Forum releases ESG reporting metrics and disclosure standards," Briefing Governance, October 5, 2020, https://www.briefinggovernance.com/2020/10 /world-economic-forum-releases-esg-reporting-metrics-and-disclosure-standards/.

198. "Truvalue Labs launches new AI-powered product suite to help investors analyze companies and portfolio alignment to United Nations Sustainable Development Goals," Truvalue Labs, October 15, 2020, https://truvaluelabs.com/news/press-release/truvalue-labs-launches-new-ai-powered -product-suite.

199. "IRIS catalog of metrics," Global Impact Investing Network, accessed January 25, 2021, https://iris .thegiin.org/metrics/?page=5.

200. Richard Barker, Robert G. Eccles, and George Serafelm, "The future of ESG is . . . accounting?" *Harvard Business Review*, December 3, 2020, https://hbr.org/2020/12/the-future-of-esg-is -accounting.

201. Robert G. Eccles, "Purpose of the IBC/WEF stakeholder capitalism metrics initiative: A conversation with Brian Moynihan," *Forbes*, December 19, 2020, https://www.forbes.com/sites/bobeccles /2020/12/19/the-purpose-of-the-ibcwef-stakeholder-capitalism-metrics-initiative-a-conversation -with-brian-moynihan/?sh=2b6361ce71bd.

202. Johnson, "ESG outperformance narrative 'is flawed.'"

203. Samans and Nelson, *Integrated Corporate Governance*.

204. Samans and Nelson, *Integrated Corporate Governance*.

205. "SW-846 test method 1311: Toxicity characteristic leaching procedure," United States Environmental Protection Agency, accessed February 13, 2021, https://www.epa.gov/hw-sw846/sw-846 -test-method-1311-toxicity-characteristic-leaching-procedure.

206. "UN Guiding Principles Reporting Framework," UN Guiding Principles Reporting Database, accessed February 13, 2021, https://www.ungpreporting.org/.

207. "Corporate reporting dialogue," The International Integrated Reporting Council, accessed February 13, 2021, https://corporatereportingdialogue.com/.

208. "Impact Management Project," Impact Management Project, accessed February 13, 2021, https:// impactmanagementproject.com/.

209. "Task Force on Climate-Related Financial Disclosures," Task Force on Climate-Related Financial Disclosures, accessed February 13, 2021, https://www.fsb-tcfd.org/.

210. "Investors can now compare ESG scores on new ESGHub app," Sustainable Brands, September 27, 2018, https://sustainablebrands.com/read/finance-investment/investors-can-now-compare-esg -scores-on-new-esghub-app.

211. Jeffrey Hollender and Bill Breen, *The Responsibility Revolution: How the Next Generation of Businesses Will Win* (Hoboken, NJ: Wiley, 2010).

212. Bruce Berman, "$21 trillion in U.S. intangible assets is 84% of S&P 500 value—IP rights and reputation included," IP CloseUp, June 4, 2019, https://ipcloseup.com/2019/06/04/21-trillion-in -u-s-intangible-asset-value-is-84-of-sp-500-value-ip-rights-and-reputation-included/.

213. Timothy Nixon, "Opinion: 7 promising signs we're moving toward a more sustainable world," Ensia, March 2, 2016, https://ensia.com/voices/7-reasons-the-world-will-be-sustainable/.

214. "Transparency in corporate reporting—assessing emerging market multinationals," Transparency International, accessed December 4, 2020, https://images.transparencycdn.org/images/2016_Tran sparencyInCorporateReporting_EMMs_EN.pdf.

215. "The Sustainability Consortium's CEO reflects on its 10-year, trillion-dollar impact," Sustainability Consortium, August 8, 2019, https://www.sustainabilityconsortium.org/2019/08/the -sustainability-consortiums-ceo-reflects-on-its-10-year-trillion-dollar-impact/.

216. Stephanie Klotz, "Can transparency alone transform the fashion industry?" Sustainable Brands, May 28, 2018, https://sustainablebrands.com/read/organizational-change/can-transparency-alone -transform-the-fashion-industry.

217. Klotz, "Can transparency alone transform the fashion industry?"

218. Joe Lindsey, "The dark secrets lurking inside your outdoor gear," *Outside*, February 21, 2020, https://www.outsideonline.com/2405448/outdoor-gear-factory-abuse-labor-practices.

219. "Forced labor & human trafficking: Patagonia's approach for remediation," Patagonia, accessed May 18, 2021, https://www.patagonia.com/static/on/demandware.static/-/Library-Sites-Patagonia Shared/default/dwb48d6b02/PDF-US/human_trafficking_child_labor.pdf.

220. Abha Bhattari and Hannah Denham, "Stealing to survive: More Americans are shoplifting food as aid runs out during the pandemic," *Washington Post*, December 10, 2020, https://www .washingtonpost.com/business/2020/12/10/pandemic-shoplifting-hunger/.

221. Steve Pearlstein, *Can American Capitalism Survive?: Why Greed Is Not Good, Opportunity Is Not Equal, and Fairness Won't Make Us Poor* (New York: St. Martin's Press, 2018).

222. Oliver Balch, "The curse of 'white oil': Electric vehicles' dirty secret," *Guardian*, December 8, 2020, https://www.theguardian.com/news/2020/dec/08/the-curse-of-white-oil-electric-vehicles-dirty -secret-lithium/.

223. Amanda Yeo, "8 ways climate change is already impacting you," *Mashable*, November 18, 2020, https://mashable.com/article/climate-change-effects-2020/.

224. Anupam Nanda, "Sustainable cities after COVID-19: Why Barcelona-style green zones could be the answer," *Fast Company*, December 18, 2020, https://www.fastcompany.com/90586749 /sustainable-cities-after-covid-19-why-barcelona-style-green-zones-could-be-the-answer.

225. Adele Peters, "How Jeff Bezos is spending his first $791 million on climate action," *Fast Company*, November 18, 2020, https://www.fastcompany.com/90576554/how-jeff-bezos-is-spending-his -first-791-million-on-climate-action.

226. "Giving Tuesday: A global generosity movement," Giving Tuesday, accessed January 25, 2021, https://www.givingtuesday.org/.

227. Toby Hill, "Delta lifts off with $1 billion pledge to become carbon neutral," *GreenBiz*, February 20, 2020, https://www.greenbiz.com/article/delta-lifts-1-billion-pledge-become-carbon-neutral.

228. "Eco-Skies alliance," United Airlines, accessed May 18, 2021, https://www.united.com/ual/en/us /fly/company/global-citizenship/environment/ecoskies-alliance.html.

229. Clifford Kraus, "Oil refineries see profit in turning kitchen grease into diesel," *New York Times*, December 3, 2020, https://www.nytimes.com/2020/12/03/business/energy-environment/oil -refineries-renewable-diesel.html.

230. Deborah Lockridge, "2016 top 50 green fleets," *Truckinginfo* (blog), Heavy Duty Trucking, November 15, 2016, https://www.truckinginfo.com/157071/2016-top-50-green-fleets.

231. Dave R. Baker, "Safeway's trucking fleet shifts to biofuel," *SFGATE*, January 19, 2008, https:// www.sfgate.com/business/article/Safeway-s-trucking-fleet-shifts-to-biodiesel-3232185.php.

232. "20 more companies from around the globe join The Climate Pledge," Amazon, February 17, 2021, https://www.aboutamazon.com/news/sustainability/20-more-companies-from-around-the-globe -join-the-climate-pledge.

233. Gill Hystop, "Kellogg's, PepsiCo, General Mills take bold steps to curb devastating effects of climate change on global food supply," *Bakery and Snacks*, September 30, 2020, https://www .bakeryandsnacks.com/Article/2020/09/30/Kellogg-s-PepsiCo-General-Mills-take-bold-steps-to -curb-devastating-effects-of-climate-change-on-global-food-supply.

234. Megan Schilling, "Pepsico announces 2030 goal to scale regenerative farming practices across 7 million acres," *Successful Farming*, April 20, 2021, https://www.agriculture.com/news/pepsico -announces-2030-goal-to-scale-regenerative-farming-practices-across-7-million-acres.

235. "Acting with purpose for sustainability," Mars, accessed March 29, 2021, https://www.mars.com /sustainability-plan.

236. Hallie Levine, "Johnson & Johnson Consumer Health commits $800 million through 2030 to make its produucts more sustainable for a healthier planet," Johnson & Johnson, September 8, 2020, https://www.jnj.com/latest-news/johnson-johnson-commits-800-million-to-making-more -sustainable-products.

237. "Apple commits to be 100 percent carbon neutral for its supply chain and products by 2030," Apple, July 21, 2020, https://www.apple.com/newsroom/2020/07/apple-commits-to-be-100-percent-carbon-neutral-for-its-supply-chain-and-products-by-2030/.

238. Alisa Priddle, "Ford nearly doubles its investment in electric vehicles," *Motor Trend*, February 5, 2021, https://www.motortrend.com/news/ford-ev-investment-2025/.

239. "Ford expands climate change goals, sets target to become carbon neutral by 2050: Annual sustainability report," Ford, June 24, 2020, https://media.ford.com/content/fordmedia/fna/us/en/news/2020/06/24/ford-expands-climate-change-goals.html.

240. "Reaffirming Starbucks' commitment to a resource-positive future," Starbucks, September 23, 2020, https://stories.starbucks.com/press/2020/reaffirming-starbucks-commitment-to-a-resource-positive-future/.

241. Alyssa Rosenblatt, "Mastercard and partners launch Priceless Planet Coalition to act on climate change," Mastercard, January 17, 2020, https://www.mastercard.com/news/press/press-releases/2020/january/mastercard-and-partners-launch-priceless-planet-coalition-to-act-on-climate-change/.

242. "Unilever sets out new actions to fight climate change, and protect and regenerate nature, to preserve resources for future generations," Unilever, June 15, 2020, https://www.unilever.com/news/press-releases/2020/unilever-sets-out-new-actions-to-fight-climate-change-and-protect-and-regenerate-nature-to-preserve-resources-for-future-generations.html.

243. "Climate change," Marks and Spencer, accessed January 25, 2021, https://corporate.marksandspencer.com/sustainability/business-wide/climate-change.

244. "JPMorgan Chase adopts Paris-aligned financing commitment," JPMorgan Chase & Co., October 6, 2020, https://www.jpmorganchase.com/news-stories/jpmorgan-chase-adopts-paris-aligned-financing-commitment.

245. Sundar Pichai, "Our third decade of climate action: Realizing a carbon-free future," Google, September 14, 2020, https://blog.google/outreach-initiatives/sustainability/our-third-decade-climate-action-realizing-carbon-free-future/.

246. "Environment," AT&T, accessed January 25, 2021, https://about.att.com/csr/home/environment.html.

247. Bryce Buyakie, "Goodyear to phase out petroleum-based tires with soybeans by 2020," *Daily Record*, May 15, 2021, https://www.the-daily-record.com/story/news/2021/05/15/soybean-oil-in-petroleum-out-goodyear-phasing-soybean-tires/5055397001/.

248. "Vision," OS-C, accessed May 18, 2021, https://www.os-climate.org/#vision.

249. Michael Grothaus, "Coca-Cola, PepsiCo, and Nestlé lead the '10 worst plastic polluters' of 2020," *Fast Company*, July 12, 2020, https://www.fastcompany.com/90583252/coca-cola-pepsico-and-nestle-lead-the-10-worst-plastic-polluters-of-2020.

250. "About us," Institutional Investors Group on Climate Change, accessed January 25, 2020, https://www.iigcc.org/about-us/.

251. Shanny Basar, "Transition bonds needed to meet Paris targets," Markets Media, September 9, 2020, https://www.marketsmedia.com/transition-bonds-needed-to-meet-paris-targets/.

252. Masercola, "Corporate climate pledges proliferate."

253. Pichai, "Our third decade of climate action."

254. "Walmart reports substantial emissions reductions in China as suppliers set ambitious targets," Walmart, April 18, 2019, https://corporate.walmart.com/newsroom/2019/04/18/walmart-reports-substantial-emissions-reductions-in-china-as-suppliers-set-ambitious-targets.

255. Walmart, "Walmart announces 20 MMT of supplier emission reductions through Project Gigaton; unveils plans for expanding electric vehicle charging stations and doubling U.S. wind and solar energy use," *3BL CSRwire*, April 18, 2018, https://www.csrwire.com/press_releases/40947-walmart-announces-20-mmt-of-supplier-emission-reductions-through-project-gigaton-unveils-plans-for-expanding-electric-vehicle-charging-stations-and-doubling-u-s-wind-and-solar-energy-use.

256. Elizabeth Segran, "Madewell, Patagonia, and Eileen Fisher want to buy your old clothes," *Fast Company*, June 26, 2019, https://www.fastcompany.com/90368774/madewell-patagonia-and-eileen-fisher-want-to-buy-your-old-clothes.

257. Adele Peters, "Levi's wants your old jeans back," *Fast Company*, October 5, 2020, https://www .fastcompany.com/90559552/levis-wants-your-old-jeans-back.

258. "Shell invests in nature as part of broad drive to tackle CO_2 emissions," Shell Global, April 8, 2019, https://www.shell.com/media/news-and-media-releases/2019/shell-invests-in-nature-to-tackle-co2 -emissions.html.

259. Eillie Anzilotti, "General Mills has a plan to regenerate 1 million acres of farmland," *Fast Company*, March 4, 2019, https://www.fastcompany.com/90313818/general-mills-has-a-plan-to-regenerate -1-million-acres-of-farmland.

260. Adele Peters, "This new marketplace pays farmers to fight climate change," *Fast Company*, June 12, 2019, https://www.fastcompany.com/90361030/this-new-marketplace-pays-farmers-to-fight -climate-change.

261. "Premium produce for everyone," Iron Ox, accessed May 18, 2021, www.ironox.com.

262. John Koester, "The future of farms is vertical: 400x more yield, 95% less water, 99% less space," YouTube video, 27:04, https://www.youtube.com/watch?v=0uXdnjXIGjI.

263. "Fetzer Vineyards releases first sustainability report, road to regeneration, ahead of 50th anniversary in 2018," Fetzer Vineyards, November 8, 2017, https://www.multivu.com/players/English /8206351-fetzer-vineyards-road-to-regeneration-sustainability-report/.

264. "Carbon neutrality makes a difference today," Natural Capital Partners, accessed December 4, 2020, https://www.naturalcapitalpartners.com/solutions/solution/carbon-neutrality.

265. "Making the leap to circular fashion," Forum for the Future, accessed January 25, 2021, https:// www.forumforthefuture.org/Handlers/Download.ashx?IDMF=0e19a301-b2e9-40c6-a034 -59cc1c5eb337.

266. "Rethinking our food chain," Patagonia Provisions, accessed January 25, 2021, https://www .patagoniaprovisions.com/.

267. "About us," The Carbon Underground, accessed January 25, 2021, https://thecarbonunderground .org/about-us/.

268. Kate Raworth, *Doughnut Economics: Seven Ways to Think Like a 21st Century Economist* (White River Junction, VT: Chelsea Green Publishing, 2017).

269. Raworth, *Doughnut Economics*.

270. "EU taxonomy for sustainable activities," European Commission, accessed January 25, 2021, https://ec.europa.eu/info/business-economy-euro/banking-and-finance/sustainable-finance/eu -taxonomy-sustainable-activities_en.

271. Esther Whieldon, "SEC acting head explains why voluntary ESG disclosure regime is not enough," S&P Global, March 1, 2021, https://www.spglobal.com/marketintelligence/en/news-insights/latest -news-headlines/sec-acting-head-explains-why-voluntary-esg-disclosure-regime-is-not-enough -62934422.

272. Biden for President, "The Biden Plan for a clean energy revolution and environmental justice," accessed January 25, 2021, https://joebiden.com/climate-plan/.

273. "Financing the circular economy: Capturing the opportunity," Ellen Macarthur Foundation, 2020, https://www.ellenmacarthurfoundation.org/assets/downloads/Financing-the-circular-economy.pdf.

274. Adele Peters, "Corporate climate commitments are now common. Next is nature restoration commitments," *Fast Company*, September 22, 2020, https://www.fastcompany.com/90553398 /corporate-climate-commitments-are-now-common-next-is-nature-restoration-commitments.

275. "Adepeju Jaiyeoba," Meaningful Business, accessed January 25, 2021, https://meaningful.business /team/adepeju-jaiyeoba/.

276. "Inna Braverman," Meaningful Business, accessed January 25, 2021, https://meaningful.business /team/inna-braverman/.

277. "Latifa Al-Khalifa," Meaningful Business, accessed January 25, 2021, https://meaningful.business /team/latifa-al-khalifa/.

278. Katie Kindelan, "Old Navy, Tory Burch, Target paying employees to be poll workers: 4 things to know about helping on Election Day," *ABC News*, September 11, 2020, https://abcnews.go.com /GMA/News/navy-tory-burch-target-paying-employees-poll-workers/story?id=72800752.

279. "From system shock to system change—Time to transform: The future of sustainability," Forum for the Future, accessed February 13, 2021, https://www.thefuturescentre.org/wp-content/uploads/2020/11/Future-of-Sustainability-2020_Time-to-transform.pdf.

280. "Business: News at a glance," *The Week*, January 22, 2021.

281. Ad Council, "Gaming is the future of social good integrations," Ad Age, November 19, 2020, https://adage.com/article/ad-council/gaming-future-social-good-integrations/2295786.

282. Afdhel Aziz, "How Riot Games and the League of Legends community are gaming for good," *Forbes*, April 10, 2020, https://www.forbes.com/sites/afdhelaziz/2020/04/10/the-power-of-purpose-how-riot-games-and-the-league-of-legends-community-are-gaming-for-good/?sh=46f2f6b76591.

283. Wai Yen Tang, Felix Reer, and Thorsten Quandt, "Investigating sexual harassment in online video games: How personality and context factors are related to toxic sexual behaviors against fellow players," *Aggressive Behavior* 46, no. 1 (January/February 2020), https://onlinelibrary.wiley.com/doi/full/10.1002/ab.21873.

284. Richard Edelman, "2021 Edelman trust barometer: Trust in technology," Edelman, accessed May 18, 2021, https://www.edelman.com/trust/2021-trust-barometer/trust-technology.

285. Cade Metz, "Competing with the giants in race to build self-driving cars," *New York Times*, January 4, 2018, https://www.nytimes.com/2018/01/04/technology/self-driving-cars-aurora.html.

286. Cade Metz, "A.I. shows promise assisting physicians," *New York Times*, February 11, 2019, https://www.nytimes.com/2019/02/11/health/artificial-intelligence-medical-diagnosis.html.

287. Paul Mozur, "Inside China's dystopian dreams: A.I., shame and lots of cameras," *New York Times*, July 8, 2018, https://www.nytimes.com/2018/07/08/business/china-surveillance-technology.html.

288. Cade Metz, "Good news: A.I. is getting cheaper. That's also bad news," *New York Times*, February 20, 2018, https://www.nytimes.com/2018/02/20/technology/artificial-intelligence-risks.html.

289. Cade Metz, "How will we outsmart A.I. liars," *New York Times*, November 10, 2018, https://www.nytimes.com/2018/11/19/science/artificial-intelligence-deepfakes-fake-news.html.

290. Bernard Marr, "10 wonderful examples of using artificial intelligence for good," *Forbes*, June 22, 2020, https://www.forbes.com/sites/bernardmarr/2020/06/22/10-wonderful-examples-of-using-artificial-intelligence-ai-for-good/?sh=8f79c722f95e.

291. Kristine Liao, "A global assembly on the climate crisis is inviting citizens from around the world to participate," Global Citizen, December 10, 2020, https://www.globalcitizen.org/en/content/global-assembly-cop26/.

292. Hope Enterprise Corporation, "Historic partnership makes significant investment into small business in the Deep South," *PR Newswire*, February 9, 2021, https://www.prnewswire.com/news-releases/historic-partnership-makes-significant-investment-into-small-businesses-in-the-deep-south-301224973.html.

Chapter 8: Transcendence

1. Per Espen Stoknes, "How to transform apocalyptic fatigue into action on global warming," TEDGlobal>NYC video, September 2017, 4:52, https://www.ted.com/talks/per_espen_stoknes_how_to_transform_apocalypse_fatigue_into_action_on_global_warming?language=en.

Index

About the Author

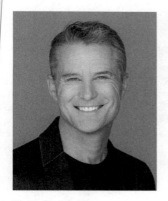

Photo by BrioFive

Simon Mainwaring is the founder and CEO of We First, the award-winning strategic consultancy that has worked with many of today's most iconic, purpose-driven brands including TOMS, Timberland, VSP Global, VF Corporation, Avery Dennison, Mammut, and leading foundations. We First is a Real Leaders "Top 100 Impact Companies in the US" and B Corp "Best For the World" Honoree. He's a Featured Expert and Jury member for the Sustainable Development Goals at the Cannes Lions International Festival of Creativity; host of the *Lead With We* podcast and the "Brands With Purpose" series with Harvard Business School Association of Boston; member of the Steering Committee of Sustainable Brands and Forbes Business Council; and a Fellow of the Royal Society of Arts in London.

Mainwaring has been featured in BBC World News, *The Guardian*, *Advertising Age*, *Fast Company*, and *Inc.*, among others. For *Forbes*, he writes an influential column called "Purpose at Work."

Mainwaring is a sought-after international speaker who has addressed business leaders and entrepreneurs around the world including at the United Nations Foundation, Cannes International Advertising Festival, SXSW, TEDxSF, Conscious Capitalism, Sustainable Brands, Social Good Summit, World 50, National Association of Broadcasters, National Speakers Association, National Press Club, and top brands and business schools globally. Real Leaders recently named him to its list of "Top 50 Keynote Speakers in the World."

His first book, *We First*, is a *New York Times*, *Wall Street Journal*, and Amazon bestseller that was named Best Marketing Book of the Year by strategy+business. It will come out in a substantially revised new edition in 2022.

Visit SimonMainwaring.com for speaking and training. Connect on Facebook, Twitter, and Instagram: @SimonMainwaring